Walter Trohan

In 1929, when a gang of Chicago hoodlums staged their historic Valentine's Day massacre, a young reporter named Walter Trohan was there for his first big scoop. A fitting prelude to Trohan's Washington career where, as reporter and later bureau chief of the Chicago *Tribune,* he reported for more than thirty years on the slightly less bloody, but decidedly fearsome, combat of Capitol Hill politics.

Now this top-ranking journalist reveals the inside stories he never printed: how he first blew into FDR's New Deal Washington slightly right of center and wound up a self-professed liberal who covered some of the most dramatic events in U.S. history.

POLITICAL ANIMALS

Memoirs of a Sentimental Cynic

POLITICAL ANIMALS

Memoirs of a Sentimental Cynic

WALTER TROHAN

Doubleday & Company, Inc.
Garden City, New York
1975

Library of Congress Cataloging in Publication Data

Trohan, Walter, 1903–
Political animals.

1. Trohan, Walter, 1903– 2. Journalists—Correspondence,
Reminiscences, etc. I. Title.
PN4874.T7A32   070'.92'4
ISBN 0-385-01786-3
Library of Congress Catalog Card Number 74-2835

*To my wife, Carol,
who was the best part of it all*

CONTENTS

FOREWORD

I AM NOT NOW, and never was a great or an important man. Count me, rather, as among those favored by fortune. I spent almost a half century as a newspaperman, the eyes and ears of a number of my fellow men who otherwise could not see their elected betters perform, not only at home but around a troubled world, with their money, their lives and even their sacred honor.

I am writing these memoirs, not because autobiography has become as common as undressing for public display—and often is about as uninteresting—but out of sheer enjoyment. This is the first book I have written for myself and about myself. I do not consider myself a wholly admirable character or one better than most I knew or met, but one more fortunate certainly than many of his fellows.

In my youth, it was my happy lot to serve as a police reporter in Chicago, the crossroads of America. It was bawdy and bossed and it was lusty and wonderful as well. Not the least of its wonders was its interest in the preservation of beauty and its advancement of learning and the arts. Yes, Chicago.

My earliest associates were crooks and their lights of love, gangsters and their molls, and police and their anxious and child-ridden wives. There were lawyers and shysters, pimps and whores, saloonkeepers and bartenders. In fact, many of my best friends in those days were entrepreneurs engaged in catering to the evasion of the prohibition law, a law that only the do-gooders of two generations ago wanted as the fulfillment of man's mission on earth.

In a sense I was a member of this motley crew or, at least, recognized as one of the family, privileged to move among them as one who had a role to play, something akin to that of the recording angel. It never occurred to me in those gangland days to be afraid. Actually, I was less of a recording angel than a frisky pup, generally wagging a friendly tail, but always wagging his adjectives behind him.

From the lofty beginnings of police reporting, I descended into politics. My progress has been steadily downward ever since. At first I associated with ward heelers, but soon graduated to elected officials. Most of my reportorial life has been spent among politicians at local, state, national and international levels. I have eaten their bread and salt and drunk their water and wine. More often than not I have paid for it, because politicians generally are afflicted with an impediment in their reach, no doubt nature's compensation for their overindulgence in speech. Also I was taught by an early and revered mentor, James Leo Doherty, star reporter for the *Tribune*, never to let a politician believe he has bought your soul because you dodged calling for a round; always buy back.

Over the years I have death-watched elections and danced at the joyous nuptials of inaugurations. Twice, I have seen Washington taken over by self-acknowledged great men, deep thinkers, youthful exuberants, assorted mystics and self-appointed popular champions —replete with charts and equations, money and spending theories, and promises—promises of the perfect nation and the world millennium.

I tried to elect some and worked to defeat others, without too much success in either direction. I have strung platitudes together for politicians, so that they might shine before their fellow men. I have nursed their egos, which makes me something of an expert on the love life of the Brontosauri. I have written the tales of their lives, their most shining deeds and their darkest hours. In short, there is no joy or woe of the political animal that I do not know. Politicians, like other men, are compounded of good and evil, weakness and strength, folly and wisdom. If there is some scandal in the pages to come and much trivia, let it be remembered that the vices of the ancients have long been regarded by the first and grandest chronicler of them all, Plutarch, as keys to their characters and times, and that politicians are occupied with trivia far oftener than with thinking great thoughts.

Politics is one of the oldest professions, if not the oldest. It is not unlikely that Adam told Eve, just before they stepped out of the gates of the Garden: "We are standing on the threshold of a new era."

It has ever amazed me that good and true people can fall in love, to the point of fanaticism, with politicians they have not met and whose principles, if any, they do not know and cannot know, because the politicians don't often know themselves. Many politicians shed party or ideology as we might throw away an old coat, but only when their own advantage is at stake.

Politicians are forever tearing tatters from the flag to enhallow some chosen course of action. They love country, flag, home, honor and mother, not necessarily in that order. We know this because they are forever telling us so. What they are really after, in most cases, is to gain and stay in office. This goes for most practitioners of the great art in every country in the world and of every race, creed and color—black, red, white or yellow.

Often politicians have hitched the national economy to the chariot of war, while professing to cherish peace above all things. For years they have been buying our votes with our money, claiming to be interested only in advancing the common welfare. Most of all they say they love to serve us. No sacrifice of time and effort is too great for them to make us happy. They love to serve us so much that few can bear to leave the public payroll by choice. "Till death do us part," could be inscribed on most political crests.

Let me make it perfectly clear that I like politicians, just as I like most of my fellow men, and just as I am especially fond of most women. However, I hardly ever take politicians seriously. No man can take most politicians as seriously as they want to be taken or as seriously as they take themselves. Almost every politician likes to regard himself as the irresistible charmer and the immovable man of principle. This would seem to indicate that there is an internal struggle going on in the breast of every politician, except that, as a class, they can almost invariably rise above principle.

Maybe it is because we are simple folk at heart that we honor none among us so much as the orators, because we turn over our money, our rights and our national honor to even the poorest of the eagle spreaders. Or, it may be, we all have a sneaking admiration for the rogues among us.

Let it be strictly understood that politics should be, and sometimes is, a most honorable and noble profession. There are men of honor and principle among politicians, although we don't seem to encourage them any more than we do in the trade of newspapering. Frequently politics has degenerated into a game practiced by genial characters, but nonetheless confidence men out for the fast buck. There are times when it seems that all one needs to join the political ranks is an ingratiating manner and a devious mind.

Along with politicians, I have spent most of my life in the company of newspapermen, but I would not pretend that the association was mutually advantageous or even salutary at all times. I would not say that all or even most of the interesting people I have met in the pursuit of news have been newspapermen. Nor would I condemn all while elevating a few.

I am not as cynical about the press and politicians as was Hilaire Belloc, who became so disillusioned with the parliamentary system that he abandoned his seat in the House of Commons, saying: "I am relieved to be quit of the dirtiest company it has ever been my misfortune to keep."

This is not the story of my life, but rather of my life among leaders. I hope it will not be regarded as signifying nothing and merely one echo of the sound and fury of our days even though it is not entirely free of bias and prejudice. I often wished that I had had enough talent to plow some of that talent under, but Washington was so large a field, to say nothing of the world, that I had to spread what little I had very thin indeed.

Unless a man is completely ignorant, he cannot be totally unprejudiced, and unless he is absolutely indifferent, he cannot be wholly impartial. One can love good, but can hardly be dedicated to it, unless he hates evil. I like to think I am prejudiced for truth and biased by sentiment and humor. Everyone becomes a part of what he sees and hears.

Carrowmeer House
Newmarket-on-Fergus
County Clare, Ireland

POLITICAL ANIMALS
Memoirs of a Sentimental Cynic

THE FOUNDER
OF THE FEAST

———

SATURDAY NOON, January 20, 1945, Washington was mantled by a wet snow, which put white cuffs on the bare limbs of the trees on the White House grounds. On the South Portico of the Executive Mansion, Franklin Delano Roosevelt, drawn and weary, raised his right hand to take his fourth oath of office as President of the United States. Around him stood many members of his family, high ranking dignitaries and those in his Cabinet. On the driveway and grounds below, several hundred lesser officials shuffled in the sun-splashed slush, jockeying to improve their view of the precedent-breaking ceremony. All eyes were on the Chief Executive, seeking confirmation or denial of the rumors about his declining health.

Solemnly Chief Justice Harlan F. Stone asked Roosevelt if he would swear to support the Constitution of the United States. Before the President could answer, I said, *sotto voce*, "Till death do us part." My voice was loud enough to send a ring of officials scurrying away and leaving me alone with George Rothwell Brown, the dean of the Hearst newspaper correspondents. George looked at FDR's scrawny neck and said simply, "A gone goose."

Roosevelt's inaugural address, on which playwright Robert Sherwood had employed considerable verbal sandpaper, struck no fire then and is forgotten now. It might have received a better response had the President not been so tired, cold and preoccupied. There were few in the audience who knew that he was planning to leave in three days for the last act of his hapless and hopeless quest for peace —in his time and for all time—at the Yalta meeting with Joseph V. Stalin and Winston S. Churchill.

When the brief ceremony was over, I splashed two slushy blocks to the Washington office of the Chicago *Tribune*. There, waiting for me, I found a characteristically curt wire from my editor and publisher, Colonel Robert Rutherford McCormick.

Fix Europe, it commanded.

It wasn't the first, nor was it to be the last time, that I got a global order. This particular message was inspired by my earlier confidential report of the impending hegira to Yalta, which could not be disclosed in a news story because the travels of the Commander in Chief were proscribed by the censorship code. What had aroused the colonel was my report that the agenda would include a modification of the plan to divide and pastoralize a floundering Germany, and that the conference would decide the fate of Poland, Czechoslovakia and other countries about to be liberated.

The message, which seemed to direct me to solve the problems of postwar Europe, was not unlike that which my predecessor as chief of McCormick's Washington bureau, Arthur Sears Henning, got on Inauguration Day, March 4, 1929, when he braved a cold rain to view the outdoor ceremony for Herbert Hoover. As the drenched new President began outlining measures for reconstruction and development, the reforms of social and business life and a program for reorientation, all of which were quite startling for that day and hardly in keeping with the reactionary image fastened on Hoover after the Depression, Henning hurried to the *Tribune* bureau to begin writing his inaugural story. He had completed his lead when a telegram, timed at 12:20 P.M., was thrust before him, which read: *This man won't do.*

This telegram bore the signature "McCormick," which I would come to know all too well. At times the signature could be beneficent and kindly, below a friendly message, but it could crackle with Morse sparks or bite like the knouts of a cat-o'-nine-tails. Henning recalled that all he had to do was pull his lead out of his typewriter and begin a new one. My problem was far more complicated; I had to deliver or find a diversion.

Fortunately, there is a good angel in the lives of many newspapermen, or perhaps it is the good St. Francis de Sales, their patron, who comes to their rescue when they are confronted by editors, who all too often confuse themselves with God. So it was with me. While I was seeking to arrange a meeting with Fleet Admiral William D. Leahy, an old friend who had revealed the impending Yalta trip a few days earlier, I got a cryptic call from Secretary of Commerce and Director of the Reconstruction Finance Corporation Jesse H. Jones, asking me to come to his office the next day.

There the man of cold steel-blue eyes, who had done so much to set business and industry back on its feet by cautious administration of RFC loans, showed me the letter he had received from FDR, informing him that Henry Wallace, who had been dumped as Vice President for Senator Harry S Truman of Missouri, wanted the Department of Commerce as his consolation prize. The letter was dictated by Roosevelt shortly before the inaugural ceremonies of the day before and was delivered while Jones was smiling on the scene with his fellow Cabinet members.

Jones had been summoned to the White House, he confided, shortly after the letter of dismissal was received. FDR, he said, first offered him the post of ambassador to France and then the chairmanship of the Federal Reserve Board. He turned both down.

Although his steely eyes were clouded in anger, they softened when Jones confided that he doubted that FDR would ever come back from Yalta alive. Jones expressed sorrow for the country and the world that FDR was going to Yalta to deal with so wily, so calculating and such an unscrupulous character as Stalin. But the softness died as Jones went to work on his letter replying to the Chief Executive, a letter drafted in consultation with other friends as well as myself. Jones bluntly told FDR he did not agree with Wallace's thinking that he could do the greatest amount of good in the Department of Commerce, nor with Roosevelt's belief that Henry was "fully suited for the post."

While I was sorry for Jones and considered the Wallace appointment a bad one, I must confess I welcomed the diverson that his ouster gave me on the command to "Fix Europe," and the confirmation of my private reports to the colonel on the state of FDR's health.

However, this was hardly the most pre-emptory assignment I

ever received from the colonel, nor the most taxing on my capabilities. When General Douglas MacArthur was fired by President Truman, I got the words:

Impeach Truman.

When I replied that I would have to explore the situation, he added: *America has never been in greater danger.* Then the colonel said he would do it himself and ran an editorial calling for impeachment on the ground that Truman was "unfit morally and mentally for his high office."

I waited for another telegram suggesting I employ the editorial as the basis of an impeachment resolution, but it never came, for which favor I could be grateful.

Another time, the colonel phoned to ask which was Rhode Island's star in the flag. When I identified it, I was puzzled by the inquiry, so I called the local room in Chicago. The colonel had ordered workmen to cut the Rhode Island star out of the large flag on display in the lobby of Tribune Tower.

I was told the colonel was displeased over a decision of the state's Supreme Court giving what he considered an unfair advantage to horse racing tracks. Fortunately for him, the colonel was advised of the penalties for defacing the flag—this was in the days before burning the flag in public became something of a national pastime—and replaced the national emblem before rival papers could photograph the McCormick version of Old Glory. I congratulated myself that I had not volunteered the information that the last stripe in the flag also represented Rhode Island or there would have been further mutilation.

When Frank McKinney of Indiana was chairman of the Democratic National Committee under Truman, the colonel sent me a note saying: *McKinney ought to be in jail.* When I didn't send him to jail within a week, the *Tribune* ran an editorial stating bluntly that McKinney was "a crook." Just why McKinney didn't sue or threaten to, I don't know except that he might have feared McCormick could prove it.

Such imperial announcements were a constant source of concern to the paper's law firm, which the colonel had helped to found. For more than a year, I was under orders to lock my drawing-room door every time a presidential special train passed through the state of

Pennsylvania enroute between Washington and Hyde Park, New York, Roosevelt's home town, for fear I might be served as the *Tribune* representative in an action threatened over an unfavorable editorial on a state judge. I ignored the order, aware that a process server would have had difficulty in piercing Secret Service and police cordons and because the train seldom stopped within Pennsylvania's borders. The colonel did lock the doors on his trips through the state, but it was his editorial that had opened the threat.

Court decisions have since flung open news columns to almost any criticism of any public figure, which hasn't always encouraged responsible reporting. This wouldn't have been considered a great boon by McCormick, because he was not only given to calling a spade a spade, but often branded it as a bulldozer, sweeping away rights and liberties he seemed to feel that he alone was interested in preserving.

At the end of one of his postwar world trips, the colonel got me into one of the hottest of critical blast furnaces with a note on scratch paper I still treasure. It read: *I have it right out of the Horse's mouth, the secret government is Morgenthau, Frankfurter and Lehman.* For years McCormick had dedicated himself to uncovering the leaders of a small group he was convinced was pulling the strings of government.

When I stalled, he called and identified his source as the Latvian-born wife of Loy Henderson. He was the American ambassador to Iran and one of the country's ablest diplomats, but that didn't exempt him from having wife problems. I argued that Henry Morgenthau, Jr., then Secretary of the Treasury, was not known as a mental giant so that he could hardly be considered a mastermind; that Felix Frankfurter, the former Harvard law professor who became a Supreme Court Justice, was never a confirmed New Dealer, and that Governor Herbert Lehman of New York was no strong man. I was abruptly ordered to write the story.

This I did, making it as strong and violent as I could, confident that the colonel would see the limb he was pushing the *Tribune* out on. This technique had worked in the past and I was confident it would work again. However, I failed to reckon with the managing editor William D. Maxwell, who was so anxious to keep in McCormick's good graces, being hopeful of succeeding him as editor, that he put the story on page one on a Monday morning.

When the roof caved in under criticism, the colonel left me to face the indignation alone. Also he let me become the darling of the lunatic-fringe press, an admiration society I didn't need or crave. Various representatives of Jewish organizations called on me in my office. I couldn't expose the colonel's hand, so I had to launch a counteroffensive.

During the war, William K. Hutchinson, the able chief of the International News Service, was bent upon impeaching Frankfurter. He enlisted my aid in compiling a dossier. This included the fact that Frankfurter had placed his ex-convict brother in charge of war alcohol purchases for the Treasury, getting a wartime taxicab gas allowance for an auto used by himself alone, and various other activities, which could have been made to look bad. Hutch couldn't get anyone to introduce his resolution. I got Representative Jessie Sumner of Illinois to agree to do so, but I let her off the hook when it became evident there was no chance of getting anywhere with the resolution. But this enabled me to raise a smoke screen, along with criticism of Morgenthau and Lehman's tie with international bankers. What saved me, as much as anything, was the fact that about that time I had to go to Chicago. There I was dining in the Tavern Club under the glowering eyes of the Chicago head of the Anti-Defamation League. The wife of Foreman M. (Mike) Lebold came in, spied me and greeted me with a friendly kiss. Since Mike was a heavy contributor, the Chicago official called her over to ask her if she knew whom she was kissing. Peggy said she did and dismissed as nonsense his suspicion of my anti-Semitism.

The colonel never bothered to say thanks. Shielding him from his own mistakes was considered one of my duties. I paid my debt to Mike after his death by working with Carl Sandburg to help get Mike's brother, Nathan Leopold, out of Joliet state penitentiary, where he was sent with Richard Loeb for the murder of the schoolboy Bobby Franks. Nathan was released on March 3, 1958, and took his first auto ride in almost a quarter of a century. It made him sick and he had to stop. During his stop he phoned me and thanked me for my help. I told him that while I was interested in his release because I felt he had earned it, I was really more interested in lighting a candle for his brother, Mike, who had visited him every month for more than two decades. Nathan died a free man after almost ten years of dedicated service on the outside.

When the White House was undergoing extensive repairs in the Truman administration and it was announced that some of the rubble of the original structure would be sold to interested Americans, I was ordered to get "a good stone for the Tribune Tower." I was lucky. The builder in charge of the project was John T. McShane of Philadelphia, a friend, who assigned a foreman, named Kelly, to get anything within reason that I wanted. We didn't take the cornerstone, but did get a goodly stone against it.

This was placed in the wall of Tribune Tower, which is studded with stones from various edifices of historic interest from the Great Wall of China to the Taj Mahal and Hamlet's Castle at Elsinore. I was not invited to the unveiling, but the colonel himself pointed it out to me, saying that it was keeping better company than when I first saw it.

I was never one to suffer fools gladly or easily, although God knows I had more than my share of practice with various editors. In almost a half century of newspapering, I worked under scores of editors and watched many others. Some were good and others were not as good as they should have been or thought they were. A few were great. The worst fault I found in editors, as a class, was in pretending to knowledge they did not have and stubbornly refusing to consult with knowledgeable subordinates. This fault is hardly confined to the newspaper trade.

The higher some editors rose, the more omniscience the less able assumed. Few editors these days have extensive reportorial experience and fewer Washington experience, although that didn't stop many from knowing everything, before and after it happened. It would not have been so bad if they had been content to be experts after the fact, but many editors clung to their own forecasts of events which had no basis in fact or grounding in history. These came to them, as near as I could make out, from conversations with the uninformed and their own interpretations based on hasty reading.

This made life difficult at times. I frequently found that being right with an editor brought no honor and less influence. A few were jealous of my acquaintance and friendly relations with many men I was paid to know. I suppose it is only natural that some editors should be jealous of those who can approach the great with familiarity and write rather quickly and easily what the great have to say with proper stress on its real importance.

However, this was not the case with the colonel, who was the most exasperatingly difficult man I have ever known but a truly great editor and a fascinating personality in his own right. Over the years I spent many days and hours in his company. When we were not together I was always as close as the nearest telephone and the Washington end of a leased teletype wire. If I left the office, I had to let my deskman, Leland Forrester, who really ran the details of the bureau, know where I could be reached, because McCormick called so frequently.

Very often when I reached my hosts in a receiving line, whether in a home, an embassy, a club or a hotel, there would be word that I was wanted for a most important telephone call. Invariably it was the colonel. Every day brought assignments scrawled on the margins of clippings from the *Tribune*, two- or three-line letters, either on *Tribune* stationery or half-sheet scratch pads, telegrams or messages.

I would be a prince of liars if I pretended that these gave me joy or provoked admiration at all times. While some were complimentary, many demanded the impossible, others spelled hours and days of work, and many more required a considerable amount of genius in interpretation. All in all, when these assignments began exploding over my days, my life took on a frenzy that makes James Thurber's *The Years with Ross,* as uneventful as the meditation hour in a Trappist monastery.

One assignment commanded: "Write a series on the invasion of America from Europe so that the fools in Washington will see how silly such talk is." Another was: "Tell the readers how Mussolini's invasion of Ethiopia is going to come out." A better one: "Draw up a peace plan that will not repeat the mistakes of Versailles."

The fact that I survived was not only a testimonial to mental agility and physical endurance, but also to an abiding affection, deep respect and the stimulation of perpetual surprises. There was seldom a dull moment and few idle ones in the Gatling gun spray of orders, comments and suggestions. The pace quickened when the colonel began dividing his time between Washington and Chicago, after the purchase of the Washington *Times Herald,* following the death of his cousin, Eleanor "Cissie" Patterson, its editor and publisher, who also was a character in her own right.

(This point will be developed in time, but to pin point it here, I can recall that she once said of herself: "The trouble with me is that I am a vindictive old shanty-Irish bitch.")

I knew the general circumstances of the colonel's life. McCormick supplied most of the details. Others I got from friends and enemies. I became something of an expert on his life, not because I wanted to write its story, but because I was sure that anything I learned would help me in dealing with so complex and demanding a man. He was born in Chicago July 30, 1880, and always spoke of himself as a Midwesterner. His father, Robert Sanderson McCormick, a nephew of the inventor of the reaper, was a diplomat serving as ambassador to Austria-Hungary, Russia and France after the turn of the century. His mother was Katherine Van Etta Medill, daughter of Joseph Medill, the vigorous supporter of Abraham Lincoln, who bought an interest in the *Tribune* in 1855, gained control of the paper in 1874 and served as its editor and publisher until his death in 1899.

McCormick told me of his school days in England where he was lonely and took to wandering over battlefields of the British civil wars in order to study history at first hand. He knew history, considering it essential to an editor and to newsmen generally. His own approach was stimulating, if controversial, in his publications which included *With the Russian Army*, published in 1915, and two volumes on the American Civil War—one on the war as fought by Ulysses S. Grant, the other lumping the campaigns of all the other Union generals as less important.

The colonel spoke of his days at Groton, where he was a schoolmate of FDR but no chum. Roosevelt told me McCormick hated him because FDR had stolen a girl from McCormick at a school dance. The colonel branded this tale as "Another of Frank's shallow lies," adding that in those days he was slow in appreciating the female sex. He dwelt on his days in Yale, confiding that he picked that university after reading the exploits of Frank and Dick Merriwell in the dime novels Gilbert Patten wrote under the pen name of Burt L. Standish.

In his lifetime, as far as I know, the colonel never gave a dime to Yale, although he saw to it that no member of his class ever suffered from want. In much the same spirit he sent a Christmas package to every hospitalized veteran of the First Division, which he served as an artillery officer. This contained sweets, tobacco and a five-dollar bill.

As his interest in education was restricted to Yale, class of 1903, so was his religion equated with the Presbyterian Church. In his own mind, McCormick considered himself a religious man, although he was not a churchgoer. I am sure he considered God a Presbyterian, although what He was before that church was founded the colonel did not make clear. McCormick did not pretend to speak for God, nor to employ Him for profit or argument. I never heard him mention God in a reverential way but, at least, he wasn't critical, nor forever telling Him what course of action He should take on the advice of one who had studied the situation. In his last days he was given to expressing his devotion to the Church. Even then he did not attend services, but this could have been due to his physical problems.

After leaving Yale, the colonel founded the law firm of McCormick & Patterson, now Kirkland & Ellis, and entered politics, becoming president of the Chicago Sanitary District. He launched the drainage canal to dispose of the city's sewage, although he acknowledged later he might have done better if he had built sewage disposal plants. After the first decade of the century he began interesting himself in the *Tribune* along with his cousin, Joseph Medill Patterson, the son of the editor-publisher's second daughter, Elinor, and Robert W. Patterson, Jr., a *Tribune* reporter, who became the paper's editor after Medill's death.

The colonel was a tall and awkward boy. At Yale he reached his full height of six feet four inches. His head, hands and feet were large, a fact which may have contributed to his shyness. But other contributory factors, according to his confidences, were that he was considered an outlander in English schools and had no intimates, and that his mother favored his elder brother, also named after Joseph Medill, who became a congressman and a senator. The colonel was clean-shaven until he came home from the war with a neatly clipped mustache, which became a trademark of sort.

His size made for some awkwardness in movement. It also confronted him with the threat of weight. As it was, he had to ride hunters rather than polo ponies, when he played that game. He tried to keep his weight down by boxing, riding to the hounds, swimming and taking to the trail in the Canadian woods, which properties he developed as a source for wood pulp. Later he was given to boasting that he could get into his World War I uniform, but it would have been a struggle.

He was proud of his career as a soldier, seeing service on the Mexican border with the Illinois National Guard in 1916 and with the First Division in France in World War I. When he was on the Mexican border with the Illinois National Guard, he purchased a Lewis machine gun from the British and had it sent to his regiment. Lieutenant General Lewis Crittenberger, then a lieutenant, told me the colonel exhibited the first such weapon army regulars had ever seen. Later critics were to distort this introduction into a McCormick claim that he had invented the machine gun.

In later life, McCormick was remarkably frank about his relations with women. He recalled he had a flamenco dancer brought to his quarters for the night during his border service.

"Imagine my surprise," he confided, "when I found out she wasn't Spanish but Mexican."

It didn't strike me as making any difference, and I told him so, observing that all sleeping dictionaries, whatever the language, were invariably opened at the same page.

There were conflicting stories of McCormick's war service. I tried to get at the truth, but never could, because the sources were biased. One of the most controversial stories was that the colonel had never been present at the Battle of Cantigny, after which he renamed the family estate of Red Oaks in Wheaton, Illinois, and where a museum was erected to commemorate the First Division.

He wore the insignia of the division, the big red "1," on a blue sports jacket, around his estate. He gave a yearly party to division members of the Chicago area, particularly those in veterans' hospitals. There is a story, which persists to this day, that he came to one reunion mounted on a horse in a van, whose tail gate was let down so that he could ride down a ramp and wave to his guests. The tale was manufactured out of whole cloth by Ray Quisno, a reporter for the Chicago *Herald and Examiner*, in the Cook County press room. Later Quisno joined the *Tribune* staff and was ever fearful McCormick would learn he was the author of that lasting jest.

The story told of the battle was that McCormick had run off, without leave, in search of his dog, which he suspected had left him to return to Paris. According to the tale, the colonel's absence from his artillery unit was covered by a young lieutenant from Princeton, Arthur Schmon, who made his fortune as a result, becoming the chief executive of the *Tribune*'s Canadian properties. Schmon indignantly denied the story. The colonel, less indignant, said it had been manufactured by a disgruntled Paris correspondent of the paper.

In the last days of that conflict, McCormick told me, Pershing planned to send him back to the States so that the colonel could return in command of a brigade which would have put a general's stars on the McCormick shoulders. The colonel confided that he was most disappointed that the war ended before he could get his brigade, until he realized that he would have had men die so that he could be a general. This realization, he said, awakened him to the terrors of military ambition.

For services in France the colonel was awarded the Distinguished Service Medal. The citation included mention of his personal bravery in action. He often harkened back to this service. One letter to me read:

"My portrait has me in the uniform of a colonel of artillery with a cannon. After that was painted I was appointed to the general staff. I would not want to take the cannon off.

"Find out if it would be proper for me to have the braid around the cuff painted black, as it is on the general staff, or to put it another way, would it be objectionable to do that?"

I did not dare tell the colonel what the Army said he could do with the cannon.

McCormick was devoted to the First Division and its various commanders, including General Charles P. Summerall, whom I had met as far back as 1928 when he was chief of staff. We called on Summerall in his final illness several times in the VIP quarters of Walter Reed Hospital. After one of these visits, I got a message from Chicago reading:

"Do you think Summerall would welcome some further gift like a bushel of apples or less, or would it look too much like subsidizing him?"

Because I knew the colonel had given his Asheville, North Carolina, home to the general, I couldn't understand the extreme caution over a gift of apples. Anyhow, I got the bushel, and by arrangement with Summerall, the apples were divided among nurses in his suite, a gift which was to serve me well, when President Dwight D. Eisenhower underwent his operation for ileitis in that institution, because a nurse phoned me reports on the progress of the operation and gave me bulletins on the President's condition.

In his European service, the colonel met General Douglas MacArthur. He was fond of telling that he was present when the stars of a brigadier general were pinned on the West Pointer. "McCormick," said the new general, "commented smilingly that I had gained on him, as I was a major when he was a colonel and became a colonel while he was still a colonel."

During World War II, the colonel had me send a personal message of congratulations to MacArthur through Colonel Larry Lehrbas, a former *Tribune* reporter and later an AP correspondent in Washington, who was flying to join the general on his campaign toward Japan from Australia. In his cordial reply, MacArthur expressed the complimentary wish that McCormick was serving with him.

It took quite a bit of convincing, on my part, to keep the colonel from taking his old uniform out of moth balls and setting off to join what I was sure would have been a flabbergasted commander. MacArthur confessed as much when I mentioned the episode to him after the war.

McCormick gave up playing cards during his college days, considering the pasteboards a waste of time. He also gave up smoking because he did not want to be chained to a habit. His table at Cantigny was always set with the finest of lace cloths, acquired in Paris at the turn of the century by his mother, and woe to one who dropped a lighted cigarette and scorched one. Such a guest was never, but never, invited again.

Maxwell wore out his welcome during his first visit, but for another reason. The managing editor was a bit nervous about the impending ordeal, so he fortified himself at home and in stops on the way, with generous lashins of scotch. At the table, shortly after being seated, he rose to inquire: "Where is the little boy's room?" The colonel was a stickler for the proprieties and while he enjoyed an occasional off-color story, if it were funny, I never heard him tell but one.

McCormick was fond of the theater but on his own terms. If he wanted to see a movie, his office would have to arrange to have a number of ushers sit in choice seats until the colonel and his party arrived. McCormick once made a rather spectacular exit from a performance of *Hamlet* in Chicago, which he attended with his chauffeur and personal bodyguard, Bill Bockelman, a former Chicago policeman. They were late and had to stumble over the feet of those in their row to reach their seats. Hardly had they settled themselves to look upon Horatio, Bernardo and Marcellus moving about in the bluish darkness outlining battlements of Elsinore, when the colonel rose again and started out, crying in his booming voice:

"Come on, Bill, I saw this play in college."

He was a regular theatergoer in New York, invariably wiring the New York advertising office of the *Tribune* to get him tickets. Before he acquired his own plane, he rode the Twentieth Century Limited. On the train he occasionally met acquaintances and invited them to join him and Mrs. McCormick at the theater. Then he would instruct the office to get more tickets. One such wire forced Eugene Struhsacker, the advertising representative, to exhaust all his theater friends and mortgage *Tribune* advertising space to get four seats for each of four smash hits. When we called on the colonel together, the more abashed Struhsacker begged me to ask McCormick how he enjoyed the show the night before.

"Last night's show was the greatest I ever saw," McCormick exclaimed.

Struhsacker beamed. The words rewarded his superhuman efforts. Then the colonel added:

"How did it come out?"

Struhsacker swallowed, his mouth dropped, but he managed, at length, to stammer: "How did it come out?"

"Yes, I left before the last act."

The colonel rarely carried money. On his travels a secretary was designated as treasurer to pay all bills and hand out all tips. In Washington I was expected to do it. Once at dinner he reached into his breast pocket, pulled out a wallet and began fingering some bills. I reminded him I was getting the check.

"What do you think I brought you along for?" he asked with a smile.

McCormick was accustomed to service all his life. He worked his servants hard but they had much free time when he traveled. I saw him ring for a servant and ask him to pick up a pencil some inches out of his own reach. He seldom bothered to housebreak dogs, leaving it to servants to clean up after them.

He rarely read any paper but his own, but he read that to the last line. He tore and scattered *Tribunes* like autumn leaves, making notations on clippings he saved for the instruction of editors and writers.

He was fond of good food, but didn't like surprises. In his own home he insisted on having the menu written for him on a porcelain stand. The colonel was a consistent drinker. He enjoyed an occasional cocktail, but usually drank scotch before dinner. He was not without idiosyncrasies in his drinking. Every now and then he would insist that some brand or other was being cheapened. George, his Swedish butler, would take the scotch away and bring back another, which the colonel always pronounced as infinitely better. When we became friendly, George took me into the pantry where he showed me how he poured the same scotch from one labeled bottle to another to meet the colonel's whims.

During the Second World War, when I managed to secure a case of rather rare fourteen-year-old scotch, McCormick insisted I take it back the next day because, while it tasted fine in the first drink, he said, it declined thereafter. Another time, he ordered me to have a liquor closet put in the suite he occupied in the Shoreham Hotel on his Washington visits. With considerable difficulty I had it stocked and was commended on his next visit. But when he returned the following week, he found the closet empty, because he had neglected to lock it. I have often wondered what lucky guest got that windfall. Fortunately, I was above suspicion because for some twenty years I drank nothing but an occasional glass of wine at dinner.

Some of his drinking provoked anecdotes. Shortly after the end of World War II, the colonel undertook a private plane trip to South America. The first stop was Jamaica, where the governor, Sir John Huggins, was in a dither because, as he explained to an aide, "I've invited Colonel McCormick to lunch and can't move the picture."

The aide, who thought his chief had been touched by the island sun asked, "What picture?"

"The painting of King George III," replied the governor.

The aide suggested that the governor seat the colonel with his back to the king, but the governor protested: "I can't do that, you know; it's the governor's chair." Finally, the aide observed that the colonel was a gentleman, after all, and had gone to school in England; the official could proceed with the luncheon, picture or no picture.

When time came for toasts after the meal, the governor proposed, "To the King." The colonel joined in the traditional toast. When it came his turn to respond, he rose slowly, being mindful that Truman, who was in the White House, was no friend to the paper or himself. The colonel looked at the portrait of the king who lost the colonies, at the ceiling and then back to the king, raised his glass and said, "To the father of my country."

The colonel told me of an earlier experience with British toasts. At a quiet and private dinner in the home of Winston S. Churchill, whom he had once employed to write articles for the Sunday *Tribune*, the host said: "I assume you'll want to begin with one of those abominable American cocktails."

McCormick allowed he would relish an old fashioned.

"Good," Churchill exclaimed, "the only sensible cocktail because it's almost straight whiskey."

Dinner proceeded with white and red wines. At the end of the meal the butler set a bottle of port on the table. The colonel waved it aside, saying he couldn't take anything more.

"But this port was laid down by my father in the last century," Churchill protested. "You would insult any British host by refusing his port."

Under the circumstances, McCormick was forced to accept. After the bottle had been passed to the left, in accordance with tradition, Churchill asked, with a twinkle in his eyes:

"Now, how about a spot of brandy?"

"I don't care if I insult the King, the Queen and the whole empire," McCormick exploded, "but I won't take any brandy."

"Good!" Churchill approved. "Then we'll go directly to the scotch and soda."

McCormick was long dismissed and still is, out of our penchant for labels, as anti-British. This he was not, but he was militantly pro-American which often brought him into conflict with British interests.

The colonel was not above jesting on the score of being anti-British. Once he barged into a meeting of the board of governors of the staid Chicago Club. He said he had taken note of the large number of portraits of red-coated British aristocrats and military figures on the club walls.

"Gentlemen," he said, "I see so many portraits of Englishmen here that I conceive you have an admiration for them. So, in the belief the club would like more, I am presenting five that I possess."

With perfect deadpan humor, he identified the subjects of his prints as:

Captain Sir Richard Pearson, who commanded the British frigate *Serapis,* when it struck its colors in 1779 to the *Bon Homme Richard,* commanded by John Paul Jones.

James Richard Dacres, who surrendered the HMS *Guerrière* to the USS *Constitution.*

General John Burgoyne, who surrendered his invasion army from Canada to the Americans under General Horatio Gates at Saratoga in 1777.

General Charles E. Cornwallis, who surrendered his army to forces under George Washington at Yorktown in 1781.

General Sir Edward Michael Pakenham, who was defeated and killed at the battle of New Orleans by American forces under Andrew Jackson.

Before his startled fellow club members realized that McCormick was pulling their legs, he turned and stalked out.

McCormick had more facets than all the jewels he bought his charming and vivacious second wife, Maryland Mathison Hooper McCormick. In addition to founding a law firm and directing construction of the drainage canal, he was a sound businessman. He was the first to recognize the potential of North Michigan Avenue in Chicago, although the credit is generally and mistakenly given to William J. Wrigley, Jr., the gum manufacturer, but the latter didn't buy his property and build until after he learned McCormick had purchased a site for the Tribune Tower.

The vision McCormick displayed built the *Tribune* into the largest full-sized newspaper in America, a position it has lost under his successors, but possibly through circumstances somewhat beyond their control. As a publisher he had the vision to conquer Canadian forests, erect paper mills, establish his own towns, construct a private TVA dam and launch a whole fleet of vessels so that trees could grow into *Tribunes.*

He also pioneered with color, experimented with readability of type and fostered experiments which produced rubber out of wood as a step toward meeting the World War II tire shortage. I tried to persuade him to end this experiment, when the group of wood chemists he had brought over from Poland produced potable alcohol from wood pulp as their first step toward synthetic rubber.

His vision made him the first to propose elevated highways as the solution of Chicago's growing traffic problem in the '20s. His rivals killed the idea by ridicule at a time when such a highway might have been launched for five million dollars. The development did come after his death at a much greater cost per mile. He saw value and necessity for a lake-front airport and a lake-front exposition hall. He was the first person I knew to adapt airplane seat belts for automobiles. He was interested in all mechanical phases of newspapering, being one of the first employers to install air conditioning in the Tower, even to the soaring city room.

But he was not in the least mechanical himself. He would have an engineer from WGN-TV, the paper's television station, drive thirty miles to Cantigny in order to change channels on his viewing set.

Not all his experimenting was successful. In the late '20s he embarked on a project to reform the often prolix and confusing orthography with which we all have struggled and which drives so many foreign students to despair. He even dropped the final "k" off his own name to encourage his program of calculated elision, but not for long. He put his plan in charge of James O'Donnell Bennett, a masterful writer, who had to battle for every change with stubborn resistance from editors. The program was abandoned after McCormick's death except for a few of the more common and accepted contractions, like "tho" and "thru."

Over the years he had a constant battle with the Tribune Tower's elevator service. These were never fast enough to suit him, although he replaced them a number of times. When he stepped into an elevator, it went directly to the editorial department on the fourth floor or to his office on the twenty-fourth floor. The service was fine for him, but he wanted to improve it for his employees.

The colonel's office on the twenty-fourth floor held terrors for many visitors because there was no knob on the door, which fitted into the wall paneling so closely it was almost impossible to detect. It was opened by kicking a brass plate.

McCormick's place in history is and will be as an editor. He didn't found the *Tribune*, but he took control in a critical period, surviving a threat of extinction by a renowned former editor, James Keeley, and defeated him in a battle for supremacy in Chicago. Under the colonel the paper exercised a tremendous influence upon the thinking of an area he regarded as Chicagoland, including all or portions of Illinois, Indiana, Iowa, Michigan and Wisconsin.

To me, his greatest quality as an editor was his courage. He did not, for a moment, believe in pandering to the tastes of his readers, but rather he strove to lead them. Under him and his cousin, Joe Patterson, the *Tribune* opposed entry into World War I. When the war came both went to the front, not wanting it said their opposition was based on concern for personal safety. They were consistent in their opposition to war, fighting to the last against entry into World War II. When war came McCormick and Patterson were dedicated to victory.

McCormick was a conservative, one who drew his principles and scale of values from the wisdom of generations that have gone before. The colonel was constantly seeking, reasonably and prudently, although it must be confessed, with some impatience, to reconcile the best of the wisdom and experience of his ancestors with the changes which are, perhaps, essential to a vigorous social existence. He had no patience with throwing the teachings and experiences of the past out of the window.

McCormick did not see that anything was holy merely because it was new. He was aware that whatever it was, it had been tried in the past and found wanting. Despite this composure he was a great believer in stirring up the animals, including myself. He kept all of us in his far-flung empire on our toes with letters, wires and phone calls.

In his time the *Tribune* was Colonel McCormick and it was known and read around the world—favorably or unfavorably, but it was known. As its Washington representative I shared this hate and adulation. In fact, I rather gloried in it, because I had no craving to be a nonentity. My paper was known and, therefore, I was known. The colonel's paper was always in the White House, even when the news columns and the editorials were most critical. It was at the elbows of such foes as Roosevelt and Truman, and a host of lesser officials. They might hate it, but they felt they had to read it. When I called in person or by phone I was always recognized as a personality.

Whether or not the colonel enjoyed cultivating hate, I cannot say, although I suspect he did not, but he could not tolerate indifference and seldom met with it. He was a personage in his own right so that on his travels he was invited to Buckingham Palace or the executive mansion of Liberia. No doubt he was the last of the great personal editors and merited reading by friend and foe for his courage and his battle against the inevitability of gradualness.

I have always found it difficult to resent people I don't know and whose workings I don't understand. McCormick had no such trouble. If a known or an unknown enemy did the right thing, he was confident that it was only by accident or the result of reading one of his editorials. He suspected any and all campaign promises, by friend or foe, as the only currency never affected by inflation, because they are generally valueless from the moment of issuance. He was convinced that Washington's only approach to any problem—national or international—was to fling money at it in hope that it would disappear.

Always, he suspected do-gooders, being aware that once a man dedicates himself to what he professes to be the ultimate benefit of humanity, there might be no restraint on his capacity for villainy. He firmly believed that dedication to doing good was even more corrupting than power. In this he agreed with Henry David Thoreau, no conservative, in the declaration: "As for doing good, that is one of the professions which are full. Moreover, I have tried it fairly, and, strange as it may seem, am satisfied that it does not agree with my constitution."

The colonel was my boss but he became my friend, despite a

twenty-three-year gap in our ages, partly because of our fondness for history and a common approach to national and international problems. We achieved a more intimate footing than he ever had with his various editors, but that didn't mean I could unduly drag my feet on any assignment or presume to ignore them. I would not say the colonel was "the man we hold the best, wisest and most just of his age," as Plato did of Socrates. After all there were times when I could have cheerfully strangled him. As much as I revere Plato, I love truth more, so that I might possibly conclude of the colonel, as James Boswell did of Samuel Johnson, that his "talents, acquirements and virtues were so extraordinary that the more his character is considered, the more he will be regarded by the present age, and by posterity, with affection and reverence."

Although ducal and even imperial, the colonel considered himself a member of the middle class—and in the very middle, not at its right. He included me with him in this company, even though I told him I considered his scale of living and way of life a rich mixture for our class.

The colonel was given to enlivening dinner parties in his home with the declaration "All the McCormicks were and are crazy except myself." Then with that humor which was always at war with his pomposity, he would add: "You wouldn't agree with that, would you, Walter?"

I had to admit that I wouldn't at all times, which would evoke a hearty roar of laughter.

EARLY DAYS

I was born with a silver spoon in my mouth on July 4, 1903, in Mount Carmel, Pennsylvania, a pleasant town on the edge of anthracite fields. The spoon didn't remain there long because my father, a prosperous and enterprising merchant, who not only operated a grocery and meat shop, but sent a fleet of wagons to sell in the area's coal patches, went bankrupt. He had given credit to support mining families in the great strike of 1907. He tried to stage a comeback after the settlement, wiping his books clean of the debts, but his former customers were ashamed to return. My mother was the daughter of a grocer in neighboring Shenandoah, where she was something of a belle, being quite pretty and possessing a pleasant voice.

My memories of the area are dim. I can see, in my mind's eye, my great-grandfather, an omniverous reader (who got his first pair of glasses at the age of ninety-three and died five years later), playing chess with the blind pastor of the church to which the family contributed several stained-glass windows. I recall wandering over green foothills of the Appalachians with Dan, a handsome black and white setter. I guess I was a bit of a snob because I best remember taking friends and schoolmates into our home to show them electric lights, steam heat and our bathroom, and because I could read before I went to school.

In 1910, my mother took me, a younger sister and my baby

brother to Chicago where my father became a wholesale grocer. At first we lived in a brownstone at 553 East 37th Street, a stone's throw from the mansions of some of the city's wealthiest families, but more importantly to me an even shorter distance from the tomb of Stephen A. Douglas, a lifelong hero. In time we moved further south, generally within walking distance of Lake Michigan.

It was not long before I became a Midwesterner in speech and thought and so I have remained despite thirty-eight years in Washington and two in the friendly magic of Ireland. About all of Pennsylvania left in me is my birth on Independence Day, a fact which has colored my life toward the virtues of patriotism.

I embarked on a newspaper career by accident rather than choice. First, I became the editor of the Bowen High School monthly magazine. As such I was enlisted to write editorials urging an increase in teacher pay for the *Daily Calumet* in South Chicago, a publication unknown to me until then because we lived further north. The night of my graduation, William A. Rowan, the paper's city editor, offered me the role of reporter—in fact, of being his entire reportorial staff.

Since I was planning to enter the University of Illinois to study law in the fall of 1921, I declined with thanks. Bill pressed me, saying that among my duties would be the coverage of the branch of the Municipal Court above the South Chicago police station. That convinced me. After a few weeks all thoughts of law and Illinois vanished. I remained a reporter for some fifteen months and then entered the University of Notre Dame in the fall of 1922.

I found reporting my dish of tea and took to it like a duck to water. I was flattered by the respect it brought from my elders. I gained a new insight into the lives of police and they have retained my sympathy ever since, despite those who yield to temptation and power. As a class I found them far better than those who revile them.

My schooling on the *Daily Calumet* was good. Its editor, George W. Bolling, had been city editor of the Chicago *Interocean*, then defunct, and was of the same Virginia family as Edith Bolling Galt Wilson, President Woodrow Wilson's second wife. He was kind and helpful, but I learned the trade from Bill Rowan, who subsequently became an alderman and then a congressman. It could be said that the two of us left the banks of the Calumet for those of the Potomac; we became lifelong friends.

Notre Dame is a pleasant memory. My days were filled with friendships and instruction and happiness. However, the most I can say for the institution and many good professors is that my thirst for knowledge was increased rather than dampened, so that it continues even to this day. I served as secretary to John M. Cooney, Ph.D., in return for private lessons in Greek rather than the customary allowance on tuition and board, which will indicate why I gathered enough credits but not the residence or thesis for a master's degree. I was offered an instructorship in history, but chose to see what I could do in the newspaper world.

After graduation I spent a few months in the New York City area, which I found unattractive, and returned to Chicago where I went to work covering police for the Chicago City News Bureau, a local press service familiarly known as the City Press, operated by the then six Chicago newspapers, two morning and four afternoon. Later I went on to cover every beat in the service.

I started covering the western suburbs of Cook County from Oak Park for $18 a week. I worked from 9 A.M. until 11 P.M. at night as well. And I got every other Sunday off! Yet I did not consider myself abused or overworked. I gloried in it and managed to leave some myths behind me which I am told live to this day.

This was in the days of gangster warfare. Many a dull gray dawn found me on a country road beside the bullet-riddled body of one who had served the rival gang of Al Capone or Roger Tuohy, too well but not too wisely, perhaps. Once because a coroner's physician had no taste for it, I grasped the slimy hair of a smelly corpse found in an abandoned auto in a cornfield and sawed off the top of his head in order to determine whether he had been killed by shotgun pellets fired by guards at fleeing bank robbers or by gangland bullets. Joe Lavandier, veteran City Press rewrite man, insisted I find out. There was no other immediate way.

I had my triumphs and my failures, but was considered a good reporter, getting $32 a week and had the promise of a two-dollar raise before I left to join the *Tribune*. Before leaving I directed the bureau's coverage of gangland's greatest story, the day Chicago's hoodlums graduated from murder to massacre.

I was covering the Cook County Building at the time and one of my duties was to relieve a rewrite man for his noon hour. It was St. Valentine's Day, February 14, 1929. John Pastor, a young lad who had been collecting marriage licenses, births and similar vital statistics, was being given a trial at police reporting. He was alone in the Detective Bureau because the ace regular reporters had gone to the City Hall to confer with Chief of Police Morgan Collins.

Johnny was on the phone stuttering with excitement: He reported five men were killed in a garage. Isaac Gershman, the city editor, wouldn't believe him, and turned Pastor over to me, but instructed that I write a bulletin that five men had been injured in a fight. So I wrote the bulletin of which I am not proud: "Five men are reported to have been injured in a fight at 2022 North Clark Street."

A moment later Johnny was back on the line swearing by all that was holy it wasn't five men dead but six and one was on the way to the hospital dying, and all had been cut down by machine-gun fire. Pastor bypassed the unbelieving desk and gave it to me. I pounded out a second and more accurate bulletin, flung it at Gershman and announced I was on my way, without asking for approval. As I went out the door I turned to ask if I could take a cab, City Press being most cautious about expense accounts. "The Clark streetcar runs right past the door," Gershman said.

Even so, I was the first man on the scene of carnage, being careful to avoid the lunging of the crazed police dog chained to one of the garage trucks. The most memorable remark of the day was that of Willis O'Rourke of the Chicago *Evening American* who looked down at his feet after tracking around the garage and said: "I've got more brains on my feet than I have in my head." Other staffers joined me in tracing the path of ambush and the story of the slaying of six members of the George (Bugs) Moran mob, rivals of the Al Capone gang. I topped off the St. Valentine's Day murders by attending an all-star performance of *Macbeth* in Chicago's Auditorium Theater, the old opera house, with Carol Rowland, whom I was to marry the next St. Patrick's Day, and my sister Irene and brother Lee. After all, the massacre was no more than a fitting prelude to the ten violent deaths in *Macbeth*.

I was hired by the *Tribune* a few days later and went to work covering the County Building on February 25, 1929. I'd like to say

that the selection was due to brilliant and industrious reporting, but
that would not be true. Reportorial ability played a part but the fact
that I was no respecter of authority, whether Mayor William H.
(Big Bill) Thompson, a Republican, or County Board President
Anton J. Cermak, a Democrat, or anyone else in power, played a
large part.

Not long before St. Valentine's Day, I was unwittingly involved
in a scene outside the Club Alabam on Chicago's near North Side.
This night club was then owned and operated by one Carter Blatch-
ford, a friend of Big Bill's, who ran a gambling room on an upper
floor, with the mayor's protection. Late one evening, Carol, Milton Fairman of the Chicago *Evening Post*, and I had stopped next
door to the club to call on John Drury of the Chicago *Daily News*.
He was not in, we were told by his landlady, who came to the door
in a garish bathrobe with her hair tied up in leather curlers. She was
something of a sight.

We restrained our laughter until we left her door. Since it was
raining, we stopped under the club's sidewalk awning for a moment,
still laughing. A couple of overzealous club bouncers charged up
and ordered us to move on. When we tarried, the bouncers flung
me to the ground. Carol straddled me and fended off further assault
—there was nothing I could do subsequently but marry the girl.
When I got up, I went into action with Fairman, who had also been
overpowered.

I had a bystander call the police. When they came I demanded
the club be raided because it was a gambling dive. They, of course,
were aware of this, as well as of the mayor's interest, so they de-
layed. I demanded to be taken to the East Chicago Avenue station.
There I called the Detective Bureau, Circuit Judge Joseph B. David,
E. C. Yellowley, chief of prohibition agents, Corporation Counsel
Samuel Ettelson and the office of the chief of police. I got plenty of
action, but there was no raid. I mention this, at some length, only
to demonstrate that, even in those distant days, reporters considered
themselves a special breed.

Naturally enough the story got around. A day or two later,
James L. Doherty, a reporter for the *Tribune*, sought me out in
the press room of the City Hall, which I was covering at the time.

"Quite the bantam battler, aren't you?" he chuckled. "You're just what we need on the *Tribune*."

This endorsement did much to gain me a place on the staff. In those days the reportorial staff of the *Tribune* was something of a club, because no newcomer was accepted unless he had the approval of his fellow reporters as well as that of the editors. I had no trouble adjusting to the team. However, let me be entirely frank and acknowledge that I was a trial then and through my long years of services. I have always resisted uninformed and capricious authority and have been something of a rebel. My independence was heightened by knowledge that I could accept offers from other papers in Chicago and in Washington. In fact, I consider myself a true liberal, not one who binds himself to any faction, but who is convinced the least government is the best government.

In these early days McCormick was a dim and distant figure in his twenty-fourth-floor office. Yet, his spirit was in the local room at all times. He was known affectionately as "the Colonel," but not without a tinge of awe and even fear. He was an admirable boss, because he was convinced, or at least convinced those in the vineyard, that every employee with whom he dealt was the best possible man in his post. He was demanding and exacting, but he was also forgiving; he seemed to enjoy the making of mistakes by those about him, so that he could be forgiving.

Although distant, he was not inaccessible. We met when I began filling in on the day city desk, going to his office for assignments and instructions or taking them by phone. He figured so much in our daily lives, and was so benevolent and generous a patron, that the late Edward Scott Beck, the best of the many managing editors I served, often said he was going to write a book, entitled *The Colonel Told Me*. And, with a characteristic twinkle in his eye, Beck would add that Louis Rose, then circulation manager, would write the sequel, *I Told the Colonel*. Rose was given to half-hour discourses on what he had told the colonel in a five-minute conference. These were generously sprinkled with malapropisms. We liked his reference to "an ego with a six-foot wing spread," he had mounted in his office. It was an eagle of course.

The colonel seldom appeared in the local room until after Alfred (Jake) Lingle, a *Tribune* crime reporter, who was reputed to be an

intimate of Capone and other gangland figures, was shot by a gun-
man in the pedestrian tunnel of the Illinois Central Railroad's sub-
urban service off Michigan Avenue at Randolph Street. The slaying
precipitated a violent exposure of municipal and county misgovern-
ment that reached into newspaper offices and tarnished some reporters and editors. I have no intention of dwelling on it, except
that the case was to be one of my stepping stones to Washington.

Jake Lingle was shot by Leo V. Brothers, a St. Louis hoodlum,
imported to do the job for the North Side gang, known as the
Aiello-Zuta-Moran mob after its more important figures. These gangsters suspected Lingle was taking advantage of his long friendship
with Police Commissioner William F. Russell to raid and close their
gambling establishments in order to help Capone advance and extend his gambling empire. Lingle, who was never more than a leg-
man, cultivated a mysterious manner, which could be taken as proof
of such suspicions and of rumors which, even in his lifetime, reported he was profiting from questionable connections.

A few days before his death Jake went to Robert Morton Lee,
the competent if somewhat flamboyant city editor of the *Tribune*,
to demand that I be fired because I had accused the reporter of being
a racketeer. I had done no more than make an airy reference to a
favor Jake had asked me to seek for two women friends as "evidently one of his rackets." When Lingle's heavy spending was revealed by examination of his finances, I was credited with more
knowledge or insight than I possessed. Also I served notice on day
city editor J. Loy Maloney and Lee that if either were involved in
Lingle's activities, I would resign from the staff.

I was an idealist then and have always been, despite a generous
salting of cynicism acquired over the years. Lee, whose position in
the local room and with McCormick was in danger, took to cultivating me, evidently figuring if he won me over this would help him
rebuild staff morale. I was flattered and may have been taken in a bit,
but this contributed to my education.

Colonel McCormick began frequenting the local room. Now and
then he would make a speech, which was aimed at restoring confidence, and he would talk over coverage of major stories, asking
me to fill him in on such things as bank failures and the political
manipulations of Cermak, who had become mayor.

The colonel sent a former army captain, Maxwell D. Corpening, to the fourth floor to keep an eye on the editorial department. Corpening, who had been brought to Chicago as a polo instructor at the Onwentsia Country Club, was a pleasant fellow who knew nothing about the newspaper business. After the uneasiness that followed in the wake of Lingle's death had stilled, Corpening traveled the world as a military expert, although he never mastered any of the essentials of newspapering, but always found someone to do his work or copied articles from the Encyclopaedia Britannica, as he once did on the Philippines, which was pointed out to Lee by an alert copy reader.

"Proves Corpening can read, at any length," Lee remarked sententiously.

Brothers, Lingle's murderer, was sent to prison. John Boettiger, a personable and competent reporter, followed and at times directed the investigation. Among others, I frequently worked under him on this quest and did considerable traveling, because the *Tribune* was determined to leave no stone unturned in its efforts to bring the slayer to justice, regardless of Lingle's operations.

My contributions to the solution of the case were unimportant, being no more than clearing up tips that proved to be unfounded. My only happy recollection is the time I persuaded Police Sergeants J. F. (Jiggs) Donohue and Frank Reynolds, attached to the coroner's office, to let a suspect, who had been found guiltless of the Lingle crime but was being returned to a Minnesota prison on an old robbery charge, enjoy the favors of his wife in the washroom of a Cook County jail interrogation room.

"Thanks a lot," he told me as I left. "I'll never forget you. Believe me, I didn't push Jake. I'd tell you this if I had, but I really didn't and I tell you this on my wife's body."

During the Lingle investigation, I was put in charge of a *Tribune* project to harass the city's gangsters. Some twenty-six of them were sought or tried on charges of vagrancy. All but one of those tried, Edward (Spike) O'Donnell, were found guilty, but their convictions were overruled by the state Supreme Court. I may as well confess here and now that Spike got off because I persuaded him to undertake his own defense and wrote his final plea to the jury, just for the sake of a good color story. Also I played a major role in another

Tribune anticrime project, persuading judges of the Circuit and Superior courts to give up their vacations and come home to clean up the criminal court dockets. This was so successful that lawyers began pleading their clients guilty, shortly after arrest, rather than face juries that were handing out death sentences and prison sentences up to 244 years with prompt and effective regularity.

But this is not the story of crime and corruption in Chicago, nor of my newspaper days in that turbulent era. It is, rather, the tale of some thirty-eight years in Washington and world capitals. However, some explanation of my preparation for the national and international scene is an essential of my story.

In those days Washington was not the goal of reporters that it has become today. Nor had Washington become everyone's city hall as it is today. I can remember men being elected to Congress, mostly as a reward for faithful party service. They would be given a farewell banquet and forgotten. Few knew the names of their congressmen or cared about them. Senators were known as godlike dwellers in the nation's political Valhalla.

Of course, the total federal budget was under five billions a year, including the Army and Navy, as against more than two hundred and fifty billions today. Deserving and itching palms were not all turned to Washington, nor were states, schools, cities and a whole gamut of projects and administrations demanding federal financing. Washington was little more than a sleepy town where editorials of its leading newspaper, then the Washington *Star*, called on the citizenry to save its beautiful dogwood trees and advised all who could, to leave town in July and August in order to escape the sultry heat.

The 1929 Depression changed the pattern. More people and more groups began turning to Washington for help. Although I was more interested in the national scene than most of my fellow newsmen, because I had played a minor role in covering the 1932 conventions and had interviewed many capital figures on visits to Chicago or when they changed trains in the city, I was in no hurry to pull up stakes and try my fortunes elsewhere. After all I was making $75 a week, a handsome salary in those days, had an impressive stable of sources, my roots in Chicago were deep and my family was growing, then numbering a daughter and a son.

Boettiger had been assigned to coverage of Franklin D. Roosevelt's political campaign after his Chicago nomination, as a reward for his part in bringing Brothers to justice. After FDR's victory Boettiger continued to follow the President-elect and joined the Washington bureau of the *Tribune* after Roosevelt's inauguration. The rapturous advent of the New Deal played havoc with the bureau, four members joining what they considered the dawn of a new and great day. These were John Herrick, the able second man; Genevieve Forbes Herrick, his talented wife; Guy McKinney, who undertook to publicize the Civilian Conservation Corps, and George Barnes, who held a number of public relations posts, including a term with UN in its founding years.

Since the bureau was small, replacements were an immediate necessity. Chesly Manly, the *Tribune* man covering the federal building in Chicago, was considered a natural. Eugene S. Duffield, an extremely competent master of federal finance, was hired in Washington, a rare departure for a paper that believed in promoting its own, because money and its uses and problems were one of the major operations of the new Administration. The *Tribune* never fully appreciated Duffield, because he was unknown in Chicago, so he left, eventually becoming publisher of the Cincinnati *Enquirer* and other publications. Boettiger took over for Herrick and began importuning me to join him, because he felt quite confident I would resist New Deal wiles and because I had something of a reputation for incisive questions. I dropped my resistance in the fall of 1934 and a beautiful October day found me awed by the sun-lighted capital, the avenues of limestone federal buildings with their green trees and the charm of the White House.

Henning, the bureau chief, who had a rare genius for getting others to do his administrative work, was an envied figure in those days because he was the highest paid reporter in the capital, receiving $20,-000 a year and another $10,000 for a weekly radio program, in a day when top reporters were getting around $75 a week.

Henning was a scholar, a gentleman and a gourmet, but hardly a bureau chief. I can say this because I never considered myself much of a bureau chief either, except, when my time came, for welding together a group of highly competent newsmen and trusting them to do their work well, which they did, and leave me to reporting, my great love, although I did fight for them and get them far above the

Chicago pay levels. Also I built the bureau from four to fourteen men, operating a tight but efficient news service, as the capital end of a press service the colonel founded in promoting his paper.

Being a bureau chief is a thankless job at best, because one makes many unhappy when he passes out a coveted assignment and reaps no gratitude from the recipient of the favor, who is generally convinced the chief couldn't pass him over without doing worse. I could never get any sense of accomplishment out of putting others to work, no matter how good a news package they delivered, so I knew I was not conditioned toward being an editor. The greatest attribute I possessed for chiefdom, in addition to a nose for news and a gregarious nature, was a good memory. It is not as good as it was and still is fabled to be, but good enough to serve me well even to this day, because I can recall a great deal. And I had top investigative reporters like Philip L. Warden and Aldo Beckman, and men who could be sent almost anywhere, like Larry Burd, Bill Moore, Joe Hearst, Philip Dodd, William C. Strand, Lloyd H. Norman and Robert C. Young.

I will say for Henning that he never did, as so many of his colleagues were given to doing, steal the best story of the day from the reporter who covered and wrote it, and slap his own name on it before sending it to the office. He was one of the leisurely school of covering the capital, having come to Washington shortly after the turn of the century when life was quieter and news much slower. As Henning stepped off the train from Chicago, he walked unknowingly by the coffin of the bureau chief he had come to serve, Raymond A. Patterson, an uncle of Eleanor and Joseph Medill Patterson, who had died while Henning was enroute and whose body was being returned to Chicago for burial. Henning served John Callan O'Loughlin, the succeeding chief, who was a great favorite of President Theodore Roosevelt, who later made him an Assistant Secretary of State. Still later he was the owner and editor of the *Army and Navy Journal*.

Henning never became accustomed to the explosive character of the New Deal, under which stories were bursting all over town like fireworks tied to the tail of a dog. His greatest contribution to the *Tribune* was a weekly review of the Washington scene, which was invariably carried on column one of page one and ran for several thousand words. This ran for years and years. In Chicago I had been impressed by his erudition, background and perspective. I was shocked and surprised, therefore, when it became my Sunday duty to put these stories on our leased telegraph wire to Chicago. Then I learned that he merely wrote a lead and occasional introductory sentence to pages of editorials clipped from the New York *Herald Tribune* and the New York *Times*.

Not once in all the years I served Henning was he ever confronted with an accusation of plagiarism, evidently because no one in Chicago read the New York papers or the editorials in those papers. Correspondents of the two New York papers were given to saying no one ever read their editorials and I was prepared to believe it when I saw Henning going unchallenged.

I did not appear in Washington a full-fledged reporter of the national scene, as Minerva sprang fully armed from the forehead of Jove, for all my brashness and my seven years in the hurly-burly of Chicago's machine politics and gang warfare. Still, I had been trained to act as a spectator, not as a wielder of power. I was aware of the pomposity of mediocrity. I had been schooled to know that when impious men hold sway in politics and when vice prevails, as it did in the Prohibition era, the point of honor for a reporter is to maintain his private reputation spotless. It was no problem for me to learn that he who sups with the President might do well to take a long spoon, lest he find himself enlisted or captured. The danger in dealing with Presidents is not so much that they sell you their programs as that you sell them interest in something close to your heart, like preservation of wild life or advancement of ecology, and they have you for all time.

Once a Chicago politician offered me $3,000 to forget a story I uncovered on an attempt by him to shake down the Chicago Title and Trust Company by promoting an alleged rival organization. I ran the story but didn't dare tell Maloney of the bribe, until years later, because I was sure he wouldn't believe I had been offered and refused so large a sum. Another time I rejected the offer of a $250-a-month payment as a lake level consultant when I was covering the Chicago Sanitary District, for City Press and few newspapers bothered to assign men to cover sewage. Only a few years later I had reason to thank myself, when the job files of this governmental agency were flung open, because the disclosure of my name among payees would have ended my newspaper career.

Not all the credit for my honesty was due to training I received from God-fearing parents or from insatiable reading in days when the old virtues were honored and respected. I was schooled by great and good newspapermen, like Bennett and Doherty and Parke Brown and Philip Kinsley and Orville (Nimble Orville) Dwyer. The latter got his nickname from the Western Union code word for payment of $50, because on out-of-town assignments he regularly requested money and its delivery followed messages which read "Nimble Orville Dwyer." After their teaching it was easy to refuse the ten-dollar or twenty-dollar bills lawyers, politicians or hoodlums were given to tucking into reportorial pockets.

My first press conference was on Capitol Hill within hours of my arrival in Washington. It nearly became my last. Boettiger took me to the office of Senator Joseph T. Robinson of Arkansas, the majority leader, who had just returned from Europe with Senator Tom Connally of Texas. We were a bit late, entering as the impressive statesman was answering a question on farm price supports. He was leaning back in his chair with his eyes closed dictating his answer, as though we were a battery of stenographers, noting paragraphs, colons, semicolons, commas and periods. Every question was so answered. I had never seen such a performance. I didn't understand the questions, which were highly technical, nor the answers which were even more so. I was crushed and left with my shoulders sagging, because I doubted that I could ever master the issues of such a technique. All my elation over being assigned to the capital evaporated; I was ready to ask to be allowed to return to Chicago.

Dejectedly, I followed the reporters into Connally's office, where Charles Michaels of the New York *Times* opened the questioning by asking the Texan what he proposed to do about the nuisance taxes in the coming session. Connally stammered, finally saying he didn't remember them.

"You voted for them, didn't you?" Michaels challenged. "And now you tell us you can't remember them. You better go home and study what you did in the last session of Congress and then come back and schedule a news conference on what the country is thinking. You better forget Europe."

I was home. This kind of questioning and this sort of approach to politicians I understood. From that conference, Charley, whom I had met several times before in Chicago, was an idol and remained so in a press corps that was conceded to be at least 95 per cent New Deal by its members.

My arrival in Washington came more than a year after the drama of the Hundred Days, as that period came to be known in which FDR closed and reopened the banks, called Congress into special session and unloosed a whirlwind of laws, projects and orders that began coming from a mushrooming of alphabetical agencies. I had covered aspects of the banking crisis in Chicago and the workings of various federal agencies, particularly the National Recovery Administration.

So that there might be no mistaking my position, I had not voted for FDR, like so many other reporters, who were then, as many have done since and are doing today, hailing the dawn of the millennium. I did not hold Hoover responsible for the world-wide depression and I was less than enthusiastic about the regulation of prices and production under the Blue Eagle, which I considered nothing more or less than a borrowing of regimentation from Adolf Hitler, then the socialist some admired rather than the dictator all were to dread.

However, the mad snake dance of the self-admitted great minds, deep thinkers, professorial pundits, panacea philosophers, monetary miracle workers and strange schemers was still going on when I arrived. Never were so many, who knew so little, so sure of their answers to everything. New truths, largely old heresies, were being offered by a wide variety of alphabetical agencies as the true political faith, but were to prove to be old superstitions.

The public had been dazzled by the furious succession of novelties, restrictions and regulations. The NRA alone was turning out daily stacks of press releases of orders and regulations, more than a foot high. The AAA was promising to end the farm problem forever, but had, up to my advent, succeeded only in ending the lives of millions of piglets.

FDR offered as his pet project to end the Depression, the Civilian Conservation Corps, which was to put a million youths into the nation's forests at a dollar a day to preserve and enhance their beauty and usefulness, a pioneering in ecology. He created the Federal Relief Agency, which later became the Works Progress Administration, but which still was concerned with leaf raking on highways and other made work programs. This change in names was one of the first of a pattern of creating new agencies for the same tasks, whenever the promise of earlier agencies failed to mature. The NRA was launched as the great charter for free business and free labor, but was actually a program for total regimentation.

FDR did not offer these things in his campaign; actually, his campaign was nothing more or less than an exercise in traditional conservative Democratic policy. He promised to cut the cost of the federal government by 25 per cent through efficient management and consolidations in the interests of economy. He declared himself for a sound currency. Almost his only economy was to order officers in the military to take a two-week vacation without pay. And he was to cut the gold value of the dollar to 59 cents, thus launching currency manipulation which goes on to this day.

Roosevelt rode to power on the Depression, blaming it simply and profitably on the Republicans in general and Herbert Hoover in particular. In 1958, Hoover made a satirical reference to this representation, but without naming FDR, saying: "Once upon a time my political opponents honored me as possessing the fabulous intellectual and economic power by which I could create a world-wide Depression all by myself."

In his campaign FDR promised to help the needy, but without doles, through useful public works, which were to be self-liquidating. For the farms he promised control of surpluses and encouragement of cooperatives. For business, he urged strict control of antitrust laws and regulation of securities in order to prevent such disasters as the market collapse.

No one could fault his campaign program. There were grave faults in the government. The Democratic party had always opposed the creation of more government and had always called for less borrowing, holding huge federal deficits were at the bottom of all our economic troubles. Many so hold to this day, but have seen the deficits continue to mount.

In office, FDR overturned his campaign promises by inviting the professors and crackpots to launch the concept of big government, and socialist government at that. There was nothing new in his approach, although it was claimed to be new. It was the age-old game of taking from the haves and giving to the have-nots.

This practice was reported in the great Celtic Iron Age epic *Táin Bó Cualinge,* the longest and most complete of the Ulster cycle of heroic tales. And the practice was old then. According to the ancient story, Nes, who was sought for his wife by Fergus mac Roich, king of Ulster, persuaded her lovesick monarch to let her son, Conchobor, be king for a year so that they might call the latter's son, when he had one, the son of a king. Fergus agreed and the tale continues:

"Nes immediately set about advising her son and his foster parents and everyone in his household they were to steal everything from one half of the people and give it away to the other half."

The result was that at the end of the year, Fergus lost his throne, because the men of Ulster, who shared Conchobor's bounty, were grateful and stood by him against their old king.

One of the first casualties when FDR took office was the "Forgotten Man" of his campaign. The common man was neglected, as he had long been, in the race for power. Hated business, on the other hand, was receiving more attention and greater benefits, although it remained a favored oratorical whipping boy. Class was pitted against class, even though FDR was promising to make all men equal. The favored ones were to be more equal than the others. The favored were the new federal aristocracy of planners and managers, who were wired into permanent jobs under the extension of civil service. In time, most deserving Democrats—and weren't they all?—were so wired.

By the time I arrived on the scene, the grand carousel of the Hundred Days was still whirling, but some of the planners were being revealed as prophets without honor and some of the plans were grinding to a halt. Critics were beginning to raise the cries of socialism and communism.

My arrival almost coincided with the visit of Dr. William A. Wirt, famed originator of the Gary, Indiana, system of public education. Wirt was entertained at a cocktail party and a dinner in the home of a former secretary. At this dinner were Larry Todd, the mild and scholarly American correspondent of Tass, the Soviet news agency, and a few American leftists who were looking toward the great day of liberation.

One of the guests told the good doctor they had Roosevelt racing in the middle of a stream from which he could not escape. The plan, they boasted, was to keep him there until he could be replaced by an American Lenin or Stalin because, after all, FDR was only the Aleksandr Kerensky of a revolution that the insiders were controlling and manipulating, while letting Roosevelt believe he was making the decisions himself.

On his return to Gary, a genuinely horrified Dr. Wirt wrote to a number of friends in an effort to mobilize them against the threatened revolution. One of his letters was read in Congress where it created a sensation. New Deal champions were outraged by what they denounced as an attempt to besmirch the President. Republicans professed to believe every word of it. A congressional investigation followed in which the man who made the statement confessed to doing so, but declared that the whole affair was a jest, that he was merely pulling the good but gullible doctor's leg.

Representative John J. O'Connor of New York, a brother of Basil O'Connor, FDR's onetime law partner, who became head of the campaign against infantile paralysis and later of the American Red Cross, ridiculed Wirt at the hearings. Later he was to apologize publicly for his part in the sorry smearing of the educator, but only after his defeat in 1938 as the only man purged for his opposition to FDR's ill-fated plan to pack the Supreme Court. How much of O'Connor's apology was due to honest contrition and how much to vengeance against FDR for his defeat, only O'Connor knew and he went to his grave without telling.

The Wirt incident inspired the Republican opposition, none too bright, to charge that Roosevelt was drifting toward communism when the drift was actually toward socialism, a less maligned but no less dangerous form of government to traditional American liberties. Communists had gained a foothold in the New Deal at its outset and were to extend their influence. They were to exert considerable power and to shape thinking, but largely through their dupes and starry-eyed fellow travelers. There were many wild thinkers around the Chief Executive who were convinced that the capitalist system was doomed and that our traditional system of representative government needed drastic overhauling.

Many of these men were wild and radical, but were not necessarily Communists. Most of them were parlor pinks, who talked glibly and violently of revolution, but had a horror of shedding blood, especially their own. They were ready to man the bars and hors d'oeuvres tables at capital cocktail parties, but in no hurry to expose themselves on the barricades. Only a few of these had made any study of communism or acknowledged acceptance of its philosophy. Most of them professed to abhor even the term "socialism," although they were promoting it. They claimed to be interested in planned economy, which has a spectrum of its own from the deep red of communism to the pale pink of socialism.

It is evident now that Roosevelt did effect a revolution in the American way of life at home and abroad. The only room for argument is whether the revolution was good or bad or whether it was inevitable under the circumstances. At home it is debatable whether the lot of the common man has improved as rapidly as his taxes, or whether he has merely kept his place on the treadmill because of mounting prices and slumping dollars. Abroad the wars in Korea and Vietnam were the natural result of FDR's dedication in World War II to intervention in any corner of the world.

Almost none of the joyous planners had ever seen the Russia they so admired. Those who had were interested in one aspect or another of the Communist system, such as farm co-ops, housing programs, schools or whatever, so that they were blind to what was going on behind the front they were led to see. Most of the projects that entranced admirers were in the planning stage and far from completion, even as they are some forty years later.

The dreamers could not see or refused to believe the terror, the brutality, suppressions and other evils that characterized the Soviet system. These have increased rather than lessened, because the war brought such nations as Estonia, Latvia and Lithuania into the Soviet Union and others like Poland, Czechoslovakia and East Germany into captivity as satellites.

The enthusiasts could never see the Russian leaders as just another kind of politicians, a new and more terrible aristocracy than that of the czars, climbing to power by the easiest means at hand—terror. The dreamers professed to see the Red leaders as just and dedicated men, motivated by nothing but unselfish concern for the common good. Then and even now many men, some at the highest levels of government, education and the arts, seem to be convinced that the only way to approach the Kremlin is in a spirit of generous conciliation so that they will be led out of evil ways by good example into one world, which they are certain is the happiest and best of all possible worlds.

In my first weeks in Washington, a corner of the rug was lifted on Communist infiltration into the New Deal. The disclosure came with a mysterious one-line announcement from the Department of Agriculture late one night that the legal staff of the AAA was being reorganized. I was new and alone in the office, but the briefness of the item piqued my curiosity, as it had that of far more knowledgeable persons. These helped me to discover there had been a wholesale house cleaning of the more radical members of the farm unit's legal staff. The next day the list of enforced partings included Alger Hiss, then known as one of the zealots of planned economy. My story bluntly branded him as a Red, one spawned in the Harvard classrooms of Felix Frankfurter.

I don't claim any particular prescience on the Communist conspiracy or infiltration, but cite this incident in the early fall of 1934 to support my statement that Communist activities were recognized from the start of the New Deal, although not as widely as they should have been, perhaps.

This disclosure didn't figure in the 1934 congressional campaign, nor in the 1936 presidential campaign, although House committees had long been concerned with the Red menace. Subsequently, it was disclosed that there were two strong and influential Communist cells in the Department of Agriculture and another, even more potent on fiscal matters, in the Treasury. Washington didn't have to be loaded with Red agents, however; there were fanatics enough, innocent fanatics, perhaps, but still advancers of the interests of the Kremlin and there were swarms of conscious and unconscious fellow travelers and sympathizers.

The firing of Hiss from the AAA didn't check his career the slightest. He was able to get a job with the staff of a Senate committee, headed by Gerald P. Nye of North Dakota, which was engaged in an inquiry into the activities of "merchants of death," as those profiting from the sale and distribution of arms came to be known. Naturally Communists favored the inquiry, supporting anything that would brand capitalists as warmongers. It wasn't long before rumors of Hiss's alleged Communist connections reached Nye. He summoned Hiss to his office, as he told me, and said that he was satisfied with the lawyer's work, but wouldn't stand for any Communist connections.

Hiss looked Nye in the eye and solemnly swore he was no Communist, but offered to resign in order to spare Nye, the committee and the investigation possible embarrassment. Nye said he would not sacrifice an innocent man and persuaded Hiss to remain.

It is not my intention to go into the Communist conspiracy or weigh its merits and abuses. Others who lived with the investigation are more qualified to do so. I merely want to emphasize it was known early, but did not become a national issue until some twenty years later, when it brought many men into prominence, even to the White House, and others into disrepute and prison. Also the myth of conversion of Russia to Western ways and ideals by conciliation and good example played a profound part in the conduct of American foreign policy.

So much was myth that Joseph E. Davies, ambassador to Russia, as much for the wealth of his second wife, Marjorie Post Hutton Close Davies, as for his party service, wrote a book on his experiences without the slightest knowledge of the language and no more acquaintance with the country than the suburbs of Moscow. He glorified the purge trials as a great display of justice. He had only one visit with Stalin and that was when he came to say farewell after he had been assigned to the court of Belgium, which his wife preferred for its gay social life. Yet, Davies wrote that Stalin was radiant with such inner benevolence that little children instinctively wanted to climb into his lap.

No Russian had ever written such nonsense. In the de-Stalinization campaign, Stalin's face was characterized as the cruel symbol of ruthless individual rule. Davies was to repent having the volume ghosted for him, or so he confessed to me in 1947 when he asked me why I was always right on Russia and he was invariably wrong. My answer was: "Joe, I didn't want anything."

In all fairness to Davies he did try to see Russia, but wasn't allowed to travel as he wished. No doubt the Russians knew why he wanted to travel because it was subsequently revealed they had tapped the

Davies bedroom. Davies confided to me that his much married wife was a demanding woman. Since he was no bedroom athlete, being sixty in 1936, he wanted to get away now and then. When the Russians would not co-operate by granting travel permission, he confided that he was forced to arrange for frequent visits home for supposed departmental consultations. This vigorous and dynamic woman shed Davies and a later husband for failure to meet her demands, she told intimates.

ROOSEVELT

I FIRST MET FDR on Sunday, April 17, 1932, when he was governor of New York and on his way to make a speech in the Minneapolis-St. Paul area in order to advance his quest for the Democratic presidential nomination. At the time I was keeping a diary for the first time in my adult life, because our first child, Carol, had been born two months earlier and might some day have some interest in my doings. In it I noted an interview, observing Roosevelt was "very affable but said nothing," which could have been an epitaph for his customary relations with the press.

We met the governor in the lounge of a private car, which had been placed at his disposal. Although he could not walk, he had the face of a marching man. His chin was tilted high in confidence, his eyes were bright with purpose, and his spirits were gay. Near the end of the interview he asked the Albany correspondents, who were accompanying him to leave him because he wished to talk privately to the three local reporters. Then he asked if any of us could arrange a meeting with Mayor Cermak. I was the only one of the three who knew Chicago's political leader intimately so I said I could.

However, I told FDR a meeting would not do him much good, because Tony was devoted to Mayor James J. Walker of New York City, whose political career FDR was driving on a tumbrel through the nation's front pages to the guillotine of defeat. FDR waved my observation aside airily. He asked me to have Cermak come to his private car in the Union Station the following Tuesday night.

This mission was an easy one. I saw FDR on his return and told him I had Cermak waiting outside. I waited for Tony until their meeting ended. The mayor confided that he found FDR engaging and persuasive, but resisted the governor's blandishments. They did not meet again until after FDR's nomination and for the briefest of congratulations on Tony's part. They met for the third time, almost a year later, when Cermak paid with his life for his effort to establish closer relations, in the interest of obtaining patronage, with the man whose overtures for enlistment he had declined in Chicago.

Many in Chicago preferred to believe, and the report persists to this day, that it was Cermak himself, and not FDR, who was the assassin's target. Tony was doing his very best, perhaps not entirely for the best of motives, to drive Chicago's predominantly Italian crime syndicate out of business. Giuseppe Zangara fired six shots where FDR's automobile was parked on Miami's waterfront. Cermak was beside the car. None of the shots hit FDR but one fatally wounded Cermak. The name "Zangara" was the only basis for the Chicago rumors. In the assassin's pockets were clippings that gave evidence that he had first contemplated encompassing the death of President Herbert Hoover and then switched to Roosevelt, when the President-elect announced his plans for a southern vacation.

As the Democratic convention was getting under way, I was in Cermak's Congress Hotel hideaway, in search of news, when Alfred E. Smith, the 1928 Democratic standard-bearer, who was seeking a second nomination, paid a surprise visit. Tony introduced me and I moved to leave them alone, but the Happy Warrior waved me back to my seat, saying he had nothing to say that I couldn't hear. He begged the mayor to help "Stop Roosevelt" and left as abruptly as he had entered without one word about his own candidacy.

The 1932 conventions were the first of a span that covered almost forty years of political gatherings. The Republicans met in the shadow of certain defeat to renominate Hoover; the Democrats were in a festive mood in anticipation of regaining the White House after twelve years of longing. My role in both conventions was minor, but I can never forget the dramatic appearance of a somewhat unsteady Mayor Walker in the early hours of a balloting morning. He came from revelry in the Lake Shore Drive home of Vincent Bendix, inventor and industrialist, to cast his vote in person, rather than through an alternate, against Roosevelt and for Smith. The picture of the slight, dapper figure, a study in proud courage, is etched in my mind. Some years later Walker and I became friends. I found him a delightful companion with a wit as sharp as it was spontaneous.

Once he presided at a Circus Saints and Sinners luncheon in New York City's Waldorf Astoria Hotel, at which Secretary of Commerce Jones was being led over the coals of wit that toasted but did not burn, principally for his interest in the accumulation of money, both for its own sake and the power it brought. When it came to the turn of Fall Guy Jones to speak in his own defense, the Secretary whispered in Walker's ear and then started down a right aisle to a door.

"It's the third door on your right," Walker shouted after the silver-haired financier. The remark provoked a gale of laughter.

"Just a minute, just a minute," Walker checked the laughter. "He isn't going there for what you think; he's going to count the take of the nickel machines on the doors."

Only a few conventions stand out in my mind as at all memorable. Mostly they were confused and disorganized spectacles, demonstrating considerable imbecility. News accounts often make them more exciting than they were, because the ritual was generally dull and long drawn out.

I can still see a sadly smiling James A. Farley, who twice nominated and elected FDR and then broke with him over the third term, waving farewell as Democratic national chairman to the 1940 convention that punctuated cheers with boos for him in their ecstasy for FDR. I can hear "the voice from the sewer" that Mayor Edward J. Kelly of Chicago planted at a microphone below the Chicago Stadium's main floor, screaming for "Roosevelt and humanity." Kelly thus repaid FDR for getting him off the income tax hook for arrears that ran into six figures, even though it meant cutting the political throat of the man who arranged the tax deal, Farley. The voice was that of an official in charge of the city's sewage system.

And I can well remember the seesaw battle in the early hours of a summer morning, again in Chicago, in 1956, when the relatively unknown charmer Senator John F. Kennedy of Massachusetts was vying with Senator Estes Kefauver of Tennessee for the Democratic vice-presidental nomination. Adlai E. Stevenson was about to make his second unsuccessful race for the White House. Adlai had precipitated honest excitement by letting the convention decide on the choice of his running mate. However, the convention actually didn't because Speaker Sam Rayburn of Texas, then presiding as permanent chairman of the convention, swung the pendulum toward Estes, as the more malleable of the contenders, perhaps.

After writing my story of the drama, I jumped aboard a bus carrying the Mississippi delegation from the Stock Yards Pavilion to their hotel. The delegation mortally feared and dreaded Kefauver as a southern liberal. The group was in deep dejection until Governor White roared from the front of the vehicle:

"By the way, did anyone ever find out where Kennedy stands on civil rights?"

No one had.

All in all, whenever I think of conventions, I can only recall the vivid and apt description of a campaign train by Pierce Butler, newsman son of the Supreme Court Justice of the same name, who said: "It's like nothing so much as a whore house on Saturday night with the madam away."

Conventions have always been popular because of the American love for spectator sports. Now that we have TV, they frequently attract more spectators than less zanier sports. Before TV and radio, participation was largely by way of the endless book—the American newspaper—which alone of the media provides a record while it informs, although the record is rarely consulted because few are interested in learning from the past. Henry L. Mencken, with whom I covered many conventions, summed them up better than anyone else when he said:

"A national convention is as fascinating as a revival or a hanging. It is vulgar, ugly, stupid and tedious, to be sure, and yet there suddenly comes a show so gaudy and hilarious, so dramatic and obscene, so unimaginably exhilarating and preposterous that one lives a gorgeous year in an hour."

To me, one of the best features of those revivals with their prayers, singing and incantations was Mencken himself. He was forever rising up to shout some quip that came to him as orators spouted like volcanoes, flung spume like whales or tried to charm in imitations of the voice of Orpheus.

His last conventions were in 1948 at Philadelphia where he and I and Westbrook Pegler, the great phrase-making columnist, enjoyed a hilarious lunch, reviewing the antics of Republicans scenting victory and Democrats casting spells to ward off impending defeat. A few days later Mencken suffered a massive stroke, which did not bring death but a fate even more terrible, impairment of his faculties. The next time I saw him was in Baltimore's Maryland Club, where he approached me to ask my name, saying that he knew he knew me, but could no longer remember names.

"Of course, of course," he said when I told him. "I'm sorry I didn't remember, but I can't even remember the beginning of a sentence when I reach the end in reading. The doctors did me no favor when they saved me."

The only name he mentioned in the eight years he survived the stroke was that of Ludwig van Beethoven, for whom he had as great an admiration as I have for Wolfgang Amadeus Mozart. In debating the merits of our favorites he told me how he and a group of musicians had resolved to play all nine of their idol's symphonies in a single evening. They began with great verve and enthusiasm, but bogged down in the middle of the evening when they began feeling the effects of pauses for liquid refreshments that inspired improvisations which turned their heroic efforts into something of a classical jam session.

Conventions are often featured by the antics of favorite sons, a curious breed of political hopefuls who seem to promote the idea that they generally have one thing in common—unmarried fathers. As a rule politicians, including favorite sons, don't welcome advice, but can always be made to stop and listen if you offer them the White House. Most politicians think time flies when they are talking, but lags when someone else has the floor, but then many of us only listen for a speaker to stop so that we can break in with what we have to say, which we know to be brilliant, fascinating and interesting, at least to ourselves.

Often politicians cannot be persuaded to hold their peace on any issue, fancying themselves as instant experts on any subject that comes up. I don't know how many honest and well-meaning friends, including myself, have begged Hubert H. Humphrey, senator, vice president and presidential nominee, to confess just once that he didn't know the answer when asked a question, but we were unable to persuade him to do so.

When he spoke for eight hours in the Kremlin with Nikita S. Khrushchev, I wrote him a kidding letter about his marathon. In reply I got a letter asking me what I expected him to do. I replied that I expected him to laugh because I was jesting. Right back came a second letter, saying he had reread my first letter and found it most amusing.

Over the years, conventions have given me many laughs. I can remember in 1940 when delegates were smoldering over being forced to swallow Secretary of Agriculture Henry A. Wallace as FDR's second running mate. Governor E. D. Rivers of Georgia turned to Governor Leon C. (Red) Phillips of Oklahoma in the delegation behind him to ask what Red thought of Wallace.

"Why, he's my second choice," said Phillips.

Rivers thought that he may have overlooked some redeeming feature in Wallace, but then asked: "Who's your first choice?"

"Any son of a bitch—red, black, white or yellow—who can get the nomination."

The Chicago convention of 1932 brought me the greatest of personal dividends, which was and is the friendship of the genial gentleman from Grassy Point, New York, Jim Farley, a politician of impeccable personal integrity although a master of expediency and other tricks of the trade. We met at his first news conference in Chicago, when he asked me to stay behind. When we were alone he asked if there was any chance of winning Cermak's bloc of Illinois delegates. I told him there was none, but said that if he would approach Senator James Hamilton Lewis of Illinois, he would find him itching to lead a revolt that would chip a few votes from the Cermak bloc.

This was done and the Illinois phalanx was split. I don't claim to have been a Roosevelt kingmaker in that convention, although almost everyone else did. Farley was aware, I am sure, that Lewis, who had been elected to a second Senate term, after an enforced and unwelcome absence of twelve years, was ready to break step with Tony's political dictation. I have read and listened to hundreds of stories by men who claimed to have turned the tide for FDR—usually by persons accusing him of ingratitude—by suggesting he make a deal with William Randolph Hearst, the publisher, to get the California and Texas delegations to switch from Speaker John Nance Garner to FDR in return for the second-place nomination. Actually, this gambit was obvious to Farley and Roosevelt long before the convention was gaveled to order, so that they were working on it long before Chicago.

All I claim is my advice brought me the friendship of Farley, a personal prize beyond measure as well as an invaluable contact when I came to Washington. I knew that Lewis was looking for an excuse to break away from Cermak because he told me so. I knew and liked this pink-whiskered dandy, who possessed a keen political mind for all his exaggerated courtliness and flowery oratory. All of us have something of a weakness for the actors and orators among us, as well as a sneaking admiration for the rogues, even though we might hesitate to admit it to ourselves. Lewis was no rogue but he had a roguish eye for a trim figure.

Once he stopped a pretty young miss in front of the Senate Office Building, raised his hat, made a courtly bow and asked: "My dear, can you direct me to the Senate Office Building?"

"Yes, I can," she replied fluttering her eyelashes until he beamed broadly in anticipation of a conquest. "And I can tell you that the number of your suite is 111, Senator."

The Lewis reputation for flirting was well established in the capital. One evening a man attempted to approach "Gypsy," the senator's attractive wife, while she was window shopping on F Street. She froze him with a haughty stare, which prompted him to exclaim:

"You needn't get so hoity-toity with me; I saw you out with Jim Ham Lewis last night."

I first talked to Lewis one wintry evening in 1928, when I was on rewrite in the City News Bureau, pounding out the story of the chase and capture of three youths in a gun battle following a theater hold-up. Larry Mulay, who was on the desk, was beating out the tale of a gangland murder. Lewis entered, removed his hat and stood humbly behind a railing. I snatched a few seconds to explain our problem and asked him to be patient.

"That's quite all right, young man," he said. "I used to work here; I'll write the story myself."

And he went on to prove he had worked there by picking up a stack of stencils and writing a story, which was mimeographed and sent to the various newspapers by pneumatic tubes. The story he wrote was an interview with himself on an international problem. He left this with me and bowed his way out.

I came to know him very well. He was a familiar figure in the courts and at banquets, always given to making an entrance. When he was engaged in a trial, he would delay his entrance until the presiding judge had mounted to the bench. Then he would enter, remove his hat with: "Good morning, your honor," lay down his walking stick with: "Good morning, Mr. Clerk," pull off his gloves with: "Good morning, Mr. Bailiff," remove his coat with: "Good morning, gentlemen of the jury," and face his opponent with: "Good morning, counsel."

He was cured of this practice by the late Walker Butler, who was to end his career as a judge. Butler saw that these tactics were impressing a jury in a civil case. One morning Butler outwaited Lewis and came into the courtroom after Lewis had gone through his act.

Butler removed a worn sealskin cap and trilled in a high falsetto; "Good morning, your honor." He laid down a battered umbrella with an exaggerated: "Good morning, Mr. Clerk." He pulled his hands out of leather mittens with: "Good morning, Mr. Bailiff." He removed a heavy streetcar motorman's overcoat with: "Good morning, gentlemen of the jury." Then he leaned over the counsels' table toward Lewis and exclaimed: "Kiss me, sweetheart."

The stage missed a luminary of the first magnitude when this slight man, who was addicted to yellow vests, chose law and politics. He was one of the greatest of storytellers in a profession that has many adepts at the game, because politicians find that gaining laughs gets more votes than taking positions on issues. I covered Lewis on the stump in his Senate campaign. He had an absolute genius for leaving out the commitment clause on any controversial issue, so that listeners on both sides of any question could feel that he was with them heart and soul.

For all his acting and posturing, Lewis was shrewd and courageous, especially where his own interests were most concerned. Therefore, he was a good and important senator. I used to visit him regularly in search of news in his office on the Hill. After he had outlined his position one day, he went into what I recognized as an act and settled back to enjoy it.

"You don't see me often at the White House," he began, reaching for a red telephone on his desk. "All I have to do is to pick up this instrument and it rings at the President's desk, so I can consult him. And all he has to do is pick up the matching phone on his desk and get the benefit of my advice and experience and . . ."

By then Lewis saw the smile on my face and realized he was talking to the *Tribune*'s White House correspondent, who could be expected to know better.

"Oh hell," he exclaimed. "Why in the world am I trying to impress you of all people with that pleasant bit of fiction."

There was an often told tale in the capital that Lewis was dropping a year from his age every time a new Congressional Directory came out with the biographies of members of Congress and top officials. When Lewis died April 9, 1939, it became important that I learn his correct age, which I did by going back to the directory which appeared in his first year in Congress, as a young representative from the state of Washington. The Virginia-born Illinois senator was first elected to Congress at the age of twenty-one. It was obvious that this birth date was correct or he would not have been eligible to serve in the House. Thus it was evident also that he had cut but two years from his age instead of the reputed half dozen or more.

Many members of Congress begin dropping their ages from their biographies as they approach and pass seventy, being aware voters may be moved to shy away from senior representatives. Politicians are much alike, regardless of color, creed, race or nationality. Most of them want to stay in office as long as they can draw a breath, even in a hospital bed. They enjoy power and adulation. Also they like being supported at a level they generally could not establish for themselves in any other line of endeavor. When he was premier of Russia, Nikita S. Khrushchev remarked, rather wistfully, of Marshall Tito of Yugoslavia: "Tito isn't a dictator; he's a king."

Many and many a time I have heard men, seeking favors, tell one politician or another that he could make millions in the practice of law if he had continued in that career instead of embarking on public service. I heard it told many times to my friend Senator Alben W. Barkley of Kentucky, the man with a resounding pipe-organ voice who became Vice President under Truman.

When Barkley failed to get the nomination for the presidency at Chicago in 1952, because he was dismissed as too old at seventy-four by his chief, who loved him not, he returned to the practice of law. He found that the charming people who spun pretty tales of his potential had lawyers of their own and had no intention of changing them. Barkley went back to the Senate as soon as he could, evidently to protect his own money as well as to make a living, because when he died in 1956, proclaiming in a speech at Lexington, Virginia, he would rather be a servant in the house of the Lord than sit in the seats of the mighty, the federal government moved in to attach almost his entire estate of some $400,000 for unpaid income taxes. Sometimes it is a very handy thing to be in office when the tax collector comes around as at least one Republican senator can similarly report today.

Barkley was one of the greatest storytellers in Congress. He had a magnificent mesmerizing voice, so that when he spoke what he said wasn't as moving as the way he said it. Often listeners were moved to believe they had heard the greatest of speeches, until they analyzed what he had said and found they had heard nothing but an array of purple passages and shimmering clichés.

But even this celebrated orator met his Waterloo. The Kentuckian was a candidate for the post of majority leader of the Senate in 1937 against Senator Pat Harrison of Mississippi. The leader, Joseph T. Robinson of Arkansas, who had run on the ticket with Al Smith in 1928, had died suddenly. Roosevelt promised to keep hands off the choice of a successor, but had no intention of keeping his promise because FDR knew that Harrison had opposed the New Deal secretly at many a turn and had given the White House many a stinging defeat. In his manipulations, Harrison made a great man of Senator Charles McNary of Oregon, the Republican minority leader. Pat found the monkey wrenches McNary tossed into machinery of New Deal legislative schemes, and also pointed out the closets in which McNary found New Deal skeletons. Republicans were to take the amiable McNary so seriously as an omniscient leader that they gave him the party's vice-presidential nomination with Wendell Willkie in 1940.

After FDR defeated Harrison's leadership hopes by persuading Senator William H. Dieterich of Illinois to run out on his pledged vote to Pat in return for the power to name a federal judge, the Mississippian found himself president of the Alfalfa Club, a Washington dinner group, which featured oratory and political humor. That year Barkley was the club's mock candidate for the presidency. Barkley was given to speaking in twenty-minute bursts, having no shorter terminal facilities.

In his first twenty minutes Barkley had his audience rolling in the aisles. Then he asked Harrison, in a whisper, how he was doing. Harrison told him that he was going great and urged him to give the audience more. Alben went into a second twenty minutes. This was good but hardly as spectacular as the first twenty minutes. Again Harrison urged him to continue. Barkley launched into his third oratorial stanza. By this time many in the audience were restless. Those who had drunk deeply, but not too wisely perhaps, were squirming in their seats. Many left for the men's room. The exodus became general, so that diners were shuttling back and forth like commuters in a railway station.

Barkley was oblivious to the movement, being entranced with the sound of his own voice. Harrison suggested Alben launch into a fourth movement of his oratorical symphony. There were groans the speaker did not hear or took for applause. Then one of the diners, who had sipped liquor even more deeply than the roots of the alfalfa plant, tossed a roll at the Kentuckian. Soon he was on the receiving end of a dinner roll barrage, but he couldn't stop until he had run down like grandfather's clock.

Barkley served FDR well as leader. Whether he understood legislation or not, Alben gave the impression of being completely informed. However, there is reason to believe the country would have fared better under Harrison because Pat would doubtless have curbed New Deal excesses and slowed the drift toward socialism in the critical prewar years.

Curiously enough, Senator James Francis Byrnes of South Carolina, who was later to become FDR's champion in the drive for a third term, a powerful wartime administrator, Supreme Court Justice and

Secretary of State, was battling the White House in Harrison's leadership contest. This was in 1937, but by 1940 Byrnes was dreaming of the presidency and hoped to gain it by the back door of the vice presidency, not knowing FDR had ruled him out. FDR spread the story that Byrnes shouldn't be given a place on the ticket, because although the senator had been born a Catholic, he had left that faith. With customary guile FDR blamed the spreading of the story on others, including Jim Farley.

The New Deal, at my arrival in Washington, resembled nothing so much as the Mad Hatter's tea party in *Alice in Wonderland*. The national economy was being dosed by a wide variety of panaceas. Roosevelt was knocking heads off and creating new agencies. Many observers were gazing apprehensively at their watches, like the White Rabbit, because time was running out. FDR had an apparently inexhaustible supply of rabbits, but even so some were going back into his hat, having failed to realize their promises.

Where else could a stenographer's mistake add 300 million dollars to make a pump priming spending bill 3.3 billion dollars instead of 3 billions without even raising a parliamentary question of the rather irregular total? Where else could FDR raise the price of gold one day by 21 cents because he had a "hunch" that three times seven was a lucky number?

Secretary of the Treasury Henry Morgenthau, Jr., whom FDR called Hennypenny, wrote in his diary after the gold price decision: "If people knew how we fixed the price of gold, they would be frightened." After publication of the diary revealed how casually the gold price was fixed, FDR apologists attempted to explain that he was merely teasing Hennypenny and had sound reasons for his price action, but they never attempted to explain what the sound reasons were.

FDR had am impish or elfin streak that admirers considered endearing, but inclined him to the dramatic rather than the considered. He loved to watch the jaws of associates drop when he announced some new and startling policy or program. His dramatic move kept the Republican opposition forever off its feet. Every time there was a crack in the New Deal ceiling, FDR would rush to prop it up by creating some new agency without bothering to abolish the old one which had failed, or he would propose some new legislation, frequently in direct contradiction to his campaign promises.

Every time he did so GOP leaders would shout: "Now we have him!" in their strategy sessions and prepare to make an issue of his latest prop or proposal, which they would drop as soon as he came out with some new action. They seldom seemed to find an issue to latch on. Meanwhile, the Administration was as full of props as an old house shored up against collapse.

From the first days of the New Deal, men who favored setting the printing presses rolling out paper dollars as the best means of ending the Depression were honored prophets. After Roosevelt was inaugurated he was given vast powers over management of money, a course he had pretended to abhor. The money powers were not spelled out in a considered fiscal program, but were tacked on to the Agricultural Adjustment Act, almost as an afterthought, including authority to devalue the dollar by as much as 50 per cent.

The extent of these powers shocked some of his most trusted advisers, so he assured them the powers were merely discretionary, but he did devalue the dollar to 59 cents by raising the price of gold from $20.67 to $35 an ounce. Dean Acheson, the Under Secretary of the Treasury, who insisted this could not be done legally, left the little Cabinet in protest, but he was welcomed back as an Assistant Secretary of State, when he buried the hatchet with FDR by plugging for American participation in World War II. Thus gaily, FDR maneuvered another break with the fiscal past, as he had smashed many another precedent. He changed the pattern of government from one of fiscal responsibility to one of free spending, and he changed the American way of life, in my opinion, from emphasis on virtues and earning one's way to glorify the acceptance of handouts.

Almost invariably there was some personal touch in any recommendation he proposed. Roosevelt once suggested limiting all incomes to $25,000 a year. Why $25,000? Because that was the most he had ever made, although few knew it, when he demanded and got that salary as executive of a Maryland insurance company, as his price for running for Vice President on the ticket with James M. Cox against Warren G. Harding and Calvin Coolidge. Another time he lashed out at large holders of railroad stocks, but said railroad bondholders were fine people. Why? Because his father had invested money in bonds of the New York Central Railroad.

In the mad madrigal of professors and dreamers and schemers, it was no wonder Secretary of Agriculture Henry A. Wallace could call for the reading of a list of great books as a short cut to the millennium, even though he was forced to confess, under questioning, that he had read only a few of them himself. FDR could blithely make votes for his "must" legislation a condition for getting federal projects for bigger government and more spending, although he had promised in his campaign to force a 25 per cent cut in federal spending by streamlining government and curbing its activities.

FDR changed the face of government and upset the balance between the three branches of government, reducing the role of Congress and encouraging the courts to legislate by decree. All of these innovations were more or less criticized at the time, but so much was going on and so few realized the significance and enormity of his changes. Few do even to this day, although the government bears the stamp of Roosevelt as it does of no other President. FDR's devaluation of the dollar was a sensation, but it paved the way for changes no less startling, almost without question. Gold backing was ended for the dollar. Silver was taken out of coins entirely or in part by John F. Kennedy and Lyndon B. Johnson. Richard M. Nixon ordered two devaluations of the dollar within fifteen months without any great outcry.

FDR stripped Congress of its constitutional power by inducing its members to surrender traditional control of the purse strings, which forced them to come to the White House with hat in hand to beg for portions of appropriations they had voted, at his request, for spending in their states and districts. Many members of Congress were bitter about it but there was little they could do except talk about it among themselves when they gathered on the sprawling porch of the Wardman Park Hotel to rock away many a lazy summer afternoon. At one especially acid session on FDR, Senator Henry Fountain Ashurst of Arizona sought to pour a bit of oil on troubled waters.

"After all," he said, "Roosevelt is his own worst enemy."

With that, Senator Ellison D. (Cotton Ed) Smith of South Carolina, who was apparently dozing but was, in reality, listening, opened his eyes, threshed his arms about like a drowning man treading water and snorted:

"Not while I'm alive, he ain't."

They were giants in the Senate in those days. I realize this is easy for an old man to say from a distance of some forty years, but there were many in the Senate whose names were household words, at least a third of that body and perhaps as much as half the ninety-six members. There were many well-known men in the House as well. The Senate then was truly the most exclusive club in the world. Its members carried the aura of the toga with them. Few were running for President, as so many are today. Almost all were satisfied to be dwellers in their political Olympus.

In addition to the Democrats named earlier there were William Gibbs McAdoo of California, Walter F. George and Richard B. Russell of Georgia, Huey P. Long of Louisiana, Millard E. Tydings of Maryland, David I. Walsh of Massachusetts, Bennett Champ Clark of Missouri, Burton K. Wheeler of Montana, Key Pittman of Nevada, Robert F. Wagner of New York, Josiah W. Bailey of North Carolina, David A. Reed and James J. Davis of Pennsylvania, Kenneth D. McKellar of Tennessee, Morris Sheppard and Tom T. Connally of Texas and Carter Glass and Harry Flood Byrd of Virginia.

On the Republican side of the aisle were Hiram W. Johnson of California, William E. Borah of Idaho, James Couzens and Arthur H. Vandenberg of Michigan, Henrik Shipstead of Minnesota, George W. Norris of Nebraska, Gerald P. Nye of North Dakota and Robert M. La Follette, Jr., of Wisconsin.

I knew them all, because my first assignment in Washington was on Capitol Hill. I knew many in the House as well. In those days many men in Congress were aware of what was going on in the government and were master manipulators, who could get things done, often without disclosing their own hand. Many a member of Congress was the making of many a favored reporter by feeding him inside information. Frequently it was far easier to break White House or departmental news from the Hill than from the White House itself or from the department concerned. Often some members of Congress knew more about what was going on in the government than many top federal workers in the Executive Mansion or in the establishment of Cabinet members.

In all my years in Washington only one man ever exercised the full power of a senator and no President has ever exercised the tremendous power of his office to the hilt. The lone senator was Kenneth McKellar of Tennessee. He was not at all prepossessing, in fact often appearing uncouth. Nor was he at all magnetic or charming. But he knew what he wanted and how to get it and he invariably did as the chairman of the powerful Senate Appropriations Committee.

I COVER
THE WHITE HOUSE

I WAS ASSIGNED to Washington to cover the House of Representatives, but I wasn't to remain on Capitol Hill long. I was
shifted to the White House when John Boettiger left the *Tribune*
in order to accept a role in the motion picture industry in advance of
him impending marriage to FDR's only daughter, Anna Roosevelt
Dahl. Boettiger's wife, who had joined him in Washington, returned
to Chicago with their family. She was persuaded to sue for a divorce.
There was no mention of the romance with the President's daughter,
which was no secret in the capital.

Naturally, I was introduced to FDR at the first news conference
I attended in the White House proper, because the Executive offices
were being renovated. He didn't remember our earlier meetings, but
he soon came to know me well, although not always with pleasure.
At this first conference FDR was asked if Rexford Guy Tugwell,
the controversial professor of the experimental AAA, had been sent
to Europe to get him out of the way of the current congressional
campaign, where he might be expected to cost the Democrats votes.
Tugwell and Wallace were responsible for the killing of millions
of piglets, a major program of planned economy which was then
backfiring. FDR gave a ringing denial to the charge.

As we left the White House, Kenneth Clark, then head of the
now defunct Hearst Universal Service, told me: "You have just
heard the President of the United States lie." He referred to the

denial of the purpose of the Tugwell trip. In his Washington reportorial days, Turner Catledge, retired editor of the New York *Times*, used to say that FDR's first instinct was to lie when asked a probing question at his news conference, but often the President would realize he could tell the truth and so he would execute a 180-degree turn in mid-paragraph and come up with the truth or a good bit of it.

I got an early introduction to the operations of FDR's mind when I accompanied Roosevelt on an inspection of power projects which included Muscle Shoals, Wheeler Dam and the then-building Tennessee Valley Authority Dam. The journey ended with his traditional Thanksgiving Day visit to the Georgia Warm Springs Foundation he had helped to establish for fellow polio victims.

As we were steaming in the presidential special across the state of Alabama, Ken Clark and I cornered Dr. Arthur E. (Tennessee) Morgan, one of the TVA directors, in the club car and questioned him on his plans for remaking society, which, he explained, were largely to free rural areas from dependence on urban areas like Chicago. When urban areas got into trouble, he said, in response to my questioning, it would be a simple thing to launch city TVA units. There was no doubt about this scholar's good intentions, but Morgan paved a road to hell of discarded accepted economics.

Two days later at an informal news conference in the living room of the summer White House, FDR repeated almost all of what Morgan had offered without noticeable pruning or addition. Later that same week, Tugwell, a leaner and surer scholar, arrived from Europe to report to the President on his findings in Germany, France and England. Clark and I rose early to tackle him in an hour's questioning. At the next news conference, FDR gave us a complete replay of Tugwell. Mrs. Roosevelt sat in a corner, knitting like Mme. Defarge in *A Tale of Two Cities*, and putting in sharp observations and incisive questions to the annoyance of her husband, because she exposed his lack of background on Europe.

Thus, I came to recognize early that FDR had a mind like a sidewalk in the rain, which can retain moisture until the passage of time brings out the sun and dries up the moisture or, in his case, the borrowed ideas. It was something I was to get considerable evidence of in later years, especially toward the end when he was more interested in the past than in the war at hand.

Curiously enough, neither Tugwell nor FDR seemed alive to the menace of Hitler, although Mrs. R. was. However, both were borrowing from Hitler's socialism and at that time Hitler and Benito Mussolini were the heroes of some liberals because they were socialists going for made work projects and doles. FDR went so far as to exhibit an ersatz suit made of wood fibers at a news conference.

Roosevelt and I became chummy from our meetings at Warm Springs. After all I had been friendly with Tony Cermak and Ed Kelly in Chicago without joining their ranks. FDR was gregarious, full of small talk, loved to laugh and genuinely liked people, even as I did. He was a gentleman, which I have always tried to be. It was not important to me that I share a man's political beliefs to be his friend. I had liked many a politician in Chicago personally, although I was prepared to strip off their masks or check their depredations. I must say for them that they expected me to do it, if I could, and respected me for it when I did. This was not true of FDR.

So I genuinely liked the man, and I must confess I was flattered being friendly with the President. I cooked for him, although I must say he was no gourmet, but rather one who ate to live. I poured drinks for him—and loaded them—although he was one who could take liquor or leave it. I shared many of his hours of leisure, where he could be the best of company. I don't pretend I was his favorite reporter, although I might have become so had I forsworn my loyalty to McCormick and pledged allegiance to him.

Nor was I the best of the reporters who covered FDR. It has been said of me that I was a born reporter. I don't quite know what that means, but I do know my work was by no means as hard or as difficult as many thought. Even though I was a representative of FDR's most powerful and most consistent enemy in the press, I scored many scoops. And I was scooped quite often, altogether too often in my opinion, because I could never become one of that breed of reporters who share their news because they have convinced their editors that it isn't what they write that is so important, but the way they write and present it. To me no matter how you write it, it is still pretty much journalese and hardly literature.

In addition to covering the White House I was responsible for almost all the executive departments, except the Treasury and those dealing entirely with fiscal matters. It was a good bit of territory, but there were only four working reporters in the bureau. The fact that I was the representative of FDR's greatest press foe was my making rather than my handicap. Persons within the Administration, even Roosevelt himself, leaked stories to me in order to further their feuds, gain the advantage in their struggles for power or to embarrass their enemies within the establishment. There were others who had no love for the Administration or its chief actors and who were eager to get unfavorable news in print. And there were reporters who dared not print stories they had uncovered for fear of involving their papers or services, or who knew their editors would not back them in any controversy with authority; they gave me some of my best stories. All I had to do was to be grateful, check the facts and have the courage to face the critical music.

In those days I was accused by the Administration, and by many of my press colleagues who were devoted to the Administration, of slanting the news. Now slanting has become the fashion, under the dignified term of interpretation. I tried to let readers interpret for themselves news that Administration idolaters didn't think was fit to print. I might have been guilty of undue slanting; I don't think so. Nowadays interpretation is supplied by reporters in their twenties who do not have the experience or historical background for their pontification.

Like most Presidents, FDR couldn't get away from the White House often enough, once he got in, although he may have been tempted to pledge his immortal soul to get in. Lyndon and Lady Bird Johnson referred to the Executive Mansion as "the compound." Harry S Truman, on a morning walk with reporters from the Blair House, pointed to the White House across the street and said: "There's the big white jail." Dwight D. Eisenhower looked out of his office window and sighed over the squirrels cavorting on the lawn: "They have a freedom I personally would dearly love." On my first trip with FDR to Warm Springs, we watched him bargain for two mules. While other reporters concerned themselves with solemn assessment of the philosophy of New Deal directives, I concerned myself with the purchase of the animals that I promptly christened "Tug" and "Hop," after Tugwell and Harry Hopkins, then head of the Federal Emergency Relief Administration, who was to become the No. 1 White House intimate and who supplied me with many a story, unfavorable to his enemy Secretary of the Interior Harold L. Ickes.

At Warm Springs, the regulars of the press generally staged some sort of party for the President. At the first one I attended, he was enjoying himself so thoroughly we had to tell him to leave after 2 A.M. because our singing was disturbing the patients. I composed a song, which he greeted with delight; he was given to singing himself in a pleasant baritone. It was to the tune of "My Country 'Tis of Thee," and ran:

> My country 'tis of thee,
> Sweet land of liberty
> FDIC.
> AAA, NRA,
> CCC, RFC,
> PWA and WPA,
> HOLC,

While cruising down the Potomac, FDR used to sing another song I wrote. This was the school song of a mock university, the White House regulars named after J. Russell Young, White House correspondent of the Washington *Star*, and later the chairman of the District of Columbia Board of Commissioners. Russ, who looked more like a senator than most of the duly elected solons, was given to oratorial delivery, which inspired the creation of the mock college. The song I wrote for the annual commencement of the university was to the tune "Celito Lindo," and the words were:

> J. Russell Young School of Expression,
> Perfect enunciation, diligent application.
> J. Russell Young School of the Silver Tongue,
> Our alma mater, Oh, so true,
> We lift our voices high to you.

FDR was awarded a coveted diploma at the first commencement. Jesse Jones led the daisy-chain parade in cap and gown for years. In trying out for a diploma, Justice William O. Douglas recited a poem he created for the occasion, right after his appointment in 1939. Unhappily for him, the poem had more four-letter words than sense or rhythm, so that his diploma was held up for years by our dean. I don't say the school or song got Young named district commissioner, where he established a record for longevity in service, but they didn't hurt his political career either.

Also on my first trip to Warm Springs, I visited nearby Magic Hill, a most interesting optical illusion, where the road appears to be going up but actually goes down. Governor Eugene Talmadge of Georgia came to pay a courtesy call on the President. I knew he was critical of the New Deal and persuaded him to liken the alphabetical agencies to the hill, because they gave the appearance of going up but were really pulling the country down. FDR was told I had coined the comparison and it amused him.

This was the beginning of a game of name calling that we were to play for some years. I was addressed as "a prince of privilege" or an "economic royalist," while I retorted in kind about "Dr. New Deal" or "Chef of Alphabetic Soup." FDR was sure he always won our exchanges, but I considered that conclusion open to debate.

FDR's relish of humor did not always include quips directed at himself, as I was to find out early in my White House days. It seems strange now, but at that time budget sessions were conducted by the President in person with the Secretary of the Treasury and Director of the Budget sitting at his side. One such session was held in the Cabinet room, because there was relatively little interest in the financing of New Deal experiments.

I was a bit late in reaching the room and the only place I could find was at the end of the Cabinet table. When FDR was wheeled in, by Morgenthau, he spotted me and broke into a derisive laugh.

"Financial expert. Ha! Ha! Ha!"

"Budget balancer. Ha! Ha! Ha!" I retorted, pointing at the budget before me.

Morgenthau nervously buried his head in the budget, not daring to look at me for fear of bursting into laughter. The lines on FDR's face switched from humor to anger. He didn't speak to me again during the session or recognize me for a question.

FDR did enjoy laughing at those who ridiculed him. At a picnic on the family estate one Sunday, he read aloud from *Frankie in Wonderland,* a satire on him and his Administration which was popular on Wall Street in 1934. The scene beside the swimming pool of his cottage; the company, he was flanked by his dowager duchess mother and his wife, and his ironical rendition of the critical lines made for a colorful news story.

Only two reporters recognized this. We left for Poughkeepsie, where we had some difficulty but succeeded in getting copies of the booklet, by getting a bookseller to open his shop on Sunday. While we were writing in the telegraph office, Marvin Hunter McIntyre, the frail but likable White House secretary, came in to inform us that the incident had been put off the record. Later we learned that one of the idolater reporters had asked FDR, after we left, whether the reading wasn't off the record. Thinking he was advised by experts not to make the incident public, FDR said that it was. Many a good story was spoiled by some newsman, who was hoping to ingratiate himself with the President without concern for the right to know—a phrase unknown in those simpler days—by asking if something or other wasn't off the record.

Once, a couple of years later, at the same spot, Francis Marion Stephenson of the Associated Press picked up Mrs. Dorothy Storm, wife of Fred Storm, the United Press correspondent, and dropped her fully clad into the swimming pool, before the startled eyes of the President and his guests. This was immediately put off the record although not without challenge.

There were eight of us who traveled regularly with the President in those days. These were the representatives of the four press services—the Associated Press, the United Press, the International News Service and the Universal News Service. The newspapers represented were the New York *Times*, the New York *Herald Tribune*, the New York *News* and the Chicago *Tribune*. When the Universal service folded, the Philadelphia *Inquirer* joined the regulars. We were wet-nursed by Carroll S. Linkins of Western Union, who not only saw to it that our copy reached our offices, but also performed miracles of service.

This is a far cry from the many who follow the Chief Executive by plane today. Although FDR was the first President to fly, or at least the first party nominee to fly, he preferred to travel by train or ship, a naval vessel whenever possible. On longer stays our number swelled and on transcontinental journeys, there might be as many as twenty-eight reporters—a goodly number then but small today.

In addition to the newsmen, the National Broadcasting Company and Columbia Broadcasting System manned every trip in case the President might want to address the nation. There were cameramen and photographers but no television crews, because that media was unknown.

On his trips no one was permitted to photograph FDR getting in or out of his automobile. So successful was this protection that few of his countrymen knew that FDR could not walk without his braces and the assistance of canes or a friendly arm. Many a hapless cameraman, who knew nothing of the ban, had his box smashed by alert Secret Service men when he attempted to take a picture of the President being lifted from his limousine. At Indianapolis hundreds of yards of white muslin were wound around the spiral ramp of the George Rogers Clark Memorial to hide the fact that FDR was brought to the speaking podium in a wheel chair.

Even on the shorter trips, we continued the news conferences twice weekly, one for the morning papers and the other for the afternoon papers. There was no transcript except what we provided for ourselves and no direct quotation of the President was permitted except by his authorization. The conferences in his high-ceiling study at Hyde Park were the most intimate and relaxed, but were hardly any more rewarding. For all his gay camaraderie, FDR distrusted the press as most Presidents had and still do.

This suspicion of the press extended to his top aides concerned with the press. Almost invariably he never told Stephen Tyree Early, his press secretary, or McIntyre, who acted in that capacity on travels in addition to being appointment secretary, much more than he wanted the press to know. This became quite clear one day when we were pestering Early in his White House office about the filling of the first vacancy on the High Court after the defeat of FDR's plan to pack the Court with justices favorable to his legislation.

Steve, whose temper was as short as his ability was long, roared that he had told us a thousand times but would tell us again, that the President had not made up his mind. He added that he, Early, would let us know when there was any news.

At that very moment, the bulletin bell of the UP-operated Washington City News Service began ringing in its closet off his office. A reporter went over and pulled the bulletin off the machine. This reported that Senator Hugo Lafayette Black had just been appointed to the High Court. Early flushed with anger because he had not been taken in FDR's confidence.

Neither Early nor McIntyre ever claimed to have any influence on appointments or policy, except in rare instances. Neither was a New Dealer at heart although both were personally loyal to Roosevelt. Early, a former Associated Press reporter who had scored a great scoop on the death of President Harding in San Francisco's Palace Hotel, had covered FDR's vice-presidential campaign in 1920, and McIntyre, also a former newsman, was a newsreel contact man in the Navy Department during FDR's time as Assistant Navy Secretary.

Poughkeepsie, where we regulars spent most of our time when FDR was at Hyde Park, is not the most engaging of river towns. There was little for us to do when FDR began going to his family home nearly every weekend in the spring until he headed south for Warm Springs. We were forced to keep company because we never knew when there might be some news developing. We drank together and we ate together or haunted the temporary White House office in the Nelson House Hotel. With little to do, we spent many hours singing together.

McIntyre was convinced that "Home on the Range" was the greatest song ever written. So great was his love for the song that he convinced every band leader in the country that it was the President's favorite and it was played as often as "Hail to the Chief" at banquets. FDR confided that he actually disliked the song, and that his favorite was "The Yellow Rose of Texas," which I do not remember ever being played for him.

Roosevelt's knowledge of music was fragmentary at best. When Vice President Garner gave a dinner in FDR's honor in 1937 in the Washington Hotel, I attended as president of the White House Correspondents Association. A violinist asked FDR to select the next number. FDR thought and thought, then his face brightened and he came up with *The Fire Bird Suite*. The pained musician knew that he couldn't represent an entire symphony, so he asked the President if he would be satisfied with Fritz Kreisler's *Liebesfreud*, and FDR exclaimed, "That would be fine." I doubt whether he recognized it.

FDR liked to play poker, but on his own terms. Now and then he would play with us regulars at Hyde Park. Most of my colleagues were delighted to be able to put this line in their expense accounts: "Lost playing poker with the President . . ." I wasn't delighted and never used the line, but then I didn't have to. Roosevelt was a great bluffer and a driver in command of the game, calling on this person to ante up, bet or fold up. Nothing delighted him more than a successful bluff, although he never seemed to suspect there was some hesitancy to win on the part of most of his opponents, including his staffers. He was most unhappy when one of his bluffs failed, almost childishly so. My delight was getting a pair, back to back at stud poker, a great favorite with him, and calling his bluff. One of the first signs of his declining health came when he became vacant and forgetful at the poker table and often had to be invited to make his play.

FDR enjoyed knowing what the regulars of the press were doing when we accompanied him. He loved to twit anyone who put a sheet too many to the wind. One Sunday morning he looked down at the press men seated in front of him at a public church service and speaking appearance in Tupelo, Mississippi, and asked who had drunk a toast to General Grant after midnight the previous night in Corinth. He didn't know the microphone was on until an angry roar came from the crowd, which wasn't pleased. The guilty Stephenson and I didn't relish the attention.

FDR enjoyed our humor and encouraged his staff to relay the best of the press quips to him. In 1937, Boettiger, then married and editor of the Seattle *Post Intelligencer,* came with Anna to the drawing room I shared for years with George Durno of International News Service. We were enroute to Yellowstone Park. John complained he had joined the party in hopes of getting some news for his paper from his father-in-law, but all he could get out of FDR was a replay of my latest quips.

On that trip FDR summoned me to his side at every one of the tourist sights we visited in three days. Each time he would point to something like a boiling pool and say he was saving it for stewing robber barons like myself, and I would counter by saying I was thinking of using it for making alphabet soup. Or when we looked at the spouting Old Faithful, he told me he was reminded of fulminating *Tribune* editorials and I answered that it reminded me of Harold Ickes on one of his happier days.

So often did FDR call me that the nine governors of western states, who were in the cavalcade, assumed that I must be a person of great importance and tried to enlist me in helping them sell their favorite projects, which of course required federal outlays. Sistie and Buzzie Dahl, Anna's young children by her first marriage, were along too. Every now and then the cavalcade would stop and Lyle Wilson, the UP's Washington bureau chief, and I would race up in the high altitude from our position at the end of the cavalcade, only to find John taking Buzzie into the woods at one side of the road and Anna taking Sistie to the other side. "It's gotten so on this trip that I don't know whether to run up with a notebook or a pail," Wilson remarked.

During one of our long stretches at Hyde Park, I conceived the idea of forming the Poughkeepsie Protective Association with the help of George Durno. This was an adaptation of the protection rackets of Chicago gangsters. Members of the White House staff and those covering the President were invited to join and pay a fee of two dollars or face the ingenuous if compelling consequences.

Most members joined willingly, but some held out. One of the latter was Roberta Barrows, McIntyre's beautiful redheaded secretary. Where gangsters met opposition by applying lighted cigarettes to the toes of the hesitant, we put a match to newspapers piled against Roberta's door and yelled: "Fire!" This brought her around. It also brought around the hotel manager, a confirmed Republican, who gave the scorched rug a look that might be best described as marked by bigotry and prejudice. It then brought around the fire department. The sponsors of the organization were unable to report what happened after that because they had pressing business elsewhere. FDR thought it was great.

The association also met with some reluctance on the part of Dewey Long, the White House telegrapher and trip arranger. Twelve packages of assorted hardening Jell-O in his washbowl, in which his shaving and toilet articles were put to rest, effected a speedy change of heart. FDR's pleasure was heightened by the discomfiture of the hotel manager, who made no secret of his dislike of Roosevelt and all associated with him, including the President's only critic in the group, me.

When Norman H. Davis, the dignified American financier and diplomat, invited himself aboard the presidential special on a trip from Hyde Park to Washington, FDR invited me to his side and with great glee confided that he was submitting the free rider to the tender mercies of the Poughkeepsie Protective Association. It was the day after my birthday, which is the Fourth of July, and I had provided myself with plenty of firecrackers. These had already got me into some trouble, because I threw a lighted one out of a limousine window and into the boot of a motorcycle policeman who happened by. The officer didn't relish the explosion, but could hardly proceed against a member of the presidential party. I set off a packet behind a stone outdoor fireplace at Val-Kill, Mrs. Roosevelt's cottage, which brought Secret Service men racing to the area with drawn guns. FDR seated me beside himself in recognition of my natal day so there was nothing they could do. He was not at all alarmed; rather, he regarded the incident as a great joke.

Needless to say, the President's entrusting of Davis to our care was considered a great challenge by the association members. For a time, we contented ourselves with inserting firecrackers in the cracks and keyhole of his door. This was all right in its way but hardly spectacular. Then I got an idea of dazzling brilliance. Packets of firecrackers were strung together and set off in the shoe box of the Davis compartment, where he had put his white buckskins to await the attention of Sam Mitchell, our regular porter. When several hundred firecrackers combined to sputter, fizz and burst, they gave the shoes a smelly and lurid patina that might have come from the sulphur and brimstone of hell with a detour by way of Hiroshima and Nagasaki, then in the future.

This pyrotechnical display so inspired envy in the breast of a Secret Service man, who knew of our presidential directive, that he managed to open the door of the Davis compartment, lift the pajama coat of the sleeping—at long last—Davis and drop a twenty-five-pound cake of ice on his stomach. The ensuing scream from Davis brought answering wails from every female locomotive on the New York Central Railroad. Davis left the car the next day with hot feet and a cold tummy, while the President, who had received a full and complete report, howled and sent back a message of congratulations on a job well done.

"Never, never again, will I ride a presidential special," Davis confided as he disembarked in Washington. And he never did.

Messages were frequently passed between the President and the press, because of his interest in our doings. Once, when he was going to Harvard for the induction of his third son, Franklin, Jr., into the Fly Club, an old fraternity, I wrote Roosevelt a note saying that I had gone to Notre Dame, where I might have joined the Knights of Columbus, so I could not help but be impressed by association with such distinguished clubmen as his son and himself.

"Shoo fly, don't bother me," he scrawled in reply.

Robert Post, a socialite reporter who covered the White House for a time for the New York *Times*, donned his Fly Club tie for his first presidential trip. FDR didn't recognize the stripes and it wouldn't have helped Post if he had. Post died in a bombing raid over Germany, which he was covering as a war correspondent.

A few months later, another trip provided great amusement for FDR. He invited Felix Frankfurter, then a Harvard law professor, to accompany him to watch young Franklin pull an oar with Harvard's sophomore crew in boat races at New London, Connecticut. The professor was not assigned to our care in the press car, as Davis had been, but was given a compartment in the President's private car.

Frankfurter wandered into the diner from the private car for a nightcap. Edward L. Roddan of Universal News Service rounded up Ernest K. Lindley of the New York *Herald Tribune*, a Rhodes scholar, and myself, saying the three of us could take Frankfurter on and cut him down to size. After considerable banter and several drinks, Frankfurter challenged us to name three important books he said he should have read but had not.

"*Das Kapital*," ventured Lindley, who had specialized in Russian affairs at Oxford.

Frankfurter was somewhat taken aback, but acknowledged that Lindley was right.

"*Alice in Wonderland*," Roddan put in.

Again the surprised Frankfurter nodded.

"The Constitution," I shouted.

Frankfurter's astonishment indicated another bull's eye. Whether or not he had read the books, they were the three he had in mind. I must say that the professor was game and continued drinking with us into the night, but the next day he stayed below deck on the presidential yacht *Potomac*, with a magna cum laude hangover. It amused FDR no end and so did the tale of the three books. FDR pretended astonishment that anyone had missed any of the books, although I doubt that he was serious.

FDR was no great reader. I have a camera eye for books and always examined the books he took along with him on the *Potomac*. None of these were ever disturbed except a few detective stories, which were the favorite reading of his military aide, Colonel Edwin W. ("Pa") Watson. What quotes FDR employed in speeches were given to him by ghost writers like Ray Moley, or were supplied by literary admirers like Carl Sandburg, the poet-historian.

On still another trip from Hyde Park, FDR became interested in a little red hen, which Fred Pasley of the New York *News*, bought from the back of a farm truck in Poughkeepsie. Fred led the creature around barrooms on a string and taught it to drink beer and whiskey. Then he brought it aboard the diner of the presidential special, where he set up a pool on the time the hen would yield to a call of nature. FDR joined in the pool and asked for bulletins on the hen's progress. Unfortunately, the bets were never settled because a frantic dining car steward realized what could happen to his gleaming linen and banished the hiccupping hen to the baggage car ahead.

Presidential specials are a thing of the past today, almost as ancient as the wagon train and far less glamorous in the public mind. However, they had their moments and took more planning and security precautions even in peacetime than jet travel does today. Train travel involved far more people. Once the Chief Executive determined on a trip, the chief of the White House Secret Service, Colonel Edmund W. Starling, went over the route, checking on presidential accommodations as well as those of members of his party and the press, if he were staying overnight along the route.

Crews of the special were carefully selected from the engine cab to the President's private car in the rear. The same porters were on duty regularly on all cars. My first ride on a presidential special was a short run with President Hoover, on which I met Samuel C. Mitchell, a porter who was to become one of my best friends and later a White House employee. He was assigned to the private car built for the Chief Executive in the last days of train travel, under Truman. Later still, he became a White House receptionist.

Sam went to his grave refusing to reveal his private thoughts on the Presidents he had served, even though White House staffers enlisted me to persuade him to put his recollections on tape. Sam was free with his observations on Presidents and the other great men he came into contact with at the White House and aboard trains, but could not be induced to have a book written on his experiences or to talk about them for posterity. He had a deep respect for the presidency. I must preserve his confidences although I can say no President was a hero to this valet of the railroads except Herbert Hoover.

The roadbed of every inch of track, especially bridges on which the presidential special traveled, was carefully inspected in advance and a short time before the passage of the train. A pilot train with engine, tender and caboose went on a mile ahead to be certain that the road was clear, even though no journey was undertaken without careful regard to the schedules of regular passenger and freight trains. On longer trips there was a following engine, which could pull out the President's private car in the event of an accident.

As limited a trip as the journey to Hyde Park required eight cars for the special. There was the President's car, another for his staff and the Secret Service as well as some guests, the diner, the press car, a club car, a car for the railroad men, a communications car, and a baggage car to carry equipment for any temporary White House, as well as the engine and tender. Longer trips brought as many as eighteen cars and two engines. However, one jet today carries more than the trains of yesterday, taking 150 and more in the press plane, including some Secret Service men and other staffers.

Ordinarily the payment of 125 fares was exacted for a special train. This requirement was waived for the White House when the frugal Calvin Coolidge objected to such a charge and boarded a regular passenger train between Washington and Chicago. This gave railroad men the fidgets because it played havoc with security.

Every rider on a presidential special, including the President, was billed for a regular fare and whatever Pullman accommodations he occupied. There was no charge for the private car. Those who were invited to go along for part of the journey, such as local newsmen and various politicians who wanted to accompany the Chief Executive through their state, paid the fares and Pullman charges they would have had to meet on any top train.

FDR wasn't a heavy tipper at any time, but was less so aboard trains. He gave five dollars to the porter on his car for the round trip from Washington to Hyde Park, which included payment for what guests he might have in his car. In the press car we each gave two dollars for the trip, but there were about twenty of us all told. Sam soon begged off the private car; the honor of serving the President faded for a man raising a family and sending a boy to college as well as paying for a home, when he could count on forty dollars in the press car as against five dollars in the private car.

In campaign years, FDR was a more frequent churchgoer than in noncampaign years. At Warm Springs, an Episcopal clergyman with a large family in a relatively poor parish in Gainesville was induced to conduct services for the President, who would drop one dollar into the collection basket with a flourish and go out to have his picture taken leaving the Foundation chapel. Earlier in the morning Catholics among the staff, Secret Service and press would drop no less—without flourishes—at their service in the same church.

Another cautious tipper in Washington was one of its wealthiest men, RFC Chairman Jones, who could never forget the days when a dime was a good tip. When he was forced out of government service by FDR, he set up an office in the Statler Hotel, where I lunched with him regularly. Uncle Jesse, as I called him, would leave a dime. It didn't take long for waiters to busy themselves elsewhere when he ordered. One of his secretaries had to serve us.

Uncle Jesse was generous with liquor, however. When I went on the wagon for some twenty years, Carol would join him in a couple of scotches, her limit, while I sipped water in his Houston apartment. He poured the drinks dark with liquor. When we went from his apartment to the home of his nephew, John Jones, who was the son of Jesse's brother of the same name, Carol refused a third drink, saying she just had two from his uncle and was feeling them.

"You know why he pours them so heavily?" John asked. "His friends give him the liquor and he has to pay for the soda."

Uncle Jesse once showed me a table of his worth, about $285,000,-000, and an aerial photo of Houston with the buildings he owned marked and numbered. I pointed to an impressive structure and asked him why he didn't own it.

"That's the federal court house," he explained.

"Oh," I said, "you own that one indirectly."

One Sunday afternoon he took us through his bank, where there was a large portrait of himself, which seemed to be looking directly at every teller and employee in sight. We found the bank president working in his office. As we left, I told Uncle Jesse that if I were he, I'd begin worrying.

"You mean because the president is working on Sunday?" he mused. "I wonder why."

Another time he took me to the Petroleum Club in a building he had just sold to an oil company.

"I suppose you think I'm going broke," he said.

"No, Uncle Jesse," I said. "I think you were afraid they might build a big clubhouse alongside the Shamrock Hotel and shift the pattern of growth in this town some miles away from your holdings."

"You're a smart fellow," he conceded.

But I really wasn't and I knew it. Jones frequently offered me a tool company or some other business the RFC controlled, offering to lend me the money to operate it. I turned these offers down, because I didn't know anything about such businesses and because I didn't think I would be honest in accepting.

Uncle Jesse told me how he made his first million; it convinced me that I was never cut out to make money. He was born in Tennessee, as so many Texans were and are, and came to Texas to work in the lumberyard of an uncle. He made his first trip to Europe before World War I and on his way home stopped in New York to see Robert Scott Lovett, the Texas lawyer who had become general counsel for Edward Henry Harriman's Union Pacific Railroad. Jones said he told Lovett he had $50,000 to invest and asked his advice on how to invest it. Lovett said he had put a similar question to Harriman and the financier told him to buy Union Pacific Railroad stock.

Jones stopped off in Kansas City and bought $50,000 worth of the stock on margin. At this point I interjected a question to ask Uncle Jesse where he got the $50,000.

"I stole it from my uncle," he said calmly. "He wasn't paying me enough."

It wasn't long before Jones began getting wires for more margin, because the stock was easing downward. These telegrams aroused the curiosity of the office manager, Jones said, so he told him the story of his visit to Lovett. The office manager told him he was a fool to play the market, so he wired Lovett for advice. Lovett's answer was that he was sorry but he couldn't advise Jones.

"So, I bought another $50,000 worth of Union Pacific on margin and the office manager bought the same amount."

"Don't tell me, Uncle Jesse," I said. "I know you stole the money from your uncle and so did your office manager, who probably felt he wasn't being paid enough. But why did you buy? I would have sold out."

"Well, I figured, if I had done wrong, Judge Lovett would have told me so. When he didn't I knew something was up and it was. Union Pacific divided and went up and I had made my first million."

I told him I was glad that he had told the story because it explained why I didn't have a million. I was also glad to learn he paid his uncle back after he made his million.

"It's easy to make a million," Jesse said. "The hard part comes in keeping it. Look at Jack Garner. He's worth a million and he's working harder to keep it than he ever did as Speaker or Vice President."

My first concentrated presidential campaign was Roosevelt's greatest, that of 1936. I covered most of his stumping on the theme of flood control and drought control. He invariably favored a leitmotiv for this purpose. He masked his tours for votes as some form of presidential business, which was his right, but he fooled no one in politics.

Just before the 1936 campaign Roosevelt undertook what I have always regarded as his strangest train journey. In June 1936, he planned to go to Texas as part of his re-election campaigning and with some hope of blanketing the Republican convention. Four days before his scheduled departure, Speaker Joseph Wellington Byrns died of a heart attack in his sixty-seventh year. The Speaker is one of the officials who commands presidential presence at his last rites, so a hasty journey to Nashville, Tennessee, was arranged. The funeral was held there on Saturday, June 6.

The congressional train, bearing the Speaker's body, set out about the same time as the presidential special. It was a curious conceit of such train trips, whose expenses were borne by the taxpayers, that all chits for drinks and meals be signed in the name of the departed leader.

A great many chits were being signed for drinks, we noticed when our special paused beside the funeral train from time to time. Senators and congressmen in the funeral party would lift their glasses in salute. Needless to say, members of the press did their best to match the legislators in their liquid respect for the departed.

We arrived in Nashville on a blistering morning. A National Guard band, playing Chopin's *Funeral March*, led the mourners headed by the family, the President and the congressional delegation slowly through the streets and up the hill of the state capital to the city's War Memorial, where a huge crowd was gathered as far back as the capital lawn, where President James K. Polk is buried.

For some strange reason, the President and his immediate party were relegated to a corner of the vast hall. The main aisle was given over to the congressional delegation. The press had more prominent seating than the Chief Executive in an aisle to the right of the main aisle.

The arrival of the congressional delegation was preceded by a cloud composed of the aura of the distilled fruit of corn, the juice of the barley and the tang of juniper. The members filed to their seats, most of them unsteadily, in a strange pattern of dress. Some wore white tie and tails, others, dinner jackets, still others, frock coats and striped pants, but the majority were in business suits, not all of them dark.

Two members of the press, George Durno and Charles McLean, of the New York *Times*, were hardly better off than the more redolent members of the congressional delegation, so a couple of the Secret Service men left Roosevelt to watch over them.

On the stage to the right were a mass of floral wreaths, including gates ajar, cracked hearts, broken wheels, fractured pillars and a siz-

able map of Tennessee in white roses with red roses indicating that
it was split by grief.

On the stage, to the left of the audience, was a clump of palms,
behind which were two men and two women, obviously composing
a mixed quartet. In the center were the Reverend James Sherra
Montgomery, the chaplain of the House, in Roman collar, and two
associates, in dark suits, whom I assumed correctly were the local
clergy. When I saw one of these draw a bulky manuscript from his
breast pocket and begin reading, smiling to himself in satisfaction,
I knew we were in for it. So I called a Western Union boy, gave
him money and told him to bring two bottles of whiskey to the
cemetery.

The flag-draped coffin of the dead leader was wheeled into the
memorial from the right along the front aisle and parked inches
from his widow and his family. The widow fainted and had to be
revived. The services began with a song from the quartet. The two
women looked like fugitives from Grant Wood's painting *Daughters
of Revolution*. The tenor was short with a wisp of hair grown for
the purpose of concealing his baldness, but not successfully. The bass
was tall and thin and as dour as a Scot at his own funeral. They
didn't rise up with any apparent effort, but seemed to float up, from
time to time, when called on for "Lead, Kindly Light" and other
lugubrious hymns.

The first of the local clergymen rose and took the podium, de-
positing a bulky manuscript. He began by saying that when he was
first assigned to Nashville, he took the pulpit of the Third Baptist
Church and was later called to that of the First Baptist Church,
where he organized a men's Bible class that grew from a handful to
more than three hundred members, including Byrns when he was
at home.

"I shall never forget the day in 1934, when our dear departed
brother [here the widow collapsed again] came into the back of the
church, right after Election Day," he continued. "I could see him,
but the class couldn't, so I announced: 'Once again Tennessee has
written on its slate, "I love you, Joe."' Members of the class turned
around and recognized him and then realized the import of my line.
Well, sir, you should have heard the applause."

This went on and on. So did the second local clergyman, also a

Baptist. Several times the widow had to be revived. It was growing hotter and hotter. Members of Congress were paling, and Durno and McLean were swaying. Both clergymen told the story that when Byrns was riding a presidential special on FDR's visit to TVA in 1934, FDR sent William Donaldson, superintendent of the House press gallery, to bring the legislator back to the private car one night. They made much of the fact that Donaldson found the good man on his knees. They hailed him as a great but humble man seeking divine guidance in a time of crisis. Actually, Byrns was on the floor searching for his false teeth, which he had dropped on the swaying train, and all of the presidential party knew it and had difficulty in maintaining composure.

But the services had only begun after more than an hour and a half. Montgomery, a Methodist, had been absent from the capital when Byrns died so that services in the House well were conducted by a young stand-in. The young man had done very well, indeed, too well for Montgomery because one and all told him how beautifully the young clergyman had recited Alfred Lord Tennyson's "Crossing the Bar," a recital in which the House chaplain considered himself second to none.

Montgomery went to the podium, without manuscript, and paused for effect. Then he began: "In my Father's house there are many mansions." Again he paused for effect. The loud speakers in the memorial plaza, where many who could not get in were gathered, brought the echo of his words back to Montgomery.

The delivery didn't satisfy Montgomery, so he began again, stressing the word "Father's." He waited for the echo and still was not satisfied. The third echo brought a smile of approval to his lips, so he plunged on, ever conscious of the echo and repeating a line here and there when he wasn't satisfied.

Montgomery felt he had to be longer than either of his local colleagues so he did his best to match both their times. He launched into the close of his sermon by pulling out all of the stops on "Crossing the Bar," when the undertaker and his assistants, evidently realizing the sagging widow was near exhaustion, began wheeling the coffin out.

Montgomery matched their pace in finishing the poem and then called: "Good-by, brother of mine! Good-by, leader of mine!

Good-by, Joseph E. Byrns!" He was unaware he had given the wrong initial to the dead. Then, as mourners began to follow the coffin, Montgomery rose to his full height and called on them to stop. Most of the startled mourners did so.

Montgomery realized he had committed a grave breach of protocol that might imperil his sinecure, so he urged them back to their seats. Not all did so, but Montgomery turned and pointed to a man in the audience. He told the drifting audience that while Byrns was gone, the country was fortunate that he would be succeeded by no less a great man in the person of Representative William B. Bankhead of Alabama.

Outside the band again took up the lead and the procession followed to the mournful notes of the *Funeral March*, played over and over again on the dreary miles to the cemetery. Radiators steamed and boiled over. Finally, the party reached the receiving vault, where Byrns was to rest until his tomb could be prepared.

My Western Union boy was there with the two bottles. I revived my stricken colleagues, McIntyre and a few choice spirits, including myself. Just as I lowered the bottle behind the vault, there was a round of rifle fire, which brought me around to the front crying: "Thank God, they've shot James Sherra Montgomery." I was embarrassed when my voice carried to all in the hushed stillness.

When we got back to the special, FDR called me to his car, where he told me: "You missed the worst of it. Just as we started to leave the cemetery, Montgomery rushed up to my car, stuck his head in the lowered window, and ran alongside shouting: 'Good-by, beloved President of mine! Good-by, beloved President of mine!' I wanted to spit in his face."

A few weeks later I was with FDR in Philadelphia when he delivered his acceptance speech in the Philadelphia National League baseball park on a black night. By that time I was used to the tremendous ovations he inspired and had studied them. He was one of those gifted people who are capable of rousing listeners to wild enthusiasm and fanatic ecstasy. It wasn't so much his words or his ideas as it was the personal and hypnotic magnetism that came through his mellifluous tones, perhaps through his flesh or bones, but certainly not through his mind because the words were not his own but the studied work of others. I suppose Hitler and Mussolini had the same sort of animal magnetism, but not for me because they didn't vibrate in my rhythm as German and Italian opera does.

But there never was a setting for FDR more dramatic than that night in Philadelphia and he milked it for all it was worth. He told the story to us aboard the yacht *Sewana*, which he had chartered for a voyage in the Bay of Fundy and off Nova Scotia, with three of his four sons. His skipper was a German sailor who had served at the Battle of Jutland in which Kaiser Wilhelm's forces actually defeated their British opponents, but had lost the engagement by retiring and bottling themselves up in port for the duration of the war. FDR wouldn't have even talked to a German sailor three years later. The press regulars were aboard the chartered schooner *Liberty*, a sturdy and stanch vessel which at one time served as the craft of Boston pilots who waited off the city's harbor to guide in merchant ships.

Hall Roosevelt, Mrs. Roosevelt's brother, who had a fondness for gin, was on the cruise for the first few days. Hall's drinking was a matter of concern to Mrs. R. and something of a problem for FDR, because it probably inspired Hall to arrange a White House meeting between FDR and Henry Ford, the auto manufacturer. Ford was one of the most dedicated foes of the New Deal in the summer of 1935, but the meeting was a fiasco rather than a meeting of minds.

Ford had no cause to love the *Tribune*, having been made to look ridiculous in a libel suit brought against the paper. He won a few cents and the *Tribune* gained a moral victory. Edsel Ford, who had sat beside his father throughout the trial, told me he never expected to see the day when he and his father would respect the *Tribune* above other papers, but they did for its opposition to the Blue Eagle of the NRA. Edsel and his wife were generous contributors to the Warm Springs Foundation from its beginnings, before FDR gained the White House, because they were interested in helping the stricken wife of a Ford executive.

In the *Tribune* trial, Ford made his famous remark: "History is bunk," a statement cited with scorn for a half century. Yet, in many ways, the remark is entirely justified. Some tell us that history is the story of great men, yet there have been few truly great men and a lot of lucky ones. Historians profess to see this or that event sparking this or that action, but man is so complex an animal and every day is so full of events, that it is impossible to say just what action or what thought inspired any particular decision by a leader.

History is timely opportunity as well as the man. We can wonder what Napoleon would have been had he been born ten years earlier. We can ponder who else could have pockmarked the facade of St. Roche by firing the whiff of grapeshot that ended the French Revolution. Or who would have wintered at Valley Forge had George Washington been born ten years later. And, finally, where would FDR have been if Al Smith had taken the advice that he forget the Democratic nomination in 1928 and let it fall into his lap in 1932?

When Hall left the *Sewana,* FDR invited us aboard, explaining: "Hall's gone so we could take the lock off the gin locker." While we rocked at anchor off Shelbourne, Nova Scotia, James, John and Franklin vied with one another in making and pouring Martinis for their father and urging him to drink up. He was moved to tell us the long but fascinating story of how his acceptance speech almost became a major disaster because the pin came out of one of his steel braces.

FDR was coming to the podium, having been introduced by Vice President Garner who bungled his Chief's middle name. Roosevelt could see nothing but blackness because the bright lights, all turned on the stage, blinded him to the audience. When the pin came out, FDR knocked the speech out of the hand of his eldest son, James, on whose arm he was entering. Jimmy let go his father, when he dived for the speech and scrambled about the floor for its pages. Gus Gennerich, the New York policeman, who left the force to become FDR's bodyguard when he became governor of New York, saved Roosevelt from falling on his face and valiantly held him upright by massive muscular strength.

"There I was hanging in the air, like a goose about to be plucked," FDR told us, according to notes I made at the time, although he charged us not to write the story, "but I kept on waving and smiling, and smiling and waving. I called to Jimmy out of the corner of my mouth to fix the pin."

" 'Dad,' Jimmy called up, 'I'm trying to pick up the speech.'

" 'To hell with the speech,' I said, again from the corner of my mouth. 'Fix the God-damned brace. If it can't be fixed there won't be any speech.' But I didn't lose a smile or a wave.

"By this time, I was mad clean through. First, I was mad because Jack Garner had mangled my name in his introduction, calling me 'Delaney,' and then 'Deluno.' Then I was mad because Ed Halsey, the Senate secretary, got in front of me when I was waving to the crowd, and I must confide to you that Ed has the broadest beam in a body renowned for its posterior spread.

"I was mad at the mayor of Philadelphia, who kept leaning over to confide how many police they had on duty in the park, at the station and along the route. I have to tell you that the mayor has one of the worst cases of halitosis ever blown in my face. I was mad at the lights which were so bright I couldn't see a soul in the blackness beyond.

"I was mad at the speech which had scattered on the floor. Finally, and above all, I was mad at the damned brace, which had picked that particular moment of all moments to break down.

"I could feel Jimmy fumbling and then I heard the pin snap back into place. My balance was restored and the weight was lifted from poor Gus. Jimmy shuffled the pages into their proper order, but with some difficulty because he was flustered.

"I was still mad when I began, never missing a wave. It wasn't until I reached the line about 'economic royalists' and 'princes of privilege' and heard the mighty roar from the crowd that I knew that I had them, so I gave them the business."

He beamed in recollection of the triumphant scene he had played.

It was at this session that FDR confided that he would have preferred that the Republicans nominate Hoover again. I never knew whether he felt he hadn't licked Hoover badly enough in 1932, but suspected that he probably thought that Hoover would have been easier to lick than Governor Alfred M. Landon of Kansas, even when others had no doubt about the outcome of that contest. FDR always ran scared.

FDR had a deep and abiding hate for Hoover, which is not unusual among Presidents for men who dare to run against them. Defeated men are less bitter toward men who have beaten them, but almost never as hostile toward men who have beaten other candidates in their own party.

Truman could be friendly toward Hoover and employ him to direct world-wide relief and launch a program of governmental reorganization, where FDR could not even give Hoover—by personal direction—a Secret Service man to accompany the ex-President back to his Palo Alto, California, home. Johnson could embrace and support Nixon where he was less than cordial to Senator Barry Goldwater, who opposed him in 1964.

Roosevelt dearly loved to play a game of cat and mouse with the press, so it was with studied casualness that he announced, in a news conference in his Hyde Park study, his intention of meeting with the governors of Iowa, Missouri, Nebraska, Arkansas, Oklahoma and Kansas on one of his first 1936 flood inspections.

"Alf Landon?" I asked in a voice that went to falsetto in surprise.

"Yes, Landon," he roared with delight over our astonishment.

Few had any doubt about the outcome of the campaign, except the *Literary Digest*, whose poll, conducted by Dr. George A. Gallop in his early tabulating days, indicated a landslide for the Kansas governor, but that magazine polled its own readers and telephone subscribers, missing the lowest levels of income.

Farley gained a great and lasting reputation as a prophet, because he said the Democrats would carry every state except Maine and Vermont. Others were not far behind. I had included Connecticut in the Republican column, because the turnout was not as large or as enthusiastic in that state as in others, but I failed to account for a drizzling rain. Also the state was one not tied to either party but swung back and forth between Republicans and Democrats.

The state had one Democratic senator, Francis T. Maloney, and a Republican, John A. Danaher, who later became a judge of the Circuit Court of Appeals in the District of Columbia. This representation was one of the most effective in Congress. Quite often senators from opposing parties work together in the same state better than some from the same party, not being plagued by jealousies and not engaged in wrangling over seniority.

Danaher's father had been a Democratic state leader, who switched to the Republican party. A few days after his switch, John told me, two ladies met on a street corner in an Irish neighborhood in Hartford.

"Didja hear the news?" one asked the other excitedly. "Connie Danaher's turned Republican."

"Aw, go'way widja," exclaimed the other, "I saw him at Mass last Sunday."

FDR won as handily as Farley predicted, although he didn't hail Farley for it. Roosevelt relished a torchlight victory celebration given him by townsfolk at the family estate. He did take time out to send his mock condolences to "Bertie McCormick," through me.

THE NEW DEAL
GOES GLOBAL

I n November 1936, Roosevelt celebrated his re-election by heading for South America to attend a hemisphere peace conference in Buenos Aires, with stops in Trinidad, Rio de Janeiro and Montevideo. Colonel McCormick, who always sent men where the news was, ordered me to cover. FDR boarded the USS *Indianapolis* at Charleston, South Carolina. Three press service men boarded the accompanying cruiser, USS *Chester*. They were Durno of INS, Storm of UP and Harry D. Oliver of AP, a newcomer to the regulars.

I secured a seat on a Pan American Airways Clipper, which had been chartered for the trip. There were a number of Secret Service men and a postal inspector, who arranged mail pickups and deliveries by diplomatic pouch. Carlton Smith represented NBC and Paul White, CBS. William Murray, a cameraman, and Ben Box, a sound man of Fox Movietone News, represented all newsreels and Tom McAvoy of *Life* magazine, then about to make its bow, came along with his bride on a combined honeymoon and business trip. William McEvoy of Pan American Airways publicity staff completed the party.

No other paper faced up to the importance of the first extended presidential visit outside the continental United States to the southern hemisphere as McCormick had. Thus I became the first and only reporter to cover the first White House plane charter.

A few days before his departure, FDR posed on the White House lawn with members of the White House Correspondents Association, with me seated at his left as that group's vice president. I confided to FDR that the taking of the picture was indeed a historic occasion, because it marked the first time that he was ever to the right of me, a jest he enjoyed. What I did not tell him was that the photograph, which was to appear in the second issue of *Life* a few weeks later, had not been arranged to promote him with the press so much as to establish me in the good graces of McCormick.

The colonel had ordered a new picture of the newly re-elected President in color with which he was experimenting. Early knew that FDR wouldn't sit still for the colonel, but the press secretary wanted to help me, so he arranged for the photograph with newsmen. The *Tribune* was able to smuggle in a color camera team, under E. Harrison Johnson. The photograph, taken outdoors in bright sunshine, wasn't too good, but it was a color exclusive so the colonel was happy and I got the assignment to South America.

The plane journey from Miami down to Buenos Aires took most of five days at that time, because there was no night flying and we made the journey in an amphibian plane with a top speed of about 150 miles with a strong tail wind. We had a rendezvous with FDR at Port of Spain, Trinidad, where the skull and crossbones banners of pirate ships had fluttered in off-shore breezes some two centuries before.

As we flew into Rio, Fred Clark, our pilot, hugged the green mountains until the panorama of that lovely city unfolded before us. It is still the greatest bay I have seen, making those of Acapulco, Naples, San Francisco and Vigo, beautiful as they are, fade by comparison. On the marble dock at the foot of the Aveniedo Rio Branco, my fellow travelers pointed me out as the chief of the party, for a musical salute from a band and an exchange of speeches. Little did they realize that this designation put the green Packard automobile of the foreign office and its chauffeur at my disposal. I was given a twenty-four-hour watch of three Brazilian foreign service officers, all of whom had served as consuls general at one city or another in the United States.

Our first evening in Rio was a gay one, ending at the sumptuous gambling casino, the Atlantico, where I became a multimillionaire for the first and only time in my life by winning more than two million reis, about $125 U.S. currency, at roulette and making as much for my consul general attendant. Whiskey and champagne flowed like buttermilk; orchestras rose from the stage floor to play for a time and be succeeded by other bands. I was enchanted and inspired and not a little under the influence of the bubbly and barley squeezings. I was moved to report on glorious Rio to FDR. Naturally, the consul general was enchanted and put Brazil radio at my disposal. My message to the President read:

FORGET BUENOS AIRES HOLD CONFERENCE RIO
STOP TROHAN

FDR relayed the radiogram to my colleagues on the *Chester* with the observation that it was obvious someone was having quite a time in Rio. The next morning my door was besieged by a platoon of Brazilian newspapermen, who had been advised of the message by the consul general. These saw an opportunity to promote their country above Argentina. National pride had been evoked and after the enthusiasm of champagne it was not easy to quiet by the cold water of truth.

Echoes of the episode were to reach Cordell Hull weeks later. There was some concern in the State Department that FDR might have been slighted in Buenos Aires, which led him to prefer Rio. Hull took one look at the distorted reports from American missions to the south and walked across West Executive Avenue to lay the Latin American messages on Roosevelt's desk. FDR took one look, threw back his head and laughed heartily:

"Why, Cordell," he exclaimed, "all this is nothing but Walter Trohan having a night on the town in Rio."

FDR gave me a broad wink, during the exchange of national anthems, on his arrival in Rio, in recognition of my message. His appearance in the city was a personal triumph, as it was in Buenos Aires and Montevideo. I had grown accustomed to the enthusiasm he inspired in America, but to the south he was regarded as an even greater hero than he was at home, because they saw him as cracking down on the rich and distributing money to the poor. And the Latin temperament is more given to enthusiasm. Never had I seen crowds go so wild with joy and I was not to see its like again for almost a quarter of a century when I accompanied President Dwight D. Eisenhower on his visit to New Delhi, India, in 1959.

In Philadelphia in the 1936 campaign, I saw a policeman get so excited that he threw his watch, a treasured memento from his father, into FDR's car. This action brought him discipline and almost cost him time in jail because the Secret Service were fearful that it might be a bomb. In Rio, crowds broke ranks and jogged behind the American Chief Executive, tying up traffic into hopeless snarls.

Buenos Aires was a bit more formal, but not much. In Montevideo, throngs again broke all controls. I rode in a car with the movie camera team, alongside the President's car. He was ecstatic, waved to me and shouted, above the roar of the crowd: "Did you ever see anything like it?" I never had.

In Montevideo, FDR was taken on a road the government was building in imitation of American public works projects. The road ended abruptly in the middle of a field and it took considerable jockeying to turn the presidential car around in the auto jam, so that he could get back to his ship. I couldn't resist sidling up to the car and telling FDR that the Latin American version of the New Deal was just as confused as its American counterpart.

I believe that FDR became a bit intoxicated with the reception he received, as well he might. I am sure it played a great part in convincing him that he was indispensable not only at home but to the world. I am equally sure that I was in on the birth of the third-term decision, although I was not to realize it until later. I was aware that one of the first persons to come under the magnetic power of Roosevelt's oratory was himself. He often looked on himself as a man of destiny sent to right the nation and later the world.

One of the greatest regrets of my life is buried in Rio. When FDR lunched with the Brazilian President we were feted in the home of one of the country's wealthiest families. Never have I seen a more sumptuous table, glowing with a huge central mound of flame-colored orchids, a gorgeous lace cloth and rows of solid gold cutlery on either side of the finest French china. The wines were the finest of Germany, France and Portugal, and the menu was staggered over two hours for three dozen guests.

At the end of the meal, I asked for and was led to a bathroom, where the furnishings were carved from solid blocks of green onyx with solid gold taps. Briefly, I considered taking a bath in such a tub, but decided to give way to others. I have never forgiven myself for passing up that tub.

FDR transferred from the *Indianapolis* to a destroyer to make his way into the rather shallow harbor of Buenos Aires. However, he arrived for the peace conference on a ship of war and was met by Argentine President Justo who appeared in a white general's uniform. The ironic display of military might did not go unnoticed at the conference.

Roosevelt addressed a joint session of Congress as he had in Rio. I was seated on the steps of a dais immediately below him. As he began to talk I saw a figure leap to the front of one of the boxes in the visitors' galleries and shout, *"A bas imperialisme!"* before he could be restrained and led away. A Scot in the Argentine equivalent of our Secret Service, who had been assigned to me, explained that the man who had shouted: "Down with imperialism!" was Justo's son, who was something of a parental problem.

When I went to the cable office to file my story, I asked if there were any censorship in Argentina. I was assured by the indignant British manager that there was none, so I put young Justo's outburst well up in my lead. The manager came back with my copy, somewhat abashed, saying that while there was no censorship, there were questions of the exercise of good sense. He added that I shouldn't expect him to send such a story and keep his office open.

The manager did agree to send a message, if I could compose what he considered an innocuous one, which might alert the *Tribune* to the incident. Mindful that the *Tribune* cable desk had often told me how alert and alive they were to any hints of news, I sent a message stating that I was unable to interview Justo's son as requested on the shouting in the gallery, assuming they would recognize that the shout that I reported anonymously had come from him. Within a short time I got a reply, which read: "Did not request Justo interview." However, the son did get into my story because the news services phoned a full report of the incident to Montevideo, from which city it was sent north without question, so the cable desk could pick it up.

By specific direction of the colonel, the *Tribune* never employed any form of code communication in his time. The only identifying notation we ever used was an "RRMC" on the slug of any story he ordered. During the war this was changed to "Special," presumably to protect the colonel, although just how this would have fooled any inquiry was never made clear.

The only time I ever employed a code was at the behest of the French Deuxieme Bureau early in 1940 when I was about to sail from Genoa aboard the *Conte di Savoia* of the Italian lines. I was approached by Henri Blanche in the French foreign service. Blanche, a Lavalist, confided that French intelligence had received word that Hjalmar Schacht, the German financier who had helped Hitler to power, was being smuggled to America aboard the vessel in order to confer with American financial leaders in New York.

Blanche knew I was friendly with Pietro di Carbonelli of *Il Corriere della Sera* of Milan, a ranking Fascist, who was returning to Washington. Blanche wanted to know if I would help him by reporting on the rumor. Aware that if I found Schacht aboard the ship, I would certainly mention it in my dispatches, I agreed and we arranged a simple code. If Schacht were aboard I would radio Carbonelli I was sorry I missed him at the pier. If Schacht were not aboard I would wire to thank him for seeing me off. And if I found that either of my first messages were in error, I would send a second inquiring about lost luggage.

I sought out the captain to whom I had letters of introduction from Italian compatriots and asked if he had any secret guests. He told me he had none. I got the same report from Carbonelli, so I radioed the code message that Schacht was not aboard. The French were satisfied, but the British, who had the same report, were not. They held up the Italian liner for fourteen hours at Gibraltar, while they searched the ship from stem to stern. The captain assured them he was not hiding anyone, but that if he were, they would never find him, because a secret guest could be so shuffled about in connecting cabins, no small force could uncover him.

When the British officers gave up their unsuccessful search, the exasperated Italian bartenders refused to accept British pounds as payment for drinks they needed. So John O'Donnell of the New York *News* and I, who had been irked by the delay they occasioned, came to the rescue of the weary and stained officers, swallowed our anger and stood for a couple of rounds.

Buenos Aires was some ten hours by air from Rio. On that leg of the journey we were joined by Oswaldo Aranha, Brazilian ambassador to the United States, later a contender for his country's presidency and finally head of the UN General Assembly. We were already friends in Washington, partly because the embassy had been built by Colonel McCormick's mother and was her home for many years.

Naturally, we arrived a day or two ahead of FDR. When I greeted him at the dock, I had a story which provoked a hearty guffaw. Robert Clark, a Secret Service man, had won himself a berth on the South American detail by representing himself as fluent in Spanish. When I went down to the room of Colonel Starling, who had flown down ahead of our party, I found Bob sweating at the phone over the ordering of ham and eggs for breakfast for fellow agents. They, like so many American travelers in so many places, seemed to be dying for that American eye opener they seldom have at home. I tried to tell Bob that the City Hotel had placed English-speaking operators on our phones, but he waived me aside, deeming it imperative that he justify his presence.

Some fifteen minutes later, a white-tied waiter entered the suite, carrying a covered silver salver. Triumphantly, he raised the dome to reveal a whisk broom. Evidently Bob's pronunciation of "*jamon y heuves*," had been accepted as "*tapon de paja*."

One evening after FDR's arrival, I dined with Bill Murray and Ben Box in the Bal Taberin, a night club to which I was taken for local color. It was a resort to which one would not take his sweetheart, wife or mother because any number of beautiful young ladies awaited a nod. As I left around midnight, Gus Gennerich, FDR's bodyguard, entered with several Secret Service men. They wanted me to remain, but I was tired and needed rest, so I returned to the hotel. No sooner had I fallen asleep than I was awakened by the ringing of my phone. It was Jimmy Roosevelt, who was acting as his father's Marine aide and press secretary. He informed me that Gus had dropped dead of a heart attack in the night club. I promptly dictated stories for my three colleagues, who could not be found because they were dining late, and one for myself.

Seldom have I seen Roosevelt more moved than he was at the services for Gus the next day in the embassy drawing room. His face was drawn by grief and weariness, because the death of Gus marked the passing of an era. Many times had Gus carried FDR singlehandedly, although he generally carried the President with another assisting, in a sort of cradle made by crossing hands and permitting FDR to put his arms about the shoulders of his bearers.

At one point FDR lost traction when he tried to turn away from the coffin. The parquet floor was almost a mirror and the rug on which he was standing was small. FDR threshed about wildly, for what seemed a long time, apparently unaware of what was going on about him. Those in the embassy staff didn't know what to do, so I moved in, but Jimmy got to his father's side first and steadied him. While he was deeply moved, FDR was not one to brood long and soon regained his gaiety.

In the relaxing company of intimates, FDR made no secret of his inability to walk. Many of us knew the light touch of his arm when he propelled his braced legs or the light weight of his body because of the wasted legs, although his chest and shoulders gave him the appearance of being massive.

FDR enjoyed harassing nervous bearers, especially Morgenthau, by an unseemly but not ineffective application of a forefinger where he thought it would do the most good.

"I'll drop you!" Hennypenny would shriek.

"You do and you'll be job hunting," Roosevelt would warn with a laugh.

Those were far simpler days, as I have indicated before, than newsmen know today. The President and his Cabinet officers were far more accessible than they are today, not only at press conferences but privately. If one had a query when Jimmy was acting press secretary, he would break in on his father and demand an answer, no matter what the President was doing, while Early or McIntyre would pocket the query for a time and come back with a purported "no comment" reply.

Larry Lehrbas of the AP, who went down to cover the conference ahead of the Roosevelt party, and I gave a dinner to Secretary of State Cordell Hull and Under Secretary of State Sumner Welles in the Chicken Ranch one evening and questioned them on their hopes and aspirations for the conference and on problems around the world. Today, I am sure, no two newsmen could corner their successors for such a private session.

I must admit we didn't get much from Hull, whose knowledge of foreign affairs was limited and FDR was his own Secretary of State, one who didn't always inform his ranking Cabinet officer of decisions. I knew Hull was anti-Japanese, but I never knew until years later that his views were influenced by Tennessee cartoonists, who were given to sounding alarms on the "yellow peril" on Sundays when material for their art ran short.

Welles, who was the embodiment of diplomatic aloofness, was thoroughly informed and helpful in his guarded way. Hull held a daily press conference at the State Department in those days, to which I delighted in taking visiting firemen. Hull was often more cryptic than the sulphur-fume breathing Pythia at Delphi. Invariably, I would observe, after we left his conference, that Hull had cleared up the situation. Generally, the all-knowing editors agreed, but now and then, a more honest editor would confess that he didn't understand the Secretary. Fewer than a dozen reporters attended the daily briefings, including correspondents for European papers, who were most interested in American foreign policy. We had difficulty rounding up a soft ball team to play a team of younger career men in the department.

After our return from South America, FDR was given to referring to me as an expert on Latin America, which I knew I was not. I was certain that this was calculated flattery, aimed at getting me to soften my dispatches on the New Deal. FDR went so far as to cite me as an expert to General George C. Marshall, who called me to his office for a chat on South America. He had made a brief visit there before he took over as chief of staff of the Army. I suspected the President was behind the offer of a post with the Office of Inter-American Affairs, headed by Nelson A. Rockefeller.

This was unquestionably the peak of Roosevelt's fame. He had won his greatest election victory. He was vigorous, colorful and handsome. He had only to command to get billions from Congress. He could get almost anything he demanded in the way of legislation. Members of his court strove to outdo one another in flattery, hailing anything he said or did as worthy of being engraved on stone.

Persons seeking preferment, politicians pressing for advancement, industrial leaders looking for contracts and leaders of organizations in search of shares of the federal bounty joined in extolling him. If ever a political leader became a legend in his lifetime, it was FDR at this moment. It is no wonder, then, that he came to believe in his own myth; that his vanity grew by what it fed upon.

But at the height of his popularity, he was engaged in secret manipulations, which were to bring him his greatest defeat at the hands of the subservient Congress. FDR had long smarted under adverse decisions of the Supreme Court, especially those which outlawed the NRA and the first AAA. On Thursday, February 4, 1937, just two weeks after his second inaugural, he summoned four members of Congress to meet with him and his Cabinet in the White House. At that meeting he offered a bill which would give him power to appoint a justice for every member of the Court who reached the age of seventy and did not retire. He didn't wait for any reaction from the stunned congressional leaders or his startled Cabinet, saying he had to attend his afternoon press conference.

Until that moment, the plan was a carefully guarded secret known to Attorney General Homer S. Cummings alone of those present in the Cabinet room. It was not surprising that the Court decided as it did because FDR had swept the Constitution aside in his race to push measures he had been encouraged to accept and propose. What was surprising was that he was to put the most revolutionary Court-packing plan before his Cabinet and congressional leaders so casually and without consultation.

The night before the press conference, in which Roosevelt hit the High Court as operating in "the horse and buggy days," I had been in the company of the one man fully in the know, Attorney General Cummings. The highest legal officer, his plump second wife, Cecilia, John O'Donnell and his correspondent wife, Doris Fleeson, and Carol and I went to see a performance of John Gielgud in *Hamlet*. Cummings never gave a hint in the theater of what was impending, even at the line "Something is rotten in the state of Denmark," nor in his home overlooking Rock Creek Park where we repaired for a review of the play and a chat on politics. But never did Cummings in the line of the play "With arms encumbered thus, of this head-shake, or by pronouncing some doubtful phrase" give us any inkling of what was to come. Cummings was much better at locking his lips than FDR. That same evening there was a dinner in the White House at which FDR told Russ Young and another newsman: "Enjoy yourselves; you're going to be very busy tomorrow."

The manner of the unveiling of the Court plan did much to injure FDR in Congress. He had already begun to acquire a reputation for being unreliable and even shifty. It was being whispered that he was arrogant and unreliable, not given to seeking advice on the Hill and being hard to pin down, because he was given to breaking not only understandings but also agreements. Congressional grievances were nursed in silence until he offered the Court plan as an accomplished fact.

For once the Republican opposition adopted a wise course but not until after a heated battle within the party. They agreed to let the fight against the plan be carried by Democrats, who were alarmed that the Court proposal would put the Constitution in grave danger. The brunt of the struggle was carried by Senator Burton K. Wheeler of Montana, a liberal in his own right, but one who regarded the attempt to dominate the High Court as dangerous to the liberty not only of that time but in future generations. Wheeler was also a liberal who regarded war as the greatest of evils.

He had the support of many senators, who dared not oppose FDR publicly, but could not go along with the experiment. He also received the help of members of the Court, including Chief Justice Charles Evans Hughes and Justice Louis D. Brandeis. Curiously enough Wheeler did not know either man personally—although he had served in the Senate for twenty-four years—so scrupulously did members of the Court preserve their aloofness from the political scene.

Frankfurter, who was often at FDR's side, hoping for a Court appointment, did not favor the plan, although he dared not cross Roosevelt. Nor did Frankfurter, for all his legal liberalism, like the NRA or AAA, but his complaints were neither loud nor deep.

The Court battle occupied the nation for more than five months, dominating the press and air waves. Defeat came on July 22, 1937, when a weary Senator Marvel M. Logan of Kentucky, chairman of the Senate Judiciary Committee, rose to move the recommital of the Court bill to his committee. I was in the gallery.

"Is the Supreme Court out of this?" asked Senator Hiram Johnson of California.

"The Supreme Court is out of it," Logan conceded sadly.

"Glory be to God!" shouted the dignified Californian.

The galleries applauded wildly. The country was relieved. FDR's defeat at the hands of Congress came some seven months after the landslide election victory of November, which had led him to believe he was above Congress, the Supreme Court and the Constitution. It was not only a bitter blow to his pride, but destroyed the invincibility he had enjoyed in Congress as well. For it was known in Congress that Roosevelt could have gained his end by other legislation, which Congress would have passed readily and easily.

It was known that Justices Willis Van Devanter and George Sutherland were prepared to retire if they could do so on full pay rather than half pay. FDR at first approved the legislation, which would have enabled him to get a majority of justices who could be expected to favor his programs, but then spurned it, preferring his packing plan. Many members of Congress considered the Court too conservative and would have favored the retirement pay plan, but they could not swallow what they considered a revolutionary and unconstitutional program.

When defeat came, FDR didn't blame Wheeler as much as he did Vice President Garner who, he said, had not tried for any compromise, and Mrs. Lulu White Wheeler, the senator's wife, whom FDR described as Lady Macbeth. Actually, Wheeler had the votes to defeat any compromise and Garner knew it.

The defeat was a great but not a fatal blow to FDR. After all, he got his way in the long run, naming a Court that ultimately favored his views. He was successful in gaining the Court he wanted but at a great price. The campaign undermined public confidence in the High Court and initiated the policy of legislating by decision, which many feel has done so much to upset the constitutional provisions for a balance of power among the executive, legislative and judicial branches of the government.

Roosevelt's first appointment to the Court after his capitulation was that of Senator Hugo L. Black of Alabama. The appointment was not dictated by love or respect for Black and his legal ability as it was designed to make the Senate lump it and like it. Roosevelt knew that Black was not too popular with his colleagues, particularly those who opposed the Court plan, but he knew also that senatorial courtesy would impel them to vote for the man who would not oppose the measure yet dared not fight for what he secretly favored. Black was then fifty-one years old and looked upon seventy as ancient and deserving of nothing so much as retirement. Yet he regarded seventy as spry when he reached that age and he continued on the Court until death took him at eighty-five after thirty-four years on the Supreme Court bench.

Shortly after the nomination the country was disturbed by the disclosure that Black had been a member of the Ku Klux Klan. This was hardly a strange alliance for a southern politician, although many had courageously opposed the organization which enabled some to profit from bigotry. The story of Black's association was hardly new, but became so on his nomination. One of the newspapers put aboard FDR's train on his 1934 visit to southern power projects carried a reproduction of Black's membership card.

Black was abroad when a Pittsburgh newspaper disclosed his association with the Klan. He came home to make a radio address to the nation on his membership. FDR planned a trip to the Northwest that September and October, partly to get as far away from the senator as he could. When Black was about to deliver his speech, Roosevelt pointedly switched from an automobile equipped with a radio to one without such an instrument in the state of Washington. Thus he was able to tell the press that he had not heard the speech, although we were sure he had cleared it before delivery. Later Black, who became a good and even admiring friend, told me he had joined the organization when he was just embarking on a political career at the suggestion of his law partner. He soon found it to be of little help and lost interest in the group.

In addition to getting far away from Black, FDR also undertook his passage to the Northwest in order to divert public attention from a financial slump which was tormenting his New Deal and to test his personal popularity. He wanted to see whether he had suffered personally from the defeat in the Senate. The rousing receptions he got everywhere inspired him to undertake a purge of those who had opposed him. This effort, undertaken in the 1938 congressional campaign, was a complete failure, so far as Senate races were concerned. Not one of the senators whom Roosevelt opposed was defeated. This demonstrated what had been made clear many times before and a number of times since, that a Chief Executive cannot rub his popularity or prejudices off on the electorate in any congressional by-elections nor on congressional campaigns when he is running himself. FDR could not defeat Democrats for all his personal popularity, just as Eisenhower and Nixon could not elect Republicans for all of theirs.

One episode of the Court-packing plan, never hitherto made public, has always intrigued me. Roosevelt was at Hyde Park when Governor Herbert Lehman of New York, until 1937 a stalwart supporter of the New Deal, decided to speak out against the Court-packing plan that spring. FDR was furious because he considered the issue none of the governor's business and would have denied him the right of personal expression. The morning the story of Lehman's opposition broke, we had a press conference beside the specially equipped automobile which enabled FDR to drive around his estate and inspect his crop of Christmas trees. Roosevelt was asked what he had to say about Lehman's statement. He lost his smile and snapped:

"What I have to say will have to be off the record."

We had no choice, so we had to agree, knowing that whatever we got would serve as a guideline. However, we were taken aback when he thrust out his chin and sneered:

"What else could you expect from a Jew?"

I was not too surprised, however, because he had made similar remarks about some of his most devoted supporters before and was to do worse when he told Ibn Saud, during their wartime meeting, he would like to send the Arab king a half million or more Jews from New York. What did surprise me was that he made the statement with such anger that he failed to take note or regard of the presence of Henry M. Kannee, a White House stenographer who was taking down his words. I have often wondered whether Kannee let the words survive in press conference records.

I am not alone in regarding Washington as heavily tinged with anti-Semitism at high as well as low levels. Many visitors have expressed surprise at finding a host or hostess take them aside and point to a fellow guest, saying cryptically, "He's one," or to hear another exclaim: "Thank goodness, there's none of them here tonight." One of Washington's better known hostesses once said she would not have married her husband had she known how other Washingtonians felt about his race. There were some raised eyebrows, because she was accepted as sharing the same blood. The feeling is unfortunate, probably more unfortunate because it is more in the capital than elsewhere, but it is true and should be faced.

I used to tell Bernard Baruch, the financier, who preferred to be known as the park bench statesman, that he was anti-Semitic where I was not when he spoke frankly about his own people. I am sure he felt that his race kept him from being the power behind the White House throne, a position he coveted, when he was denied the confidence of the Presidents he courted because they didn't trust him, feeling any confidence or power he enjoyed would go toward adding to his fortune.

The years of 1937 and 1938 were not good ones for FDR. He lost the Court fight and the purge he had attempted against his opponents. More importantly, the economy was in a slump. He was not threatened by a repetition of the 1929 Depression, but the New Deal was hanging on the ropes. It could be said that the New Deal Santa Claus had struck out in the 1938 elections, because Democrats lost many Senate and House seats.

Roosevelt's twice-weekly press conferences—Tuesday morning and Thursday afternoon—sparked a flood of capital news sessions. Everyone but Secretary of War George H. Dern and Secretary of the Navy Claude Swanson held regular conferences. Dern held none. Swanson held only a few. Officials below Cabinet level also held conferences.

The former Virginia senator, who presided over the Navy, will always be remembered by me for a great political observation. When he suddenly changed position on a major political issue before his appointment to the Navy post, he said: "My constituents can't change their minds any faster than I can."

One of the most popular among the second level of conferences was that of RFC Chairman Jones. These were given over more to racy stories than news. They became so talked about that some women reporters, then feeling the first growing pains of the Lib movement, began attending with the result that Jones had to give up his conferences to wide regret.

Mrs. R. had her own press conferences, which were strictly limited to women. The distaff brigade would gather about her on the floor of the White House living quarters, where there was much tittering and cackling and very little news. When Mrs. R. was named to the Civil Defense Agency, along with Mayor Fiorello La Guardia of New York, these conferences were shifted to her agency office in the DuPont Circle Building.

At the first of these conferences, the gentle but determined Dewey Fleming of the Baltimore *Sun* showed up, to the horror of the ladies of the press. Mrs. R. attempted to show him the door, but he stood his ground, insisting that she was no longer First Lady but the co-chairman of a newsmaking agency and, therefore, subject to coverage and questioning by any and all interested. He determinedly took a seat and would not budge. How I envied him for a brilliant news gambit!

I did get into the act on my own, however, when I was tipped off by a secretary, now an important government official, that Mrs. R. led her staffers into the hall of the fifth floor of the building. There they joined hands and danced around the central corridor. I showed up with a photographer. One story and a picture ended that gay practice as effectively as Fleming's appearance had ended her news conferences in the building.

Although I did not see too much of Mrs. R., I did see enough of her at Warm Springs and Hyde Park to know she had as good a grasp—if not better—of political fundamentals as her husband and she had a far warmer and more generous heart. For all his gaiety and courtesy, FDR was a snob. It always disturbed me that photographers and movie cameramen were rarely drawn into his more intimate gatherings, as reporters were, because they were considered "below stairs." Perhaps reporters shared some of the responsibility, because there were, and still are, social levels in the trade, which put photographers, who often made more money, beyond the pale.

FDR let Mrs. R. bring an occasional Negro into the White House, but almost never saw one himself. Roosevelt had his personal valet, Irwin McDuffie, thrown into the Navy brig for looking on gin when it was white. That smacked more of Simon Legree than the friend

of the common man. Mrs. R. persuaded her husband to give McDuffie a number of last chances, but finally had to agree to his replacement. Mrs. R., like most of us, was susceptible to flattery, which
was evident to opportunists. We can say she was curious in her
choice of friends of both sexes and be more than charitable. She had
her eye out for an easy dollar, working with politicians to pack her
lectures, and firing the man who put her on the lecture platform
to replace him with more amenable if less competent admirers. She
undertook to write a newspaper column and magazine articles, knowing she was selling the White House rather than herself.

The last time I went horseback riding was with Mrs. R., years
ago on the mountain trails around Warm Springs. She had a good
seat, which I hadn't, and my horse, Tom, remembered to this day,
recognized it. He tried to brush me off by straining to get me under
branches that might hold me. He didn't succeed, but it wasn't for
lack of trying or her encouraging laughter. But I had the last laugh
when I whipped the weary mount home.

There was little love lost between the President's mother and her
daughter-in-law. A number of times at Hyde Park picnics Mrs. R.
handed me a charred hot dog on a stick with "Here, please take this
to my mother-in-law." I never heard her address Sara Delano Roosevelt as "Mother," and the dowager duchess of Hyde Park seemed to
ignore her.

Mrs. R. came from a family given to looking on wine and wishing
it were whiskey. When FDR carried the day for repeal, she forced
adoption of some strange drinking regulations in the capital. Among
them were provisions that bartenders mix drinks outside the sight of
customers in an improvised booth, where some could and did employ
cheaper brands than those ordered. This was dropped in time as a result. Another of her regulations barred customers from carrying a
drink from one table to another. Still another prohibited standing at
a bar.

I met the President's mother a number of times, but she never
knew me. She was even more of a snob than her son. She ignored my
friend J. Arthur Mullen, the son of FDR's floor manager of Chicago,
Arthur Mullen, until she discovered that his mother-in-law was a
Spanish marquesa. I had to give her Girl Scout points when she
startled a luncheon group in the Hyde Park home, at which Senator

Huey P. (Kingfish) Long was holding forth, by observing: "I never wanted Franklin to go into politics because he has had to associate with such strange people."

One morning when I was wandering about the Hyde Park home, I was stopped in my tracks by this grand dame. She looked down on me from a porch.

"Young man," she exclaimed, "I presume you are one of the press."

I acknowledged I was.

"Well," she continued, "I wish you would stop calling this place Krum Elbow, even though Franklin likes it. My husband named it Springwood and I prefer the name he gave."

At that time FDR was involved in a quarrel with a neighbor, Howland Spencer, who claimed the name "Krum Elbow" for the name of his place, which was across the river. FDR controlled the coast and geodetic survey and had the name switched to his side of the river. Spencer tried to interest newsmen in his claim but lost to the idolaters, so he sold his property to Father Divine, the New York black cultist, to Roosevelt's ill-concealed annoyance.

The ebullient Long was one of the first men to recognize the Lorelei nature of FDR's charm. He had been persuaded to go along with FDR in 1932 by Wheeler, but broke with the President early, far earlier than Wheeler. In no time at all Long was strutting in the Senate aisle denouncing Roosevelt while many a Democrat glowered, as he roared:

"Hoover is a hoot owl. Roosevelt is a scrooch owl. A hoot owl bangs into the nest and knocks the hen clean out and catches her while she is falling. But a scrooch owl slips into the roost and scrooches up to the hen and talks softly to her. And the first thing you know—there ain't no hen."

About this time the wiry, bantam rooster Senator Carter Glass of Virginia, who fathered the Federal Reserve Act, rose from his seat, marched over to Long and snarled into his face. The words could not be heard in the press gallery, but Long was so taken aback he sat down and was silent.

"I called him a son of a bitch," Glass boasted later. "That's what I did."

Glass was not given to such language, being a courtly Virginia cavalier as a rule, and Long undoubtedly recognized it.

Huey was gaining a national reputation with his slogan "Every Man a King," which he used for the title of a book. He was considered a wild man on fiscal as well as political matters. Yet anyone bothering to read the book will discover that he proposed to make every man a king by spending two and a half billion dollars. This is ironic when one considers that former Secretary of Housing and Urban Development George Romney recently charged that we have flung away some 246 billion dollars over the years without substantially improving the housing and the lot of poor people.

Roosevelt shed no crocodile tears over Long's assassination in 1935, even though he deplored the method of his taking off. The death of Long spared him a possible challenge in 1936 and a certain challenge in 1940. In anticipation of his bid for the presidency, Long was collecting a war chest, which reputedly contained two million dollars at the time of his death. The story is that it went to the first man to reach Long's room in a New Orleans hotel, after the senator was cut down by a bullet from the gun of a grievance-nursing dentist. At least I was told so by one who said he missed winning the race by the length of the victor's foot.

In anticipation of this third-term drive, FDR went to Louisiana in 1938 for what was widely described as the "second Louisiana purchase," because he wanted the state's delegation. During that visit FDR found himself seated at a table in a private dining room in Antoine's restaurant, between Governor Richard Leche and Mayor Mastri, neither of whom was celebrated for statesmanship or honesty. The governor eventually went to jail. I was at the far end of the table when Colonel Starling came to me and whispered:

"The President wants you to sit across from him."

I couldn't believe Starling, so I looked up and caught FDR's eye. He nodded and so I went to the indicated seat; Doris Fleeson joined me. Leche and Mastri sat woodenly, while FDR exchanged banter with us.

However, I was in the presidential doghouse a day later. FDR left New Orleans on a fishing trip off the coast of Texas, during which he found time to meet with two Texas financiers to advance the fortunes of his second son, Elliott, who was at the luncheon in Antoine's. I wrote a story listing the cost of the operation of the presidential yacht, accompanying naval vessels and other arrangements to estimate that the President's fishing excursion was costing taxpayers several hundred thousand dollars. This story evoked one of the few critical wires I got from McCormick. He told me I was being petty. FDR was furious, but softened when he heard of the colonel's telegram.

We were based in a Galveston hotel during the fishing trip. One day we received a summons from Roosevelt to join him in a press conference aboard the *Sequoia* at Aransas Pass. Eight of us were driven more than two hundred miles in the President's own automobile with McIntyre, which was unusual in itself. We narrowly escaped death or serious injury when the road on which we were speeding abruptly ended in a T. Dick Flore, the President's chauffeur, drove into a ditch and then swung out to set us on the new road.

We went aboard the yacht in time to see FDR landing a tarpon, which gave him quite a tussle, dancing on its tail and running off with his line. When he came aboard his yacht, puffing from his exertions in a small boat, FDR had nothing to tell us. All of the two hundred miles back we pondered on why the conference had been called.

We were not to learn until we returned to the capital and went to a conference in the President's Oval Office. With studied innocence, he said that what he was about to say was more our problem than his. Then he read from a private newsletter, distributed by Richard Waldo of the McClure Syndicate, in which it was said that FDR was found in a coma at his desk recently with a significant rash on the back of his neck. It went on to say the President had not gone fishing in the Gulf of Mexico but was actually confined, under guard, in a naval vessel. Roosevelt said the incident was one requiring action by newsmen themselves rather than by him, but stressed that those who accompanied him south saw him land a fish on the day the newsletter was issued.

I was president of the White House Correspondents Association at that time and was induced to call its executive committee into special session twice to consider a course of action against Waldo. All the members of the committee, except myself, were militant New Dealers or apologists, although some were to change later. I resisted a resolution to expel Waldo from the association on what I thought was the most logical of grounds—he was not a member. I was openly accused of allowing *Tribune* thinking to influence my decision. It was said I was using the association to advance myself with my paper, which knew nothing about the incident. Another resolution was offered at the second meeting, which declared that Waldo could not become a member of the association if he wanted to, which I held to be ridiculous. I must say that the other members of the committee were as interested in breaking the story as they were in courting FDR's favor.

Early, who was consulted by my colleagues, agreed that my position was sound; that a man could not be expelled from something he had not joined. So two members of the executive committee went before the board of governors of the National Press Club of which Waldo was a member with a resolution calling for his ouster. They got a favorable reaction because the board was loaded with New Dealers. Waldo was summoned to show cause why he should not be expelled, which allowed newsmen to break the story. Waldo appeared, but was not in the least contrite over his obviously faked report. He threatened every member of the board with a libel action, saying he would seize their savings and homes if he was successful. I am sorry to say most newspapermen are not as brave as they pretend to be, so the board hesitated and never expelled Waldo. He subsequently left voluntarily. The ground for expulsion was that Waldo had maligned a fellow member, Roosevelt, who had been given an honorary membership, as all Presidents are, on his inauguration. If this provision had been carried to its logical conclusion the club would have been reduced to a membership of one, because newsmen do not always speak well of one another.

Roosevelt's famed luck held, in his calculated denial of the story, because when we were brought to the scene, solely to testify he had been fishing on the date of the confidential letter, he landed a tarpon in front of our eyes. And also because he persuaded idolaters in the press to pull the chestnuts of a smear out of the fire, which he should have exposed himself.

FDR had many friends, a very great many, most of whom didn't know or understand him. But he also had his enemies. These may not have been nearly as numerous, but they were bitter and even violent. These were not all concerned about being fair. Some were not content to hiss his mistakes, but invented indictments against him, and I say this as one who was not in his political corner and did not feel that any invention was needed to draw up an indictment against him.

Among FDR's good friends in those days, but later to become an implacable foe over involving America in World War II, was Captain Joseph Medill Patterson, first cousin of McCormick, who supported Roosevelt in 1932 and 1936, as editor and publisher of the New York *News*. By way of reward the captain was invited to spend a night in the White House. After dinner, FDR took him into his study for a private chat, setting a bottle of Danziger Goldwasser for his guest and himself. Patterson took one drink, thinking it would be followed by whiskey, but it was not. Patterson found the drink cloying but concealed his irritation as a good guest should.

Late in their session, Mrs. Roosevelt interrupted to ask the editor what time he wanted to be called and what he wanted for breakfast. Patterson said he would suit himself to the hours of the house. She so pressed him to name a time that FDR put in that he liked to loll in bed, over breakfast and newspapers until nine or ten o'clock. Patterson said that being a morning newspaperman, the time would suit him well. Mrs. R. made a note on a pad she brought in with her.

Then she pressed him as to what he desired for breakfast. Again he sought to adapt himself, but she insisted he could have anything he wished and poised her pad. He selected orange juice rather than tomato juice, fried eggs rather than scrambled, bacon soft, not crisp, unbuttered toast and black coffee. At each decision, she made a note. Then she bade him good-by, saying she was off at 6 A.M. on a trip to the West Coast.

At nine the next morning I got a call from John O'Donnell, the captain's man in Washington, saying Patterson wanted to see us both immediately in the lounge of the National Press Club. I hastened to find Patterson in something of a temper. He would not talk until we had all consumed a couple of double scotches, at an hour which was early for me even in those youthful days. This was good drinking because the club measure was then two ounces.

Then the mellowed Patterson unfolded the story of his White House visit and what had followed in the morning. He was awakened, he said, by thumping at his door and a cheerful voice saying: "Good morning, Captain, it's six o'clock." He grunted and turned over, but had to get up, because his breakfast was wheeled in on a table almost immediately after the knock. He walked around it, picking up various dishes to find that he was being served tomato rather than orange juice, bacon so crisp that it crumbled at the touch, scrambled eggs instead of fried, toast so heavy with butter that it was limp and coffee with cream and sugar.

"All I have to say," the captain turned to me, "is that if they are running the country like they are running the White House, you and Bert may be right."

PRECEDENT SMASHED

SOCIAL LIFE in Washington, while demanding and time consuming, is highly important. It is not without its influences on government and it is often a good source of news. Society reporters frequently write hard news, because officials let down their guards under the relaxation of rare viands, fine wines and generous potions. It is not rare to come upon a knot of ambassadors, deep in discussion of some world development that has called one of their colleagues or a high American official from their midst. To those scrambling for recognition and influence, it is important to be seen and to capture hard-to-get invitations.

In my earlier days the capital was much more formal than it is today. "Informal" on invitations spelled black tie and not business suits as it now does. Business suits were correct for cocktail parties, but even these had their now-discarded rituals. Tea and coffee were invariably served and discriminating hostesses selected friends to preside over the cups and pour for stated intervals. These functions were confined to homes, not to clubs or hotels.

White tie and tails were the social uniform. I wore out two sets in my earlier years, but more recently I have had one for almost twenty-five years and it spends most of the year in cold storage.

The reporters who covered the White House regularly were not only invited to all receptions in the Executive Mansion, but also to formal and intimate affairs given by Cabinet members and other high officials. Since I also covered the State Department, we received invitations to many functions of the diplomatic set. Strangely enough, when I first came to Washington, a luncheon or dinner invitation to the British embassy was coveted more than one from the White House. The British ambassador had long been a major social lion in the capital, but in the '30s Sir Ronald Lindsay was even more important than most of his predecessors, because he was dean of the diplomatic corps as well.

This is strictly an honorary post, but one which brings invitations to most important social functions in town, because the dean is the representative of the corps. Where it is impossible to invite more than a hundred ambassadors to an important function, it is sufficient to invite the dean of the corps.

Calling was a strict formality of the day, even at newspaper levels, and a major obligation among the striped-pants set of the State Department. A newcomer to the department or a career officer shifted home from abroad was given a list of those on whom he or his wife had to call and leave cards. Cards were also left by the socially established and climbers, as well, at the White House and many embassies. At the beginning of the winter season there were parades of cars about town, the heaviest being under the lion- and unicorn-topped gates of the British embassy and at the White House.

Probably the most widely publicized social event in my time was the garden party for King George VI and Queen Elizabeth, who came to the capital in June 1939, at the invitation of the President. In one of his characteristic machete jobs on protocol, FDR extended an invitation to the King by letter when he heard that the royal couple were planning a visit to Canada. With war clouds gathering in Europe, the monarchs eagerly embraced the proffered opportunity to cement and extend British influence in America.

Sir Ronald precipitated the maddest of maneuverings for invitations the capital had known when he announced a garden party would be held for the King and Queen on the embassy lawn. The towering and dignified envoy, under a bombardment of questions from the press, likened the function to heaven, saying: "Many are called but few are chosen." While many an uninvited heart was broken, the affair went off smoothly enough and made a good color story. The well-prepared and coached King gracefully accepted a pat on the back from Vice President Garner and confounded Senator Ellison D. Smith of South Carolina, who was preparing to twist the British lion's tail a bit to win votes at home, by recognizing the lawmaker with: "I know you; you're the one they call Cotton Ed." The senator was so pleased by this royal identification that he wasn't aware his critical guns had been spiked.

In advance of the function, I had lined up an amateur reportorial staff, including Senator Arthur H. Vandenberg of Michigan and his wife, Hazel, as well as several members of the capital's established social set, known as cave dwellers for their long establishment on the Washington scene. One of these purchased a special hat for the occasion, created from living flowers and leaves.

On her way to the garden party, the socialite had to attend a funeral. She was aware that she couldn't wear her dashing creation to such a solemn function, so she set it on a table in the entry and donned a scarf of somber hue and settled sedately in a pew.

When the coffin was wheeled down the aisle behind the officiating clergyman and acolytes, the woman gasped in horror, for there on its center was her treasured creation, which an unenlightened sexton had taken as the due property of the dead.

However, the most memorable remark made at the garden party was not widely reported at the time. It was not made by royalty and was not considered prophetic, although it soon proved to be so. Count Jerzy Potocki, the able and personable Polish ambassador, spotted Hans Thomsen, the German charge d'affaires, on the lawn.

"I wonder," he mused aloud, "how long he will be coming to British parties. For that matter, I wonder how long any of us will even be speaking to the Germans."

In a few months Potocki was an ambassador without a country and was speaking neither to the Germans nor the Russians, who had divided his outraged land between them and for the second time within two centuries.

Potocki was being used as protective coloration at the time by Franklin D. Roosevelt, Jr., who had married a member of the DuPont family, but who had become interested in a socialite of the Warrenton, Virginia, horse country. When FDR questioned his son on photographs taken with the socialite at horse shows, Franklin identified Potocki, who was often in the pictures, saying she was the Polish ambassador's girl. When he found that his son was not telling the truth, FDR resolved to have it out with Franklin.

The President said he was going to Charlottesville, Virginia, where Franklin was attending the law school of the University of Virginia. FDR insisted the visit was a purely personal matter and tried to bar the White House regulars from accompanying him. We knew the story of Franklin's amour and determined to go along in a hired car and a couple of private cars.

The trip was something of a nightmare because the roads had not been cleared, which was the customary procedure on presidential motorcades, and we had no police escort. There was much weaving in and out of traffic in our frantic efforts to keep up. When we got to Franklin's home, just behind the smoldering father, Franklin was at the door with a traveling bag in hand. He explained to his father that he was sorry he could not stay to entertain him because he had to attend the funeral of a distant cousin, thus escaping, for a time, the blast of parental ire.

The laxity of members of the President's family and their rather flexible ethical standards occasioned much talk in Washington and around the country. The antics of his children disappointed many and disturbed others, since it was obvious that while he professed to know how to rule the nation, FDR could not control his own family.

The third-term campaign is now history, along with the war that saved the New Deal from fiscal collapse and aided him in smashing the two-term precedent. Few today can appreciate or understand the doubts and fears about FDR's intentions that swirled about Washington, almost from the second inauguration, but became the major topic of 1939 and early 1940. It seems strange now that the country was baffled for months and many of the nation's best and ablest politicians, including Garner and Farley, were positive for so long that he would not run. Doubts that he would run were common in the White House and in the highest Administration circles, but these were inspired, in part, by fears of loss of power and prestige.

In the summer of 1939, FDR had solemnly whispered to Farley that he was not going to run and Farley took him at his word. Farley had secured Roosevelt's consent to submit his own name for selection as the favored candidate of Massachusetts. And FDR was encouraging many others by telling them they would make great Presidents.

Harry Hopkins, the architect of made work, went back to his native Iowa and rejoined the Presbyterian Church as a way of putting up his lightning rod. Solicitor General Robert H. Jackson, who was to become Attorney General and a Justice of the Supreme Court, was contemplating making a bid for New York's slate of delegates although, as Farley said, he could have walked along the Erie Canal from Buffalo to Albany without being recognized.

FDR was given to offering to others what he most wanted himself. In addition to Hopkins and Jackson, he encouraged Hull, whom Farley favored, Wallace and God alone knows how many others to dream of succeeding him. He didn't hesitate to pick candidates of the opposition Republican party, setting Vandenberg purring by telling him he should be his party's unanimous choice. One evening in the White House, Hopkins told me, Roosevelt asked Senator Joseph H. Ball of Minnesota to stand up and turn around slowly.

"Stop there," Roosevelt commanded. "From that angle you look remarkably like Lincoln. I wonder why the Republican party doesn't recognize it."

I never had the slightest doubt that Roosevelt would run. I put together the script of a movie for a White House correspondents' dinner, with Richard Harkness, newsman and radio correspondent, which as much as said so. The movie, put together by Universal News Reel Company, was a great White House favorite, FDR showing it in the Executive Mansion many times and it was borrowed by news groups around the country.

I was certain that Roosevelt was fixin' to run, because I had come to regard him as something of a stranger to truth and a dramatist. Also FDR never took himself anywhere near out of the race by any positive action or statement. FDR wouldn't say "yes" and he wouldn't say "no," but he never missed a single opportunity to enhance his own candidacy.

One story FDR gave me exclusively in 1938 indicated, at least to me, that he wanted to shatter the two-term tradition. Steve Early called me into his office. When I got there he told his staff he was not to be disturbed. I knew he was most serious because he never gave such orders, except when he was trying to pick winners at horse tracks.

"You're a good friend of Joe Kennedy's, aren't you?" he asked.

"Yes."

"Would you write a critical story, if we give you all the facts?"

"I'd write a story against any New Dealer and I haven't hesitated to aim higher, as you know," was my reply.

"The Boss thought you would," Steve laughed. "Here it is. Joe wants to run for President and is dealing behind the Boss's back at his post in the London embassy, sending one set of reports to the State Department on the situation in Europe and an entirely different set, contrary to our policy, to Arthur Krock of the New York *Times*. Krock innocently sent his reports to the Boss, thinking he might find them interesting."

Early laid the two sets of reports in front of me. The reports to the State Department were quite formal and restrained. Those to Krock were highly critical of British foreign policy, which Kennedy saw as encouraging war.

I wrote the story, saying Kennedy was aiming at the White House by setting himself up to counter FDR's policy. The story didn't create much of a stir, but did hit a highly sensitive nerve in Kennedy, who did want the presidency, although he must have known his chances were slim. However, Joe didn't complain to me or to Colonel McCormick, a close friend, with whom he saw eye to eye on foreign policy, but wrote to the editor-publisher of the Detroit *Free Press*, which carried my story, recommending that I be fired. This letter was sent to the colonel, who asked me to report on it and was satisfied with my story although it involved a friend.

A short time later, on one of his visits home, Kennedy spotted me at a cocktail party and drew a finger across his throat as a way of accusing me of trying to cut it. Being mindful of his letter, I drew my index finger across mine. Later, the ambassador to Britain came to realize that I couldn't have got the story if it hadn't been fed to me by FDR, so that when I went to London in the summer of 1939 and the winter of 1940, he went out of his way to make amends by introducing me to his powerful British friends and having his closest associate, Edward Moore, after whom Senator Edward M. (Teddy) Kennedy was named, take me under his wing.

The night of Kennedy's appointment to the Court of St. James's in January 1938, he had arranged a dinner party for the White House press regulars, at which I was the guest of honor as the president of the Correspondents Association. When Roosevelt broke the news of his appointment the morning of that party, Joe expressed his thanks and then exclaimed:

"My God! I'm having the White House press boys to dinner to-night and Walter Trohan will lead them in taking me over the jumps."

"God help you," Roosevelt laughed, "but don't forget the knee britches."

Then he sent word to us to give Joe as hard a time as we could.

At the dinner, in his rented estate, Marwood, on the Potomac, near the town of that name, Joe stationed a butler behind me and charged him to see that my champagne glass was never empty. It was always filled to the brim but he couldn't make me drink it as fast as he would have liked, so it was a rough night for Joe. FDR called for a report on the evening and found it worthy of many laughs. Joe didn't wear his knee britches that night, but he and Eddie did don them for another press party to the delight of all.

Kennedy was no favorite of the politicos, who suspected him of trying to buy the White House. Farley was among those who didn't trust the tall redhead. When FDR named Kennedy to the chairmanship of the Securities and Exchange Commission in 1934, Farley protested. The Democratic party chairman considered the appointment a bad one in view of the fact that Joe had made a fortune selling short and helping to precipitate the market crash.

"Set a thief to catch a thief," Roosevelt remarked airily.

I got another hint of the President's intentions on the 1938 trip to New Orleans. George E. Allen, then District of Columbia commissioner, who later became known as the White House jester, joined the train, presumably because it was going through his native state. Allen was an accomplished coattail rider and enjoyed hitchhiking on presidential specials, employing them to his advantage. In 1944, he was astute enough to latch himself on to Truman's campaign train, when Truman was running for Vice President, being fully aware he would succeed to the presidency, and still later attaching himself to Dwight D. Eisenhower when he loomed as a Republican candidate for the White House.

At the first stop of the special in Allen's native state, Mississippi, I was seized by a humorous impulse to make a speech proposing Allen for Congress to a group of curious citizens come to catch a glimpse of the President. Allen loved it; others found it amusing. At the next stop I proclaimed Allen as "The man to beat The Man, Senator Theodore Bilbo," who was no White House favorite, being a lesser Huey Long. At the third stop I proposed Allen for election to the Supreme Court, ignoring the required presidential appointment. FDR was taking an interest in the campaign and offered me the use of the back platform of his private car for the next speech.

I declined for the best of reasons; I was running out of offices. But at the last stop I was prevailed upon to make another speech and launched an Allen boom for the presidency. Allen fled. FDR lost all interest in Allen and in my oratory. It seemed clear to me that FDR didn't consider running for his job the subject of wit and humor.

Roosevelt had a high regard for the presidency, although he had none for Hoover. Nor did he care much for those who dared run against him, referring to Landon as a bumpkin, Wendell Willkie as the barefoot boy from Wall Street and Thomas E. Dewey as a choirboy.

In Yellowstone Park, where Paul Y. Anderson of the St. Louis *Post-Dispatch* was invariably late for any of the scenic wonders on the 1937 tour, the reporter stopped beside FDR's car while the rest of us were looking at Tower Falls. Roosevelt asked Paul how he was getting along with a reactionary like me, knowing Paul and I were riding the same bus. Paul was a bit unsteady, being engaged in a scientific project to prove that one could drink at high altitudes without passing out any quicker than at low altitudes, for the benefit of FDR's personal physician, Navy Captain Ross T. McIntire.

"Fine! Fine!" Anderson replied. "I am going to teach him that Herbert Hoover is a son of a bitch."

"I wouldn't say that," FDR cautioned.

"Proves my point," Anderson exclaimed. "He's just the kind of a son of a bitch who would call you a son of a bitch, even if you wouldn't call him what he is."

FDR broke down in the face of such alcoholic logic, but he was the one who told the story, despite his professed regard for the presidency.

One of the most interesting and dramatic men in Washington at that time was John Llewellyn Lewis, the beetle-browed labor leader, who could quote Shakespeare as well as Will himself. He was among the first to recognize FDR would run for a third term, seeing that Roosevelt was counting out everyone but himself, saying Garner was "too conservative," Jones's health was "not too good," Hull was "too slow," Farley was "a Catholic," Byrnes was a renegade Catholic and so on.

The dynamic head of the United Mine Workers Union was a fountain of information, knowing more of what was going on than most senators and representatives, and most heads of executive departments, not to mention businessmen, who are generally children when it comes to politics. Lewis was excellent company as well as thoroughly informed. We became close friends when he began realizing that Roosevelt, whom he had supported strongly, had no political philosophy and could not be trusted.

"You tickle my risibilities," he often said when he called me by phone or invited me to his office, after reading my stories critical of FDR and the New Deal.

Lewis had been a great White House favorite, being summoned often to the President's office and to the White House living quarters for social visits. Lewis began becoming disenchanted with the Chief Executive when the latter tapped him for a half million dollars in the 1936 campaign and ran out on pledges to aid labor.

The mine union leader had offered a much smaller share of union funds, but FDR put him off, saying he would prefer to call on Lewis when funds were needed. Lewis recognized at once that FDR was aiming at taking a larger bite than had been offered. However, there was nothing that he could do but assent. Soon he found himself being called on for funds from a wide variety of Democratic sources. He was wise enough to insist that every request for funds come from FDR himself, but these were sizable enough.

On one occasion Roosevelt called Lewis to the White House with his wife, Lewis told me. The wife was no Roosevelt admirer. It was strange to me that many a woman came to distrust the gay reformer instinctively, long before their husbands learned the hard way. In addition to Mrs. Lewis, others were Mrs. Wheeler, the wife of the Montana senator, the first wife of Senator Bennet Champ Clark of Missouri, Mrs. Garner and Bess Farley.

In the living quarters on the second floor of the Executive Mansion, FDR told Lewis that he had a great plan for building power projects in the East and West. First, the President explained, a suitable hilltop would be leveled off; railroad tracks would be laid around the circumference of the artificial mesa, and on these flat cars with sails would be installed. When the wind blew, FDR reported triumphantly, the cars would go round and round and turn a shaft down the center of the hill to generate power.

"What happens when the wind don't blow?" Lewis asked.

"That's where you come in, John," Roosevelt beamed, producing a sketch of the project. "About halfway down, we have a plant fired by coal that will generate steam to turn the shaft when the wind doesn't blow."

"Mr. President, I'd like the plan a lot better if you just forgot the hills and mountains and concentrated on coal-burning plants."

That observation apparently killed the plan aborning, Lewis told me. And a good thing, too, because in addition to the ill-fated plan to harness the tides at Passamaquoddy, Maine, we might have had FDR as a modern-day Don Quixote of flat-car windmills.

In describing his negotiations with coal operators, Lewis observed, "Scowls are my business." He was to turn them on FDR, but with no effect on the third-term campaign.

I shall never forget Lewis at Paul Anderson's funeral. The reporter died by his own hand, a hand that would have enjoyed writing up one of the capital's strangest funerals. It was Anderson himself who arranged it, requesting that Lewis, Senator George W. Norris of Nebraska and George Holmes, INS bureau chief, speak and that there be no religious rites.

Norris was engaged in a battle on the Hill, which was uppermost in his mind so that when he spoke he forgot his solemn obligation. Instead he outlined his position in the floor fight, presented his resolution and called upon all in favor of it to raise their right hands. Most of the hands in the funeral chapel went up, to my not inconsiderable astonishment, but to Norris' satisfaction, so he smiled and sat down.

John L. then approached the coffin and looked down.

"Hello, Paul," he intoned.

Then he went into a dramatic recital, one which appeared to have been inspired by Edgar Allen Poe's poem "The Raven." In tones charged with drama, he described how on sleepless nights the raven sat outside his door.

In those sleepless vigils, he went on, he was comforted by the fact that as a young man he plunged into an icy river to save the life of another young man, who had decided to take his own. This was not exactly a fortuitous simile, at least to me, because Paul had taken his own with an overdose of sleeping pills.

Lewis went on to say that he was also comforted on such nights by the memory of the time he saved a young girl from being trampled by a team of runaway horses. The thanks of the mother still comforted him when the raven was at his door, he said. Then, after almost no mention of his deceased friend, Lewis returned to the coffin and intoned:

"Good-by, Paul."

Holmes gave Anderson his due as a reporter and writer, in a graceful and moving elegy.

I never tired of hearing John L. tell of his participation in a high school play in his early days in Illinois and often importuned him to repeat it. The play was a Western melodrama in which a stagecoach driver burst into a frontier saloon in the third act, raised clouds of dust by slapping his clothes with his hat, and electrified its dozing denizens by announcing the drinks were on him, insisting he was so dry he could drink poison from a sidewinder's fangs.

"We played three nights," John L. said. "All went well on the first two. We were veteran troupers by the third night and doing our best—up to the saloon scene. The script called for three drinks in rapid succession.

"When the drinkers reached for their glasses, they discovered that someone had substituted whiskey for the tea employed the first and second nights. Well, sir, you never saw such registering of emotion. It was worthy of Sir Henry Irving. First there were looks of surprise, then of delight and finally of enthusiasm.

"After the three quick drinks, one of the actors was moved to improvise. Then others decided to improve their lines. All forgot their parts and the curtain had to be rung down on what was a lasting fare-well tour for all.''

By the early summer of 1940, Farley came to realize, as had many others, that Roosevelt was going to run. I was at Hyde Park a Sunday before the opening of the Democratic convention in Chicago when Farley called on FDR for a showdown on his plans. FDR had been evading him.

In this conference FDR threshed about in his own duplicity. He said positively he would not run, detailed how he would eliminate himself and then disclosed that he would accept the nomination in a radio speech before the delegates could leave the hall.

Having been pledged to secrecy, Farley could not reveal what he had been told. He didn't need to when I saw him alone, because Farley's manner told me the story, so I wrote that FDR had made it clear to Farley that he would seek a third term, because most people still were in doubt about his plans. After talking with me, Farley left for his New York office where he dictated a full report on the conference, which I was not to see until 1947 when I helped the genial gentleman prepare his memoirs.

At the Chicago convention, Roosevelt, the 1932 hero of the common man, was revealed as the darling of the big-city bosses. All the city machines were beating drums for him and filling their own pockets—Mayor Edward J. Kelly of Chicago, Ray Miller of Cleveland, Frank Hague of Jersey City, Tom Pendergast of Kansas City, Dave Lawrence of Pittsburgh and all the rest.

Curiously enough the bosses never realized that FDR's welfare programs and handouts would spell the end of their power structures reared on paternalism and patronage. Only eight years before, FDR had posed as the champion against the machine corruption of Tammany Hall. New Dealers who professed to abhor bossism flung verbal halos around the heads of political profiteers who herded votes for their hero.

The 1940 gathering was unusual because it was the one convention in which many were running for the vice-presidential nomination and no one dared be a candidate for the presidential nomination but FDR. In furthering his mythical draft, Roosevelt had encouraged many to believe they had his endorsement for second place. I was in the lobby of the then Stevens Hotel when Louis A. Johnson, Assistant Secretary of War, came charging in, fresh from a Washington plane, unaware that Wallace had just been picked for second place.

"I got the green light, Walter," he said. "Where are all the reporters?"

"Green light for what?"

"Vice President."

"Well, you better go over to the Palmer House and clear it with Wallace; he's just been cleared by Sidney Hillman."

The convention had a hard time accepting Wallace, even with the endorsement of the powerful labor leader. Everyone, but a few in the know, was stunned by the choice. More than stunned was Byrnes, who was operating in the third-term-draft headquarters in the Blackstone Hotel with Hopkins, and expecting to be tapped. Hopkins, by then Secretary of Commerce, was hardly less surprised than Byrnes and just as ambitious.

Why Wallace? was the question heard on every hand. History has echoed, "Why Wallace, indeed?" There were explosions of wrath in various delegations but, while many were angry, few dared to challenge the President. Jones could have had the nomination if he had allowed his name to be entered, as friends urged. He might well have become President because had he been nominated, had he displayed courage, he may not have been dumped in 1944 as Wallace was.

Jones was angry over the choice, but not angry enough to challenge Wallace and risk losing control of RFC funds, and he may have been counting on succeeding Hopkins in the Department of Commerce, which he did shortly. Speaker Sam Rayburn was unhappy. Paul McNutt, former governor of Indiana, who was a candidate for the post, was indignant. Secretary of the Interior Harold L. Ickes was as close as he ever came to open revolt. Every time Wallace's name was mentioned in the convention, many delegates booed. When he was nominated, I heard the shouting of one impassioned delegate: "Just because the Republicans have nominated an apostate Democrat [Wendell Willkie], let us not for God's sake nominate an apostate Republican." Others expressed fears that the selection would split the party in a most delicate campaign situation, because FDR was making a controversial break with the third-term tradition.

In that convention I spent many hours with Farley, who was

being shunned because of opposition to the third term. The Post-master General arrived at his decision after many hours of walking the streets of Washington and more in prayer. To him the party and its traditions were second only to his devotion to the Roman Catholic Church. I was with him when he told Jones he could be Vice President if he would stand up to the President. The steel-blue eyes of Jones dropped and he went out with his tail between his legs. I was outside Farley's inner door when he convinced Mrs. R., who came to make a graceful speech at the convention, that Wallace would not do. She called from Farley's desk to tell her husband his choice was a most unpopular one. FDR asked her to put Farley on the phone.

"I've given my word to Wallace," FDR protested. "What do you do when you give your word?"

"I keep it," Farley snapped.

Farley told me of the call immediately after Mrs. R. left. He was sad rather than jubilant when he reported how he had reminded Roosevelt of his many broken promises to the man who put him into the White House in 1932 and to all to whom he had denied third-term ambitions.

Ickes was violently against Wallace for second place. They had long battled over the forestry service, which was in the Department of Agriculture but Ickes felt should be in the Interior Department. But he had an even more important reason for his opposition—he wanted the nomination himself. The Chicagoan wrote a letter to FDR just before the Chicago gathering, proposing Robert M. Hutchins, then president of the University of Chicago, for the nomination. However, the letter ended by noting that many people thought that he, Ickes, would be the best possible candidate! The letter closed with a declaration that Ickes, like Barkis, was willin'.

Wallace gained a first-ballot nomination, but not impressively. The successful candidate wanted to deliver an acceptance speech before the Democrats, I learned, but was persuaded not to show himself because he would have invited a hostile demonstration.

In a comic convention interlude, accepted with relief by all, Bascom N. Timmons was offered as a compromise candidate for the vice-presidential nomination by an exuberant delegate from Ohio. The convention member stripped off his coat in the hot hall and handed it to a perplexed Permanent Chairman Barkley, and called for the selection of the Lincolnesque Texas reporter for the Houston *Chronicle* and other newspapers. A few of us mounted a demonstration for him.

The day after the convention ended, Timmons and I were breakfasting together in the diner of the Capitol Limited, returning to Washington, when Wallace and Hopkins entered and took the table across from us. Wallace mockingly offered condolences to the defeated Timmons, a greater display of humor than most people thought he had.

"We both came to Chicago with one man supporting our candidacy," Timmons replied with greater wit and even more penetrating truth. "Somehow it turned out you had the stronger man."

Wallace was a much maligned man, who paved his own hell with good intentions that were ever going astray. Every time he packed an idea on his horse of thought, it seemed to ride off in all directions. He was a greater experimenter than FDR, but totally lacking in political sense, although his father had been Secretary of Agriculture under Warren G. Harding. He was anxious to please everyone and was convinced that things needed changing, but seemed to be completely unable to differentiate between sound and unsound change, with the result he pleased no one.

Once, he confided to me, he had considered joining the Roman Catholic Church. He was impressed by the ritual, the sonority of Latin and the clouds of incense, but repelled, he said, by the dogma. No doubt he found scholastic philosophy based, in part, on the inquiries of Plato and Aristotle into the mind of man, altogether too rigid for him. Also he was out of tune with the contention of the Greek philosophers that the freedom and dignity of man should not be subjected to the coercions of political power.

During the 1936 drought-inspection campaign trip to North Dakota, this generally shy and often confused man, approached me aboard the presidential special to say he had a friend who wanted to entertain the press at that night's stop. Knowing Wallace did not drink and assuming his friend didn't, I thanked him and said I would pass his invitation on, but cautioned him that the newsmen might be very busy writing.

"But my friend has bought a lot of liquor," Wallace said ruefully, "and will be sorely disappointed."

I asked him why he had not said so in the first place. There was no trouble in rounding up most of my colleagues. The party was a good one, but the host served scotch mixed with ginger ale.

"Mr. Secretary," I told Wallace after the party was over, "you have absolutely no political future."

"Why?" he asked in puzzlement.

"Because you have friends who serve scotch with ginger ale."

"Is that bad?" he asked with even greater puzzlement.

I wasn't much of a prophet. I have been wrong many times, but seldom more wrong on a political prediction.

To me it was no great surprise that Wallace should be captivated by Nicholas Constantine Roerich, an adventurer, who pretended to knowledge of mythical Asian philosophy. His disciples, of whom Wallace was one, addressed Roerich as "Guru." Among other things he was the originator of a thing called the "Roerich Pact and Banner of Peace," which he succeeded in having signed by about twenty nations, since it professed great love for peace and was without involvement of any kind. Wallace was induced to bring the program to the White House where FDR let Wallace sign it as the plenipotentiary of the United States. It may be assumed that the other signers were plenipotentiaries of equal power, which was none at all. One wonders, in view of this episode, why FDR didn't knock Wallace's name off his list of vice-presidential candidates instead of putting him at the top.

The association with Roerich did much to discredit Wallace. The more he saw of the guru the less he grew in political stature. Westbrook Pegler, the phrase-coining columnist, had a field day with Wallace and his guru. Peg labeled Wallace "Bubblehead," an appellation which stuck and helped to discredit him. In 1948, Wallace accepted the presidential nomination of the Progressive party, a third party splinter, which was nothing more than a blend of visionaries, Communists, fellow travelers and crackpots. Senator Glen Taylor of Idaho, a one-time guitar-strumming folk singer, was named his running mate.

At one point in my story of the group's convention in Philadelphia, I was concentrating on the acceptance speeches delivered in the Philadelphia National League Park at night. This was the same park in which FDR had accepted his second-term nomination. There any resemblance ended. In my haste I wrote that Taylor appeared on the platform with his "two-headed baby." In reading over my copy, I discovered the error and dashed off a correction, changing the reference to "a tow-headed baby."

"We were about to let it go into the paper as written," telegraph editor Arvid Westling wired in acknowledgment. "The way the convention has been going, we were convinced that anything could happen."

The last time I saw Wallace was a few years before his death in 1965, when he greeted me, on a visit to Washington, as though I were a long lost brother and confided that he had returned pretty much to my way of thinking. I was not the least surprised that he had completed his circle of political thinking.

Although he got Wallace, FDR didn't get what he really wanted. What he wanted above all was to get the nomination of both the Republican and Democratic parties. He was not satisfied with breaking tradition; he wanted everyone to celebrate its shattering. At his insistence, a number of columnists and commentators were persuaded to urge Republicans not to contest the election because of the war which had started the year before. It did not seem to have occurred to the New Dealers or to Roosevelt that they were advocating that the best way to fight dictatorship abroad was to introduce it at home. Many were still so enchanted with FDR they could see no hint in this suggestion: that Roosevelt might dearly love to have been offered a crown. I am sure if he had been, he would have pushed it away, but no more finally than he pushed away the maneuvered third-term nomination and the fourth that inevitably followed.

Roosevelt tried to lure Alf Landon into his Cabinet, but the honest, if not brilliant, Kansan took himself out of consideration by delivering a speech which was critical of the President after he had been urged not to do so. Landon was invited to the White House before making the speech. Landon, however, forced FDR to reinstate the invitation when he disclosed that he had received an appointment —which had been snapped back—because he would not support FDR's re-election. It was not a happy meeting, I learned from Landon.

FDR did get part of what he wanted. He induced Henry L. Stimson, Hoover's Secretary of State, and Frank Knox, Landon's running mate, to join his Cabinet as Secretaries of War and Navy respectively, because both were strong for entering the war on the side of Britain and France. This was the sort of move FDR relished because it did upset the Republicans in their convention and throw them off stride in the campaign. The GOP nomination went to Wendell Willkie, whom I knew as attorney for the Commonwealth & Southern Corporation power interests. Willkie often urged me to criticize New Deal power projects but wouldn't stand for any quotes.

The Republican gathering was stampeded for the former Indianan by the eastern interventionist bloc, which was suspicious of the foreign policy positions of Governor Thomas E. Dewey of New York and Senator Robert A. Taft of Ohio. While professing to be against American involvement in the war, as FDR did, Willkie was actually as keen for intervention as the President.

On his return to Indiana to launch his campaign, Willkie encountered former Senator James E. Watson of Indiana, a legislator of flexible ethics but impressive appearance. Willkie rushed up to seize his hand, but Watson was less than cordial. Willkie demanded to know why.

"The first time I ever saw you," Watson said, "you were a young boy peddling socialist tracts around Rushville. The next time I saw you, you were a Democrat and now you say you are a Republican."

"Come now," Willkie pleaded, "you're a good Methodist and believe in conversion."

"Sure, I believe in conversion," Watson said. "I believe that even a whore can be converted, but I don't want her singing in the choir on the next Sunday."

I covered every mile of FDR's campaign against Willkie. The theme of the 1940 campaign was that Roosevelt had kept the country out of war. He coupled this with inspection of defense plants and some defense operations. FDR didn't like it much when I put a stop watch on him in Pittsburgh and clocked him as spending a minute and a half in a steel plant and an hour waving to potential voters in the streets. But he didn't mind it at all when I took to telling crowds not to vote for re-election of Senator Joseph Guffey, because FDR had no particular affection for the Pennsylvania statesman, looking on him as no more than a skillful coattail rider.

FDR was not a little aroused over a quip I made during his campaign. In the spring of 1940, he had referred to Mussolini's entry into the war on the side of Hitler as "a stab in the back," in a line he interpolated into an address at the University of North Carolina. When he toured New York City for votes, he found crowds were sparse in Italian neighborhoods, because they resented what they considered a racial slight.

So, by one of those coincidences common to politics, we just happened to be in Columbus, Ohio, on Columbus Day. At high noon Colonel Watson staggered under the biggest wreath I have ever seen and placed it at the foot of the statue of the great navigator in the plaza of the State House. My car happened to be right behind the President's in the circular driveway. I couldn't resist turning down my window and shouting:

"Hey, Pa! What are you trying to do—pull the knife out of that wop's back?"

During the campaign I was unintentionally to get my friend Steve Early into very hot political water. FDR was boarding his special after a New York address. George Durno and I were stopped by a policeman when we tried to get in our car. This was not an unusual experience, because local police and National Guardsmen were frequently given orders to let no one pass. They ignored all credentials and were deaf to explanations. In searching for Secret Service men we ran into Early coming down the steps of the Pennsylvania Station.

Early went to the officer and ordered him to let us pass. When the uniformed policeman refused, Early's hair-trigger temper exploded. He pushed the officer and the latter pushed back, setting Early off balance. In attempting to right himself, Steve threw up his knee. By this time a police captain appeared and pitched into the policeman, who under this barrage crumpled and said he had been kneed.

Strangely enough, some New Dealers in the press, who evidently didn't like Early, wrote up the incident, magnifying it into a major assault, especially because the officer was a black and Early a Southerner.

There were some fears that the policeman might be egged into filing a suit against Early, so he did not accompany FDR on the next trip through New York. It turned out the fears were groundless, because the policeman announced from his hospital bed that he was still voting for Roosevelt. So I wrote a story, the lead of which was something like: "Stephen Tyree Early, grandnephew of the great Confederate cavalry leader Jubal Early, did something his distinguished ancestor would never have countenanced—retreated in the face of the enemy." When Election Day passed, I wired Steve from Hyde Park that I had little to be thankful for, but could rejoice that he didn't have to blame himself for defeat. Steve never forgot my message.

To me, FDR's victory in that campaign, never much in doubt, was sealed at Boston, where at a huge rally he told the mothers of America he had said it before but would say it "again and again and again" that their boys were not going to a foreign war. Never have I heard such a thunderous roar of approval from an audience—political or nonpolitical. There was no doubt this is what they and America wanted to hear.

I was a bit late getting back to the special. Instead of going to my car, I climbed aboard the second private car, which had been put ahead of the President's own car, expecting the train to pull out momentarily. The second car had been added to accommodate an overflow of distinguished guests. Already aboard were the frail Harry Hopkins, Pa Watson, the presidential ghost writers and others. As I entered lugging my portable typewriter, Early asked:

"Well, Walter, what did you think of that?"

"He won re-election," I answered, "but I don't believe him for a minute."

"The drinks are on me," Watson announced. "If the Chicago Tribune says the Boss is elected, it's all over."

The drinking went on into the early morning. Early informed FDR of my prediction and the President relayed his thanks, although Steve did not mention that I had added I didn't believe the pledge. By that time my relations with FDR were chilling but had not gone into the deep freeze that was to follow.

Michael F. Reilly, chief of the Secret Service detail, wrote in his book, Reilly of the White House, that I "could and would curl the Boss's hair about six mornings a week" with my news stories. Reilly continued:

"Yet FDR respected Trohan as a pleasant traveling companion, who was good company when he wasn't working and an adroit foe when he was."

Mike said Roosevelt was "completely contemptuous of O'Donnell, whom he considered mercenary," a characterization of the John Barrymore of Washington with which I could not, then or now, agree. Reilly went on:

" 'You know, Mike,' the Boss told me once, 'Trohan and O'Donnell hate my guts. Trohan comes up here to every press conference and politely spits in my eye, he doesn't seem to mind when I spit back. I wonder why O'Donnell rarely comes?' "

Actually O'Donnell was a regular when he was in town, although FDR chose not to think so, but I, being more gregarious and more fond of my fellow men, fared better at the White House, although not much better in the press corps. O'Donnell had once been a New Dealer and I never had, so he suffered the stigma of traitor.

O'Donnell and I were shunned by many of our colleagues. Some genuinely hated our exercise of the right to disagree and others feared they might suffer from any association. Guilt by association was not unknown then, at least to me, although it was said to have been discovered later. This avoidance was highlighted one morning by Lyle C. Wilson, UP bureau chief, with whom we had left a White House press conference. We walked, with Wilson between us, past the White House and the Treasury, where I tossed a couple of pennies over the railing to the grass below saying: "I'm helping Henry Morgenthau balance the budget." This jocosity had reduced the elder Senator Harry Flood Byrd of Virginia, the stout advocate of sound fiscal policy, to paroxysms of mirth, but had no effect on Wilson and O'Donnell except for wan smiles.

Lyle threw up his arms and stopped us in our tracks, saying: "Look, fellows, I can take one of you or the other; it's asking too much of friendship for me to take you both. So, why don't you toss up and see who wins me. I don't much care; one of you is just as objectionable as the other."

The Washington press corps has long run in a jackal pack at the heels of lions. Those who are loners and do not choose to accept the pack's enthusiasms or ideologies are not popular. I made no secret of my belief that newspapermen are glorified gossips and that too many make a profitable living interviewing one another, but I invariably delivered my criticism as a quip, while O'Donnell did not. I had the reputation of being a wit, although in a city where the truth is often considered the best of jokes.

I have always believed with Ambrose Bierce that politics is a strife of interests masquerading as a contest of principles. It has always amazed me to find people giving themselves, body and soul, to a politician they do not know and whose principles, if any, they do not understand.

This seemed to me to be especially true in the 1940 campaign, when FDR was low on political philosophy and high on keeping out of the war. He continued to lambaste interests and churn up class strife. FDR was the gay reformer, whose New Deal had been hailed as the dawn of a new day and the answer to all of man's political exploration, but it was actually being rescued by the war he was telling people he didn't want.

At heart FDR was no political or economic radical. In fact, he was without any deep-rooted convictions. Everything was on a personal basis with him and his paramount concern in the 1940 campaign was to get re-elected by any means. He had dipped his toe in the political waters under Woodrow Wilson and found it to his liking. At the time he accepted Wilson's theories of liberal political reform, yet these did not permeate his thinking.

He was a Democrat and voted for and supported most Democrats because that was the thing to do. No doubt he had been confirmed in his Democratic faith by the fact that so many of his wealthier neighbors along the Hudson were Republicans. Just how he escaped the magnetism of his distant cousin, Theodore Roosevelt, is not clear.

The positions he took on political questions in the third-term campaign were not based on any code of fundamentals nor any deep reading of history or study. His knowledge of history was sketchy, even of American history, except for anything involving his family. Thus, he was able to call for a sound currency in this first campaign which meant a monetary system based on gold, and then take the country off the gold standard as soon as he settled in the White House. In 1940, he claimed he had saved the country by his fiscal tinkering.

Frances Perkins, the first woman in the Cabinet as Secretary of

Labor, was one of the first of his intimates to discuss FDR's lack of political convictions and political philosophy. She related a conversation she overheard between a young reporter and FDR.

"Mr. President," the reporter began, "are you a Communist?"

"No," said Roosevelt.

"Are you a capitalist?"

"No."

The puzzled reporter then asked the Chief Executive what his philosophy was.

"Philosophy?" the President was puzzled. "Philosophy? I am a Christian and a Democrat—that's all."

It was enough to win him a comfortable re-election, although nowhere near as impressive as that in 1936. I was on the front steps of the family home at Hyde Park when he came out to bask in the third torchlight serenade of his fellow townsmen. I mused then on how difficult it was to get an appraisal of his mind, his philosophy and his ethics. I was convinced then, as I am now, that he didn't know what it was all about, having no firm philosophy or convictions.

I left wondering, not whether the country could survive the war he was aching to join, but whether history would ever learn the truth about him. I knew he had told William R. Castle, the able career diplomat, with whom he was walking across the White House driveway in World War I, when FDR was Assistant Navy Secretary: "Bill, it must be a great thing to be President in time of war." And I remembered he had confided on board his private car in 1935:

"The British who gave us no credit for winning the war [World War I] would like to get us in on their side if they get into another; but they'll have to come crawling on their belly buttons before we do."

SEX SPICES
CAPITAL LIFE AND POLICY

W HEN A MAN SAYS he had pleasure with a woman, he doesn't mean conversation, said the learned Dr. Samuel Johnson. Sex has been of absorbing interest to man from the Garden of Eden. Sex is not for any one administration but for all time. And let it be clearly understood that interest in sex is not always prurience. There is nothing more boring than a man recounting an episode that can be of interest only to two persons. More often than not it is highly exaggerated. What is important is to know who may be exerting influence and why, or to know whether men can discipline themselves and hold themselves above temptation and flattery.

Also there are times when sex becomes the greatest of life's jokes. It is hardly the most dignified of operations at best, but when men, who should know better sigh and simper like schoolboys and their partners wax coy and kittenish, almost everyone knows their most guarded secret and laughs.

Plutarch of Chaeronea, the first and greatest biographer of them all, salted his lives of great Greeks and great Romans with their foibles in his aim to present the rounded man. It is evident that in his day and those that have followed, the pace was set by leaders. If extramarital sex was good enough for Louis XIV, Augustus the Strong of Poland and Charles II, it was also enjoyed by their courtiers.

With FDR not without interest in a trim ankle or the soft rise above the female waist, one could hardly expect others to eschew stolen sweets. And they did not. There was more preoccupation with sex rearing its lovely head all over the New Deal than in preceding or succeeding administrations.

I did not cover Woodrow Wilson or Warren G. Harding, but Secret Service men who had served them both and knew their traits were around in my time and talked freely. During his brief period as a widower, Wilson was reputed to have more than an avuncular eye toward girls in vaudeville, which he attended regularly. When he married Edith Bolling Galt, he fired a Secret Service agent who knelt to tie his wife's shoelace, because he was convinced the man had feasted on the ankle above.

Nick Hayes, long-time Democrat, who was around in my early days, knew them all. On his ninety-first birthday in 1972 he reminisced that Wilson began life as Thomas W. Wilson, looked upon the wine when it was red and chased chippies. So when his reputation got more than he could bear, according to Hayes, he took his middle name, Woodrow, and went on to become governor of New Jersey and President, but he didn't give up his interest in femininity.

Harding was no angel, but one could hardly class him as a rake because he had an illegitimate daughter before he became President. I knew James Sloan, whose days in the Secret Service began under TR and ended under FDR, who told me he paid off the mother with thirty thousand dollars, but would never permit the story to be printed. Calvin Coolidge was a stern Puritan and Herbert Hoover a self-contained Quaker. Neither was given to the games FDR played.

The story of Roosevelt's attachment to Lucy Mercer, the socialite daughter of a former marine colonel, during World War I, was published after his death, but had been known long before. I first heard the story one evening in the fall of 1934, when I was walking across the White House grounds with John Boettiger, then courting Anna Roosevelt. John pointed to the family dining room on the second floor, which was glowing with lights, and said:

"There's an interesting dinner party going on there tonight. Roosevelt's entertaining an old girl friend, a Mrs. Winthrop Rutherfurd, probably to show her what she missed. It's a woman he wanted to marry and was prepared to get a divorce from Mrs. R. so he could."

I asked John how he knew. He told me Anna had filled him in on the situation. John, a tall handsome married man, had met the vivacious Anna on FDR's campaign train. She had divorced Curtis Dall and

John divorced his wife so they could marry. John said Lucy Mercer had been engaged as Mrs. R.'s secretary when FDR was in Washington as Assistant Secretary of the Navy. He became smitten with her and took her as his own secretary. He wanted to marry her, but she would not do so because she was a Catholic, he said. Also his mother opposed it and friends who knew—in those times—it would ruin his political career.

I wasn't particularly interested, but I could not avoid the story. It was a frequent subject of conversation by various insiders, who wanted to show how much they knew. I wasn't concerned, but I couldn't escape the gossip, any more than I could that about his personal secretary, Marguerite LeHand, better known as Missy.

From my earliest days around the White House, I came to recognize that the Executive Mansion was divided into two factions, the Missy faction and the Eleanor faction, with most of the staff in the former's corner, and that faction included myself. Missy was a charming person, thoroughly and completely devoted to FDR. Now and then she may have been taken in by some of the persons who cultivated her as the quickest and surest route of access to FDR. Some did this so assiduously that there were occasional rumors of romantic entanglement, such as William C. Bullitt, the first American ambassador to Soviet Russia, who wanted to be shifted to France.

She made no secret of her attachment. Once after one of the intimate Sunday-night dinners of scrambled eggs and bacon, we retired to her quarters in the White House, where she sat on the bed, kicked up her heels and said joyously:

"Thank goodness, he spent most of the evening with my friends, not with hers."

I had a genuine affection for Missy and not a little admiration for the manner which she conducted a difficult situation. I had none for FDR in his affair, because he brought Missy into his home at Hyde Park, into the governor's mansion at Albany and into the White House, no doubt with the knowledge and consent of Mrs. R., but Louis XIV, who was for FDR the personification of reaction, did no more.

Cyrus Curtis, the publisher of *The Saturday Evening Post*, would not purchase a story from an author he knew to be hunting off the trail, saying: "If he cheats on his wife, he will certainly cheat on me."

No one can know the secrets of the Roosevelts' bedrooms, although their second son, Elliott, recently professed to in a book; but he was far from a model husband and she may have been less than a model wife.

Missy had an aura of saintliness. This and the loyalty of friends did much to protect her from gossip. Among others, I indignantly denied there was anything questionable in her relations with FDR. I had no such compunction about Lucy Mercer Rutherfurd. I saw her but once, in the middle of a night in New Jersey where the presidential special paused while she paid a brief visit to the President. At that time she was a fine-looking woman and a worthy wife to her New York financier. The Secret Service men told me of her visit and I wanted to see the heroine of an old romance.

My interest was kept alive by the fact that I purchased a home, two doors from the house the Roosevelts occupied when he was Assistant Secretary of the Navy. I often thought of Lucy and Franklin in walking past the red brick house on R Street. I knew that Louis McHenry Howe, FDR's gnomelike companion and adviser, had come home one afternoon to find Eleanor sitting on the doorstep crying. She explained that Franklin wanted to divorce her and marry Lucy. She asked Howe what she should do.

"Why don't you go in for politics?" Howe suggested, a proposal which I did not think had always been of benefit to the nation.

I began collecting everything I could about this romance with the help of Lucy's friends and members of her family. Strangely enough, I found wide variations in estimates of her character. To some she was an angel and to others not a whit better than she should have been. Colonel McCormick wouldn't print any part of the story, saying the *Tribune* didn't fight that way, a refrain I was to hear from time to time.

So I turned over my files to Westbrook Pegler when the columnist approached me on the story and put him in touch with my sources. His stories on the relationship, the first to be published, resulted in his being assailed as the worst of gossipmongers and the epithet of "God's angry man." Subsequently Jonathan Daniels, a onetime White House administrative assistant and press secretary, and later Elliott confirmed every line of Pegler's stories.

Peg didn't stop at rattling skeletons in FDR's closet, but also rattled some bones in Mrs. R.'s. He made much of her relations with a much married New York state trooper, a romance also confirmed by Elliott. One facet of this romance I can never forget. The trooper decided to remarry and won Mrs. R.'s permission to hold the wedding at Hyde Park. When Sistie, Anna's daughter, was introduced to the bride, she exclaimed: "I thought he was going to marry Grandma." Out of the mouths of children!

Another romance of FDR's was whispered about Washington, but was never mentioned in print, except by me. It attracted virtually no attention, although it may have had more effect on American foreign policy than any of his other affairs. Certainly it sent Missy into a decline and, some friends suspected, hastened her death.

After the fall of Norway, FDR invited Crown Princess Martha of Norway with her young children to Washington from England where she and the Crown Prince had taken refuge. She became a great favorite at the White House and at Hyde Park—but not of Missy's, Mrs. R.'s or of the press, most of whose members were more attracted to her lady in waiting, a prettier if less exalted person. We met them both when we gathered about FDR's auto at Hyde Park to ask his opinion of a Hitler speech. We heard him tell her, in answer to the same question, "He held the door to peace open that far." And he extended his hand, holding his thumb and forefinger about an inch apart.

In the fall of 1941, I was tipped off that Martha was accompanying FDR to Hyde Park every weekend, although her name never appeared on the official list, which included the President, his staff, the press and cameramen. This concealment, of course, piqued my interest, especially since it was already being whispered that Martha was FDR's latest light of love.

Ordinarily, the handful of press regulars drove from the railroad station at Hyde Park to the Poughkeepsie Hotel in the same car, each charging his office the full fare of four dollars in order to help defray the long and costly hours of waiting in the hotel's bar. I chose to go alone in a second limousine, saying I could not leave until I had seen FDR from the train to the gates of the family estate. I said such coverage was my solemn duty to Colonel McCormick.

Week after week, I would watch FDR make his way slowly down the ramp of his private car, the Magellan, to his auto. Then the train door would open and Martha would dart out, invariably in high-heeled slippers and black silk hose, muffled somewhat against the morning air if not from the gaze of any curious, like myself. She would race to the car, leap in and off it would go.

I would describe the scene, not omitting the black slippers and hose, noting that Mrs. R. was away at one city or another. My lead numbered the visits so that my story would say something like: "For the fifth time in as many weeks, Crown Princess Martha joined President Roosevelt for a weekend in his family home on the upper reaches of the Hudson."

After the first of my stories, the Secret Service men began offering to take me to town in the car of the off-duty crew, which left before FDR could disembark. I insisted that I, like Frederic in *The Pirates of Penzance*, was a slave to duty and would see FDR to the gates of his home. Still later my colleagues tried to persuade me to go with them, because some were being questioned about my stories, but were denying them. The White House staff became frigid and they and my colleagues dropped me from their gatherings. I was put into Coventry, but I was enjoying myself.

Captain Patterson of the New York *News* was particularly indignant, insisting that if FDR were carrying on with royalty, his paper should be the first to tell the story. He was unable to move his correspondent Fred Pasley, a good reporter and a great writer, but such a devoted idolater that he almost quit speaking to me over my stories.

I had no idea what FDR was carrying on, but I know I was getting very unpopular. Steve Early called me into his office and begged me to cease, after the gentle and scholarly William Hassett, a former New York *World* reporter, had failed to move me. Steve was no admirer of Mrs. R. so that his final plea was: "My God, after Eleanor, isn't he entitled to a bit of femininity?" I mused on this when Mrs. R. came to the graveside for final rights for Steve in 1950.

At Warm Springs, Georgia, when I attempted to call upon Missy, who had been ill for months in her cottage there, I was stopped by a Marine who almost planted a fixed bayonet in my navel. I let out a roar of indignation that could be heard almost as far as the Little White House. Another Marine called the officer of the day, who had no book to go by such a situation, so he called the Secret Service.

In no time Mike Reilly was at my side trying to pull me away. I was not to be denied my act. I protested that "this Cossack," who was actually a flustered and embarrassed young Marine, was about to run me through and that all I wanted to do was call on my old friend Missy.

"You know why they don't want you to go in there," Reilly argued.

I protested I didn't and refused to leave.

"All right, then," said Mike, "they don't want you to hear what she says about Crown Princess Martha."

"OK, Mike," I responded and walked away with him. "I just wanted to hear you say it."

I never did get to talk to Missy about the princess, although she came north and was hospitalized in Washington, for a time, before she returned to her native Massachusetts to die. Roosevelt called on Missy only once during her illness and then in Doctors' Hospital in the capital. Early told me of the visit. We shook our heads over the fact that FDR took Mrs. R. with him on that visit, an incident of truth stranger than fiction—a man taking his wife to call on the mistress for whom he had betrayed their marriage, a mistress who was lying in illness partly because she had been betrayed in turn.

In her last days, Missy had little money and great expenses. She was provided for by Bullitt, Baruch and Joe Kennedy, the founding father of an amazing family. All were moved by compassion and regard, they confided to me. They took turns in making monthly deposits to her account and told me FDR never contributed a red cent. That didn't surprise me because he and his family weren't given to charities. In fact, FDR wasn't given to spending his own money for all his liberality with tax dollars.

Roosevelt did visit Martha in her Washington home, but not with Mrs. Roosevelt. Most of these visits were not publicized. I can only remember one on the record.

My stories of the visits of Crown Princess Martha changed the lives of the press regulars. When the war came, FDR barred coverage of his movements, including all trips to Hyde Park. Naturally we knew when he left the White House and where he was, because in those days a group of White House regulars lunched regularly with Hassett, whose principal function was to answer presidential mail which did not warrant FDR's personal attention but still demanded his signature. He was an assistant to Early and was designated to make minor trips because Early thoroughly disliked the social life and travel that went with his post.

We knew that when Hassett did not show up, the President was away, obviously at Hyde Park. When Hassett showed up, after such absences, we asked if he had been at Hyde Park and he acknowledged he had. He missed the companionship of the press and blamed me for it.

"Bill," I asked him on his return, with feigned innocence, "by any chance was . . ."

"Yes," he would cut in, "she was there, you son of a bitch, and there isn't a damned thing you can do about it."

"I can dream of what happens in the dream house, can't I?"

I had named the cottage FDR had built for himself on the grounds of the family estate the "dream house," because FDR told us the plans came to him in a dream, but the President didn't like the designation.

On another occasion when FDR was dedicating his library and deeding over part of the estate to the federal government, he called me to his side.

"I suppose you're going to do a poison-pen piece on this story," he said, laughing.

I acknowledged that I was. Then I spotted some poison ivy growing around an oak. I rubbed some copy paper on it and said:

"Now I'm going to write a real poison piece."

FDR howled, but he didn't laugh when he saw my lead which was: "President Roosevelt today dedicated the memorial he is building to himself on his family estate."

Early told me FDR was furious. I pointed out that the story was accurate and true.

"Yes," Early acknowledged, "but when a Dutchman gives away anything he loses all sense of humor."

Just before the war ended coverage of Hyde Park trips, Hassett made a final pitch at shutting down my coverage of Martha's visits. Marshall Field III was preparing to launch the Chicago *Sun* to counteract *Tribune* isolationism, with the blessing and assistance of the White House. Hassett, whom I had helped to place in Early's office, asked me to take a walk with him to the cemetery south of the Nelson House Hotel. Naturally we were friendly. He importuned me to accept an offer, which had been made, to join the *Sun*.

"You know, the President likes you," he said, "and you and he could go back to your old relationship, if you were on another paper, a friendly paper."

"Hold it, Bill," I broke in, until then not aware he knew of the offer. "You go back and tell him I hate war, a phrase he may recognize, more than I hate the New Deal and that he can't buy me with someone else's money."

I am sure that Hassett didn't repeat my words, but FDR got the message, because he became quite cold to me. Hassett began avoiding me, being a timid fellow, for which he was the loser because he could smell a New England boiled dinner and could be counted to knock on our door whenever the dish was served.

Early did not drop me, nor did the ailing McIntyre, who was stricken by a recurrence of an early case of tuberculosis, which proved fatal after months in a North Carolina resort.

Crown Princess Martha remained near Roosevelt throughout the war. She was among the few select personages invited to join him and his personal and official families when he took his fourth oath of office as President on January 20, 1945, and she was also one of the few persons invited to the White House for the funeral services in the East Room of the Executive Mansion less than three months later.

"I am leaving now, returning to England," she confided to a friend. "My work is done."

Whatever her work was she served her country well.

There were many young ladies in those days who played the games people like to play with as much enthusiasm as New Dealers displayed in making over America. Bess Farley was inexpressibly shocked when she attended a party early in 1937 honoring the Postmaster General and Democratic party leader for FDR's second-term triumph. This good woman sat beside a member of Washington's younger set, who ticked off those at the head table with whom she had been intimate.

Three of the young ladies had made a wager as to which would be the first to tumble bachelor Frank Murphy, former governor of Michigan, when he was named Attorney General in 1939. The one who shocked Mrs. Farley claimed the wager by secreting a couple of her hairpins in the bed in his office-living quarters in the Department of Justice, but the other two refused to pay without more conclusive evidence.

I once stumbled upon the same young lady trying to interest McIntyre in an amorous bout in his hotel bedroom. She wasn't the least embarrassed, nor was McIntyre, who giggled before I could back out, saying, "She thinks there is life, but the flame is gone."

Games have long been played on Capitol Hill where some staffers of the fair sex are chosen for friendly beauty. Quite often the best of men at home are led to fancy themselves as the greatest of lovers, when they come to the free and easy corridors of Congress. There are members of the non-Lib wing of the female sex, who are stimulated to engage in activity between the sheets by prominence and names.

Now and then the more romantic members of Congress lose their heads, at least for a time. When I learned that Senator Harry P. Cain of Washington was contemplating divorcing his wife and marrying a mattress-backed lass who was free with her favors among members of the Senate and House press galleries, I went to see him and caution him that he would be a brother-in-law of the saddle to many of the less discriminating members of the press. Cain didn't make the break, but not necessarily on my account. The decorated paratrooper came to Washington a conservative, but flirted with the liberals when he was named to the Subversive Activities Control Board, with the unhappy result neither the right nor the left trusted him and he faded into anonymity.

One of the more active capitol Lotharios was Senator Estes Kefauver of Tennessee, who often made a connubial bed of many a House and Senate committee-room table and made no secret of it. Philip L. Dodd, one of my Hill staff, chanced upon this senator's wife signing into a motel with a man, not her husband, on the lower reaches of the Potomac. We considered the turnabout by this lively redhead no more than fair play.

Estes was to the right of Louis XIV during his days in the Yale Law School with my great and good friend George Shea, the number one man in his class, who became editor of the *Yale Law Review*. In those days Estes dreamed of being a corporation lawyer. When he was elected to Congress Shea and I were surprised to find him the most ardent of New Dealers. He told us the conversion came while he was waiting in his office for clients and looked out on a factory nearby, realizing that there were far more men working for the plant than running it.

When he moved over to the Senate, Kefauver was smart enough to revive an investigation into racketeers, which had won Dr. Royal S. Copeland re-election to the Senate in New York. With the introduction of television, Kefauver became a national figure and a contender for the Democratic presidential nomination.

It was not unusual in those days for a senator, like Clyde Herring of Iowa, to bring his lady love to the Senate public gallery to hear him raise his dulcet tones on this or that issue. Whenever one did, his colleagues spent more time noting the lady's reaction than they did his words. Invariably one of them would tip off the press gallery, where such scenes occasioned as much merriment as they did on the Senate floor. Senators could and did call newsmen to their cloakroom and newsmen could always go to the entrance of the Senate chamber and request a senator to come to the cloakroom for a chat.

The sex gambit was employed to influence policy by the British on Senator Arthur H. Vandenberg of Michigan, one of the vainest men to serve in a body where egos are often king size. The commanding former editor and publisher of the Grand Rapids (Michigan) *Herald* was strongly opposed to American intervention, but made a fast switch to intervention. Before the about-face, he was a regular attendant at keep-out-of-the-war strategy sessions, organized by two of my best senatorial friends, Wheeler and Nye.

One of these sessions was held in Vandenberg's apartment in the Wardman Park Hotel. He had installed a Canadian charmer in a connecting apartment. The senator's second wife, Hazel, a former *Tribune* writer, would not tolerate the bringing of the mistress to the adjoining apartment and left for home. The Canadian woman presided at the dinner the senator gave our group and rose to leave as we prepared to get down to business. Then she went over to Vandenberg, patted him on the cheek and said:

"Good night, you great big statesman, you."

Vandenberg blushed with delight. I turned to Nye and said, in what I thought was a whisper, "Where does one throw up?" Unfortunately all conversation died in surprise over the scene at the head of the table and I might as well have shouted it. The session had to be cut short because, whenever Vandenberg or I spoke, there were snickers. Vandenberg never forgave me.

When the Canadian woman left the capital for her home, she was replaced by a British woman. The replacement convinced those in the know that the British were working on the senator. Proof came when I learned the Office of Naval Intelligence had intercepted the woman's reports to British intelligence on her progress with Vandenberg. These reports were supplied to the White House where they were undoubtedly welcome, but must have provoked many a smirk.

In the 1940 GOP convention at Philadelphia, I was among those who persuaded Joseph Pew, the Sun Oil Company executive, who had secured copies of the ONI intercepts, not to read them on the convention floor. The long-time Republican party angel felt such a reading would be necessary to block Vandenberg's planned grab for the party's nomination. I argued, as did others, that Vandenberg didn't have a chance and Pew would only hurt himself, so the reports never became public.

Other senators were beyond the age of action but not of ideas. One of these was Senator William H. King of Utah, who was known as the most persistent garter snapper in Congress. This was so common a subject of jest in Washington that a socialite told McIntyre, who bore a slight resemblance to the legislator, that she had been seated beside him in the National Theatre the night before. McIntyre looked at me, in some surprise, because we had been together at a function the night before. Before I could come to his rescue, she went on:

"I saw you," she insisted, "and near the end of the second act, I felt your hand on my knee. Just then the lights went up, and I had a good look at you, and discovered you were Senator King."

The septuagenarian Senator Arthur Capper of Kansas was one of the capital's most confirmed partygoers and could be found wherever there was dancing and free food. He did not drink. Because he was reputedly worth some nine million dollars and unmarried, he never lacked for partners, many of whom would have enjoyed helping him spend his money. For all their trying, he was never led to the altar.

Capper encountered Mrs. Junior Owens, the widow of a well-known and well-liked capital lobbyist, at a reception in the Mayflower Hotel. As they left together, he offered her a lift and then suggested they stop at her Columbia Road apartment. Thinking he was going to repay her with a dinner invitation in return for the many hospitalities showered on him by her late husband, she invited him in. Once inside he led her to a sofa, glanced at his watch and said:

"I have fifteen minutes before I have to leave for the Philippine embassy. Would you give me a kiss?" When the proposal met with a look of amused wonder, he added: "I think it would do us both good."

Sex was never a difficult commodity to obtain on Capitol Hill. Telephone operators would call on discreet members to ask them if they had any constituents coming to town that evening, who might be seeking companionship and entertainment. It was rather a simple matter to smuggle an obliging young lady on the federal payroll, if not into a member's own office, into that of a friendly colleague. On one occasion a congressman, somewhat in his cups, persuaded a secretary to strip to her waist in front of me in his office to exhibit what he claimed were the most perfect breasts in the capital. I have known far less accurate congressmen.

In the Cabinet, Secretary of the Interior Harold L. Ickes, who courted the title, "the Old Curmugeon," fancied himself as a lover, although his face was hardly one for Valentines. In his college days he had boarded in the home of James Westfall Thompson, the University of Chicago historian, who had married Anna Wilmarth, daughter of a substantial Chicago family. When he was graduated Ickes left with the professor's wife, who was better known than her husband in Illinois because of her able service in the state legislature. However, she did bear some resemblance to a frigate under full sail and Ickes soon found that power in Washington was not without side rewards, such as office wives.

I considered Ickes my special pigeon. After all we were both from Chicago. He had a number of former Chicago newsmen on his staff, who were less than entranced with him, so they fed me unfavorable stories and kept me informed on his love life. Hopkins and Wallace, who were tilting with him in power lists, also fed me similar stories.

Ickes didn't owe his post to ability or qualification. He was a former Republican who had supported FDR in 1932 as had Senator Hiram Johnson. Because of Mrs. Ickes' interest in Indian affairs, Ickes asked for appointment to the Bureau of Indian Affairs. Johnson got him the Interior Department, which bossed such affairs and a good deal more.

The Old Curmudgeon was of considerable service to FDR as a professional scold, especially in campaigns. He would say things FDR could not say himself, but they would serve to embarrass Roosevelt's opponents. However, Ickes had a genius for making his own troubles, beyond what most of us do, such as when he delivered eggs from his Maryland farm for sale to a capital grocery in his Interior Department limousine during gas rationing. And he was forever putting chips on his shoulder for others to knock off, which they, like Wallace and Hopkins, generally did.

When Pegler and later Frank Kluckhohn, of the New York *Times*, began taking out after him, I became a bit resentful because I considered him my private property. Kluckhohn, who was shifted from coverage of Spain to the Washington bureau, dedicated himself to the extermination of the project to harness the tides of Passamaquoddy, where there was no industrial demand for kilowatts and the cost of shipping power from the area to where it might be used would be prohibitive.

One Saturday afternoon, Frank waited outside Ickes' office to put another question to him about the project. As the Secretary came out of his office, Frank stepped forward. Ickes, who was being followed by the secretary he was romancing at the time, darted back and slammed the door. Frank knew that Ickes had another exit, but knew nothing of the romance.

Frank raced down four flights of stairs, just as Ickes disappeared into his limousine, the shades of which had been drawn in order to shield his inamorata. Before the car could get under way however, Frank had the door open and was pointing an accusing finger at the cringing Ickes, whose guilty conscience led him to believe his amour had been discovered.

Instead Kluckhohn leveled his question on the moon-harnessing project and got his answer, but was oblivious to the bigger story, which he could not have printed anyway. Ickes' personal secretary came to me after Ickes had tired of her and offered to sell copies of all her boss's letters and papers for thirty thousand dollars, which was a lot of money in the middle '30s. She had them in safety deposit boxes of the Riggs National Bank.

I insisted on examining the wares. There wasn't much of explosive public interest in the papers. They included a copy of the diary he was dictating almost every day and which subsequently was published in a somewhat abridged form, but constituted a Narcissus pool of self-admiration and the firing of volleys of confusion to his enemies that ultimately totaled a million words. There were reports of departmental investigators he had assigned to investigate his fellow Cabinet members, including Farley, beside whom he sat at Cabinet meetings, because the Postmaster General was interested in a New York City building materials company with a brother-in-law. The investigation found not the slightest trace of wrongdoing or undue influence on the part of Farley or any other Cabinet member, but the fact that Ickes ordered his colleagues investigated was highly interesting and an index to his mind.

I reported on the papers to Farley, who was understandably outraged. In my presence he put in a call to Ickes and asked him to come immediately to the huge office Farley occupied in the Post Office Building. When Ickes arrived Farley launched into what he termed "a Patrick Henry," that singed the Secretary down one side and up the other for contemplating, then investigating a fellow Cabinet member without the justification of any suspicion of wrongdoing, an investigation which properly belonged in the Department of Justice if there were suspicion.

I did not stay for the confrontation, but Farley gave me a replay later. Ickes sat through the display of honest indignation, evidently aware he had earned it. When Farley finished, he told me, Ickes had only one thing to say: "I must acknowledge you are frank as well as honest."

The sex life of another Cabinet member came under my purview in Chicago and Washington. He was Frank Knox, publisher of the Chicago *Daily News*, Landon's 1936 running mate and FDR's third Secretary of the Navy. Knox came to Chicago from New Hampshire to succeed Walter Strong, who died suddenly and mysteriously during the Depression and who left a million dollars in insurance to his paper and another million to his family.

When it was learned that Strong's personal library contained some well-thumbed books on poison and that he had been secretly cremated some days after a public funeral, I was among reporters who undertook to explore the possibility of suicide. I was not interested in Strong particularly, but in exposing Cook County Coroner Herman

N. Bundeson, who was the conductor of a health column in Strong's newspaper. I could never establish my suspicions.

Knox came to Chicago with a woman editor, Leola Allard, who was well known as his favorite. Her presence irked many a *News* reporter, especially when Knox gave her a car at the paper's expense and a handsome salary, when salaries of other reporters had been cut and the *News* was not generous in its pay.

Edward Scott Beck, *Tribune* managing editor, and Robert Morton Lee, its city editor, assigned me to taunt Knox over bringing Leola to Chicago. When I asked them what they wanted me to do, they said they would leave that to my fertile imagination. I was cautioned I must not disclose their hands and not to reveal the nature of the assignment to anyone on the paper, which put J. Loy Maloney, the day city editor in a dither of curiosity I refused to satisfy.

It took some cogitation, but after some days I got the germ of an idea. I had enlisted the aid of a friend on the *News* to try to get Knox's private phone number in his apartment. This failed. Then I went to the law office of Litsinger, Healy and Reid and enlisted the help of a telephone operator. After dinner, she posed as a long-distance operator in Palo Alto, the home of Herbert Hoover, whom the *News* supported strongly in 1932. She called the paper and asked for Knox. Because it was assumed Hoover was calling their boss, Knox was soon on the line. I had no idea in mind when he came on the line, but was soon to develop one.

"Hello," I heard Knox answer, being familiar with his voice.

"Is Leola there?" I asked.

"Hello! Who is it?"

"Never mind who it is. Is Leola there?"

"Who wants her? Hello! Hello! Who is it?"

"This is your conscience, Frank," I confided in what I considered awesome tones and hung up.

Very pleased with myself, I had a few more drinks and then went back to the office, where I typed a memo reporting my mission accomplished. Out of the corner of my eye, I saw Lee read the memo and grin, turn around and hand it to Beck, at the desk behind him. Beck reddened with laughter. In a short time Lee came over to my desk, pulled a chair across an aisle and sat down.

"Mr. Trohan," he began, being given to formality, "should you ever want to resign from the *Tribune,* which I hope and pray will not be the case, you will not have to write a letter of resignation. All you will ever have to do is to tell the story of the phone call and reveal the role of Mr. Beck and myself in it."

Whenever I saw Knox after that, and it was quite often in the capital, I couldn't help but wonder how much I might relieve him by telling him the story of the phone call. The story of his romance was common property in Washington when he was running for Vice President. Washington papers carried a spread of photographs on the GOP second-place nominee, including one of Knox with his wife, which prompted Mrs. Jay Jerome Williams, the wife of a capital newsman and publicist, to remark, sardonically: "Politics sure does make strange bedfellows!"

A sex story of international scope, which was widely known but no more than hinted at in the press, was to occupy my attention for some years. In the fall of 1940, Speaker Bankhead died and was buried in Jasper, Alabama, a few miles northwest of Birmingham. I did not join the presidential special to Alabama, so that William C. Strand, then a new man in the bureau, might have a bit of experience in presidential travel. An event on that journey was to echo in Washington and in chanceries around the world for years.

During the trip, one of the porters on the special, an efficient workman and a great churchman, went to the passenger agent of the Southern Railroad to report he had been approached by Under Secretary of State Welles with an improper proposal. The shocked agent had the porter dictate and sign an affidavit. Why he thought the situation required such a document we never knew.

The incident was reported to me some days later by a person unfriendly to Welles. I demanded and saw the affidavit and promptly dismissed it. Not long after I got a call from Colonel McCormick. He said he had been approached by Sewell Avery, the chairman of the board of Montgomery Ward and Company, who had been carried out of his office by soldiers during a labor dispute and harbored a grudge against the New Deal. Avery asked if McCormick were going to print the terrible story about Welles, then offered to get it for him if he didn't have it.

McCormick phoned me and asked what the story was. After I told him, he said he would call Avery immediately and tell him the *Tribune* didn't fight that way, which is what I expected.

Within the month, Cissie Patterson, editor and publisher of the Washington *Times Herald*, sister of Captain Patterson and cousin of McCormick's, had us to dinner. She confided that the night before, she had been invited to dinner by Bill Bullitt, who had often clashed with Welles.

"I thought I was going to a regular dinner party," she said, "but when I got there, I found I was the only guest at a small table, lit by candles, which hadn't happened to me in years.

"After dinner, he leaned over to ask in a whisper whether I was going to print the Welles story. I didn't know about it, so I just tried to look wise. Then he said that if I didn't have it, he would get it for me. I put him off. He told me Bert had it.

"This morning I called Bert and he told me to call you. Now, what's the story all about?"

When I filled her in, she also rejected the story. Still later Captain Patterson called me to ask about the story because a similar approach had been made to him. He also turned the story down. For this the much despised McCormick-Patterson axis, as interventionists were to brand the *Tribune-News-Times Herald* combine, got no Brownie points.

I didn't like Bullitt's approach to the proprietorship of the papers, although we were friendly or, at least, as friendly as one would get with a man who invariably turned on his leaders and associates. So I talked to Michael McDermott, the gentle and efficient State Department press officer, and told him of Bullitt's offers to expose Welles. Mike was horrified. He asked me if I would tell the story to Welles. I had no objection so an appointment was made for 4:30 P.M. in the afternoon.

At 4 P.M. I got a phone call from a flustered McDermott.

"You and your sense of humor," he sputtered. "That appointment is off."

Later he told me privately that he had never heard the story, but had mentioned it to Hull, reporting he had had it from me. Mike said Hull was amazed that McDermott didn't know about the incident because every ambassador in Washington was laughing at Hull about his top aide.

Hassett had told me that Hull marched over to the White House, as soon as he heard the story, demanding Welles be fired. Hassett imitated Hull's lisp of gutter language. Mrs. R. intervened, saying that such action might precipitate a suicide.

Meanwhile, the incident was investigated by the FBI, which found the porter involved to be thoroughly reliable and a man of exemplary habits and character.

Months later I was having dinner in Farley's suite in the Mayflower Hotel with the former Postmaster General, Hull and Jones. During the meal the cryptic Hull turned to me and said:

"I'm getting wid [rid] of that fellow down the hall."

I knew the reference was to Welles because that "son of a bitch down the hall" in Hull's book was Adolph A. Berle, another aide high in FDR's confidence. Anyway it made for a nice scoop and Welles was dropped a day or two later.

Mrs. Patterson's reference to the intimate dinner with Bullitt as something that had not happened to her "in years," served to recall the fascinating and dramatic story of her marriage to Count Joseph Gizycki, a member of an old Polish family. She was twenty and her prospective groom was twice that age, but a dashing figure, when she accepted his proposal.

Cissie, Countess Cassini, daughter of the Russian ambassador, and Alice Longworth were considered the liveliest and most mischievous young debutantes of that day. Cissie's mother sought to prevent the marriage by offering her daughter a set of black pearls, which she fingered at her neck as she bartered. Cissie refused, ran upstairs and barricaded herself in her bedroom the night before her wedding. The mother pushed notes under the door, offering Cissie sums up to $250,-000 as bribes not to marry. Cissie remained obdurate. Then the mother sent Mrs. Ruth Hanna McCormick, wife of Cissie's cousin, Senator Medill McCormick, to instruct her in the facts of life, so as to avoid immediate pregnancy.

"We were married right over there," said Cissie pointing to the marble fireplace at the right of the paneled living room of her Du-Pont Circle home. "When I went upstairs to pack, I was careful to put in a bottle of vinegar, because Ruth had advised me to employ this liquid in a douche.

"Then we went aboard our private car and on to the old Waldorf in New York City. Once in our room, Joseph charged at me and flung me on the bed. I fought and tried to escape but he tore off my clothes."

Cissie paused for emphasis and then added dramatically:

"It was rape!"

"You must have hated him," ventured Mrs. Evie Walker Robert, capital socialite and one of the group.

"Not at all," she exclaimed with a sigh. "He was every inch a man."

Then Cissie retired to employ the douche. Unfortunately her cousin had failed to mention that the vinegar was to be diluted; so Cissie used it at full strength. The end result was that the count was deprived of her for days.

Following her marriage, she accompanied her husband to the family estate in Poland, where the peasantry knelt when her carriage passed, which she rather liked. Her concern for democracy had yet to develop, if it ever did.

In prowling about, she came upon her husband's diary, which he kept in French, evidently because Polish was employed chiefly in dealing with the peasants. From this, she learned to her mounting ire, that the count was given to exercise of seignoral rights toward brides on his estate and to visits to a favored brothel in Vienna.

"I considered a course of action," Cissie said. "I realized it had to be clear and unmistakable. I also knew I had to teach him a lasting lesson."

Some weeks later she observed the count going about arching his neck and scraping the rugs. Another visit to his desk uncovered a letter he had received from the madam of the Viennese brothel, stating she had just acquired a redheaded American girl in her establishment, who was being saved for his pleasure. The count was soon off to Vienna.

In that city, he hastened to the house, where all had been arranged. He was led to a darkened room, where there was a table set for two, with two shaded candles, in a far corner and the bowed head of a red-haired woman.

"Joseph strode over gallantly, bowed and murmured 'Good evening' in English," Cissie continued, pausing for effect.

In triumphant tones she continued: "Then I looked up.

"His mouth dropped.

"I was the American girl! I had bought the place and arranged for the confrontation. I showed him!"

She left him, but the count held up the family for about a quarter of a million dollars. How much of her story was truth and how much was fiction, I can't say, but it certainly made a good story, one rivaling fiction.

Her break with her second husband, Elmer Schlesinger, a Chicago lawyer, had no less a dramatic aftermath. Shortly after they separated, he died suddenly, while visiting friends in the picturesque mountain region of North Carolina.

When she heard of his death, Cissie summoned Raymond M. Hood, the noted American architect, to her Washington home and commissioned him to build an American Taj Mahal as a memorial to her husband. For some days she joined him in pouring over suggested sketches, urging him to spare no expense, and then disappeared. After a week Hood became desperate. He knew she was there but servants insisted she wasn't in the home and her office denied she was there.

At last unable to endure the situation any longer, he said, he charged into her room, where she greeted him as a stranger. He demanded to know what the trouble was; blandly she told him she had changed her mind and asked him to send a bill. It was not until he returned to New York that Hood discovered that Schlesinger had had time to change his will after the breakup and had cut her off without a penny, so that there were no funds available, except her own, for the proposed Taj Mahal.

At my first diplomatic reception in the White House, there was an amusing incident that should live forever in diplomatic memory. These receptions have long since lost their color, but in those days they were glittering affairs, with diplomats wearing dazzling orders on red sashes across white shirt fronts, women in gorgeous gowns, and displays of dazzling uniforms, including gold-chained dolmans of officers of Hungarian hussars.

There was dancing in the East Room, after the guests filed by the President and First Lady, with a goodly sprinkling of waltzes naturally. Carol and I were somewhat awed. In one of the dances, the wife of the Turkish ambassador chanced to be paired with a young and dashing Italian naval officer. In the course of the dance there was a snap and the ample and brilliant bloomers of the horrified lady tumbled to the floor. Without a moment's hesitation, the officer scooped them up, folded them as compactly as he could, bowed and returned them to his blushing partner.

"Madame," he said with a bow, "you dropped your handkerchief, I believe."

For this truly magnificent display of presence of mind, he was awarded the Turkish Order of Chastity, second class (the order doesn't have a first class).

Now and then sex in the capital became a diplomatic problem. When important delegations came from the Middle East oil-producing nations, the State Department undertook to recruit call girls for their pleasure. The Middle Eastern guests stipulated that the girls be shaved as were the women of their harems. I am sure that young career men were not assigned to undertake such interesting barbering, but I do know they acted as procurers and American taxpayers picked up the tabs.

The girls often came from a curious institution on Connecticut Avenue, known as the Vivien Hopkins Institute, which advertised in the city's Yellow Pages offering, among other things, high colonic irrigations, whatever they may have been. The institute and its girls were quite popular in their day and way.

One of the girls, Carmel Snow, became a movie starlet, but not for long. Returning to her alma mater, which offered diplomas in massage, she testified that she returned because she was able to make three times as much in the establishment as she got in Hollywood and doubtless she got to meet more interesting people.

At least one member of Congress died in the establishment. I learned that when I investigated his death on arrival in a Washington hospital. Doubtless he died happy.

These few notes are no more than a glance at sex life in the capital, even though there will be occasional disclosures under succeeding Presidents. However, it does serve to give evidence that such things were going on among our political gods as they did among the deities dwelling—and diddling—on Mount Olympus. This has been a rather neglected pasture, although an important one. I cite a few items if for no other purpose than to make clear that those considered good and wise are often as frail and weak as the rest of us.

These are freer times, of course. Times and manners differ although there is nothing new in the games people play and hasn't been as far back as we can go in recorded time. Hoover was impeccable in habits and conversation. Once I heard him tell an off-color story which, while witty, would not shock novices in a nunnery, at least today. Lyndon B. Johnson was, as far as I knew or heard, the "parfit gentil knight," although he was not above patting the well-rounded bottom of a dancing partner in the White House, but in an open and playful way.

Then, as now, Washington led the nation in liquor consumption. It has been said that this is due, to a considerable extent, to cheaper liquor prices in the capital than in nearby Virginia and Maryland, so that residents of those areas do their bottle shopping in the District of Columbia. There may be some truth to this, although there is getting to be less as taxes rise.

Some will tell you that there are times when it appears that almost every drop of the Potomac is whiskey, although some will say that every drop is distilled history. It is true that no city of comparable size—and many much larger—has the number of cocktail parties the capital enjoys. Almost everything is launched or promoted on a river of alcohol. It got so that I went on the wagon and remained there for twenty years, except for an occasional sip outside the country, just to avoid drinks I did not want and could not enjoy.

Many Washingtonians not only freeload on liquor, but make their dinners on hors d'oeuvres offered as blotting paper. One of the more prominent of these was Senator Theodore Francis Green of Rhode Island, the multimillionaire, who continued in the Senate into his nineties and long was chairman of the important Foreign Relations Committee. When he wasn't going to eat his dinner at a party, Green could often be seen walking and eating a bag of popcorn, purchased in the Union Station. He walked regularly between his home in the University Club and the Capitol, about two miles, for exercise—and to save money. When he went to parties he rode in streetcars or buses wherever he could.

Drinking was as popular on Capitol Hill as it was elsewhere in the capital, if not more so. However, there was a self-imposed although religiously observed law that no alcohol should be served or taken while Congress was in session.

A member could come to the floor drunk and some did so. Once a senator rose on a point of privilege to ask that the record show that he was not sitting in his own seat because a colleague was slumped there in drunken slumber. He didn't want the public in the galleries to identify him as that slumping senator from the seating charts provided for visitors.

Many senators and representatives assembled for refreshments in capital hideaways or their own offices immediately after daily adjournment. Generally these groups crossed party lines in their affection for John Barleycorn, the only requirement for membership being a good capacity, an engaging manner and a devotion to Bacchus. Considerable business was done at many such gatherings.

Vice President John Garner was one of the more celebrated of the Capitol Hill hosts. Many a piece of legislation was pushed to victory or defeat at quiet sessions in his office near the Senate chamber, where he was ever ready "to strike a blow for liberty," which meant three fingers of sour mash bourbon in a water glass with a water chaser. Garner was an early-to-rise and an early-to-bed man, retiring about 9 P.M., when he could, in his apartment in the Washington Hotel. This gave him ample time for striking blows in the morning and late afternoon.

When FDR called on his Vice President to throw in the towel of defeat on the doomed Court-packing plan, Garner called Wheeler into his office and suggested "striking a blow for liberty." Then he called for a second. Nothing was said about surrender until Garner began:

"You know, Burt, the longer I've lived, and the more I've seen in Washington, the more convinced I am that in the Senate it's more important to have guts than brains. And you've got guts!"

"You mean," Wheeler teased, "that I haven't any brains?"

"I said you got guts."

Not until then did Garner tell Wheeler he could write his own ticket on the defeat of Roosevelt.

Garner had a trait which endeared him to newsmen, and especially to me; he never denied a story no matter what was written about him. I must confess I frequently took advantage of this, although not unduly, when I found his name on the White House calling list, generally on a Saturday when Congress was not in session. I knew Garner had sought the appointment, because FDR never called him, to warn against some course of action. Garner made no secret of his hopes of setting FDR straight. I knew Garner wouldn't deny my story and that the White House couldn't because my report was an accurate, if deduced, estimate of what he had to say.

On Inaugural Day, 1941, I went to Garner's office for a final taste of "liberty" he was enjoying with a few friends, very few, because he was relinquishing power and out of favor. Then he went to the Union Station with Mrs. Garner and boarded a train for home in Uvalde, Texas. No one came to see him off except the few friends. The bigwigs were lunching at the White House just before the inaugural parade and others were taking their places in the reviewing stands.

One of the most dedicated and enthusiastic capital drinking clubs was in the House. There was a group of members from both parties that met every Saturday for an afternoon and evening of drinking. If I wanted any member of the group, I always knew where to find him by inquiring by telephone until I found the office which had been selected for that day's festivities.

In the office of Paul Shafer of Michigan at one such gathering, I found him drinking with Dewey Short of Missouri and Frank Fellows of Maine, along with others. While I was getting information from Shafer, Representative Cliff Davis of Tennessee, who had been in earlier, returned.

"Paul," Cliff said, "I'm leaving for home and going through Virginia, where they don't serve liquor on Sunday. Can you give me a drop for the road?"

"Sure thing, Cliff," said Shafer, who went to his safe and pulled out a bottle of bourbon, and extended it toward Davis.

"I don't want a whole bottle," Cliff said.

Shafer opened the bottle he had taken from his safe, dug an empty bottle of the same brand from his wastebasket and solemnly poured almost all from one into the other. He put in the cork and handed it to Davis.

"Thanks, Paul," said Cliff. "I just wanted one for the road." And he walked out with the bottle in his pocket, a bit of mud for his eye.

WAR—AT LONG LAST

ROOSEVELT WAS A CONSTANT READER of the *Tribune;* his insatiable curiosity impelled him to peek at what his enemies were saying. He reacted even more quickly to criticism by friends. I was, of course, delighted to have him as a reader, because it is good to know one is read where he most wants to be.

Once, in the days immediately before the war, FDR was so roused to anger by criticism that he summoned the Secret Service and gave orders to bar a half dozen newsmen from an impending press conference by force, if necessary. He gave instructions that Early was not to be informed of his order, being aware that Steve would countermand it.

He named those to be barred: Arthur Krock of the New York *Times;* David Lawrence, columnist and editor of U. S. News and World Report; Paul Mallon, a King Features columnist; Westbrook Pegler, columnist for the same syndicate; John O'Donnell of the New York *News* and myself. Pegler was in his home at Tucson, Arizona, and O'Donnell was with the British Army in France. Krock, Lawrence and Mallon never attended the conferences, so that left me as the sole target.

James Sloan, my good friend and a veteran of the Secret Service since the turn of the century, planned to make a production of the incident. He knew I was the only one who would attend the news conference. He selected two of the tallest and huskiest of his fellow agents and instructed them to pick me up and carry me out when I came through the door of the Executive Offices. He didn't tell me, knowing I would put up a battle. He did tip off photographers that there would be a good picture story and told them to wait outside the doors.

Unfortunately for me, Early got wind of the order and canceled it. When I came to the door nothing happened, but Sloan called me into the little private office the agents had off the entrance to the White House press room. He told me what the orders had been and what he had planned. I could only thank him for his good intentions.

When the conference ended, Early pulled me into his office and told me what a great favor he had done me by cooling off the President's scheme. I pretended I knew nothing.

"With a friend like you, Steve," I said with mock seriousness, "I have no need for enemies. You just kept me from being a national figure and a great hero of the press, something like Peter Zenger, only a lot smarter."

"Well," Steve countered, "I couldn't let the Boss make a damned fool of himself, could I?"

Sloan, a young sheriff's deputy from Danville, Illinois, joined the White House Secret Service detail of two men in days when TR thought it "bully" to take dinner guests—white tie, tails and all—into Rock Creek Park on a hike, through the creek itself at times. Sloan found life less strenuous under the portly William Howard Taft and under the scholarly Wilson. The latter once asked Sloan to take him on one of TR's hikes, which he did, but he had an automobile trail discreetly behind, so that when the President tired, he was picked up and driven home. Wilson took the walk only once.

When he was about to retire Sloan asked me to help him with his memoirs, which I was happy to do, but I soon found out his respect for the presidency was so great, he would not permit the publication of his best stories because he felt they would bring the office into disrepute.

Another story, perhaps one of the most dramatic ever known to the Executive Mansion, was the time he saved Harding from committing murder in his office. I printed the story, on which I took notes at the time we were exploring the possibility of selling his life story, when Sloan died.

One day while he was on duty outside the President's office, Sloan heard a curious threshing sound in the room. He knew that Charles R. Forbes, chief of the Veterans' Bureau, who was under fire for questionable fiscal policies, had an appointment and was inside.

Forbes, who had a good war record, served in the Army. He came out of the conflict a colonel with the Distinguished Service Medal and the Croix de Guerre. He had entertained the Hardings in Honolulu when the Ohioan was in the Senate. Harding gave his friend a federal job in which he was in charge of the purchase of land, and the erection and equipment of veterans' hospitals. As administrator, Forbes became a systematic looter and profiteer.

Without knocking, Sloan eased open the office door and saw Harding with his fingers wrapped around Forbes's throat. The administrator was bent over the desk of the enraged President. Sloan pried Harding's fingers from the neck of the terrified official, who fled and didn't draw an easy breath until he reached Europe early in February 1923.

Other Secret Service men, like Sloan, would have given their lives to protect FDR but were hardly enamored with him or his policies. These gave me tips on inside shenanigans. One called me even as FDR was being made up by a Hollywood make-up artist, who had been imported to cover his worn and haggard appearance in the 1944 campaign.

My relations with Roosevelt were cooling, but had not snapped entirely in early 1941. Even in his most solemn moments FDR was ready for a laugh. At the 1941 inaugural, I left the press stands to search for a friend, Chief of Detectives McCarthy of Miami, who was among the policemen recruited from all over the country to swell presidential protection.

I went unchallenged in my search because I was known to the Secret Service men. Soon I found myself beside the podium as FDR came to take his oath. My appearance there surprised him so much that he exclaimed:

"What in hell are you doing here?"

"Looking for a friend," I explained. "I have one even though you may doubt it."

He had to laugh.

With the war coming closer, ready access to the President was shut off for all in the press, but critics were flung into coventry. There were no more intimate suppers of scrambled eggs in the White House, picnics at Hyde Park and long trips anywhere. When the war came restrictions grew even more rigid.

The sound of war drums was in the air as early as 1937 in Spain, Japan, Italy and Germany. Roosevelt revealed he was thinking of war in 1937, but the country generally refused to believe it. At the dedication of the Outer Drive Bridge in Chicago, against the background of a Tribune warehouse on which Colonel McCormick had the word "UNDOMINATED" painted in letters several feet tall, Roosevelt spoke on the foreign situation. Only eleven days before Adolf Hitler and Benito Mussolini had held their first meeting in three years at Munich, an event marked by much goose stepping, military strutting, elaborate salutes, camera posturing and verbal bombast.

In his bridge speech, the President declared that war must be treated as a contagious disease to be countered at the first outbreak or threat of an outbreak by a "community quarantine" of the infected nations, especially the bad guys who resorted to war by the good guys who hated war. He said America was prepared to act in community with peace-loving nations. Later, he was to brand nations which did not get into the war, like Switzerland, Ireland and Sweden, as nonpeace loving.

At that time liberals hated war above all things. They were not happy with the suggestion of military involvement or policy, which was to bring us into World War II, Korea and Vietnam. The change in liberal thinking was two years away, when the liberals put themselves in the front rank of interventionists for a war they were sure would bring the one world of their dreams.

The only time I have ever seen the press really take on Roosevelt was after the Chicago speech. Both the liberals and conservatives, like myself, flung a sustained barrage of questions on involvement at a session on the lawn of the family home at Hyde Park for more than two dozen newsmen who had accompanied him on the western trip. FDR did not defend himself, as it was evident that his mellifluous tones and popularity were being manipulated by those who believed the Berlin-Rome axis should be contained.

If FDR were baffled by the pace of events in Europe, we were even more so when he tried to explain them. With the return of Leon Blum to power in France in the summer of 1936, he devoted an entire press conference to an exposition of the French situation. It was so disjointed he had us reeling, because it was obvious that he had forgotten much of the lesson he had been taught, probably by Adolph A. Berle in the State Department. Roosevelt hailed the leader of the French coalition of leftists, labor and middle-of-the-road parties as the savior of France, applauding Blum's radical reforms in agriculture, banking and labor as the New Deal in France. Then, he concluded that the reforms wouldn't work because it was already too late to save France. He added that the great crime of the French was that they hadn't put Blum in power four years before, when FDR went in. It was just as well this conference was put off the record.

As a matter of cold fact, Roosevelt was not the all-wise or all-seeing father of his people his idolaters portrayed him during the war. He toyed with the idea of declaring war against Japan after the bombing of the USS *Panay* in China, as urged by Admiral William D. Leahy, chief of naval operations. Leahy argued that Japan could be blockaded into surrender, which would prove a powerful deterrent to such aggression-minded nations as Germany and Italy. Roosevelt fought the war on maps for a few days and then told Leahy he could not go to war because Charley Michaelson, who was no more than publicity director for the Democratic National Committee, "wouldn't let me."

In the Spanish Civil War he wavered in support of Francisco Franco and the radical so-called Loyalist Government. As Communist domination and support of the radicals grew, FDR came to regret actions which helped Franco. When Nazi legions rolled into Czechoslovakia, Roosevelt sent a personal message to Mussolini begging him to intervene. FDR's spokesmen were to boast that FDR was the architect of the appeasement of Hitler at Munich. Top spokesmen said Mussolini had intervened at FDR's request and five days later Hitler invited British Prime Minister Neville Chamberlain to Munich after pulling back his troops.

When the appeasement became a matter of shame, FDR was to deny any part in it. In the 1940 campaign, Willkie charged FDR had boasted of his role in the appeasement. Hull indignantly denied the

Willkie charge, but in his memoirs Hull reported that FDR had actually sent the message to Mussolini.

In this period FDR thought he had the British ambassador Sir Ronald Lindsay in his pocket, as mesmerized as many American followers. Yet, Sir Ronald, who had known FDR in his days as Assistant Secretary of Navy, was even then writing his estimate of the American President to the foreign office, an estimate which was not made public until 1970.

"In the first place," Sir Ronald reported, "he appears to be extremely obstinate and to dislike opposition, which makes him prefer men who will 'go along' with him, and in the second place, his intellectual powers are only moderate and his knowledge of certain subjects, particularly finance and economics, is superficial."

Lindsay retired in 1939 and was succeeded by Lord Lothian, who died suddenly at his post in 1940. In 1941, Lothian was succeeded by Lord Halifax, who came to his post aboard the HMS *King George V*, then Britain's newest and mightiest battleship. FDR went to greet Halifax off Annapolis, aboard the *Potomac,* as another gesture of sympathy toward embattled Britain.

Also he undoubtedly thought his cordiality and his great charm would unbend the austere envoy, but Halifax wrote his foreign office that Roosevelt was "a baffling character of only moderate ability, whose advisers were second-rate men."

These judgments were rendered even as the ambassadors were working their best to have FDR exert his powerful voice to bring America in support of the British cause. During the war, Field Marshal Viscount Alan Brooke, while finding FDR personally charming and engaging, added that he did not think "his military is on a par with his political sense." Lord Moran, Churchill's personal physician, while also acclaiming FDR's political acumen, accused him of being jealous of the British Prime Minister for assuming the role of "leader of the free world."

Nor did all the American leaders FDR courted accept him at his exalted valuation of himself. Justice Oliver Wendell Holmes, whom Roosevelt professed to venerate, said of him: "A second-class intellect but a first-class temperament."

In this uneasy period, Captain Patterson and the New York *News* became involved in an incident which illustrates the easy simplicity of the times, critical as the period was. At the time the situation was regarded as most grave, although from a period of more than thirty years, it is hardly more than amusing.

The genial and gifted Bob Conway of the *News*, the son of an American artist and his Italian model-wife, had been assigned to Washington, when O'Donnell went with the British Army. Conway found himself in the same hotel as Secretary of State Hull. Being an engaging gentleman, Conway persuaded a hotel switchboard operator to cut him in on the Secretary's telephone calls, which paid off with relatively little news, but provided background material of inestimable value.

Conway felt such enterprise should be rewarded. He wrote a letter to his editor boasting of his pipeline and inviting a raise for his good work. He left the letter unfinished in his typewriter, when two members of the White House secretarial staff, Grace Tully and Roberta Barrows, whom he had invited to drop by for drinks, knocked at his door.

While he was in the bathroom, watering the scotch, one of the secretaries casually read the unfinished letter. Back in the White House the two women promptly reported on Bob's raise gambit. At the next Cabinet meeting, FDR staged one of the surprises he so dearly loved. He cautioned his official family to exercise extreme caution of their lines of communication, announcing he had evidence that a reporter had succeeded in tapping the phone line of one of them.

Hull, who was concerned about the international situation and who considered himself above such snooping, began sifting the papers before him, being anxious to get down to business. Watching him carefully, Roosevelt sprung his surprise.

"I mean you, Cordell," he explained.

Roosevelt enjoyed the confusion of his Secretary of State and the consternation of the others. He identified Conway and his method but did so with relish rather than concern, in much the same way he was amused rather than disturbed by quarrels involving those on his team. However, the *News* did recall Conway, which was hardly the reward he hoped for, although he was not loath to leave the capital.

As war neared, my life was complicated a bit by ostracism, which I met in some official circles and among my colleagues, but not much. My friends in the military who did not enjoy seeing America stripped of powder and weapons, were concerned that the nation was being rendered impotent. I learned that FDR had ordered American submarines into infested waters, inviting attack as a means of overcoming sentiment at home against entry into the war. When this failed he was to shift his attention toward getting into the conflict by the back door of the Pacific.

Before and during the war, I found the embassies of occupied countries had excellent intelligence and were eager to share it with friends. Personal friendships endured. I was able to do more by telephone than many another reporter could by running around. I always favored personal contact to the "grand inquisitor" type of reporting in which newsmen ask sharp, irritating questions of men they do not know personally.

The only ostracism that hurt came from frightened colleagues, who thought that I was going to be jailed for treason because of my opposition to entry into the war. A few of the more timorous even crossed the street, when they saw me approaching. I lost no sleep over such slights; they left no scars. I never joined the America First movement, although I was in sympathy with its goal of keeping out of war, because I didn't like the activity of Communists in that organization before Hitler attacked Russia. Communism had become a tarnished ideology when Russia attacked Finland and when the Ribbentrop-Molotov pact precipitated the war in the resulting attack on Poland.

I continued to get exclusive stories, even from the White House. Just before the war, Early called me in to see him on what he said was a matter of importance. In his office he said Lowell Mellett, the former editor of the Washington News, who had been put on the White House staff, had been drawing up a censorship code. Early said there was nothing unusual about the code, but what concerned him was that Mellett was proposing himself as chief of the unit.

"He's a Torquemada at heart," Early snarled.

I interrupted to say that Torquemada was a much maligned figure in history.

"All right, that's what I am trying to tell you," Early went on. "Mellett's worse than Torquemada. All I'm asking is that you write the story; it will help me see that he doesn't get the job. He would be a national disaster."

I did write the story and there was a stir in Congress that cost Mellett the job. It went to Byron Price, former Washington bureau chief of the Associated Press, who gathered an able and understanding staff about him, including Nat Howard of the Cleveland *News*, Bill Mylander, later Republican publicity chief, Jim Warner, later of the New York *Herald Tribune*, and Bill Steven, who became editor of several newspapers. I had many dealings with the office, all pleasant even when the going became difficult. Mellett could never forgive me and called me during the war to abuse me late at night when he would be emboldened by drink.

In spite of our friendship, Early didn't spare the *Tribune* when he had to hit, although he generally left me out of any condemnation. In June 1940, the cryptic Hull dropped a line at his news conference, which lit a light bulb in my head. He brushed off France as though it were no longer in the war. I went around to State Department friends, employing an old reportorial bit of bait, remarking: "It's too bad about France . . ."

Everywhere this opening evoked condemnation of France, but praise for Paul Reynaud, the premier. There were remarks that the French deserved their fate, so that it became obvious to me that France was about to surrender.

I sought out Sumner Welles, whom I respected as an ideal diplomat. I had accompanied Welles on his supposed peace mission to Italy, Germany, France and England early in the year. In the course of that journey, the worried British unjustly suspected him of giving aid and comfort to the Nazis, which I was able to confound. Some high Nazis assumed that because I was against the war that I was in sympathy with them. They confided their conviction that Welles was doing everything he could to injure their cause. Welles asked me if he could report this to the department as the best of answers to the British, which action I was glad to authorize.

Welles was always aloof and dignified; when he came to Paris, the French quipped that a new cocktail had been created and named after him, the sole ingredients being ice and water. In his office I told Welles I had the story that the French were going to surrender, but Reynaud had fought the step and would be forced out. I asked him whether he would write it if he were me. He said he was sorry, but he could not advise me. That was all the confirmation I needed.

When the story appeared in the early editions of the *Tribune* and the Washington *Times Herald,* the State Department attempted to kill it. The department's press officer insisted that there was not a word of truth to it. He added that he was not asking for a denial but wanted the story killed, because a mere denial would not do.

The next morning in his news conference, Early branded the story as akin to treason.

"I am lacking in decent language to deny the story," he said. "The *Tribune* story was denied by the State Department from 5 P.M. last night. The *Tribune* disregarded that denial and continued publication of an erroneous story, knowing that it was erroneous. That leads me to wonder whether all the news in America is published from an American point of view or a foreign point of view."

Early did not mention my name.

Five days later Reynaud was forced out of office and France surrendered. Steve told me privately that he knew my story was right, which was why he didn't mention me by name, but he had to deny the story because he had seldom seen "the Boss so angry."

Later I learned that Bert Hulen of the New York *Times* had the story, but his editors decided against printing it, but whether from an American or foreign point of view I could not say.

Our last trip to Warm Springs with the President came just before the Pearl Harbor attack. Early came along, although he disliked presidential travel because the situation was critical. With Steve was a curvaceous secretary, who was cuddling up to various of the press regulars, including me, and had some of them panting. I went to Early and told him to call his girl off of me; I didn't like the role of being protective coloration. He flared up, but then had to acknowledge laughingly that I was a bit sharper than most of my colleagues. I told him that Carol didn't believe in sharing the wealth as far as I was concerned.

As a result of this incident, Early took me into his confidence. He told me we would probably return to Washington the next morning. He urged me to bake the ham which a half dozen of us living together in one of the Foundation cottages had purchased.

He liked the way I baked and glazed it with sherry, now and then inviting himself to dinner in my home for this dish.

Steve confided that we knew every move the Japanese were making. This mental bell was to grow louder in tone in the months ahead. Steve repeated we knew every move as fast as it was made. Because of this knowledge, we had to return at once to Washington; war was imminent.

Even then I reasoned that we had to have a spy in the Japanese Government at the highest level, but I didn't see how he could transmit his reports easily and quickly. So I concluded that we had broken the Japanese diplomatic code. This conclusion was one not requiring any great deductive powers. Everyone knew, but few remembered, that we had broken the Japanese naval code during the naval disarmament conference in Washington in 1921. All this was detailed in a book by the man who directed the breaking, Herbert O. Yardley, *The Black Chamber*, which I had read and remembered. I read it again with greater interest because it seemed to support my hunch. American intelligence was furious with Yardley for revealing the code-breaking coup, so much so that he was not invited to take any role in cryptology before or during the war.

It wasn't long before my suspicions were confirmed. Friends in the army and navy intelligence acknowledged that the code had been broken. There was nothing I could do about it under censorship, but I did keep after it. For four years I collected bits and pieces of the story, which resulted ultimately in a congressional investigation. The Administration maneuvered the inquiry into a whitewash of Washington responsibility for Pearl Harbor. However, they merely scotched the snake and didn't kill it, so that Pearl Harbor is becoming to be recognized more and more as FDR's road to war.

I was not to get public credit for the code-breaking story, because J. Loy Maloney, then managing editor of the *Tribune*, had let himself become involved in a censorship storm, which threatened indictment and even closing of the *Tribune*. So when John T. Flynn, a great newspaperman and a true liberal in that he detested war, got a corner of the story and asked me about it, I turned over the full story to him and put him in touch with all the witnesses. Flynn put the story into a pamphlet, *The Final Secret of Pearl Harbor*, which the *Tribune* printed after the war ended. The pamphlet launched the congressional investigation.

I was awarded the Edward Scott Beck prize, established by our former managing editor, for a story I didn't write. I did play a role behind the scenes in plotting the strategy of anti-Administration forces in the investigation, so that I knew it all, including the tremendous pressure which was brought to bear to hide Washington responsibility.

As he edged closer to war, Roosevelt began playing games with the press and with the public. He had already launched Lend-Lease, which was neither a loan nor a lease, but an outright gift of war supplies and strategic materials. He transferred fifty destroyers to Britain in return for sites for bases in that country's Caribbean islands. Colonel McCormick got the first hint of this transfer, which was of questionable legality. He ordered me to get the story, but I couldn't because it was known only to a few. When it was sprung by FDR at a Cabinet meeting, there was considerable surprise. Later the colonel sent me on a visit to all these bases.

In August 1941, the press regulars were told that FDR would go to New London, Connecticut, to inspect a submarine base there and then go fishing. We knew this could not be so, because every brass hat of any importance in the Army and Navy was mysteriously missing from the capital. We were put up in quarters at Swampscott, Massachusetts. Every day we got bulletins, supposedly from the *Potomac*, telling about good weather and fine fishing. We knew this was nonsense, but couldn't prove it. I asked my editors to check with London to determine whether there had been a similar exodus there, but censorship was so strict that nothing was allowed through.

Then on August 14 we got word that Roosevelt and Churchill had met at Argentia, Newfoundland, and drafted a joint declaration, which became known as the Atlantic Charter. This was a lot of high-sounding words about no aggression, no territorial changes and the right of peoples to choose their own form of government. I knew in my bones that Roosevelt had gone to the meeting to make commitments. I was sure of it when he told congressional leaders he had made no commitments and when Churchill made a speech in the House of Commons, clearly intimating, but not saying so directly, that the vast American potential would soon be theirs.

I knew a number of junior planners who had been taken on the trip. When they returned I found them all quite concerned and worried. I knew that they were appalled by commitments that had been made, but I could only hint at the fact. Not until after the war did Hull and Welles reveal that FDR had agreed to take over protection of the Azores, the Portuguese islands off the coast of Spain, to deliver a warning to Japan on aggression that was an ultimatum, and other co-operation which made the United States a silent partner in war. FDR wouldn't let Churchill announce the commitments and insisted on the drafting of the Charter, which was no more than a smoke screen.

In the fall of 1941, a master plan was evolved, with White House support, to offset the *Tribune*'s potent voice against entry into the war. This was the founding of the Chicago *Sun* by Marshall Field II. In order to help the paper get an Associated Press franchise, then a guarded possession, FDR had FBI agents call upon various small-town publishers and urge them to support Field's bid for a franchise. J. Edgar Hoover, head of the FBI, later showed me the order he had received to undertake a campaign, which he considered above and beyond his unit's functions. The *Tribune* knew about it because several courageous editors resisted and denounced the White House move. Roosevelt did get Field the service, however.

In anticipation of the bow of the *Sun*, Maloney ordered all members of all bureaus to produce a scoop. Some editors are scoop slap happy, yet when they find themselves with an exclusive they are often uneasy, because press services do not confirm their news. Maloney was such an editor and he always seemed to believe that tomorrow's paper would have plenty of room for such scoops, but when that morrow comes news columns are as tight as ever with events that demand publication.

About this time General H. H. (Hap) Arnold, chief of the Air Force, was concerned that America was being stripped of its defenses. There wasn't enough TNT, for example, to repulse anything more than a rowboat. Weapons were being shipped, along with the highly prized Norden bomb sight.

An air force colonel on Arnold's staff appeared at the office of Senator Wheeler, the fighting noninterventionist, who had jolted Roosevelt by charging his foreign policy would "plow under every third American boy." The colonel offered to place in Wheeler's hands the war plans, made at the direction of the President, which called for ten million Americans in the armed services to carry on a global war.

Wheeler hesitated to reveal the plans on the Senate floor, being disturbed over ethical questions posed by their disclosure. So he offered them to the *Tribune* through Chesly Manly, the *Tribune*'s able Senate man. Manly rejoiced and so did Maloney. The air force colonel brought the plans to Wheeler's home on Joslyn Street. Wheeler turned them over to Manly, who wrote the story which the *Tribune* held for about a week in order to greet the *Sun* with a major scoop.

During that week I opposed publication, not so much as a violation of secrecy but because of McCormick's military rank and record. I did not think, in view of that record, it behooved the *Tribune* to publish what Wheeler felt constrained to pass. Also I knew it is the business of the military to have plans for war in every corner of the world, even against friends, and these plans are constantly being drawn and redrawn.

I now believe I was wrong in my opposition, because the American people had a right to know what its leaders were doing: planning war when they were pretending to keep out of the conflict. Actually the plans underestimated the commitment, because some sixteen and one-half million Americans served in World War II.

When the *Sun* made its bow, it appeared on the street with an innocuous headline about a growing revolt in the Balkans while the *Tribune*'s 144-point-type headline screamed: "TRIBUNE HAS WAR PLANS." It all became academic within a week, because the Japanese hit Pearl Harbor and the *Tribune* supported victory in the war as strongly as its rival.

The *Tribune* came under heavy critical fire in the interventionist press even to charges of treason. Some thirty years later the same segment of the press was to glorify the stealing of the Pentagon papers, a secret study on the war in Vietnam. These newspapers said the people had a right to know what was in the papers, forgetting they had denied that right when it might have meant keeping out of World War II.

No one suspected Wheeler of being the source of the war plans story. However, he made no secret of his role among friends and acknowledged his role in his memoirs, *Yankee From the West*. There were only six copies of the plan, so suspicion fell on the military. Because I covered the Army and Navy, some investigators got the bright idea that the military had slipped me the plans and that I had passed them on to Manly.

My home phones were tapped—I had two lines—and the *Tribune*'s office phones were also tapped. I had a Washington police lieutenant, an expert on bugging, check the phones. He came from an examination of the lead box to my home, saying he had never seen such a setup, that I had taps on taps. He found that my telephones were being monitored by the FBI, military intelligence, naval intelligence and the Anti-Defamation League. This didn't concern me or my colleagues, although I made it known widely. Most of my colleagues felt it served me right for my opposition to the war. Today bugging seems to be the crime of crimes.

About this time, Albert C. Wedemeyer, then a major in the war plans unit, who had helped draw up the plans, collected and deposited an inheritance. When the money appeared in his bank balance, G2 jumped to the conclusion that the *Tribune* had paid him the sum for the war plans, probably through me. Al was taken over the inquisitorial jumps but was able to prove where his money came from.

I had my suspicions on the source of the leak at the time, but never breathed them over my phones or to the various military investigators who spent much time questioning me. As a result of the story Arnold got what he wanted—more arms and equipment. We were quite friendly, because I was early convinced of the value of air power. The general was the source of many a good story and generally these advanced the Air Force.

FDR often let cats out of the bag, being unable to control his love for dramatic surprises. Wallace was probably the greatest single leak of military information during the war. I don't think he ever fully realized the value of what he revealed. I got the date of the African landing indirectly from FDR as well as the original date of D-day. Roosevelt revealed the plan to invade Africa a few days before it was launched at a White House conference with labor leaders. Ben Goldstein, a Chicago attorney for AFL leader William

Green, crawled under a rug in my office to whisper the African landing would be on the next Saturday.

Green had offered me the post of publicity director for his organization, which I was able to pass on to Philip Pearl, Universal News White House correspondent, when that service folded. Philip was on vacation when his job disappeared. As another proof of the simplicity of those days, I knew that Harry Hopkins was at Belmont Park playing the horses and suspected Pearl might be with him. I called Harry and told him to get me Phil. Harry was a bit annoyed at having his presence announced over the loud speakers; when I explained he gladly became my errand boy. Neither the *Tribune* nor I was ever antilabor!

McCormick tried to disassociate himself from the war plans story, although he sent a telegram congratulating the bureau "on the greatest scoop in history." The wire was framed and hung in Henning's office but disappeared after the colonel visited the bureau early in the war.

On this visit the colonel, who didn't care for the critical heat he was receiving, asked Manly for a copy of his story, saying he had not read it. He certainly had, but evidently wanted to pretend to clean skirts if an investigation developed.

When we made our hurried return from Warm Springs, just before Pearl Harbor, I went into huddles with my military friends. They confided that the Japanese fleet was on the move, probably toward Singapore. The night before the attack, a pleasant December evening, I spent hours in the State Department, where it was evident that a crisis was impending. Several times that evening, I walked across the White House grounds, passing the lighted Executive Mansion.

I would have done far better if I had made my station there, but I saw no activity; the hurried visits of the military were disclosed years later. Late that night I wrote my story, which the Washington *Times Herald* carried the next morning under the banner line: "JAP FLEET STEAMING TO ATTACK." Unfortunately, the story was nowhere near as prophetic as the headline, because I had the Japanese headed for Singapore, where they did strike eventually, and not for Pearl Harbor.

The next day I was listening to the Redskin football game, when a bulletin announced the surprise attack. I raced to my next-door neighbor, Francis Paxton Old, then a navy lieutenant commander, later an admiral. He had recently been assigned to Washington from Hawaii. He called his superior, who in turn called Chester W. Nimitz, who was to gain five-star rank. Nimitz was ever ready to acknowledge he got his first news of the attack from me. Old and I raced to our respective offices where both of us worked through most of the night.

The following morning I learned much of the extent of the attack. I wrote the story before the censorship code could be put into operation, giving the damage and loss of life. For this I was criticized by other reporters, who had much the same knowledge but suppressed it, although why they thought the Japanese could not see and photograph what they had done, I could never understand.

My name had been listed among a dozen newsmen, who were to be offered commissions in the event of war by Alexander Day Surles, a captain in the army press branch, who later became a major general in charge of public relations. My name was stricken by Mellett because of the grudge he bore me. It turned out to be a great favor to me. I might have won a colonelcy but I would hardly have become bureau chief.

I broke many stories on price variances in military procurement and various plans and proposals. From my contacts in the embassies of occupied countries I was able to break many stories of betrayal and double cross, such as the Soviet swallowing of Lithuania, Latvia and Estonia without protest. I was advised by Jan Ciechanowski, ambassador of occupied Poland, that Britain was running out on its promise to protect that nation's territorial integrity. The Allies surrendered Polish territory to Russia. The Czechs informed me that their country was about to be raped by Russia with approval of Allies who had screamed over the outrage of freedom by Hitler.

The Polish ambassador advised me in 1943 that Hull's trip to Moscow, which the press hailed as the greatest of diplomatic triumphs, was actually a failure, because the major object of his visit was to gain a pledge for the maintenance of the freedom of Poland. Hull did not achieve it, as he later acknowledged to me.

I was informed of the betrayal of General Draja Mikhailovitch, who was captured and executed by Marshal Tito. The latter was favored to rule the consolidated country by the British and Russians. I learned of the massacre of the flower of the Polish Army in Katyn Forest, which Communist propagandists blamed on the Nazis; and I played a part in having that crime investigated by Congress. I was advised of Chinese fears that Chiang Kai-shek and his Nationalist Government would be let down by his allies. I had many close friends among military attachés and intelligence units, who fed me tips.

I had fun in chronicling the gay social life of the Washington military set, while fighting men were dying. John Callan O'Laughlin, a former *Tribune* bureau chief, told me he had been asked to cut society news to births and marriages in his *Army and Navy Journal* as a result of my stories. Officers received instructions not to turn in such items.

The best of the stories on Washington doings was given to me by Casimir Romaine, the maître d'hôtel at the Carlton Hotel. He gave me the menu of the party which Bernard Baruch, the financier, gave for Harry Hopkins on his marriage to the former Louise Macy of New York in December 1943.

I had a field day listing such items as caviar with trimmings, pâté de foie gras, baked oysters, tortue claire, truite en gelée, homard en aspic, terrapin, chicken à la king, galatine of capon, cold tongue, beef à la mode, corned beef in jelly, turkey, chicken, Virginia ham, calves heads vinaigrette and much more. There were whiskey and champagne, of course.

Housewives couldn't begin to match such a feast by stripping themselves of ration points. The story was widely run and picked up. Indignation ran high. There was no defense, especially because Hopkins had just recently written a piece for *American Magazine* for a fee, warning his countrymen that stringent belt tightening was in store. He said that Americans would have to forgo milk and tea and predicted drastic curtailment of all civilian industries except coffinmaking.

The heat hit Baruch, who picked up the tab. Being extremely sensitive to adverse publicity he couldn't take it. He asked me to come to his apartment in the Shoreham Hotel, where he explained he had been trapped by Hopkins into giving the party. I took this with considerable salt; I knew that Baruch could always spot and cultivate a man of influence. Baruch said he had asked Hopkins what he wanted for a wedding present and Hopkins replied that he wanted one of Baruch's famous parties. So, Baruch said, he had no choice but to deliver.

Then Baruch confided that his gift was nothing to that Lord Beaverbrook had sent, which was a parure of emeralds. I didn't know at that moment what a parure was, but learned that it consisted of a tiara, necklace, bracelet and sometimes also a ring and brooch.

I considered Baruch a good source, but should have known better. My second story created another sensation. The White House ridiculed the story but did not flatly deny it. Later, I learned from Early that the gift was not a parure of emeralds, but an antique diamond necklace, worth several thousand dollars. Like Huck Finn, Baruch had stretched the story a bit to get himself off the hook.

Hopkins talked of suing but not until after he had returned the gift. Friends persuaded him that he could hardly come into court with clean hands and he would do well to forget it. I was sorry that the lady lost her bauble, but happy to break the story. I was no less happy to explode the story that FDR violated his own wage and price controls to give a sizable boost to Hopkins. The story was given to me by Lyle Wilson. He knew he could not get it on his own wire, unless he picked it up from me, because the United Press wanted no battle with the White House.

Hopkins, the White House intimate was a likable and friendly fellow, although a news target. In a Sunday magazine article, ordered by McCormick, I branded him as the Rasputin of the White House. He took the description in his stride, but it boiled the blood of Robert Sherwood, who claimed relationship to the great Protestant Irish patriot Robert Emmet. Sherwood, to whom I always referred as the author of *Idiot's Delight*, because it was an antiwar play and because of its more obvious connotation, had joined FDR's stable of ghost writers. FDR had more ghost writers than any other President, but then he was in office longer. In fact, he had more ghost writers than anyone with the possible exception of Adlai E. Stevenson, who had the reputation of being a master stylist even when he was delivering speeches that he had never read in advance.

Harry's role in the White House was more than that of a yes man, although that was an important phase of it. He was given to reading the rather mild erotica of that day and hunting for a second wife, when we first met. When he found his intended, he spent a good deal of time daydreaming about her, like most lovers. Aboard a presidential special in 1941, during an argument over a South American aid program, which I considered a waste, Hopkins told me he had been thinking of Louise Macy, when he and FDR were alone together in the White House a few nights before. FDR was talking.

"Suddenly, the Boss asked me what I thought of that," Hopkins told me. "I thought he had been engaged in one of his usual tirades against Hitler and quoting the Nazi, so I said: 'It's the silliest stuff I ever heard.' The Boss's face fell, so I knew I had said the wrong thing.

"I had to think fast to recover lost ground, so I said: 'Wait a minute, let me think, that idea was too big for me to grasp at first flush. But I see it now; it is sublime.' His face lit up and he grinned, so I knew I had regained lost ground."

Hopkins was an ailing man, which is why he gave up the Department of Commerce. Yet he undertook many war missions to London and to Moscow, when he was in no shape to deal with better and more rigid minds.

Lest anyone think I regard myself as a paragon, I hasten to admit I missed many stories. Much of my work was routine, based on releases. This is no history of the war or of Washington policy in the war. All of that is available. In my time I missed many great stories. Like any other good reporter I didn't enjoy getting scooped or failing to recognize the news behind the news.

One story I failed to get over the years still haunts me, so that I have every intention of tracking it down in the next life. After he had been let out of the Administration to make room for Wallace, Jesse Jones invited me to his office to give me a story. Generally, Uncle Jesse was as tight with news tips as he was with his own money. He began by recalling that he and Baruch had served together on the World War I War Industries Board and had always preserved an intimate relationship, which began when they took sisters as mistresses. He boasted he had the prettier one. Uncle Jesse warned that Baruch was an operator and had to be watched at all times, an observation that I was sure Baruch would have echoed about Jones.

Jones confided that Baruch had told him that in trying to cement his relations with the White House the financier had carried $500,000 in cash and put it on FDR's desk. Baruch said he told FDR, Jones went on, that while he, Baruch, was a man with a gift for making money, FDR was a great humanitarian, who could undoubtedly find worthy employment for the half million. Two weeks later, Jones reported, Baruch said he went back and laid another $500,000 on the same desk.

I realized that this was going to be a hard nut to crack, so I began flattering Baruch and cultivating his friends, like Herbert Bayard Swope. When I thought the time was ripe, I tackled Baruch in a roundabout way. I got a quick denial but I didn't give up. After FDR died, I noted that the million-dollar estate left by his mother had more than doubled, but that might have been due to wartime inflation. I flattered Baruch on his own writings and tried again. I got another denial.

"Mr. Baruch," I said, "just for my own confidential information, would you answer a hypothetical question?" When he nodded, I continued: "If you had made such a gift, would you tell me about it in view of federal restrictions on gifts?"

He didn't hesitate, but answered, "I would not."

This wasn't enough confirmation for me. I enlisted Swope, the great editor-reporter, who had been kind enough to compliment me on a number of my stories, as well as Pegler and George Sokolsky, the Hearst columnist, all of whom were friends of Baruch. I wanted to get the story out, if true, because it was a good one. I was prepared to surrender any personal glory. All agreed the story was highly possible, but I couldn't get confirmation. I had to give up.

Under the New Deal the capital had loomed large in American lives. Under wartime rationing, and price and wage freezes, it became every American's city hall. Naturally, I urged increases in the staff of the bureau until I pushed it up from four men to fourteen. Usually we got the best men from Chicago, but now and then we got problems.

I was horrified when I learned a new man was about to approach a former *Tribune* man with the Office of Price Administration and offer him money for scoops. I knew the man he was about to approach, George Barnes, was above bribery, so I called Maloney and urged the reporter's recall.

I was surprised when Maloney commended the reporter for enterprise in the bribery plan, but was recalling him because the reporter had invited a former Chicago bar girl to his room after one drink, which I considered amusing. With lifted eyebrows, the girl answered: "After only one drink?" She considered the story so good she told it to a Chicago reporter she knew who relayed it to Maloney.

Maloney let himself become involved in a censorship storm, which shook the Tribune Tower. It was the closest the paper came to disaster during the war and there would have been little or no support from papers who are today concerned about freedom of the press and the public's right to know. Most of them would have rejoiced over any misfortune to the *Tribune*.

Stanley Johnston, an alert and engaging *Tribune* correspondent, was aboard the aircraft carrier *Lexington*, where he became friendly with all, especially a navy commander, who gave him a copy of the Japanese fleet's order of battle in the Southwest Pacific. The *Lexington* was torpedoed. Johnston helped carry several wounded men to safety. In fact, only Captain Forrest Sherman and Admiral Fitch were behind him in leaving the stricken vessel. Johnston was recommended for the Navy Cross, but it was withheld by the storm that followed.

When the survivors of the *Lexington* were rescued, Johnston was returned to Chicago. He was in the *Tribune* city room the night news of the Battle of Midway reached the United States. He remembered the list the navy commander had given him aboard the *Lexington* and turned it over to Maloney, saying these vessels were undoubtedly among those defeated at Midway.

Maloney, who had up to that time submitted every line of war copy to the Office of Censorship, decided to be his own censor that night. He examined the code and found no proscription on the movements of enemy ships, so he ordered a story under a Washington dateline, giving a list of the enemy ships. Had he submitted the story to censorship, through the Washington bureau, it would have been passed instantly because, as he had discovered, there was no censorship of enemy ship movements.

The next morning, a Sunday, I was taken to task by the icy Admiral Ernest King. I was not easily awed by brass and considered

King arrogant. I gave him as good as he dished out, being confident the story was not the *Tribune*'s because it had not been submitted to censorship through the bureau. I knew it had not been written in the bureau despite its dateline. I assumed it had been picked up and rewritten from the wires or another paper. I was soon to learn how wrong I was and that Maloney had originated the story.

Knox, the publisher of the Chicago *Daily News*, was Secretary of the Navy. It was only natural that he should welcome any prospect for putting the *Tribune* out of business. FDR had no love for the paper. Therefore, the suggestion that the *Tribune* had informed the Japanese that we had broken their naval code was seized by the Administration.

Many still believe that the *Tribune* carried a story saying that the Jap code had been broken. Actually, the *Tribune* story merely listed the names of a number of Japanese battleships. The spelling of these names was that used in the naval code and not that listed in *Jane's Fighting Ships*, the bible of the world naval craft. The Japanese couldn't get a copy of the *Tribune* and wouldn't have read it if they could.

The first actual word the Japanese had of the code breaking came in the interception of a news broadcast by Walter Winchell, who hated the *Tribune* and accused it of telling the enemy their code had been broken. The Japanese refused to believe the broadcast because Yardley, whose book was a best seller in Japan, had written that machine codes could not be broken. And to them, Yardley was the top code expert because he had broken their code at the Washington Conference on naval disarmament in 1921. They did not change their code. Another intercept months later enabled U.S. planes to shoot down Admiral Yamamoto, who had directed the attack on Pearl Harbor, aboard his plane in the Pacific.

A special grand jury was impaneled in Chicago to proceed against the *Tribune*. William DeWitt Mitchell, Attorney General in Hoover's cabinet, was named to bring the *Tribune* and, particularly, Colonel McCormick before a federal jury for trial and sentence. The grand jury could see no crime in the publication of a few more or less unpronounceable Japanese names, and voted a no bill. That night linotypers beat a salute of victory on their matrix cases when McCormick walked into the composing room.

Louis Rose, the *Tribune* circulation manager, took all the credit, although no one believed him. He said a sister of the foreman of the federal grand jury, a black, was killed in an auto accident, while the investigation was under way. When Rose learned she had a $2,500 *Tribune* accident insurance policy, clipped from the paper, he sent a circulation hustler out to her home to plunk the money on the coffin. Rose claimed it was his action and not the facts that influenced the jury. He could have had a point.

Maloney, who told me he had been walking beside the Chicago River, debating whether or not he should jump in, was relieved of a great burden. In time I was to wish he had jumped or that the colonel had not been so forgiving by nature, because Maloney was responsible for the regrettable *Tribune* eight-column line in November 1948: "DEWEY WINS ELECTION."

A year or so later, an editorial writer on the Washington *Post* and I sponsored Johnston, an Australian, for American citizenship. As we came out of the federal courthouse in the capital, where he had just taken his oath, I stopped the party on its steps.

"It has just occurred to me," I said, "that I have been guilty of the greatest disservice to my country since Benedict Arnold."

The code-breaking incident was to consume countless hours of my time, although I take no credit for the pleasant outcome. A far more taxing, although less threatening, censorship problem was of my own making. It was the story of the death march on Bataan, the barbaric cruelty inflicted on American soldiers taken at Corregidor on the fall of the Philippines. The march was one of eighty-five miles from Mariveles at the tip of the Bataan peninsula to San Fernando, under a merciless tropical sun, almost without food or drink, and without any display of mercy from vicious enemy guards.

One day a lawyer from Champaign, Illinois, August Meyer, came to my office for advice. He said he represented a client, one Major William E. Dyess, an air force officer, who had a story of the bloody trek in Bataan and his escape from captivity. He said *Collier's* magazine had offered $20,000 for the story, but he wondered if he might not get more. I asked him if he would take $21,000 from the *Tribune*.

Meyer, whom I had not known until that day, said his client was not interested in the money as much as the widest possible circulation for the story. I said the *Tribune* would syndicate the tale in other papers to provide a far greater audience than he could get in the magazine. I put in a call to Chicago City Editor Maxwell. He was quick to recognize the importance of the story and approved the $21,000 outlay. Later he was to claim he had been on the lookout for an eyewitness story of the death march, but all editors seem to like to pretend to omniscience.

The deal was quickly closed. Dyess was in an army hospital at White Sulphur Springs, West Virginia. Charles Leavelle, a reporter, was sent to get his story. Then the troubles began. The Army at first refused to let anyone talk to Dyess, but I broke that barrier through friends. When we got the story, the Office of Censorship refused to clear it. I was told confidentially the White House did not want the story out, because it might spark a public demand for more emphasis on the Pacific. There MacArthur was being denied men and supplies because the Administration was more interested in the war in Europe.

The excuse for not authorizing release of the story was that Dyess might be reassigned to the Pacific and would suffer for it if he ever fell into Japanese hands again. As far as I know, this bit of logic was never applied to any other story. There was also an argument that the story didn't belong to Dyess alone, but to several of his immediate comrades who escaped with him, as well, and all others who made the march. Efforts toward release went on for months. Meanwhile, Dyess died in a plane crash in California.

The *Tribune* lined up a considerable number of papers who were interested in the story. I suggested we forget the sale of the story to the papers and give it to the people. Senator A. B. (Happy) Chandler of Kentucky promised me he would read it on the Senate floor. When I reported this to the Office of Censorship, Nat Howard induced the Army to authorize release of the Dyess story. However, the Army insisted on releasing a condensed version of the story to all papers, a course I am sure would not have been adopted had any other paper than the *Tribune* had the Dyess tale.

When the *Tribune* got the story of Joe Foss, the ace marine war pilot in the Pacific, the Marine Corps, which had been helping him sell his war experiences, withdrew from the negotiations when the *Tribune* proved to be the highest bidder. Association with the *Trib-*

une wasn't regarded as the best way to promotion and pay. Foss favored the *Tribune* because his Fargo, North Dakota, home-town buddy, Walter Simmons, agreed to write it. Simmons was a *Tribune* war correspondent and became its Sunday editor.

For these and many other reasons the taps continued on my home throughout the war. My life was a tough one in those days, because Maloney was a driver. True, he drove himself harder than anyone else, but he bombarded me with as many as eighteen messages a day and innumerable phone calls. These were in addition to those I got from the colonel. At the height of the Dyess negotiations, I developed an ulcer in my left eye, which ultimately cost me all but a bit of peripheral vision in it. Overwork, lack of sunshine, no exercise and improper eating were contributory causes. Maloney gave me two weeks off, in the mountains of West Virginia, but Maxwell was to keep me hopping on the Dyess story.

Probably the main reason taps continued on my home and office phones was that it was known that I was continuing an investigation of my own into Washington responsibility for Pearl Harbor. I made it my business to know and question virtually everyone involved in the affair and thus learned of all the attempts to destroy records and change testimony. This became something of an obsession with me, because I was certain that Washington had maneuvered the nation into a war that the people did not want.

I knew that Colonel R. S. Bratton attempted to hand over a vital intercept of a code message from Japan which indicated the United States was a target, probably at Pearl Harbor, to General George Catlett Marshall, army chief of staff. Bratton had the message in a locked pouch. He was stopped at Marshall's office door by Colonel Walter Bedell Smith, who forced Bratton to open the pouch against all precedent for an "eyes only message." Smith said he would deliver it himself, after he read it. I also knew Colonel Otis K. Sadtler, who also attempted to have something done to warn the army and navy commanders at Pearl Harbor, General Walter Short and Admiral Husband E. Kimmel.

Bratton and Sadtler were never promoted although they served throughout the war. Bedell Smith became a lieutenant general and a millionaire industrialist after the war. I won't say he owed it all to the protection of Marshall, but the protection certainly didn't injure his career.

I learned that Marshall had gone horseback riding, when he should have been warning Short and Kimmel. I knew both commanders. I also knew navy Captain Laurance F. Safford, who played a major role in breaking the Japanese code and who resisted great pressure to have him deny that the key Japanese message "East wind rain," which spelled attack on the United States, had ever been received.

In the course of my investigation I found a call girl who was favored by Marshall. I thought for a time that he might have been in her apartment the night before Pearl Harbor. He claimed to have forgotten where he was that night. He had been found sitting on a log with his head in his hands on a bridle path, when searchers brought him word of the attack.

The answer was before my eyes all the time in the files of the Washington *Times Herald*, but I didn't know it. Marshall was among guests at a gathering of alumnae of his alma mater, Virginia Military Institute. For those interested, Marshall's relations with the call girl were not very exciting; the playing of classical records in her apartment.

I talked to Marshall's secretary and his sergeant. Admiral Harold R. Stark, the chief of naval operations, had been shifted to London, but other naval people were available. I knew that officers were being sent around the world in an attempt to induce many to change their stories. There were times when I despaired of hope that the truth would become known.

Not all of the military, by any means, were in my corner. There were many who would have liked to shut me up as much or more than they would have enjoyed shutting down the *Tribune*. One of these was Major General Clayton Bissell, who was chief of military intelligence. I broke so many stories out of G2, where I had many friends, that he was bent on my destruction. Most of the stories, because of censorship, were not sensational but clearly indicated I knew what was going on.

One Saturday afternoon Bissell forgot to lock his office safe, a major crime in G2. A friend of mine took a map from the safe, photographed it and gave the photo to me. The map wasn't of any importance, being a small map of Europe, one of many put out by the National Geographic Society. On six of these a reorganization by countries of the European desks in G2 had been inked. The only change was that Greece would become a part of the Russian desk's activities. I wrote a story intimating that Greece was being relegated to the Soviet zone of influence and offered the map as proof.

Monday morning Bissell ordered his five top aides into his office and called for a confession from the one who had supplied me the map. When none came he announced that he was going to have the man responsible busted and drummed out of the Army. Then, triumphantly, he announced all the maps were different because they had been inked individually. He ordered a return of the maps so they could be checked against the photo which went with my story. He really hit the roof when the map turned out to be his own. Not too long later, he was discovered loading an army plane in Europe with coffee, which he was employing as barter for valuables of the stricken enemy.

There was seldom a dull moment for me. All of my better news sources knew of the wire taps, so we had to arrange outside meetings for transmission of news.

Fortunately, I had a strong constitution; except for myopia, I had no physical problems. I could have eased my work load, having many offers of other employment, including one from Arthur Krock of the New York *Times,* and many from Mrs. Patterson, who wanted me as her editor on the *Times-Herald.* At times I did quit in battles with editors, but I was persuaded to reconsider. Eye and all, I have no regrets and I don't believe in dwelling on complaints. I would do it all over again, but I hope far better.

The situation was falling into confusion in Washington and in an election year. Having broken the third-term precedent, FDR showed not the slightest hesitancy about seeking a fourth term. At the State Department I was shown a flurry of contradictory directives, all signed "FDR." Some came from the President, but others were believed by State Department officials to come from Mrs. R. or Hopkins, both of whom were subject to suggestions from a variety of flatterers and intimates.

In 1944, the military situation was getting better all the time, so that victory was only a question of time. Things in Washington and around the nation, with Roosevelt occupied in war and conferences, were going from bad to worse. Congress was pulling away from under his thumb and from the New Deal.

Early in 1944, Roosevelt called for a 10½ billion-dollar tax boost. Congress cut it to 2.3 billions. The President let loose a blast impugning the good faith of Congress in a veto message. Senate Majority Leader Barkley exploded in anger and resigned. He called on Congress to override the veto, which it did overwhelmingly in both branches. After this victory Steve Early persuaded Barkley to withdraw his resignation.

THE STROKE OF DEATH

THE 1944 presidential campaign was a foregone conclusion even though all the politicians knew FDR was a dying man and the vice-presidential nomination became the greatest concern for many. It fell to Harry S Truman, the feisty Democratic senator from Missouri. Roosevelt couldn't have cared less about his running mate, having dumped two, and being sublimely confident he was going to live forever, not being able to imagine a world without himself.

The Republicans named Governor Thomas E. Dewey of New York and Senator John W. Bricker of Ohio. Dewey had joined the interventionist eastern establishment. Taft was not a contestant, having agreed to step aside in order to let Bricker make his pitch for the party nomination. Bricker lost to Dewey.

The major issues were the conduct of the war and the plans for peace. Dewey had most of the facts on the Washington responsibility for Pearl Harbor and was prevailed upon by Roosevelt not to use them. I was one of a small knot of speech-writer consultants—not the only one by any means—so I knew. I couldn't blame Dewey because the war was on and the first thing to do was win it, not question its beginnings.

I did become disillusioned with the governor when he did a complete about-face on Medicare. Our group got a proposed speech for delivery in Oklahoma City. When I saw the speech I was ready to walk out and so was Ben Stollberg, but John T. Flynn persuaded us to sit down and do a rewrite which was ultimately delivered. It seemed to me that if Dewey had no strong ideas of his own, he might not be an improvement.

FDR made relatively few campaign trips. In New York, he was loaded with Martinis to the point of being somewhat incoherent. It was a rather raw day and he was wrapped in a boat cloak against the weather as well as being fortified with drink.

In Washington, he attended a rally in the Statler Hotel, given by the International Teamsters Union, under the guidance of its president Dan Tobin, a combination of czar and zealot. There many teamster representatives became loaded and quite unruly. They challenged any opposition to Roosevelt to the point of beating up two young naval officers in a hotel corridor, because they did not consider them enthusiastic for the Commander in Chief.

I was rescued from possible trouble by Phil Pearl, who was in charge of press coverage, and Secret Service men. I could see that FDR was nipping more than usual. His delivery was slurred and he giggled a bit over what he considered his better passages. Roosevelt attended the AFL function as a sop for the dominant role Sidney Hillman of the CIO had assumed in the selection of Truman and was playing in Democratic politics.

FDR won the election handily, but not as well as he would have liked. His popular vote was down by two millions. He got fewer Democratic votes in New York State than Dewey got Republican votes. However, Roosevelt had done much to wreck the Democratic party in New York by his war with Tammany Hall and his support of fusion under Mayor Fiorello La Guardia. There is ground for the belief that he was the true founder of the American Labor Party in New York City.

On January 20, 1945, FDR was inaugurated for his fourth and last term. Three days after the brief rites on the South Portico of the White House, FDR went to Norfolk where he boarded the heavy cruiser USS *Quincy* for the Yalta Conference. It was to encompass the great betrayal of captive nations and defeat his impossible dream of one world.

Before FDR's departure I was scurrying about for some way to satisfy Colonel McCormick on his command that I "fix Europe." I did get an interview with Fleet Admiral Leahy, whom I had known for years and who was a near neighbor to my R Street home, as were Admiral Thomas C. Kinkaid, Pacific war hero, and Vice Admiral Alfred Johnson. Johnson had retired but was called back to serve on the joint Canadian and American defense command.

During our talk Leahy pointed to what he said was a message from MacArthur, which pleaded with the top aide to the Commander in Chief not to make any concessions in order to bring Russia into the war against Japan. The general, whom Leahy described as "our greatest, not even excepting Robert E. Lee," argued that Japan was approaching the point of surrender. He added that Russian aid could only be expected to be costly and of no value to any nation but Russia. The Communists had long hoped to make Manchuria a puppet state.

I broke the story of the MacArthur message immediately after the war ended and the Office of Censorship was shut down. I tried to get a copy of the message but could not find it among MacArthur's papers, which he had sent to the Pentagon. Nor could the general find it. It was not the first important paper to disappear from government files.

Roosevelt was a spent and exhausted man on the way to Yalta. He stayed most of the time in his cabin, although he did appear in a wardroom for lunch and dinner, and did attend nightly movies. Leahy told me that in conversations on the way over, Roosevelt kept saying that when he met Stalin, the President would insist on this or that point or this or that course of action. Every day, when he returned from meetings, Roosevelt would exhibit a memorandum, which Leahy would remind him was the exact opposite of what he had said he would insist upon. "I know, Bill," Roosevelt would say, according to the admiral. "But I'm tired and I want to go home. If I argue, they'll keep me fighting over a comma for a month or more."

What a setting for permanent peace was Yalta! Roosevelt was a broken man, only a few steps from the grave on the lawn of his Hyde Park estate. Some, who knew him well, like Jesse Jones, did not expect FDR would return alive from Yalta, but the coffin that returned aboard the *Quincy* was that of his military aide, Pa Watson, by then a major general. This death shook FDR. On his return voyage he spent most of his day playing solitaire, staring over the water or reading detective stories whose plots kept evading his comprehension.

Certainly FDR was in no shape to understand postwar problems or the significance of letting Russia into the war in the Pacific. But at his side was Alger Hiss, who did understand and who obviously didn't work to keep Russia and communism from gaining in the Far East. Harry Hopkins was also along but was so weak he spent most of his time in bed.

The host was Joseph Stalin, whose faculties were not dimming. Nor were his energies fading away. Photographs of the fateful conference reveal him as smiling. He must have wanted to laugh aloud, because he was the cat who swallowed an American canary. FDR thought he could charm Stalin. The more he tried, the more he gave in and the deeper became the winter of discontent of Churchill, who had charmed FDR himself so no one knew better that Roosevelt was being taken in by the wily Georgian.

Stalin got what he most wanted—dismemberment of Germany, domination of the liberated countries, a profitable role in Asia and three Soviet votes and a veto in UN. Roosevelt thought he got something—Russian participation in UN—and Churchill knew he had gained nothing but woe. Today it is all but forgotten that the Yalta agreement was drawn up by Sir Gladwyn Jebb, representing Britain, Andrei A. Gromyko, representing Russia and still cashing in on his service at Yalta to Russia, and Alger Hiss, representing the United States, at least technically. It is no wonder that Leahy confided on his return that he was heartsick over the outcome of this conference.

On his return February 28, 1945, Roosevelt arranged to address Congress on what he considered a diplomatic triumph. There was less interest in the speech than in the President's condition. He was wheeled into the well of the House, where he had formerly walked in his braces. He spoke from the well of the House rather than the podium. His delivery was not vibrant, but vague and even fumbling.

When he was wheeled out, he appeared to be near collapse. It seemed obvious to many that the end could not be far off, but many of the President's idolaters refused to believe it. The speech was the work of FDR's long-time ghost writer, Samuel I. Rosenman, who had been summoned from London to board the *Quincy* in the Mediterranean to lend his art toward making a victory out of defeat. Later, he acknowledged that FDR let his mind wander and was not any great help.

To me, FDR's decline was obvious at his news conferences. He didn't appear interested in the war or the presidency. His greatest interest seemed to be in planning new trips, a visit to San Francisco for the founding conference of United Nations, another visit to the Pacific and a journey to China. In his last weeks his condition came to be recognized by all reporters.

At one of his last conferences in the White House, Roosevelt was asked by Bert Andrews of the New York *Herald Tribune* to comment on a speech on the forming of UN by Harold Stassen, former governor of Minnesota and perennial Republican presidential candidate.

"Stassen?" the President asked querulously, his right hand trembling and groping uncertainly. "Who's Stassen?"

It was apparent the Chief Executive was not himself and a hurried "Thank you, Mr. President" ended the conference. Stunned reporters filed slowly out.

"What do you make of him?" asked a startled May Craig of the Portland, Maine, *Press-Herald*. She was a South Carolina born-and-raised grandmother, but the nation came to accept her as a New Englander because of her paper, although the so-called Yankee twang was more honeysuckle than lobster.

"He's like the last leaf on the tree," observed Bert Hulen of the New York *Times*.

At another news conference, Roosevelt baffled assembled reporters by going into a long exposition on flood control, which certainly had no relation to the war and little to public interest. Again the conference was cut short. Back in the office, I found a couple of paragraphs, which had apparently attracted the presidential eye and carried him back to the 1936 campaign, in which he had made flood control one of his themes.

It was about this time that he last spoke to me. He displayed a model of the floating dock used in the Normandy landing, which had been set up in a room across the corridor from the Oval Office. I was at the back of the room and left by the rear door and turned into the corridor into which he had been wheeled by a side door. We came face to face in the corridor.

His face lit up as he exclaimed, "Walter." I behaved badly and I regret it. I would not do it again and I am not proud of it, but I was sore in heart over the deaths of two young sons of friends. I looked into his eyes with stern disapproval. His eyes fell and he turned away.

MacArthur told me that he had found it almost impossible to get Roosevelt to talk about the conduct of the war against Japan during their meeting in Hawaii during the 1944 campaign. Instead, FDR chose to talk about World War I and the trip he made to Europe as Assistant Navy Secretary, when MacArthur was leading the Rainbow Division.

MacArthur and Roosevelt met at that time. The general knew FDR in Washington, because Roosevelt had continued him as chief of staff. MacArthur said he was shocked by Roosevelt's appearance in Hawaii, regarding him as a mere shell of the man he had known earlier.

Roosevelt left for Warm Springs March 29 and arrived there the next day. Admiral McIntire, his physician, who had regularly, especially in campaign years, pronounced FDR to be physically fit, did not accompany him. McIntire was to deny that FDR ever was treated for anything more than a persistent cold, a wen on his neck, an infected tooth and blamed Roosevelt's appearance on the rigors of travel. He denied that FDR had ever suffered a heart attack or a stroke, prior to that which carried him off.

Death came suddenly on April 12, 1945. FDR was having his portrait painted by Mrs. Elizabeth Schoumatoff, a Russian-born artist, for Mrs. Lucy Mercer Rutherfurd. Death was due to a massive cerebral hemorrhage, brought on by progressive arteriosclerosis, which McIntire had failed to note.

The President was not stricken while posing, as many believe. He had posed for an hour and was having lunch at a card table set up in front of his couch for himself and the two women guests, when he said: "I have a terrific headache," and slumped over.

I could never understand the flood of rumors that followed in the wake of Roosevelt's death, especially because the family might have squelched them in the beginning by adopting a policy of candor. One could understand their effort to be alone with their dead or as nearly so as possible, but, after all, FDR was President and belonged to the people.

A number of actions contributed to the flood of rumors, which were to occupy much of my time for months. I had to track them down and talk to all involved.

Mrs. Schoumatoff and Mrs. Rutherfurd were asked to leave at once. They were almost spirited away. Because the artist was Russian born, there were stories of a Communist murder plot, although she was no Red.

Shortly before Hitler attacked Russia, Mike Reilly of the Secret Service told me that a Communist plot to assassinate FDR had been uncovered. He revealed this during an evening of heavy drinking at Poughkeepsie and came to my door early the next morning and begged me not to print it because it would cost him his job.

I tried to verify the story, but never could through the FBI and intelligence agencies. It would not have been fair to quote Mike; I did want the story but not at the expense of his job. Later he confided that he never had any proof, but that was what he had been told and could not say that the information was accurate.

Reilly was at Warm Springs when FDR died and assured me that there was no basis for the wild rumors. Still, they were speeded by the fact that Mrs. R. flew down and decided against an autopsy. It became known that the food on FDR's plate was subjected to chemical analysis, which gave rise to reports the White House suspected foul play, but this was done at the order of Reilly, who was playing it safe as a Secret Service man should.

There were reports that FDR had shot himself as well as reports he had been shot by a mysterious Russian woman. It was said that he was laid in his coffin with a bloody bandage about his head. I talked to the undertaker who swore by all he held holy this was not true.

The portrait, which was being painted, also contributed to the wild rumors. Because it was being painted for Mrs. Rutherfurd, Mrs. R. didn't want it. The artist sent for it and it was returned to her. Mrs. Rutherfurd hesitated to claim it, because she evidently feared that it would not be wise to reveal her presence in Warm

Springs at the time of his death and that the artist was working for her.

When I saw Mrs. Schoumatoff, she was holding the portrait in a bank, waiting for instructions over its ultimate fate. I considered it a good idealized example of portraiture. It showed FDR in a boat cloak looking toward a future of great promise. The portrait now hangs at Warm Springs, which is a fitting place for the all-but-finished study.

I was not at my desk when news of FDR's death reached Washington late in the afternoon. I had called it a day and was going to the Carlton Hotel to pick up some friends for dinner. As I left I told my deskman Forrester not to call me unless the war ended or FDR died, which seemed to me to be imminent.

As I entered the hotel room of Timothy F. X. Duffy, a longtime Chicago friend, he told me I was wanted on the phone.

"Roosevelt's dead," I exclaimed, getting an undue reputation for omniscience. "Tell them I am going to the White House."

There Steve Early filled in details of the death. I caught a glimpse of the swearing-in ceremony for Truman in the Cabinet room and raced to the office to do my story. The next day I covered the arrival of the coffin at the White House and the brief services in the Executive Mansion.

As far as I know, I am the only newsman who reported the fact that the coffin was opened to permit Mrs. Roosevelt to bid her last farewell alone. Even if the coffin had not been opened, such a procedure would not have been uncommon, nor should it be regarded as a guideline for the measurement of grief or affection.

The coffin was not opened during the brief services for a limited number of officials, diplomats and friends, who were admitted into the East Room. I can only assume the failure to report that it had been opened for Mrs. R. was an oversight or inspired by concern for the privacy the family desired.

Nonetheless, the failure to open the coffin helped to spread the rumors of foul play and suicide which raced to the capital ahead of the body. So persistent were these rumors that Gromyko, then Russian ambassador to the United States and now his country's foreign minister, went to the State Department and asked to see the remains.

This permission was denied, politely and firmly, as it should have been.

Roosevelt was idolized, as few men have been in the White House. His death precipitated an orgy of mourning. Radio played nothing but dirges for days between accounts of funeral services and arrangements. Although he was loved greatly, he was also hated, so that curses, not loud but deep, were his lot in death.

When death came to the ailing Chief Executive, I received a telephone call from Maxwell saying he had been instructed by McCormick to call me and tell me I was right about the state of the President's health. Later the colonel told me the news came to him as he was preparing for a dinner party.

"I struck the planned wine from the menu," he said virtuously, "because I didn't want it reported that I had toasted Roosevelt's death in champagne. We drank a Montrachet instead."

I accompanied the funeral party aboard Roosevelt's last presidential special for the simple but moving last rites in the rose garden of the family home at Hyde Park. In a crisp morning sun, an honor guard of West Point cadets stood rigid. Subdued clusters of dignitaries surrounded the sorrowing family, and members of the press and radio maintained a discreet distance.

I will not pretend I was grief-stricken. I was sober and restrained, except for one remark, in the orgy of mourning. The day after the burial Mrs. R. wrote that she stood at her husband's grave dry-eyed. So when many asked me how I reacted to the services, I said:

"There stood Eleanor and I, both dry-eyed."

I don't think I would make the quip today.

Actually I stood alone at the services, engaged in thinking long, long thoughts of the great charmer and the amazing changes he had wrought, somewhat unwittingly perhaps because he had no political philosophy but personal power and self-perpetuation.

I thought then and I think now that the full story of Roosevelt's health has yet to be told. As a matter of fact, a definitive study of the health of recent American Presidents and world leaders generally has yet to be told. The people of most nations don't know about the state of health and the mentality of their idols, or don't seem to consider health and vigor as a job essential.

Woodrow Wilson was a shell of a man in his last months, with his wife, Edith Bolling Wilson, and his secretary, Joseph Tumulty, both of whom I knew and discussed his health with a number of times, fighting a furious power battle behind the shadow of his stricken vigor. Harry S Truman was plagued by tension, which moved him to seek release in the warmth of bourbon. His drinking was by no means excessive, but frequently gave him a glow of euphoria, doubtless when he made decisions. Dwight D. Eisenhower was stricken by a heart attack, underwent a major intestinal operation and suffered a stroke, all within three years.

John F. Kennedy, the apparently rugged champion of the new Camelot, was whipped by the scourge of an aching back and beset by Addison's disease, so much so that it would certainly be interesting if a table of his stimulatory shots of steroid hormones could be compared with such events as the hapless Bay of Pigs invasion of Cuba and the erection of the Berlin Wall after his meeting in Vienna with Nikita S. Khrushchev, then the No. 1 man in the Kremlin.

Lyndon B. Johnson was hit by a massive heart attack in the summer of 1955, about the same time Ike was hit in Denver, Colorado. LBJ was hospitalized for brief periods during his White House tenure as well as in his retirement. Warren G. Harding had a fatal stroke in office.

In fact, only three of the last ten Presidents have enjoyed good health during their tenures—Calvin Coolidge, Herbert Hoover and Richard M. Nixon. It would seem obvious that such driving and ambitious personalities are influenced by the swinging of their physical condition. Good health is, of course, no guarantee of perfection, but perhaps some professor may work out a pendulum theory of history, which would take into account the swings of mood in leaders from periods of heightened power to slumps of depression and exhaustion.

Winston S. Churchill was given to profound depressions, which he recognized by the name "black dog," and he spent hours in a sort of trance. He had three strokes in office, the last in 1953. Anthony Eden, who followed, was reported to have taken stimulants heavily during the Suez crisis. Neville Chamberlain was found to have cancer two months after the disastrous Norwegian campaign and died three months later. No one can tell how long the disease sapped his mind and vigor or how much it may have been responsible for the appeasement of Munich. Clement Attlee, who succeeded Churchill for a time in 1945, was tortured by a stomach ulcer.

Adolf Hitler possessed a questionable mentality when he launched himself into power, and is said to have been reduced to a shuffling wreck in his last years by Parkinson's disease. Antonio de Oliveira Salazar remained in office as dictator of Portugal after a stroke and brain operation, although power was taken from his hands without his knowledge. Other world leaders have suffered strokes in office.

Gamal Abdul Nasser of Egypt died young, at fifty-two, but had reportedly lost the ability to get a good night's sleep three years before. John Foster Dulles, powerful Secretary of State under Eisenhower, was given to grimacing under stress. This was known to intimates and doubtless to those with whom he dealt at conference tables. He died of intestinal cancer in the spring of 1959, but no one can say how much the dread disease influenced the decisions that aroused the animosity of England, France and Egypt. It would seem that Dulles' refusal to send medical supplies to Egypt after the Suez defeat was the petulance of an ailing man.

Another American Secretary of State, James Francis Byrnes, had a telltale facial twitch which became evident as he grew excited. Fidel Castro has been diagnosed as a maniac depressive by an Argentine woman doctor. Who knows how many of Stalin's cruel decisions and Khrushchev's tantrums were inspired by declining health?

Modern history is spotted with easy weepers, like President Johnson and Vice President Hubert Humphrey, who was an unsuccessful candidate for President. Ready tears are the sign of a compassionate heart, but they also give evidence of stress and strain. Tears seem to flow more easily when strength declines, but that may be a cruel statement. Still, a leader should be able to hold a tight rein on his emotions.

FDR's health was a matter of constant study and observation for me for a number of years, but became especially so when his decline became evident to my eyes and those about Roosevelt, including his personal physician, who insisted he was in the pink.

In his youth FDR was healthy, although not exceptionally robust or athletic. As a young man he sailed and played golf. But he was not one for contact sports, like football, or gifted by a fine sense of timing, which would have encouraged him to play baseball.

His temperament, so the family said, was one of buoyancy, when he was struck down by poliomyelitis in his early forties. But whether or not this natural optimism was magnified by his crippling attack has yet to be the subject of expert determination. There is such a thing as the mentality of a cripple, which may be less than salutary in leaders, according to some medical men.

Roosevelt was gay by nature, but at times he gave the impression that he felt the worst had happened to him, so that nothing could daunt him. Also he seemed to think that since he had suffered, others should do so. There is often a strange and even unnatural optimism in cripples, some doctors hold.

When FDR was campaigning for governor of New York in 1928, at the request of Al Smith, his health became a matter of public concern for the only time in his early political career. A board of four highly reputable physicians examined him and pronounced him physically fit for the office. When it came time for them to sign their findings, one of the four hesitated and read the report carefully. The others reminded him he had undertaken the examination with them and had supported their views.

"I know, I know," said the doctor. "I just want to be sure that I am not signing anything that says he's mentally equal to the office."

Only once did I ever see Roosevelt with his guard down on his affliction. It was at the Warm Springs Foundation. I was standing beside his wheel chair, at his request, because we were exchanging quips, in what had been his first cottage on the Foundation grounds. Leighton McCarthy, then a Canadian aluminum executive and later Canadian wartime ambassador to the United States, whose son had suffered an attack of the disease in one leg, was occupying the cottage and had invited FDR to a cocktail party.

Paul V. McNutt, former governor of Indiana, strode past us, unaware of our presence, to meet his host. McNutt, then U. S. High Commissioner to the Philippines, was in the White House doghouse, because he failed to report his poker winnings in Manila among his taxable earnings. It threatened to become an Administration scandal.

I watched FDR follow McNutt's bouncy progress with his eyes. Roosevelt didn't need to speak, the words were staring in his eyes: "Why can that boob walk while I can't?" FDR turned to me and recognized at once that I had read his unguarded thoughts. He flashed an embarrassed smile.

When Roosevelt became President a studied campaign was launched and maintained to keep his fellow Americans from knowing he could not walk a single step without crutches or braces and with the latter he had to make his way with the help of a pair of canes or by clinging to an arm.

Even tighter security was observed about his health, although it was acknowledged he was prone to colds. The decline in his health in his final years was kept from the people by the persistent refusal of Admiral McIntire to admit any change in his patient's condition.

Once Felix Belair of the New York *Times* and I spotted Dr. Wallace Mason Yater, leading Georgetown University Medical School diagnostician, darting into the White House. We knew the President was reportedly suffering from a cold, but a visit by a man of Yater's standing and eminence could mean something more serious. The good doctor absolutely refused to discuss the visit and the White House brushed it off as without the slightest significance. Much later it was disclosed that there was concern about FDR's condition.

Another Washington surgeon was less reticent, but refused to authorize any quotation. Dr. Peter Sterling was called in for consultation. After examining FDR in the winter of 1942–43, he suggested an operation but declined to perform it himself, explaining he was a relatively young man and that if the result were unfavorable, there would be wide criticism of those about the President for not getting the best man available.

The Washington surgeon recommended Dr. Frank Lahey, the famed Boston surgeon, who confirmed the diagnosis of his younger colleague and agreed to perform the surgery. Roosevelt put the surgery off, pleading the pressure of the war effort. Lahey returned for another examination about the time of the Teheran Conference late in 1943. Lahey then refused to operate because he felt it was too late. FDR's decline became quite noticeable after Teheran; where FDR first met Stalin, whose one abiding interest was in the launching of a second front in France. Churchill, who was also at Teheran, favored an operation against the "soft underbelly of Europe" through the Balkans, where an invasion could be expected to limit Russian influence in liberated nations.

After Teheran, Administration leaders began acknowledging that the President was not well. McIntire did not admit it, evidently, even to himself. The President's health became a matter of Cabinet concern because the Cabinet was engaged in a dispute over the fate of postwar Germany. FDR had named a committee consisting of Hull, Stimson, Morgenthau and Hopkins to decide the future of the almost beaten enemy.

Morgenthau offered a plan. It shocked his colleagues for its savagery. It would have stripped the industrial area of the Ruhr of all industrial potential and would have reduced Germany to a pastoral state. The plan, which came to be known as the Morgenthau Plan, was widely reported in the Administration to have been the work of Harry Dexter White, a top Treasury aide. He was suspected of Communist affiliations.

I first learned of the plan one fall evening when silver-haired Leo T. Crowley, chairman of the Board of Economic Warfare, called me to his office and unfolded what he termed a shocking and unworkable program of blind vengeance. Crowley knew that the industrial potential of the Ruhr could not be dismantled without disastrous consequences to all of Western Europe. He identified White as the author of the plan.

When I reported as much as I could get through censorship, Colonel McCormick ordered me to stop the Morgenthau Plan and put some sense into "these crazy people in the White House and State Department." Fortunately, the Morgenthau Plan, when unveiled and signed by FDR and Churchill at the second Quebec Conference on September 11, 1944, aroused the indignation of persons far more powerful than myself or even Colonel McCormick. Hull and Stimson were livid at the revival of the plan they thought they had killed in committee.

They also leaked the plan to the press, as Crowley had to me. The disapproval Crowley began gathered momentum like a snowball careening downhill. FDR was forced to recant and withdraw his approval. Churchill, who had been forced to sign under threat of having Lend-Lease funds cut to a trickle, was happy to get out from under the Morgenthau Plan.

Later Crowley leaked the allied zones of occupation in Germany to me by way of thanks for my part in helping to upset the

Morgenthau Plan. Crowley was positive the plan was given to White by the Russians for sale to the United States. White did turn over to Russia the plates for currency of the American Army of Occupation in Germany, which cost American taxpayers hundreds of millions of dollars. The Russians ran off this currency on their presses and bought whatever they wanted in Germany, and we redeemed what they had printed.

After the war White's operations in currency and on the Morgenthau Plan were investigated by the House Un-American Activities Committee. White died mysteriously and was secretly buried during the investigation. The full story of his operations was buried with him.

Relatively few people saw FDR in the 1944 campaign. He cut his campaign to a few radio broadcasts, having long before said that Dr. New Deal had given way to Dr. Win-the-War. Also he pretended to be too busy with the conduct of the war to devote much time to campaigning, going to meet MacArthur in Hawaii and to the second Quebec Conference.

He did open his campaign with an acceptance speech he made aboard his private railroad car before going on to the conference with MacArthur and other Pacific leaders. A photograph of the President, taken during the talk, showed his emaciated face and slumping body. In one corner I spotted the hand and lower sleeve of a naval commander. I couldn't imagine how so low a ranking officer could be the only armed services guest at such a historic address, so I went to the Associated Press and asked for an uncropped copy of the original photograph.

Then I took the photo to the Navy Department for identification of the navy officer. I was told he was Commander Howard Bruenn. Further inquiry revealed that he was a Boston heart specialist, who had been inducted into the Navy for the specific purpose of looking after the President's heart. Bruenn was at Warm Springs, but he was not at the President's side when death came.

Hopkins survived FDR by about a year. He was even more feeble than his chief in his last years because he was suffering from cancer. Death followed months of confinement in bed. He was unable to attend to his duties as an arbitrator in the garment industry and unable to work on his memoirs. He took an advance for a proposed book, but spent it all without delivering anything. His illness was costly.

Early and William D. Hassett continued with Truman for a transition period. Hassett, who had been on the wagon, took to drink. Truman protected him but won none of the affection Hassett had given to FDR. Early left the White House as soon as he could, not because he didn't like Truman, but because he felt the new President should choose his own team. Before he left, Early spotted Carol at a party for John W. Snyder who was to become Secretary of the Treasury.

"Your husband is a son of a bitch," Early said, laughing, "but he's the kind of a son of a bitch I like, because he dares to tell you what he thinks of you to your face. He's not a hypocritical bastard, who says one thing to your face and sings a different tune behind your back."

Early knew I had joined John O'Donnell in smuggling a Johns Hopkins University Hospital doctor into a White House Correspondents Association dinner, which FDR turned into a wartime fireside chat. I managed to seat the doctor directly under the Chief Executive whom I knew to be ailing. After the long evening the doctor reported FDR was failing rapidly and could not last out a year. The physician made much of the fact that the nape of Roosevelt's neck had as much sag as the front.

Steve, like me, disagreed with McIntire's rosy medical reports, but said there was nothing he could do about it. We agreed that a man who has himself for a doctor is generally a fool, but that a doctor who lets his patient diagnose himself is nothing short of a criminal.

It was difficult to get appraisals of FDR's mind and philosophy during his lifetime. Even now the story is just unfolding. Less than thirty years ago, FDR's voice could and did move the world, yet history is just beginning to pass judgment on him. Judgment is rarely passed on men in power or right after they die because the first to rush into print are the idolaters. When a man is in power critics generally can do no more than whistle against the wind. And wise men know that statues are not erected to critics. If admirers can be wrong so can critics.

Still, it is not wise to count any man fortunate, as Solon said, until after his death—perhaps, not until long after his death. FDR was the gay reformer, rather than the dictator some tried to picture him in life. His New Deal was hailed as the dawn of a new day and the answer to all of man's political explorations; yet, it was failing and had to be rescued by war.

Much of Roosevelt's program was punitive and divisive. He pitted class against class. He was relentless and unforgiving toward enemies. Much of his program was political to the point of demagoguery. And not a little of it was out and out fanciful, incapable of rendering any real benefits, and impractical in the delivery of lasting results. He turned government from its traditional channels into socialist streams, perhaps not deliberately, but he encouraged it so that, like Topsy, it "growed," nurtured by conscious planners, fanatics and dreamers.

In this he was aided mightily by his conquest of the press. Most Washington correspondents disliked and even hated the austere and aloof Herbert Hoover, partly because they didn't understand him or his problems. In those days, the press was anti-Establishment by nature, a position which is not without virtue. The gay FDR transformed all that with his broad smile, occasionally dropping a reporter's first name, pretending to love them and to hate their editors, and by throwing an annual press reception in the White House with a couple of barrels of beer, and encouraging Mrs. R. to invite a few top correspondents to square dances in the East Room of the White house. It worked wonders and still does for his memory.

TRUMAN

I n a sense Harry S Truman was the Andrew Johnson of the twentieth century. His accession to the presidency was remarkable in that he had not received the slightest information on development and formation of policy from Roosevelt, nor was he ever consulted on any matter of importance during the campaign and his weeks in the vice presidency. To FDR who felt that he was going to live forever and in the White House, Truman was no more than a trapping of his office, something like an appendix that can develop complications. After all, FDR had excised two Vice Presidents and the third was no more of a friend than the first, whom he scrapped without a sigh, and considerably less of a friend than the second, whose forced departure was hardly accompanied by weeping. There was no talk of upgrading the vice presidency when Truman came in, as there had long been and still is, because those about the President were fearful they might be suggesting FDR was a dying man.

Truman, like Andrew Johnson, succeeded as a long and costly war was ending in victory, and was confronted by the grave and challenging problems of peace. Both had to proceed cautiously in advancing the relatively unknown but vital policies of their predecessors. Truman and Johnson were distrusted by those about them, particularly at the highest levels. Johnson had his Edwin M. Staunton, Lincoln's Secretary of War, and Truman inherited Ickes and Wallace in his

Cabinet and appointed James Francis Byrnes as Secretary of State. He had to get rid of all three, as Johnson had to force Staunton out, because all three were convinced they could fill the office better than the incumbent they served.

In fact, Staunton came to Washington, as did William H. Seward, Simon Cameron and Salmon P. Chase, believing himself more qualified for the conduct of the war and the presidency itself than the Illinois rail splitter. There was hardly a man in the Cabinet Truman called into its first session with him who was not certain he could do better than the man from Missouri.

Both Johnson and Truman, who became Presidents by accident of death, were self-made men. Neither was a college man, but neither were Washington and Lincoln. Johnson had been a tailor and Truman was a former haberdasher. Both were fighters, Truman being even more of a fighter than Johnson and possessing a more engaging personality than the Democrat whom Lincoln put on the ticket to help him win the critical election of 1864. I am quite sure that Truman's devotion to the Democratic party, every bit as religious as that of Farley, would not have let him accept a Republican running mate in 1948, even if failure to do so would have spelled defeat.

Truman was devoted to the party, but hardly as blindly as some of his critics contended. He did put national interest above party, notably when he called Herbert Hoover to direct the world-wide relief program after the war, and when he named the former Republican President to study and propose reorganization of the government in the interests of economy and efficiency, although it was feared it would spell a reduction in jobs for deserving Democrats.

HST was devoted to his friends, often to his own disadvantage. He promoted his Senate seatmates Lewis B. Schwellenbach of Washington to the Cabinet as Secretary of Labor and Sherman Minton of Indiana to the Supreme Court. Truman was too quick to assume that attacks on individuals in his Administration, like Alger Hiss, were attacks on himself, but he could fire a crony, like Attorney General J. Howard McGrath, at the drop of a hat for too strict a regard to partisan interests.

Although I was no intimate of Truman, I welcomed his accession because I considered the third term a mistake and the fourth something of a disaster. To me, it is healthy to have the party in power vigorously opposed by that out of power, not necessarily supporting the opposition. I believe both parties should bring up younger men to vie for succession, not hold down by seniority or entrenchment in power. I think changes of party are generally good for the electorate. I don't generally like politicians who join the switchmen's union and change parties easily for personal advantage, and I abhor coalitions that bring politicians, pretending to different philosophies, together largely for the enjoyment of power rather than the advancement of their ideals.

I felt I understood Truman, because he was the product of a city machine and proud of it. Thus, he was the type of politician with whom I was entirely familiar, knowing his loyalties and methods of political operation.

"I never met a ward politician in my life," Admiral Leahy sighed to me in 1945, "and I certainly didn't expect to meet my first one in the White House."

Furthermore, I liked Truman because he was a fellow Civil War buff and because he was willing to learn. He read books, I know, because we often read the same books about figures in the war between the states. Truman read a great deal of history, going back to Greece and Rome, a period which has never failed to fascinate me, because men knew everything about politics they now know and acted no less cruelly than political leaders have in our time. Yet my acquaintance with the new President was slight and it didn't grow very much, because I was the representative of what he considered the arch, if not satanic, Republican newspaper. I knew he was a constant reader and what else can a reporter ask for?

Many and many a time Truman put his famous "SOB" brand on my hide. It didn't scorch but was accepted by me as a badge of honor, an indication that my stories were being read by him. I knew his attacks were politics and I know he knew it. The *Tribune* was the enemy and I, as its representative, was fair game. For all his name calling he respected me, as I did him. Near the end, he spoke of me to several visitors, saying: "Trohan is not only a good reporter, but a man of highest integrity," an opinion many, including some of my editors, do not share wholeheartedly.

Herbert Hoover, who was no politician, found Truman a strange mixture of generous man and selfish partisan. The former President was grateful to Truman for the relief assignment and the appointment to the Commission on Executive Branch Organization. Truman gave his unqualified support to the commission's recommendations, which is more than Hoover got from Truman's Republican successor, Dwight D. Eisenhower.

Truman and Hoover became friends, each with a commendable respect and understandable admiration for the other. So it was with injured astonishment, Hoover told me, that he heard HST pick up the old refrain of the Hoover Depression in the 1948 campaign and assail Hoover for it. On his next visit to the White House, after Truman's attack, Hoover felt impelled to mention his wounds.

"Oh, that was nothing but politics," Truman confided airily. "I didn't mean it personally and you shouldn't have paid any attention to it."

When he came to Washington in 1935, Truman didn't cause a single ripple in the capital's way of life. Like every freshman senator I have known, he was considerably abashed by the select company of political giants he had joined, men he regarded as towering figures on the political horizon.

Truman's experience as a county judge—county commissioner in most American areas—hardly equipped him for the Senate, but he was anxious to learn. He was interested in national rather than international issues and sat as a spectator at sessions of the Interstate Commerce Committee, because his state was crisscrossed by railroads.

Wheeler, who was chairman of the committee and a master manipulator, invited him to sit with the committee. The training Truman received, under Wheeler, was to promote Truman to the chairmanship of a Senate group. It investigated the conduct of the war on the home front. This group, which came to be known as the Truman Committee, put HST on the road to the White House.

Truman was ever grateful to Wheeler, especially because many of his Senate associates thought Truman had come from the wrong side of the tracks in his home town, Lamar, Missouri, which indeed he had. Truman married above him, a girl from the right side of the tracks, as Johnson had, but she did not have to teach him to read and write as Andrew Johnson's wife did. At the outset of his

Senate service, most of Truman's colleagues gave him short, if polite, shrift, figuring he was no more than a one termer. Wheeler was quick to recognize Truman's potential in battles the Montanan waged against some railroad interests.

"I'll never forget that period when a great many of the so-called liberals and smart boys of the Senate thought I was the wrong kind of person to be in the Senate," Truman confided. "Wheeler never felt that way. One of the great periods of my life was the association I had with him."

So also did many think that Truman was the wrong kind of person for the White House. Yet, at the very beginning, I felt his accession was wholesome in that it demonstrated that almost any American could aspire to the presidency and fill the job as well as more respected leaders.

I was surprised to find many of my colleagues letting dislike and distrust of FDR come out of the woodwork of their minds. These began openly to hail and acclaim Truman, confessing they were never quite at home with Roosevelt's calm assumption of aristocracy and demand for unquestioning loyalty.

Truman was a man of the people, but not to be underestimated as Ickes, the Old Curmudgeon, and Wallace, the barefoot tennis player, soon found out. They found the Cabinet door slammed in their faces when they tried to stake out their department as independent satrapies. Wallace tried to dictate foreign policy toward Russia in direct opposition to that of the President and was shown the door.

The first of FDR's cabinet to go was Edward R. Stettinius, Jr., the handsome silver-haired son of the powerful and capable head of the United States Steel Corporation. Few in Washington took Stettinius seriously. They knew the corporation, which had taken him on believing he had inherited his father's drive and brains, was happy to offer him for government services when he proved to be more pleasant than competent.

Stettinius' administration of Lend-Lease was less than notable. It is not hard to win popularity for giving away money and resources, because no one could fail in the role of Santa Claus to our friends and allies. No one was surprised when he was appointed Secretary of State to succeed the frail Hull, who I always felt should have married Whistler's mother. All Washington knew Stettinius would be no more than a figurehead, because FDR had long been his own Secretary of State.

When Stettinius was appointed, I went down to his alma mater, the University of Virginia, to look up his grades. They were so bad I didn't have the heart to do a story on them and point out that the American Secretary of State had been given grades far below passing in politics, economics and history.

No American official has made me so ashamed of my own countrymen as Stettinius. In the early days of UN, at Lake Success, New York, he undertook, no doubt under instructions, to level a mild attack on Russia, which was beginning to fling the veto power it wrested from FDR in the Security Council. It was his first speech before the council. From where I sat I could see his hands tremble and hear his voice shake. So pitiful a figure did he make that Gromyko, then the Soviet Union's first UN delegate, shrugged his shoulders in contempt and didn't even deign to answer.

When the Republican opposition began urging Stettinius to begin acting as Secretary of State, Truman replaced him with Byrnes. The latter enjoyed one of the most active and colorful careers in American politics—representative, senator, Supreme Court Justice, assistant president as head of the Office of War Mobilization, Secretary of State and governor of South Carolina. Byrnes was never one to underestimate himself and was ever mindful that, but for a nod, he might have been Vice President in 1940 and might possibly have succeeded to the presidency in 1945.

About this time I was slipped a photograph of Byrnes which was taken at the 1936 Olympics in Berlin. It depicted the senator, in the company of friends, giving the Nazi salute. I could not be persuaded to use it, because I was sure that the salute was given in jest, such as anyone might be tempted to undertake in similar circumstances. Jimmy and I were kissing cousins of a sort, always embracing when we met at functions around the capital in those days.

I had less compunction about circulating a photo of Senator Claude (Red) Pepper of Florida with his arms around Paul Robeson, Negro All-American football player, singer and actor, who loved Russia and all it stood for, and Mrs. R. at a New York political rally. When Bill Jibb, a worker for Representative George A. Smathers of Florida, came to me seeking advice in a contest for Pepper's seat, I asked him how badly he and Smathers wanted to win. I asked if they were prepared to play dirty without involving Smathers.

Jibb said they were. I went to my files and gave him a copy of the photograph. Several hundred thousand copies of the photo were distributed in the cracker country of northern Florida with the result that Smathers carried the counties and won the election. Smathers never thanked me, I suppose because politicians like to think they win on their charm and principles.

The day after the election Bill Daffrin, administrative assistant to Pepper, came to my office and said: "We know you beat us and can't complain, because anything goes in elections. However, we want you to know what sort of a man you put in."

Then he spread before me a half-dozen letters Smathers had written Pepper, when the representative was in the Marine Corps, seeking promotion and good assignments. These thanked Pepper for his help and pledged undying support and devotion to his benefactor. Pepper, who returned to Congress in 1962 as a representative, never held my action against me, continuing a cordial but hardly a warm friendship, we had established in 1937. I was to regret my service to Smathers later, but for other reasons.

It was not long before Truman and Byrnes, who went to Potsdam together to meet with Stalin, began to differ on fundamentals. I could not blame Truman for ratifying the concessions FDR made to the Russian dictator at Yalta, which made the liberated Eastern European nations captives of the Kremlin, because neither was awake to Soviet purpose or intentions. I would not say the persons who should have informed the leaders were traitors; they were wishful thinkers who were convinced that the best way to win the Russians to co-operation for lasting peace was by giving them all they asked for.

Both Truman and Byrnes have written their versions of the break and I talked privately with them on it. Truman said he dressed Byrnes down for failure to play the game properly, so sharply that the Secretary had to leave. Byrnes wrote two somewhat different versions of his departure in two volumes of memoirs that he published, but claimed to have left of his own volition. I have always felt that Byrnes lost out because he did not defer to the President, as political protocol dictated that he should, and because he considered himself more competent to make the great policy decisions.

Truman gave the post to the man he most admired in Washington, General George Catlett Marshall, who had the good sense to get out after two years. Marshall was no great brain but he was deferential. Furthermore, he was no great soldier, although he held the lives and fate of many in his hands, because the chief of staff controls promotion and assignments and plans. It seems to me that Marshall is destined to fade in history, as has Major General Henry W. Halleck, the Civil War chief of staff, who was flattered as "Brains" Halleck when he was in power.

Dean Gooderham Acheson, a man of tremendous ability and a remarkable sense of humor, with whom I often disagreed, became Truman's fourth Secretary of State. At the colonel's direction, I was given to annoying Acheson by reminding Americans that their Secretary of State was conceived in Canada, born in the United States a few months after his Episcopal bishop father was assigned to a see in Connecticut.

Acheson relaxed during trying days in the State Department by busying himself in the cabinetmaking workshop he had installed in his home.

"If I could only make a foreign policy," he often sighed to me, "as easily and as serviceably as I can join a table."

My suggestion was that he take a long hard look at Russia and the UN as a beginning. After his return to private life Acheson became extremely suspicious of Russia and wrote off the world organization as impotent. I frequently accused him of stepping to the right of me and warned him that the foothold there was most precarious.

I had great respect, tinged with a little envy, for Acheson as a writer, often telling him I could not write nearly so well. His style was a modernization of the eighteenth-century love for balance, precision, well-turned phrases, understatement and the right word in the right place.

Shortly after a night conference in the White House, as the United States was about to plunge into the Korean war, I was in my office, although it was a Sunday. (I did not take days off except for

Christmas and my birthday, the Fourth of July, for some fifteen years.) I received a call from Louis B. Johnson, then Secretary of Defense. He jubilantly detailed how he had attacked Acheson for policies which were leading to war.

"Walter, I had Acheson speechless," he boasted.

I began writing a story based on Johnson's report, which was a far better source than most colleagues could boast of having. I might say I considered it a joyous task, because I was against war in Korea as I had been against World War II, for all my close relationship to Syngman Rhee, Korea's first president. In my notes, which were rather sketchy, I came upon Johnson's claim that he had rendered Acheson speechless.

It suddenly occurred to me that I had never seen a speechless Acheson. I admired his speaking almost as much as his writing because his extemporaneous remarks at news conferences came out in well-parsed sentences. I stopped beating my typewriter and tried to get Acheson through Andrew Berding, a former State Department man for the Associated Press who had become the department's top adviser on public relations. The Acheson version was quite different from Johnson's, so I threw away my story and began another, considerably more accurate.

This serves to demonstrate one of the greatest problems of reporting in Washington. It is always necessary to question what one has been told, because even the highest witnesses tend to see and hear things the way they want them to be rather than what they are. The informant may not be conscious of misrepresentation, but he often can't help emphasize what he favors or believes. Men solemnly believe they have been responsible for some decision, when it may have been decided upon long before they were aware of it and for reasons unknown to them, and quite possibly but dimly remembered by the actual originator of the policy.

The problem of reporting is the more important because Washington is given to the great man theory of history by flatterers seeking advancement and preferment and by correspondents reporting it as such. The great man is, of course, the President, and the object is to credit him or blame him, when considering almost any action or policy. It makes for more interesting reading when the President's name is thrown about.

Because of the power of the presidency and the wealth of actions at his command, the occupant of the White House is credited with the origination of policies that are an Administration effort and the execution of details of plans and operations he may know nothing about. However, the ultimate responsibility is and must be his.

Under the great man theory of history, flattery flourishes. Those who employed this technique often told me that it could not be laid on too thickly. Nonetheless, there are times when it ought to arouse contempt and scorn and sometimes does. One flatterer overreached himself with Truman. He was Samuel I. Rosenman, a ghost writer for FDR, who had been retained to help in the period of transition. Fully aware that Roosevelt loved flattery, Sam turned the flood on the Missourian.

"You know, Mr. President, when you first came to the White House, I frankly wondered if you could fill Roosevelt's shoes," Rosenman said one evening. "Now, I wonder, if he came back, whether he could fill your shoes."

Rosenman was eased out not long after. Truman had no reason to be a Roosevelt idolater, and Rosenman knew it, because FDR had failed to inform his Vice President on plans and policy. Yet, Truman didn't like Rosenman's remark, White House Press Secretary Charles Ross told me, because he recognized it for what it was worth—a vat of soft soap.

Some time later Clark Clifford, the personable and ingratiating St. Louis lawyer, ended a speech-writing session with HST and a few White House intimates, by raising his right hand and saying: "May this hand wither, if I ever write the name of the great cadaver again." This was a far different kettle of fish to Truman and he added: "And may my tongue fall out, if I utter it again."

The great cadaver was, of course, Roosevelt.

However, both were to forget that solemn moment, which was reported to me at the time by Rear Admiral J. K. Vardaman, Jr., then White House naval aide. In his whistle-stop campaigning in 1948, Truman was to get all of the mileage he could out of the magic of his predecessor and no one could fault him for it.

Vardaman introduced Clifford to the White House and Washington. J.K., a St. Louis banker, knew the gifted and attractive lawyer and insisted on having him in the capital. At that time Truman

didn't particularly like Clifford and consented to his presence grudgingly on the condition that the lawyer remain silent unless spoken
to. For almost three months Clifford held his peace at various
strategy conferences, waiting to be drawn in.

When he was, his charm and ability made him almost indispensable. Clifford was never one to minimize himself and was quick
to adopt anything that might serve his purposes as his own, which
is hardly unusual around the capital. Clifford got a great reputation
around the capital as a wit, which he furthered by clipping the best
quips of Washington wits. He was aware that nothing is forgotten so
quickly as the authorship of a bon mot and that the borrowed quips
are invariably attributed to men of influence and power, a position
he achieved by virtue of his White House role, which he fattened
under succeeding Democratic administrations.

I have seldom been as sorry for a man as I was for Clifford one
evening when he followed the agile and explosive Bob Hope at a
Washington dinner. Clifford had a good speech. It would have been
great had he preceded the master comedian, but following that
adept performer, Clifford fell as flat as a poorly whipped soufflé.

Clifford got something of a reputation as a prophet and a deep
thinker, as the author of a paper warning of Russian activities and
intentions early in the Truman administration. Truman, no international expert, had been inclined to underestimate the Muscovites.
At Potsdam he ratified all the horrors of captivity for the liberated
nations of Eastern Europe. Many Washington newsmen credited
Clifford with great vision. Margaret Truman disclosed what few had
known, in her fascinating volume on her father, that this paper
was actually put together by Clifford's assistant George Elsey, with
the help of various interested government departments and intelligence units, but it went to Truman under Clark's signature.

So great a reputation did this paper give Clifford that he was
charged by John F. Kennedy, after his eyelash victory of 1960,
with arranging the transmission of administrations. He was mentioned as presidential timber himself. The bite of the presidential
bee is generally fatal; few, if any, ever really recover.

Still later, under Lyndon B. Johnson, Clifford was named Secretary of Defense. LBJ told me that Clifford courted personal popularity
by undercutting Johnsonian policies in Vietnam. He accused Clif-

ford of nursing presidential ambitions, but more in anger than fact, I always felt, because I am sure that Clifford, who is extremely competent, did disagree with the policies and believed he had to protect himself.

This has always happened in Washington and will continue to happen to the end of time or the end of the capital, whichever may come first. Men have every right to ambition. Many come to Washington deliriously happy just to be on the team. It isn't long before they come to feel that the team and its leader is fortunate, indeed, to have them. As they grow taller on the political horizon, they lose their awe, not only of the President but of the presidency, so why shouldn't they dream of standing inside the White House door where so many want to head the receiving line.

Vardaman, who died virtually unnoticed in Jackson, Mississippi, in the summer of 1972, was fond of claiming he was the only man in the Truman administration who owed his post as a member of the Federal Reserve Board to clean living. He was the son of the powerful Mississippi senator of World War I days, James K. Vardaman, when the state had two parties—not the Democrats and the Republicans, but the Vardaman faction and the anti-Vardaman faction. The father was one of Woodrow Wilson's despised "little group of willful men," being one of the twelve senators who defeated, by filibuster, the proposal to arm American merchantmen against German submarines just before America's entry into that conflict.

As a banker in St. Louis, Vardaman approached Truman early in 1939, seeking a favor for his bank. Vardaman got it, so that when Truman became involved in a closely contested battle for his party's renomination, the banker sent him a three-hundred-dollar campaign contribution, and forgot about it. When Truman became President, Vardaman was serving in the Pacific, having already served on General Dwight D. Eisenhower's staff in London and in the naval campaign against Italy.

To his surprise, Vardaman got a message ordering him to report to Washington as White House naval aide, a position of influence on naval matters second only to that of chief of naval operations. Vardaman reported promptly. The two barely knew one another.

Truman fished a bottle of bourbon out of his desk and invited

Vardaman to join him in a drink. Vardaman declined, he said, admitting he had once been a bottle-a-day man, but gave it up years before. Slowly Truman put the bottle back. Then he suggested Vardaman join a group of intimates who were coming over for a quiet game of poker that evening. Vardaman said he would be delighted to join the company.

At the poker table, Vardaman did not take a seat, explaining he had once been an avid player, but had given up cards. Truman shrugged. Later the players began telling stories. Most of these had a scatological flavor, because they seemed to end up with the butt of the joke running into an institution now all but gone from the American scene, the backhouse, and falling in.

When it came Vardaman's turn, he passed, explaining that while he had no objection to any kind of humor, he was one of those unfortunates who took a story in one ear and let it out the other, not being able to retain it. Truman frowned. Not too long after, Vardaman insisted, Truman offered the nonwhiskey-drinking, nonpoker-playing, nonstorytelling aide a vacancy on the Federal Reserve Board.

The White House poker-playing sessions were most unusual, it became my business to learn, because the stakes were not fixed until after the sessions ended. Truman then set the price of the chips, deciding how much the big loser could lose. Friendship guided invitations; but ability to play was always a factor. B. K. Wheeler, a seasoned Montana poker player, asked to get in some of the games, but Truman waved him aside, saying: "Burt, you couldn't afford it."

Wheeler considered this a strange statement, because he didn't propose to play to lose, and because it came from a man, that he knew as all Washington did, who had come into the White House broke and even in debt from the bankruptcy of his haberdashery venture. As a matter of fact, several close friends, all of whom I knew, anted up some $4,000 to outfit the former haberdasher for the White House, because he didn't have the clothes, especially the formal clothes for the job. One of these friends, Senator Stuart Symington, then a government official, showed me a check he had made out to Truman for $2,500, which he said he had lost to the President the night before.

Poker playing was not confined to the White House, but was the order of the night on stag trips down the Potomac aboard the presidential yacht. Bulging brief cases were carried aboard the yacht on Friday or Saturday evenings as though the President were going to spend the weekend cruise working on problems. The same brief cases were carried off unopened Monday mornings, because the cruises were given over to relaxation and poker, and why not?

Now and then I went down the river on other yachts and always got friendly waves from Truman and members of his party, when they recognized me. It always interested me that I often saw Truman and Treasury Secretary Snyder, sitting at the stern of the yacht with their arms around one another, for all the world like Tom Sawyer and Huck Finn on their Mississippi River raft. There was much of the young boy in the President for all his belligerency.

When Truman became President, it became important to me to know about his sex life. In the first weeks I went up to Representative Paul Shafer of Michigan to demand the complete story of what went on in Costa Rica and Mexico, during a joint junket of the Senate and House Armed Services committees. Truman was a member of the group as was the Republican Shafer. I had overheard various members make leering references to their junket, but the details didn't interest me until Truman became President. I felt I had to know for future guidance and told Shafer so. He agreed but began by emphasizing that Truman's conduct was that of the exemplary husband and father he had always been, even though others seemed to forget their roles.

In San José, the capital of Costa Rica, Shafer told me the members of the party were feted at a presidential dinner and then taken to a country club on heights above the city. There members of the party were introduced to a group of young ladies they took to be the wives and daughters of their Latin American legislative hosts, until one of the American party, a bit gay in his cups, reached down the front of a low-cut gown. There was giggling that could not be mistaken and that launched something of an orgy.

At the first approach of one of the ladies of the evening, Truman quietly rose, went to a waiting car and had himself driven to the party's hotel. He did not voice disapproval or assume a pose of superiority, which wouldn't have checked the situation in the slightest, but disassociated himself. Nor did he hold the conduct of some of the others against them such as Senator Sherman Minton who boasted he had enjoyed the favors of four of the women on locker-room benches, when Truman later elevated him to the High Court.

Truman also slipped away, Shafer told me, from similar games some legislators played in Mexico City. In a night club, Senator Elmer Thomas of Oklahoma asked Shafer to bring a Mexican dancer to the senatorial suite in their hotel. Shafer protested he was no pimp, but Thomas argued that after all he was a senator and Shafer a congressman, and it was, therefore, more difficult for him to escape observation. He begged Shafer to undertake the mission as a personal favor.

When he got to the senator's room with the girl, Shafer found Thomas' wallet on the dresser. Shafer laughed, he said, because Thomas would make a great show of reaching for his wallet whenever a check appeared, and then pretend he had forgotten it. Shafer opened the wallet and found some $260. Then he looked at the dancer and decided if she was good enough for the senator she would be good enough for him. Before he left her awaiting Thomas, he gave her $40 from Thomas' wallet, saying $20 was for him and $20 for the senator. Then he tucked the wallet in a drawer under some shirts.

The next morning an irate Thomas charged to Shafer's breakfast table, exclaiming: "I was rolled and your girl did it."

Aware that it was not unlikely, Shafer asked how much Thomas had lost. The senator said $40. Realizing the wallet had not been cleaned out, Shafer laughingly explained he had paid the girl from the wallet for her services to himself and the senator.

"That's $20 you owe me!" Thomas shouted, insisting on payment then and there.

Shafer paid him. I could never pass the senator thereafter without remarking, with feigned innocence, that Shafer claimed Thomas owed him $20.

I was pleased to learn that Truman had never thought of cheating on his wife. However, his standards were not observed by all his aides, including White House Appointment Secretary Matthew Connally, who never failed to show off his conquests to me, although he knew I was fond of his pretty blond wife. It did not surprise me when Connally went to jail for having itchy fingers.

Truman's devotion to his wife was unswerving and one of the most commendable features of his character. Mrs. Truman did not like publicity, which many in Washington regarded as one of her most admirable features. I was often amused by the expression on her face in various photographs taken when Truman was speaking with her at his side. She was aware that her air-sawing husband was no orator and, to me, she always appeared surprised that he was getting away with what he was saying.

Truman was no less devoted a son. He was fond of his mother and obeyed her every wish, whenever he could, even though he was not always in sympathy with her idiosyncrasies. One of these was that she was still living in the Civil War era and could not abide a Yankee or a Republican in her home.

In his Senate days, I learned, Truman invited his war investigating committee associate Senator Owen Brewster of Maine to Kansas City. He apologized to the Republican that he could not take him to his home to his mother, because Maine was about as Yankee as one could get.

On his first visit home, after becoming President, Truman sent an interesting letter acknowledging Brewster's congratulations. The contents were not as exciting as the cover, because it indicated Truman must have raided his mother's stamp box in order to send his reply by airmail; the envelope offered an interesting array of low-value stamps.

Before he became President, I knew of Truman's interest in the Civil War and his mother's devotion to the lost cause. So, after he became President, I looked up the family name in the monumental *War of the Rebellion—Official Records of the Union and Confederate Armies*, which came to me indirectly from Senator Tom Connally of Texas. He was a member of Congress when the government undertook to print the records and he got a complimentary copy.

To my surprise I came upon the name of Harry Truman of Jackson County, Missouri, which was the President's home county. I suspected that the mother had named her son after this figure, although his loyalty to the lost cause hardly matched her own.

The first Harry Truman was a guerrilla, who operated in the Jackson County area. Evidently when he met a Union sympathizer, he was overcome with love for the Confederacy and when he met a southern sympathizer he became the stanchest of Union men. Anyway, he robbed both without compunction.

The official records carry messages on the first Harry Truman's depredations, generally involving the stealing of livestock and looting towns. He did work with the Union army at times, but was more often on the run from Union cavalry.

When I inquired about the possibility that the President was a namesake of the first Harry, I met with a prompt denial. This didn't satisfy me, because the denial came too quickly, before there could be any investigation. I sent *Tribune* stringers in the area to look for fuller accounts of the first Harry's activities in the histories of the counties of the area. These correspondents reported that such histories had recently and mysteriously disappeared from library shelves. I wrote the story, but it attracted almost no attention.

Truman did express some interest in my Civil War collection, which was not inconsiderable. He was fascinated by the autograph album of Gideon Welles, Lincoln's Secretary of the Navy, who took his book to the White House on January 19, 1864, and had it signed by all present at a Cabinet meeting save Secretary of War Staunton with whom he did not speak. Later the album was signed by many leading military figures and many statesmen. Two of the signers, Johnson and Grant, were to become Presidents.

Truman was most interested in a page which bore the signatures of Senator J. W. Grimes of Iowa and Senator Preston King of New York, which were on the same page and obviously signed with the same pen at the same time. He knew the two senators had been together at a dramatic period in history when they barred entrance into President Johnson's office to the daughter of Mrs. Mary E. Surratt, when she tried to appeal to the Chief Executive to save her mother from the gallows for alleged complicity in the plot to assassinate Lincoln. The two senators were suicides, but it cannot be said this unkind act was solely responsible for their ends. Grimes shot himself when he failed to win re-election and King slipped over the side of a ferry in New York harbor when be became convinced his mind was failing.

Truman offered to sign the volume to give me another presidential signature, but I said it was my desire to leave it as Welles had left it; a decision he applauded and shared. Press Secretary Ross, a high school mate of Truman's, was not impressed by the signatures of the Civil War period, remarking they were all right but asking if I had ever seen a signature of Button Gwinnett?

By one of those coincidences that could not be tolerated in fiction,

I fished into the brief case which had held the Welles book, and pulled out a rare signature of the signer of the Declaration of Independence. No one enjoyed Ross's astonishment more than the President. I had been entrusted with the brief case, which I knew contained the Gwinnett signature, by Ralph G. Newman, Chicago Lincoln expert and appraiser for the White House, who had purchased it for our friend Mike Lebold of Chicago. A Gwinnett signature had been sold for as high as $30,000.

Truman could take any criticism of himself pretty well, as being part of the political game, but could not tolerate any slight to his family. His rather violent letter to a music critic, a frustrated tenor, who criticized daughter Margaret's singing is well known. The behavior of the critic, Paul Hume, of the Washington *Post*, was less than wise. Hume read the letter to a fellow critic on the Washington *Daily News*, who had much better news judgment, and broke the story. Hume sold the President's letter to an autograph dealer, when discretion might have dictated holding it. So would financial judgment, because the letter grew in value.

The letter to the critic, like many another angry letter, was dictated at the end of the day, when Truman would be confronted with the silence of the White House. At such times Truman would take a drink or two, generally in company but often alone. The warmth of the liquor would encourage him to write as he felt. One of his more violent letters went to a colleague I admired and respected, Frank Kent of the Baltimore *Sun*.

One of his famous political columns fanned the President's wrath. In return he got an explosive and violent letter. Kent put the letter in his pocket, after receiving it at his desk in his office, put on his hat and went to the Baltimore and Ohio Railroad station where he boarded a train for the capital. On his arrival he went to the White House where he handed the letter to Ross.

"Charley," the gentlemanly Kent said, "such a letter should never have been written by any occupant of the White House. Therefore, it should not be around to haunt any man in the presidency or when he leaves office.

"Now, I don't want you or anyone else to read that letter; I want you to burn it up right now, in my presence, and to tell the President what you have done."

"Thank you very much," said Ross, who was aware of the President's literary proclivities.

Kent put on his hat and left for Baltimore. I had the story from Ross and verified it with Kent, but he would never discuss the contents with me or anyone else. I must report that Truman was ever grateful to Kent, realizing that he had been carried away by anger and that the letter could only harm him.

When Truman took over as President, Colonel McCormick ordered that the new Chief Executive should be given every chance to carry on his difficult burden. Truman was shouldering a heavy load, not of his own making. Not only did he have to bring the war to an end in Europe and Asia, but he had to meet all the political and economic difficulties of peace, demobilization and reconstruction. It was not surprising, therefore, that he had a sign put on his desk reading: "The buck stops here."

However, he was to coin one of the greatest remarks ever made about the presidency by a holder of the office, when he said: "If you can't stand the heat, stay out of the kitchen."

When Truman succeeded there was reason to believe that the churning of class hatred, which marked the Roosevelt administration, might die. He sought help from all parties and all factions, particularly on foreign affairs.

Wheeler came to his desk before Truman went to Potsdam and warned him about Russian aims and intentions. Truman dismissed him by saying he could handle the Russians, but was concerned about the demands of the British and the French. Evidently the appeasers had got to the new President first.

Leahy was in the White House and accompanied Truman to Potsdam. He showed the President the forty-page memo MacArthur had sent in advance of the Yalta Conference, which pleaded that Russia be kept out of the war in the Pacific.

MacArthur outlined the Japanese peace overtures, which I was to print later. These were: (1) Complete surrender of all Japanese forces. (2) Surrender of all arms and ammunition. (3) Occupation of all Japanese homeland and island possessions, under American direction. (4) Japanese relinquishment of Manchuria, Korea and Formosa, as well as all territory seized during the war. (5) Regulation of all

Japanese industry to halt present and future production of implements of war. (6) Turning over of any Japanese the United States might designate as war criminals. (7) Immediate release of all prisoners of war and interests in Japan and areas under Japanese control.

Japan had also sent peace feelers through Sweden to Russia. No doubt the Russian suppressed those they got because they were aiming at getting into the war against Japan for territory.

Whatever the reasoning, Truman chose to reaffirm the blunders of Yalta. Also he decided to drop the first atom bombs on the cities of Hiroshima and Nagasaki. When he hinted at America's powerful new weapon, Stalin appeared to be uninterested and switched to another subject. Truman could not then know Stalin already knew what he wanted to know about the bomb from Communist spies and British and American traitors and dupes.

The first conference sessions were held with Churchill representing Britain. The war leader was defeated in the first election after German surrender and replaced by Attlee, who had given the Communist clenched-fist salute in reviewing the forces of the Red-dominated government in Spain's civil war.

Truman was impressed by Stalin, coming home to say that he "liked Old Joe," and that the Soviet leader was a prisoner of the Politburo. He would have been more correct if he had reversed it to make the Politburo the prisoner of the ruthless dictator.

Truman ordered the dropping of the bombs. Russia entered the Pacific war and communism made headway on the Asian continent. Truman has explained that he ordered the bombings in the interest of saving hundreds of thousands of American lives that might have been lost in an invasion.

Time will tell whether he will be applauded for courage or blamed for faulty judgment, not only for ordering the dropping of the bombs but for his confirmation of the evils of Yalta and for the betrayal of Chiang Kai-shek and nationalist China by General George C. Marshall. After all, the only nuclear weapons ever fired were dropped at his direction and on civilian populations.

It was after Potsdam that McCormick's honeymoon with Truman ended. Shortly after Truman's return the colonel editorialized: "It must now be recorded with regret that Mr. Truman is as devoid of diplomatic skill as he is without understanding of the problems he has been dealing with."

From then on, the *Tribune* began attacking Truman, which slowly but surely again pushed me beyond the White House gates. My invitations to functions, which had been revived, were ended. The assumption of the phrase "Fair Deal," to mark his Administration, was the waving of a red flag in front of the colonel's nose because it clearly signaled a revival of the New Deal in peacetime.

Over the years I got orders to hit HST's appeasement of Russia, failure to formulate a strong policy against the Soviets, muddling policy in China, vacillating policy toward Israel, failure to act promptly against Communists, fellow travelers and dupes in the government, failure to reduce taxes, wobbling on price controls and record peacetime spending, continued demagoguery toward business, occupation with the welfare state and corruption within his Administration.

Perhaps it might be said that all of this was not as serious as the *Tribune* made out, but it did help to elect a Republican Congress in 1946. The Eightieth Congress is remembered principally for Truman's tag, "the do-nothing Congress," yet this Congress did cut taxes and did bring the budget into balance for the first time since FDR came into power, promising efficiency and economy in government.

Truman lost Congress in 1946 because that campaign marked the first in which the Republican opposition was able to mount a sustained offensive in almost twenty years. They were able to capitalize on public impatience with wartime restrictions, such as rationing, price controls and wage freezes, as well as with scandals that were beginning to peep up all over the Fair Deal, like crocuses thrusting up their colorful heads in spring. The GOP captured the Eightieth Congress by basing their campaign largely on two words: "Had enough?"

However, the explosion of scandals came largely under succeeding Democratic administrations. The Republicans promised that every session of the Eightieth Congress "would open with a prayer and close with a probe." When they got in, they did not cash in on their opportunities, with the result they invited defeat in 1948.

There were scandals, as there always are and always will be, because men will profit in politics and are not too particular as to how they do it, regardless of party. I have always felt that the general underestimate of FDR's successor made the climate favorable for scandals. The greedy just didn't think that Truman would be smart enough to catch them. Most of them were small fry and none too bright themselves.

Given an opportunity, men will profit from influence. Others will steal. Many are caught, but one can only wonder how many more get away with it. And what is wrong for some, seems to be perfectly proper in others.

One of the worst operators in Truman's time was T. Lamar Caudle, the Assistant Attorney General in charge of the tax division, who was removed and jailed for malfeasance in office. Connally, as has been noted, also went to jail. There were other betrayers of trust but the scandals that got the most play in the press were something the public could understand more easily, like deep freezes, mink coats and other gifts.

Yet, the half-dozen deep freezes that a manufacturer distributed around the White House were sorry machines that few housewives would have welcomed into their homes. They were large boxes with compressors at their sides. The machines were improvised and, as a result, were so large and awkward that few homes could take them. Vardaman, one of the recipients, passed his on to the marine officers' club. The press was concerned only with the fact that the gifts had been made. Most of the figures involved were minor and the services rendered were relatively unimportant, yet the paramount issue was profiteering and betrayal of trust.

Shortly after the Eisenhower administration took over, I was lunching with Major General Wilton B. Persons, an old and valued friend I had known since his days as captain. Persons was high on Ike's team and destined to be his No. 1 assistant. Major General Harry Vaughan, Truman's military aide, who had been pilloried for accepting a deep freeze, came over to our table to warn Persons that I was a tough customer and would bear watching.

"Why, Harry," I exclaimed, "I never did anything to you."

"No," he agreed, "but only because you were aiming higher."

Vaughan rode the storm well and grew in his chief's estimation.

Truman was never touched by scandal himself, either in the White House or in all his service in the Kansas City machine of Tom Pendergast, who went to jail for his crimes. HST stood by his friend, however, when lesser men would have turned away, flying out to Pendergast's funeral when he was Vice President.

The only close brush with scandal was through one of his friends, a Kansas City lawyer, who had been employed by four Capone hoodlums from Chicago because of his connection with the President, to get them out of prison. The hoodlums also employed an attorney who was a former associate of Attorney General Tom Clark for the same purpose.

The Kansas City lawyer was traced to the doors of the White House and the Texas lawyer to the doors of the Department of Justice by James L. Doherty, the great *Tribune* crime reporter, but no further. Doherty testified on the release of the four hoodlums before a House committee on government operators. During his appearance Doherty was guilty of one of the greatest acts of contempt of Congress I have ever known, and nothing was done about it. Doherty was questioned at one point by Representative William L. Dawson, a Chicago congressman, who had been a Republican but turned Democrat when the New Deal swept into power. Doherty looked Dawson in the eye and declared:

"Congressman, I won't answer any question put by you, because you sell dope to school children."

Dawson's eyes dropped. There were a few moments of silence and Representative Clare Hoffman of Michigan, a Republican, took up the questioning.

Truman's loss of Congress in 1946 was regarded widely, particularly by Republicans, as the handwriting on the wall for his personal defeat in 1948. Republicans were confident that the presidency would drop into their laps like an overripe plum. Democrats were unhappy and talked of replacing HST, but few dared to propose any break. The political situation was allowed to drift by both parties.

Truman continued to do the best he knew how. One of his most boasted accomplishments came in 1947. This was the Marshall Plan, by which American dollars were poured into Europe to stem the Communist tide, Truman and others having awakened to the dangers posed by the masters of the Kremlin.

Although named after Marshall, then Secretary of State, the plan was actually launched by Acheson, then Under Secretary, in a speech in the relatively obscure town of Delta, Mississippi. When a favorable reaction was built up, Marshall proposed on June 5, 1947, that the countries of Western Europe work out a program for reconstruction for which he promised American assistance. The scheme came into operation under a congressional grant of 3.8 billion dollars. The program continues until this day, although appropriations have been cut to one third, but there are still billions available in the pipeline.

HST was no less proud of the Truman Doctrine, which gave support to people threatened by a Communist take-over, like Greece. This program had its inception in a denunciation of Russian aggression by Winston S. Churchill in another relatively unknown town, Fulton, Missouri.

British leaders generally had more respect for Truman than for Roosevelt. They considered him a stronger character, possessing a better mind, a patriotic American and still one genuinely interested in advancing the lot of all peoples everywhere.

Like most Presidents, Truman encountered very little gratitude from appointees. Therefore, he was astonished on October 16, 1947, when Edward M. Curran came to the White House, not seeking to see the Chief Executive but to leave a message of thanks on the first anniversary of his appointment to the United States District Court for the District of Columbia. When word of Curran's errand was brought to him, Truman insisted that the judge be ushered into his office.

"You know," he said, "you are the first man I ever appointed to come up and thank me for it after the passage of a year."

All appointees are grateful at the time they get their posts. However, it isn't long before they begin wondering why the appointment hadn't come sooner and in a short time they become convinced that the President is very lucky indeed because they are serving him and that he ought to do better by the appointee, if possible.

When 1947 faded, Truman entered the fateful campaign year of 1948 as cocky as ever. There were those who believed he would bow out for the good of the party, but no one dared ask him to do so to his face. There was grumbling that he ought to do so, but if he heard it, Truman paid no heed because he had determined to fight not so much for the retention of power, as for himself and his place in history, and he was determined not to let his family down by running up the white flag.

OUT OF THE JAWS
OF VICTORY

THE ELECTION of 1948 is without doubt the most astounding in all American political history. There have been closer contests and more violently fought contests for the presidency, but never has there been one more surprising. Almost singlehandedly Truman stemmed the Republican tide of victory, which was conceded to Thomas E. Dewey by all polls and almost all the experts, to emerge triumphant.

Still, there is much room for interesting speculation as to what might have happened if Truman had bowed out in 1948, as so many in his party fervently wished but dared not urge. At the time Eisenhower was being advanced as a candidate for the Democratic nomination. Ike didn't then know a great deal about either party, if he ever did. In his youth, before going to West Point, he had proclaimed himself a Democrat in Abilene, Kansas, holding it to be the party of the people rather than the party of interests.

While many men put aside childish things, it would not have been difficult for Ike to return to his original allegiance. Possibly what restrained him more than any philosophy or ideology was the loyalty in which the military are steeped. After all, Roosevelt had named him to the command of the allied forces in Western Europe and Truman had named him to command of the Western postwar military high command. Ike doubtless could not see himself as an ingrate, but had Truman withdrawn, his decision to enter the lists might have been different.

If Ike had accepted the Democratic nomination in 1948, he would most certainly have been elected, very likely by a far greater margin than Truman. He would have been re-elected in 1952 and might have been succeeded by his Vice President, possibly Adlai E. Stevenson. Stevenson might well have enjoyed two terms, being succeeded by yet another Democrat, perhaps Lyndon B. Johnson, who might well have been succeeded by John F. Kennedy, who might well be alive and in the White House.

It is possible that Truman's withdrawal in 1948 might have spelled another quarter of a century of Democratic rule, a consummation hardly devoutly to be wished. It is entirely possible that Ike would not have become involved in Korea or, if he had, would have insisted on victory, so that Vietnam might not have become our longest war. However, all such speculation is idle, if interesting.

History doesn't always pick the best man for President, any more than parties do. The best qualified men are seldom nominated, but those that are and win frequently function better than the people have a right to expect, as was the case with HST. How could Truman look into the seeds of time in 1948 and tell which grain would grow and which would not. He was most interested in demonstrating that his party had been right in picking him for Vice President in 1944, and in justifying the party's faith in himself.

The first man to predict that Dewey would be defeated, as far as I know, was Colonel McCormick. He made the declaration editorially early in 1948. However, the prediction grew out of his detection of the Republican shift to the left and his support of Senator Robert A. Taft for the GOP nomination. Nonetheless, he was the first to foresee what came just as he was the first to see the Republican trend toward spending and welfare programs.

After the colonel's prediction on Dewey, I went to Attorney General Clark and told him that if Truman played his political cards as close to his vest as he played his poker hands, the *Tribune* probably wouldn't support him but might stand aloof if Dewey were renominated. Clark thought the suggestion important enough to take to the White House immediately. Later that afternoon he reported Truman had spurned the suggestion without a moment's hesitation and in the strongest of language.

Not long after the Republicans regained power in Congress, McCormick wired me: "I'm afraid the Republicans are going New Deal. Vandenberg went that way when it looked as though it were irresistible and his authority and White's [Senator Wallace H. White, Jr., of Maine, who had become leader of the Republican majority] are going to put them into positions of leadership."

I am certain that McCormick felt that his party's nomination went to men often less fitted than himself, because he invariably forwarded letters from devoted readers suggesting that he be President. While I could agree he might be better qualified than some, my nightmares often concerned running the *Tribune*'s Washington Bureau with McCormick in the White House or as Secretary of War.

However, he was solidly behind Taft in 1948. The fall before, the colonel sent me to cover a western swing Taft made to test his strength against the Republican field, especially Dewey and Stassen. In Tacoma, Washington, Arthur (Dutch) Shulz of the Topeka *Capital* and I came upon a line of Communist pickets demonstrating around a theater in which the senator was about to speak. We volunteered to join the group. The young woman leader was happy to get recruits who did not demand pay and who didn't appear to be from skid row, so she gave us each an anti-Taft placard. When Taft came up and stepped out of his car, he was amazed to find Dutch and me marching with the pickets and chanting to the tune of "Red Wing":

> "Oh you can't scare me,
> I'm sticking by the union."

Taft roared with laughter. When a cameraman came up and pointed his Graflex, I dropped my banner and fled, not wanting the colonel to see me demonstrating against his candidate. Taft frequently asked me to sing the song for guests in his home or mine. The senator had only a shade more musical sense than his presidential father, whose military aide, Colonel Archibald Butt, would have to nudge him, in an agreed manner, so that the Chief Executive could stand when the band played "The Star-Spangled Banner."

Taft was very easy to cover. His speeches were his own; no one ever wanted to claim them any more than they did the involved, archaic and ambiguous style of Cordell Hull. Every Taft speech discussed every issue, so I could take his first speech, divide up the issues to stress on appropriate stops on his tour.

At Philadelphia in 1948, the Republican convention was the greatest political show on earth. Victory-scenting faithful thronged hotels so that it was almost impossible to get into an elevator or through packed lobbies. Tickets for convention sessions were as hard to come by as for any athletic championship.

While Taft was high in popular favor it was obvious that the Dewey forces were undercutting him on all sides. At a critical stage in the proceedings, when it was obvious that the only way Dewey could be stopped was by a coalition of Taft and Stassen, the senator called to ask me for the former governor's private phone number in his suite at the Warwick Hotel.

I was speechless for a few seconds, because I couldn't understand any team seeking to win a nomination that would not lay out essential lines of communication. I was not too impressed with Taft's strategy team of Representatives Clarence J. Brown and George H. Bender. They came to Philadelphia after a session of Congress that went into the early morning hours. When I rang the headquarters, seeking either of the strategists, I was surprised that Taft answered the phone himself.

"The poor fellows are sleeping," Taft explained. "After all they were up very late and then had to come here."

From the result—Dewey's nomination—it seemed to me that they slept throughout the convention. I guess Bender was too busy polishing the school bells he rang at so many GOP gatherings, and Brown was too busy running with shovel in hand after the baby elephant that Taft forces were leading around convention hotels in order to build up support for their hero, to consider much strategy. It has always struck me as one of the great ironies of political life that Taft should have been succeeded in the Senate by Bender, an amiable fellow, but as like to Taft as his school bells were to the trumpet of the Archangel Gabriel. Still, Bender was succeeded in turn by Taft's son, Robert, who has seemed to be busiest in running away from his father's conservative image.

Colonel McCormick was a delegate and no end of a problem to

the *Tribune* staff at the convention. At that time and for months to come, the *Tribune*, as well as all other Chicago papers, was involved in a printers' strike. Publication was maintained by involved and time-consuming processes of typing and photography, pasting and trimming. Our deadline for most of our circulation of over a million was about 9 A.M. of the day before the date of the paper. We could manage bulletins, but very few.

Maxwell, who was in charge of the staff, leaned on me because of my knowledge of the cast of characters and politics as well as my experience. Every morning Managing Editor Maloney would call before 9 A.M. to demand stories on what would happen at the convention sessions that afternoon and that night. This took a great deal of maneuvering, which was complicated by the fact that the colonel was apparently engaged in scooping his own paper. Aware of the printing problem, McCormick was issuing statements blasting Taft's opposition, and distributing them to all except his own paper. Had it not been for my friends in the news services, we would have known nothing of our own editor's campaign.

Furthermore, that convention came near to costing Maxwell his job as city editor, to say nothing of his succession to the editorship. He and I had to fight for his neck as well as perform our duties, which kept us racing around the clock.

McCormick was sold the idea that Governor Dwight Green of Illinois was about to double-cross the *Tribune* by selling out his support of Taft in return for the vice-presidential nomination with Dewey. The salesmen of this fiction were Senator C. (Curly) Wayland Brooks of Illinois, a close friend but one jealous of Green, and Alfred M. Landon, the 1936 GOP standard-bearer, who knew nothing about the Illinois situation, so that he could readily be enlisted in the scheme to downgrade Green.

Maxwell, according to Brooks and his wife, now director of the mint, was said to be secretly working with Green because both were from Indiana. The plotters approached the colonel through his wife, Maryland, who disliked the rather distant Ohioan.

An outraged McCormick phoned Maxwell and accused him of fomenting treason. Before he hung up, he ordered George Tagge, the *Tribune*'s master of Chicago and Illinois politics, to his Warwick Hotel suite. Maxwell was justifiably worried and called me into a huddle. I had been with him at all his meetings with Green and knew the story to be false. There were those in the Illinois delegation who wanted to break to Dewey for power and pay and the meetings were all concerned with holding the line for Taft.

Maxwell and I agreed that it would be a disaster for him if he sent Tagge to see the colonel, because George could not be expected to stand up to an affable McCormick, and we faced a smoldering one. So we suggested Tagge lose himself and I went instead, reporting Tagge couldn't be found. McCormick recognized this was a fiction. Obviously, he hadn't wanted to see me because he knew I would give him an argument, which I proceeded to do, branding the story as nothing but a lie.

I encountered considerable resistance, but finally I pledged my head on the truth of what I was saying. I had reason to be thankful I was born in Pennsylvania, because had I been a Hoosier, there is not the slightest doubt that the plotters would have sold their story. I left the colonel, somewhat, although not wholly, mollified. But he did know that when I gave him my word he could rely on it. As I left, Maryland called me into her bedroom. I found her much harder to convince than her husband—in fact she believes the story to this day, although Green held the line and did not take the vice-presidential nomination, which I am sure could have been his. I argued for more than a half hour, when the colonel burst into the bedroom to find me with his wife, while she was in a pegnoir brushing her hair.

"What in the hell are you and my wife up to?" he roared.

I fled.

The colonel was in his seat in the Illinois delegation when supporters of Senator Vandenberg made their play to gain the nomination for him at an afternoon session. They made their move as the possibility of a deadlock between Dewey and Taft existed, but was fading. Mrs. Vandenberg was persuaded to forget her disapproval of her husband's love life with two British young women, and came from the Midwest to join him. They posed on park benches outside the hall as a model if not an ideal couple.

The plan called for Vandenberg to march down the central aisle of the convention hall to join the Michigan delegation during a speech by the ethereally lovely Clare Boothe Luce. It was hoped this appearance at the proper moment would stampede the convention.

Vandenberg marched down the aisle, clad in white linen, like a shining if somewhat tarnished Galahad. Mrs. Luce did well, hailing him as the party's great hope, but relatively few delegates were on hand. There was some applause, but no stampede. Vandenberg sat down with a brave smile, fully aware the plan had failed.

Later he was to write in his memoirs that he never expected to be nominated, because of the opposition of the Chicago *Tribune*, giving the paper far more credit than it may have deserved, but he included in those memoirs the acceptance speech he had in his pocket, just in case lightning should strike.

McCormick was not among the applauders for Vandenberg. If the senator spoke the truth and the *Tribune* did deny him the nomination, there were many in the hall who would have hailed McCormick for the performance of a great public service. Vandenberg was afflicted with one of the most virulent cases of self-love I have ever encountered. He was generally given to quoting from his last speech and talking of the next.

In one respect, Vandenberg certainly lived in the right time. In those simpler days, newspapers were given to printing the text of many senatorial speeches or long stories, with generous quotes, running to three thousand words. Today a senator is lucky to get a few paragraphs and many prefer to be asked to say a few words on TV evening news reports.

When Mrs. Vandenberg died, she obviously felt she had done her duty by the senator, because she directed that she be buried with her family in Indiana and not in the Vandenberg plot in Battle Creek, Michigan.

When it became apparent that Dewey would be nominated, Colonel McCormick strode out of the convention hall, not wishing to join the customary motion to make the nomination unanimous. He left that to his alternate. The vice-presidential nomination that Green could have had for the asking went to Earl Warren of California. Representative Charles Halleck of Indiana, who brought his state's delegation into the Dewey camp, felt that the nomination had been promised to him and not without reason. Had he been nominated there is reason to believe that Halleck might have stemmed the farm revolt which cost Dewey a victory.

McCormick wasn't one to cry over spilt milk in politics. He had had considerable experience in sustaining defeat. He masked his disappointment by taking off on the oblique and wired me from Chicago:

"Of course the news now is in the Democratic convention—the Republican convention is history."

Compared to the Republican gathering, the Democratic convention was funereal in tone. The only life was given by the shouting of a former army sergeant, who had served under Ike in Europe, bellowing over a loud speaker for his former commander from a truck outside the Bellevue-Stratford Hotel. The galleries in the hall were not crowded. The only excitement was in the selection of the vice-presidential nominee. Supreme Court Justice William O. Douglas might have had it but was not eager in view of the clouds of Democratic defeat in the air, so it went handily to Senator Barkley. He was delighted and gave me a great victory hug because he knew I favored him over the Justice, who had been mentioned for the presidential nomination by some desperate Democrats.

I must say Barkley seemed to be confident of victory in the fall, but the campaign had not begun. So did Truman when he came to deliver his acceptance speech. He had to wait behind the scenes for a floor hassle, but was enjoying himself immensely as he made clear when he exchanged a few words.

Truman's acceptance speech was almost the only thing that went right at that Democratic gathering. Everything else was pretty much a bust with the organ drowning out the singing of the national anthem by Lawrence Tibbett and forcing him to shift keys, and the release of a flock of doves, which was to have offered a pretty scene, found the birds so sleepy they had to be prodded. When they were forced out, they behaved so that delegates had to scatter.

Although it was early morning and the convention had gone badly, Truman electrified the gathering. He sounded the first note of hope and gave a foretaste of what was to come in the whistle-stop campaign, when he boasted of party accomplishment and pitched into the Republican Eightieth Congress. I can still hear him announcing that he was calling on the Congress to come back into session on July 26, Turnip Day in Missouri, pass legislation to aid education, promote national health, extend civil rights, raise the minimum wage, extend Social Security and other programs. Truman demonstrated that he was a professional politician who knew all the tricks of his trade.

Back in Washington, I prepared to cover my third convention in a few weeks—that of the Progressive party headed by Wallace. I didn't cover the States Rights party which picked J. Strom Thurmond, now a Republican senator. These splinter parties were expected to cut so deeply into Democratic strength that Republican victory would be inevitable.

The night before I left for Philadelphia, Cissie Patterson had Carol and me to her home for dinner. We were alone. For many years she had tried to get me to become her managing editor. Knowing her fiery temper and her disenchantment with the most sought-after employees, I evaded her successfully, although not without occasional strain to our pleasant relationship. She offered me $35,000 a year, then a rather astronomical sum. When I hesitated she offered to put ten years' pay in escrow and throw in a $35,000 house she would build where I pleased. Still later, she began offering me shares in her will and finally the role of sole heir.

At our final meeting she again expressed dissatisfaction with her will, which divided her holdings among seven employees, who came to be known in Washington as "the seven dwarfs." They divided almost five millions. I must say that I didn't think she was going to die as soon as she did. I might have been moved to reconsider.

At this dinner, I again turned down the editorship. She then asked me what she could do, since she didn't like her will. I suggested that since the paper was the only thing she really liked, she endow it and leave it as a monument to her aims and objectives. I do not know whether she had such a plan in mind but she leaped at it, asking how it might be done. Knowing she had great confidence in Wheeler, I suggested she explore the possibility with the former senator, adding that he could help her pick a set of responsible and competent trustees to supervise the operation of the paper.

There was no experience quite like dinner in her home. Invitations were invariably for eight o'clock, but one learned never to come until nine, because she never put in an appearance until that hour, and the servants were given to loading predinner drinks. They knew their mistress was happiest when mellow and worked to get guests into the same condition as rapidly as possible. They shared in the drinking as well, which I learned on wandering into the kitchen on more than one occasion and finding the staff seated around a table and lapping up highballs.

Mrs. Patterson's advent was always announced by the yapping of three french poodles, who were her inseparable companions. She was a strong antivivisectionist and woe betide anyone who abused her dogs. I have seen her British butler enter with a poodle hanging from the tails of his dress coat, because the beast knew the butler dared not dislodge it. I had to tread on the toes of these animals in order to command respect, but never let her see me do it. As a result they left me alone, which she took as evidence of their regard and increased her fondness for me because, as she put it: "You can't fool dogs about people."

I would always offer Mrs. Patterson a drink when she entered the drawing room, where we generally ate. Without fail, she would respond: "I've been having a little white wine as you well know," by which she meant she had Martinis in her room, but she always accepted an old-fashioned cocktail. Then she would announce: "Let's not eat; let's all get drunk."

One such dinner was memorable. It was given for Joseph Brooks, the former husband of Alicia Patterson, who was the captain's eldest daughter. This meal was limited to friends, including George Dixon, the humorous columnist, and his wife, John O'Donnell, Evie Robert, Carol and myself, as well as Joe.

That evening she was interested in food, having acquired a Polish chef whose specialty was venison stew, which he laced with a full bottle of brandy. After the dinner, she left us, as was her custom, inviting the guests to stay all night if they wished.

Never before had she returned, but that night she came in, like a wild-eyed Lady Macbeth, but with a revolver rather than a candle in her hand. For a few seconds we were all taken aback. I was quite sure she didn't intend to shoot any of us, but one could never be certain.

"The son of a bitch," she exclaimed, biting off each word.

She was behind me, so I reached her after Brooks. He took the revolver and put it in his pocket, where I fished for it.

"It's all right," he said, "I got it."

"You damned fool," I whispered, "I want to see if it's been fired."

To my relief, I learned it had not when I broke it open and dumped out five loaded bullets. Mrs. Patterson went to the table and poured herself a stiff drink. As she sipped it, she reached into the pockets of the flowing, brocaded pajamas she effected for home wear, drew out a pair of handcuffs and then a police badge and flung them to the floor.

It was only then that we learned the story. She had gone downstairs to have her dogs taken out for an airing. On a marble bench in the foyer, she discovered the Burns Detective Agency guard she employed in a drunken sleep. She shook him awake to fire him. On being fired he turned over his gun, his handcuffs and his badge.

I left for Philadelphia but not until I learned that she had made an appointment to meet with Wheeler in Dower House, her Maryland retreat east of the capitol, for Sunday, July 25. She was found dead the day before, sprawled across her bed, having evidently reached for the bell to summon help. As so often happens in the case of sudden death of wealthy and prominent persons, there was much whispering of foul play. Most, if not all, of this was inspired by persons who expected to benefit from the will and didn't, and by others who preferred gossip to fact.

Services were held in the ballroom of her town house the following Monday. She made the place gay many a Christmas in giving an annual party with gifts for the children of her friends and not a few foes. I can never forget the gasp that went up when her hated former son-in-law, columnist Drew Pearson, marched in and took a seat near the front.

"Now I know she's dead," I whispered to Carol, "but I wouldn't have been surprised if she had risen up in her coffin and ordered him out."

She had once offered me $50,000 to do a critical series on Pearson. I refused, because I already had more than enough to do and because she frequently embarrassed me by trying to draw me into her feuds with her cousin, the colonel. He was to take over her paper within the year and bring the *Tribune*'s campaign against Truman to the White House doorsteps.

The *Tribune* campaign against Truman, in which I played a major role, was a savage one. While it wasn't pleasant reading for him,

Truman played it to his advantage, choosing to regard it as the tempo of all the opposition press. The *Tribune* beat drums on scandals, communism and a variety of issues. Among the latter was the charge that Truman was playing politics with a war scare, when he called for a three-billion-dollar rearmament that summer. It was not until later that it was learned that this call was based on faulty evaluation of intelligence reports, which provoked fears that the Russians might launch World War III almost immediately. The *Tribune* beat gongs of battle on Truman's pardoning of vote thieves of the Pendergast machine. The prosecution was hampered by the theft of impounded ballots from the county courthouse, while Truman, on a visit home, slept in his hotel room a few blocks away.

In his whistle-stop campaign Truman picked up FDR's old theme about "the Republican press," accusing the enemy of misrepresentation, when it was widely known that some 95 per cent of the members of the press were Democrats or self-styled independents who never voted for Republicans. Truman carried it a step further, being critical of "those Republican reporters." If there were some Republicans still in the press corps, in his day, they were mighty still.

The picture of the campaign, as we retain it today, is of a little man sawing the air on the back platform of an armor-plated and bullet-proof glass private car, pointing with pride to his party's accomplishments and viewing with alarm the actions of the opposition. This picture is pretty much true, because he was almost always alone.

Truman's respect for me as a reporter grew out of two great scoops I got in his time. One came in the fall of 1948 while he was fighting with his back to the wall. HST decided to send Chief Justice Fred M. Vinson, an old and valued friend, to Moscow to talk to Stalin. Truman was still hopeful, as many were before him and are today, that personal diplomacy might charm the Russians into joining with the United States to launch world peace.

This departure from the separation of powers of the three branches of government was not new. HST figured it could not be without effect in the campaign, for its sheer drama. Whether the move could have any influence on Russia was another matter because it had grown accustomed to parades of Presidents and envoys.

B. K. Wheeler, then a year out of the Senate and in law practice in the capital with a heavy emphasis on radio problems, came to my home one evening. He reported that he knew HST had asked for radio time to go before the American people with his proposed Vinson mission. This news posed a problem, because the continued printers' strike was still playing havoc with our deadlines.

I knew that if I sent the story at that hour, about 9 P.M., all I could get in the paper would be a short bulletin in no more than a few thousand late papers. I decided to hold the story for a day, although I knew Washington has more leaks than a worn-out fire hose. Inquiry the next day revealed that several colleagues were sniffing on the scent in the State Department, aware that something was in the international winds.

Before I sent my story, I phoned Maloney to tell him what I had and explain its importance. Having been burned by the code-breaking story, he was afraid of scoops and buried my story on an inner page, where the alert Chicago bureau of the Associated Press found it and flashed it to the country.

Within a matter of minutes, Alan Gould, AP editor, wired Maloney congratulations on a great scoop. Not until he received this wire did Maloney dare to bring the story out on page one. I subsequently got another Beck award for the story, which was dumped into my lap without any effort on my part and which my managing editor had hesitated to run.

Meanwhile the story hit the whistle-stop special, to Truman's great annoyance. It also hit a surprised Secretary of State Marshall in Paris. The old soldier had not been consulted on this important step, so naturally he was irked and difficult to mollify, although Truman tried to assure him that he would have been notified in time. The Republican opposition raised the cry of politics so that Truman was forced to drop the scheme. Yet, to his dying day, he firmly believed that the premature publication of his plan had blasted a great opportunity for world peace.

However, he blamed the *Tribune* rather than me personally in his memoirs. I would have preferred to have had the personal mention, but he thought to spare me, or so he said.

It has been widely reported that Truman was confident of victory every moment of the 1948 campaign. To support this contention, the victory letters he wrote his mother and sister are cited. Yet, this report isn't quite true. He could hardly be expected to write defeatist notes to those near and dear to him.

I know he shared the general sad view of his prospects, at least to an extent, because he told Sam Mitchell, the steward on his private car, that he was making a final journey to Kansas City in order to vote, which could be the last journey for which he would require Sam's services. This was no paean of victory.

For almost forty years, Sam was my good friend, until his death early in 1973. Once when Truman told him his services would be needed, Sam replied that he couldn't accompany the President because: "My boss needs me."

"Ain't I your boss?" demanded the surprised President.

"No, sir, Mr. President," Sam answered. "Mr. Trohan, he's my boss."

HST was forced to laugh. Sam's affection for me, along with that of other friends of the President's, like Farley, and close associates, like Vaughan, rather than personal intimacy, prompted Truman's regard for me as a man and a reporter.

After the election it appeared that everyone was riding with Truman on his campaign special and everyone seemed to profess to know that he would win. This is only natural, because most men love a winner, if only because it is hard to benefit from a loser. I know of only two men who predicted a Truman victory and, frankly, I didn't take them too seriously.

One was Farley. But he had predicted victory for every Democratic candidate up to that time and was to continue an uninterrupted string of Democratic victory forecasts until George McGovern ran in 1972.

The other was my good friend Representative Paul Shafer. On his return from a visit to his Michigan district a few days before the election, Shafer called me to say Truman was going to win. I couldn't believe it, although I respected Shafer's judgment. Shafer told me that he had toured his district—normally Republican—and found that HST was going to capture it.

"If that is going on in my district," Shafer said, "it's going on all over the Midwest and that means Truman is going to win."

Shafer went to Milton S. Kronheim, a Washington friend, who was hoping to have his son named to a judgeship in the District of Columbia. Paul told Milton that if he wanted his son named a judge he should make immediate gifts in the names of all his family and friends to the Democratic war chest, because everyone knew that money was not flowing into the party coffers any faster than compassion from a Communist's heart.

Kronheim valued Shafer's judgment and made his contributions, one of the very few to do so before the election. After the election Truman named the son to the coveted judgeship and put two of the Washingtonian's friends on the District of Columbia Board of Commissioners, his lawyer, Jiggs Donohue, and Rene Camalier, a high-ranking Mason.

I got my first inkling that there might be something to Shafer's prediction when I arrived in Chicago to cover the congressional phase of the election. I learned from indignant friends that some 250,000 rent-increase notices for January 1, 1949, had been sent out by landlords to comply with the sixty-day notice requirement. Many tenants assumed this was in anticipation of a Dewey victory, so they were influenced by their pocketbooks to vote for Truman.

The pocketbook, it is my solemn belief, is the most important single issue in almost any election. Politicians are given to a lot of confused talk about a wide variety of issues, but voters generally call for continuance of an administration because they are satisfied with their financial status and prospects, but vote for a change when they are not, or when they fear their pocketbooks or jobs may be hit.

If Nixon had faced the electorate a year later than he did, he would not have won as easily, if at all, as he did in 1972. I base this prediction not on the Watergate scandal, which has been magnified out of all proportion, but on the rise in the cost of living, which has hit every family and every pocketbook—and hard.

The *Tribune* committed a classic blunder in the 1948 election, which will live to embarrass it in all political history. I must emphasize that the blunder was due in large part to the printers' strike, which continued to play havoc with our deadlines, as well as to a major blunder in judgment.

Every poll and every expert, although some were to deny it, gave the victory to Dewey. My predecessor, Henning, who was writing the presidential phase of the election, was to crown an honorable newspaper career of more than fifty years with an unforgettable error. Henning wrote his story before 9 A.M., saying that Dewey had won, without any qualification.

Most of the nation's polls had not even opened, so only a handful of votes were counted in some sparsely populated districts of New Hampshire. On this basis of Henning's story, which was not a surprising one, in view of general agreement on the result, Maloney ordered the eight-column line: "DEWEY DEFEATS TRUMAN."

The photograph of a beaming Truman on the back platform of his private car, holding a copy of the *Tribune* with that headline, has become famous and all too familiar to the *Tribune* management to this day. It should have served as a warning to all editors, but didn't. In the tight 1960 election between Kennedy and Nixon, the New York *Times* held back tens of thousands of copies of their paper, which hailed a Kennedy victory, for hours, when the Kennedy bandwagon stalled in the Middle West and the possibility of a Nixon victory loomed. They were spared the *Tribune*'s humiliation but more by luck than judgment.

Henning should have qualified his story, as I did mine, saying Republicans were leading in early returns, which they were. But they soon began to fall behind and by percentages that indicated defeats. I began writing stories saying that Democrats had recaptured the Senate and House, but my stories were being thrown away, because they did not conform to the victory eight-column line. In the face of mounting Truman votes, Maloney arched his neck and grew more stubborn, hoping for change. He had made his bed and was going to lie in it.

At 9 P.M. Taft called me from the family's newspaper office in Ohio to ask for our projection on the vote in Illinois. Taft had a mind like a computer for election returns. When I gave him the projection, he said it confirmed his estimate that Dewey was beaten. This was long before any concessions were being made. Taft was shedding no tears, because Dewey had robbed him of the nomination in Philadelphia.

Even this estimate failed to impress Maloney. It was not until a weary and still wishful-thinking Maloney left for home at midnight, having been on duty some fifteen hours, that Maxwell switched to his seat and began changing the *Tribune*'s front page. I rewrote the victory story to make it Truman's triumph. My stories were dug out of the wastebasket. We did get the page changed but only for the reading of a few subscribers in Chicago's Loop and members of the staff.

It was not a happy night. It has always been a deep source of shame and regret to me that I gave, albeit unwillingly, a verbal hot foot to my crushed predecessor. Before midnight, he was called to discuss the results on the *Tribune*'s television station, WGN TV, which provided the opportunity for the fast rewrite Maxwell ordered. In his broadcast Henning continued to insist Dewey had won, hoping somehow the mounting tide of Truman votes would subside and ebb.

I did not know what Henning had said when I rushed in to report the congressional elections. An announcer asked me in how-now-brown-cow tones, how the races were going. I was a bit out of breath having run up a couple of flights of stairs, so I snapped that the Democrats had regained both branches of Congress by comfortable margins. The announcer continued by asking how I thought Dewey would get along in the White House with a hostile Congress.

"He won't because he ain't going to be in the White House," was my rather inelegant but completely accurate reply. I hadn't given the studio audience a glance, but I looked up to see Mrs. McCormick and a few friends, when I heard a murmur of approval. I saw a dejected and crushed Henning and could have bitten off my tongue. The colonel, who was accustomed to losing elections and had no great love for Dewey, was listening at home.

The next day the colonel broke the news to the seventy-one-year-old veteran that he was being replaced as bureau chief by me, which didn't spell any great change in the bureau because I had been running it for years. I was then forty-five, and seventy-one seemed to me quite ancient indeed, although today I would look on Henning as a fine broth of a lad, because he did live on for eighteen years and in such excellent mental condition that I employed him as a sort of reference library on Washington and its figures.

After he got the sad news from the colonel, Henning asked me if I would permit him to continue as bureau chief until January 20, 1949, Inauguration Day. I assured him it would be quite all right with me and he left that day sending a final message that Washington bureau messages which had been signed for some forty years with the initials "hng" would henceforth be signed "tro," which was to continue for some twenty years more.

Henning retired on full pay, thanks to his generous boss. Later this was cut to three-quarters pay, but it was still generous. When my time came to retire, I had no desire to linger, although my health was and continues good, because I had seen danger come from trusting aged judgment.

Eleven weeks after his election, I saw Truman in his most entertaining, if not his greatest, hour. It was at the dinner given him and Barkley by the presidential electors in the Mayflower Hotel on January 19, 1949, the day before his inaugural. He had his audience in stitches when he mimicked the clipped, somewhat Germanic tones of H. V. Kaltenborn, the radio commentator, who was assuring his listeners that Dewey would still win at a time when Truman was far ahead. Richard Harkness of NBC came in for a share of the spoofing, but his delivery was not so easy to ridicule.

During the dinner, HST spotted me within easy range and mouthed a derisive "You, too," to which he was certainly entitled. Farley and other Democratic stalwarts, who shared a prime table, howled.

Inaugural Day was quite cold but sunny. I remember his address only vaguely as compared with his comedy of the night before. However, I do recall that he defined the difference between communism and democracy, holding that the former is based on the belief that man is so weak and inadequate that he requires the rule of strong masters, while the latter is based on the conviction that man has the capacity and inalienable right to govern himself.

Five days later, on January 25, Alger Hiss was found guilty of perjury in the long and involved investigation into his Communist associations and affiliations. The Hiss case had figured in the presidential campaign, although the issue of communism did not prove the vital one some Republicans had expected it to be.

During the height of the investigation by the House Un-American Activities Committee, Truman was to describe it as "a red herring." However, he confided to a friend that he did so because he felt the investigation was being aimed at him rather than the Assistant Secretary of State. Privately he was furious at Hiss. Acheson hadn't helped Truman's position any when he declared that he did not "intend to turn my back on Alger Hiss."

Although I ordered the writing of the first story naming Hiss as a target of the House committee's investigation, the inquiry into communism was not actually my cup of tea. Men like Representatives Hamilton Fish of New York and Martin Dies of Texas achieved considerable prominence for their inquiries into Communist machinations. Some men profited financially from their roles, being invited to address patriotic meetings for fees. The speaking honorarium is considered a legitimate pursuit of members of Congress, even when it takes them from their jobs. Members have made more than twice their $42,000-a-year salaries on the lunch and dinner and lecture circuit.

The investigation into the activities brought promotion to the Senate, the vice presidency and the White House for Richard M. Nixon, as he recounts in his book, *Six Crises*. It also brought a Senate seat to his associate on the House group, Karl Mundt of South Dakota. The connection with the House committee brought defeat to some chairmen, like John E. Rankin of Mississippi, and jail to others, like J. Parnell Thomas of New Jersey. Members of the committee became the targets of persons who insisted they saw the end of all liberty in any move to uncover Reds and their associates.

Actually, the work of uncovering was not that of members of Congress so much as it was of committee staffers. Some of these were able and dedicated men like Robert Stripling who uncovered the whole sorry mess of the pumpkin papers that sent Hiss to prison. Records of data sent to Russia by Red sympathizers and agents were hidden for a time in a pumpkin patch on his Maryland farm by Whittaker Chambers, a recanted Communist. He leveled the accusation of Red spy against Hiss.

Members of Congress did show a grasp of the situation and the courage to brave a wolf pack of critics. These were loudest in halls of learning where professors knew little of the facts but pretended to know all.

Much of the criticism was rooted in fear rather than reason. There were many who feared that the indiscretions of their youth, such as flirting with communism or association with Communist-dominated groups, would rob them of jobs or expose them to contempt or ridicule. This is entirely understandable.

It has always been a major surprise to me that the most confirmed critics of the House Un-American Activities Committee, for example, never troubled to visit its headquarters. Had they done so in its early days, when the group was getting under way, they might easily have blasted it out of existence.

But critics never went near the offices, preferring to fulminate at their typewriters on what they portrayed as an evil which darkened American skies and made babies cry in their cribs, whenever investigators came to town. Such intemperate exaggerations were actually employed against investigators. The reportorial critics of the Un-American Activities Committee sought the company of other reporters who shared their hate rather than undertake any investigation on their own.

Had the omniscient critics ever gone to the House committee's headquarters, they would have stumbled on scenes which would have made William Hogarth's depiction of London's gin alley a tea dance by comparison. Drinking was the order of the day after committee sessions and in the late afternoons. The drinking was not only serious but sustained, and with it went frivolity, merriment and easing of inhibitions. I know because I had to stage two rescues from the wild conviviality of some staffers who had never had it so good or free.

A description of one such party might have been promoted, not entirely unjustly, into a Roman bacchanalian revel, which could have dried up funds and spelled the end of the group. This would have been most unfair, but it might have been done. This revelry was not true of all of the staffers, nor of committee members, but a description of one such scene might have been a death knell. It goes, almost without saying, that it has never hurt any reporter to exercise his legs, even in this day of geniuses, who never consider any policy or program good until they lean their minds against it.

Critics never gave any member of the House Un-American Activities Committee the benefit of any doubt or a fair shake. During the war Stripling was assigned, at the specific direction of Mrs. Roosevelt, to sweep out the quarters of German officer prisoners of war. There was no complaint against such degradation from those who professed to be concerned about the dignity of man.

The arch villain in all the inquiries into the Communist conspiracy is, of course, Senator Joseph R. McCarthy of Wisconsin, whose very name has become a byword for the lowest of tactics—guilt by association, half truths, reckless charges, wholesale distortion and trial by accusation.

How strange, then, that those who hated McCarthy and all he stood for the most should now leave themselves open to charges of employing such tactics in the Watergate investigation. I know very little of that operation, which seems to me to be a compound of stupidity and too much money, but I invite solemn and dispassionate consideration of the similarities.

It is not my intention to engage in any lengthy discussion of McCarthy and his concern for government security. That has been and will continue to be the subject of books. However, it was such an amazing political phenomenon that I must offer a few sidelights from my experiences.

Those who opposed McCarthy say that he stifled and nearly strangled American freedom for all time. On the other hand, McCarthy had his defenders, but they have not been successful in pushing their demands for factual examination of the security situation.

The cold fact is that McCarthy was a creation of the press as Watergate is a creation of the press, whether the creation be good or bad. Every word that McCarthy uttered was trumpeted throughout the land and almost every Washington story was tied into the Wisconsin senator as almost every Washington story is now related to Watergate.

Man often seems to crave a devil to hate as much or more than he desires a God to love. So it may be in part with McCarthy. Most of those who are occupied with Watergate do not remember McCarthy was every bit as dominating and pervading an issue in his time.

In all fairness it must be acknowledged that McCarthy made it easy for his enemies to spread their smears. He was never one to understate his case, from that fateful day on February 9, 1950, when he delivered a speech that he had not checked, before a Wheeling, West Virginia, audience of the Ohio County Women's Republican Club. The speech was partly read and partly extempore, so that it is impossible to be exact about what he actually did say. There is dispute as to whether he said he had evidence of the existence of 205 or 257 Communists in the State Department.

The situation would have been grave enough if there had only been a handful of Reds in the right places. McCarthy's enemies made out that he had launched a reign of terror that claimed thousands of victims and deprived the country of the services of more thousands of able servants, who feared his tactics and would not join the government service. This was nonsense, pure and simple. McCarthy's love of the sensational made life difficult for his supporters, but John F. Kennedy, who supported him in the Senate hearings, and Robert F. Kennedy, who was employed on the committee's staff, didn't find the association with the man from Wisconsin a blight.

McCarthy told me that Father Joe Kennedy had made a thirty-thousand-dollar contribution to McCarthy's campaign against communism, on the condition that the senator should not make a speech in Boston, where his campaign had wide support, in behalf of Senator Henry Cabot Lodge, who was seeking re-election and being challenged by son Jack.

The Wisconsin senator suffered under Eisenhower and was crucified in the Senate, not by censure, as was first proposed, but by formal condemnation of his methods. Not long afterward, on May 2, 1957, he died. His enemies pursued him to the grave, reporting the funeral was held in an "unfilled church," when mourners were actually standing, although there may have been an empty seat or so. There were no more in the same church for Kennedy's funeral six and one-half years later. Nor did the enemies mention that for two days mourners stood in lines blocks long in order to pay their respects in a capital in which he had been assailed savagely by the press. Nor did they mention that the White House sent two top aides to the McCarthy services. I know because I sat between Persons and Edward R. McCabe.

While I knew McCarthy well, let it be understood I was no cheerleader. I begged him to understate his case—both for his good and the country's—but without avail. When the FBI asked me to hand McCarthy some evidence they had, I refused. The FBI had been burnt when they had slipped him data earlier and he promptly identified the source. I told the FBI I didn't want McCarthy saying in committee or on the Senate floor that he got his information from Walter Trohan who got it from the FBI.

Some things amused me about McCarthy. One was that he was a Wisconsin Progressive of the elder La Follette's stripe, but the liberals were so busy hating him they never bothered to find out his political principles or to examine his votes. Certainly he was no conservative.

Also he was extremely susceptible to youthful charms in his bachelor days. He just couldn't keep his hands off young girls. Why the Communist opposition didn't plant a minor on him and raise the cry of statutory rape, I don't know.

I can only conclude that Communists were never, in my considered judgment, as smart as they were painted to be by the anti-Communists. The Reds were often too busy talking or too busy hating for the accomplishment of all the diabolical planning they were credited with instigating. They were ruthless, but they were also stupid, as evidenced by their efforts to tear down all religions while building one of their own more dogmatic and more rigid than any they sought to replace.

I must acknowledge that some anti-Communists were just as bad. They were also forever talking and seeing things under the bed. They had no more sense of humor than the Reds. However, some of the anti-Communists made a very good thing of it, just as some Communists did. The anti-Communists wrote me off as well intentioned but not serious, because I was always moved to laughter when they played their games of whipping dead horses and concocting new conspiracies to fit shifting events. However, I believe there was a Communist conspiracy and that Communists have not given up their long dream of world domination.

As for some anti-Communists, who are really anti-anti-Communist, I have nothing but contempt. They haven't the courage to acknowledge their affections and ties, so they go around whipping the enemies of communism, but never condemn the excesses of communism.

I did my best to promote McCarthy's marriage to his secretary, the pretty Jeanie Kerr, hoping she would school him in restraint. I did not foresee, as I complained to her later, that she would become his No. 1 cheerleader. He was a good husband and a fine father to their adopted child, a lovely girl.

McCarthy was an accomplished chef. No one could broil a better steak. He enjoyed creating his specialty—venison stew—which sent many into raptures. Joe would pass a knowing wink over such praise to friends whom he had let in on the secret that the "venison" was actually chain-store chuck.

Another tarnished warrior of the period was James V. Forrestal, the first Secretary of Defense, who was my good friend and one of the finest and most dedicated public servants I have ever known. Jim came from lower New York State, where his brother won an appointment as postmaster under Farley when he met with difficulty in the Depression.

Forrestal entered and graduated from Princeton, where he was a boxer, as a broken nose attested, and a good one. It is my sincere belief that this sport proved to be his undoing, because a boxer must rely on himself rather than on his teammates. He undertook a Wall Street career, becoming head of Dillon, Reed & Co. From this company he entered government service, first in the Treasury, later as Secretary of Navy and finally was named as the first head of the newly organized and not really united Defense Department.

In the Defense Department Jim was convinced that the United States, especially the U. S. Navy, could not operate without Mideast oil. He did not anger the Arabs, which some persons, including a scoundrel in the press, insisted made him anti-Israeli, which he was not. Few men were more misrepresented or vilified in some quarters than this hard-working official. Also his life was domestically and religiously complicated.

He had me to functions in the Pentagon when lesser men feared to do so. Also he invited me to breakfast at his Georgetown home, which I refused to join, because I am willing to discuss business or listen to speeches at lunch or dinner, but will not permit anything to intrude on my quiet tea and toast, the only meal that almost always belonged to Carol and myself.

Forrestal left the Cabinet in 1949 partly because he did not wish to embarrass Truman, who had recognized Israel and brought his influence on other nations to recognize the new state. He talked of returning to his church, but leaped out of his suite from the tower of Bethesda Naval Hospital, not long after he left the Cabinet, leaving behind him a book in which he had underlined a number of passages of gloomy poetry.

It is hard to say that Forrestal's call for caution in the Middle East was unwise. While the Jews are entitled to a homeland, the creation of the state by Britain and the United States has raised many problems in seeking to solve but one. It is not unlikely that the seeds of World

War III may spring from the tensions that have followed the best of intentions.

While Truman was debating a course of action on Israel, a group of persons interested in the formation of the new state approached Burton K. Wheeler, knowing his close relation to the President. They offered him $50,000 if he could swing the vote of the Philippines to Israel. Wheeler approached his friend Joaquin Elizalde, the Philippine ambassador, who had been the commissioner of the islands in Congress before the country was granted its freedom.

Elizalde said that he was sorry but his country had many Moslems, referring to the Morros, and did not wish to provoke trouble at home by antagonizing them over the creation of Israel. Wheeler so reported to his prospective clients and turned down the offer. Two days later Elizalde called Wheeler and asked him if he could reopen negotiations with the group which had tried to employ him. The Philippine ambassador said his country was going to have to vote for the new state, because Truman had called him to the White House to demand that the Philippines vote for Israel or lose American aid. Wheeler did not cash in on the information, although he might have.

The second scoop that I got, which brought Truman's respect for me as a reporter, was on the firing of General Douglas MacArthur, which story was again somewhat throttled by editorial timidity. By that time Maloney had collapsed from driving himself harder than he drove others, and had been succeeded by Maxwell. The new managing editor got a curious tip out of Tokyo that the allied commander in Japan and Korea was about to be relieved by Truman. The tip came from a radio newsman.

I couldn't believe it, but was aware of the friction between Truman and his commander, and I was enough a reporter never to dismiss the wildest of tips without checking. A few probes in sensitive areas lay bare the White House intent. I asked Lloyd Norman, then the *Tribune* Pentagon correspondent and now on the staff of *Newsweek*, to question General Omar Bradley, the army chief of staff.

I undertook to beard Joseph Short, who had succeeded Ross as press secretary at the White House. It wasn't much of a bearding because Short, who was a nice fellow personally and completely devoted to Truman, confirmed the story by his evident panic. So did

Bradley by racing to the White House, where he rushed past me without even a nod, although he knew me very well indeed.

So I wrote the story that MacArthur was about to be fired in time for our first edition. Meanwhile, Maxwell's Tokyo tipster was persuaded he himself was hunting on the wrong trail and dropped his efforts toward confirmation and advised Maxwell to do so. Despite the confirmatory spadework the bureau had done and the fact that the White House reported it would have an important announcement later that evening, Maxwell killed my story.

I went to the White House to await the promised announcement. Merriman Smith, the UP White House man, who thought he owned the Executive Mansion, came to ask me what I thought the news would be. I told him, but Smith wouldn't believe me, so he missed a chance to put an exclusive flash on the wire. He was to acknowledge it later.

When the brief announcement of MacArthur's relief came, I ran from the White House to my home, about a mile away, and dictated my story between gasps for breath. Maxwell congratulated me, but gave me no Beck award, partly because he had failed to capitalize on his own tip, but then I didn't deserve one. Truman mentioned the story in his memoirs, again hitting the *Tribune*, but not identifying me, out of what he doubtless fancied as kindness.

Truman fired MacArthur because he did not consider that the general had sufficiently subordinated himself to the Commander in Chief. MacArthur wanted to bomb above the Yalu River, in order to blast Red Chinese supply lines into North Korea, and thus win the war. Truman thought MacArthur's strategy would bring Red China into the war and possibly launch World War III.

History will judge whether the President or the general was right. In this instance Truman was abandoning his characteristic role of fighter and playing that of appeaser. Truman knew as well as MacArthur, if not better, that neither Red China nor Red Russia could launch a war at that time. How much Truman was influenced by the fact that MacArthur was a Republican and possible presidential candidate only he knew and he never told. Had MacArthur's plan of prompt and decisive action been followed, the war in Korea might have ended in victory and the war in Vietnam might never have been launched by Hanoi. If that is hindsight, what's hindsight for, as my friend General Carl A. (Tooey) Spaatz is given to saying.

After the MacArthur removal, the colonel wired me that Dwight Young, then president of the American Society of Newspaper Editors, had invited the general to address the group's annual convention in Washington. The colonel said he thought it would be better if MacArthur addressed a joint session of Congress, adding curtly, "Get busy." I do not claim that McCormick and I got the general invited, but we didn't forestall the invitation.

In advance of the great day, for which McCormick gave me full credit, I was ordered to get seats for Maryland and himself in the gallery of the House. This was no small problem, because the demand for seats was tremendous and members were allowed one guest seat each. I was given one ticket by Representative Marguerite Stitt Church of Illinois, one of the most informed and capable public servants I have ever known. Then I twisted the arm of Representative Sid Simpson of Illinois, who twisted mine right back, by wrapping his lone gallery seat in a copy of a recent speech, which he observed might interest me. He got a story on the speech and I got two seats together.

For the address I occupied the *Tribune*'s seat in the House press gallery, which was marked by a metal plate in the last century. The colonel and his wife were in the public gallery almost directly across the chamber. Over the years, I was inured to expecting the unusual from my leader, but I was flabbergasted when I saw him rise up, brush the knees of wrapt spectators and make his way up an aisle to an exit, just as MacArthur launched into his peroration about old soldiers fading away. There wasn't a dry eye in the house, nor an empty seat —except the colonel's.

"Response to 'MacArthur,' 'United Nations' and 'Hope for the Future' broadcasts shows that Congress is way behind public opinion," the colonel wired a few days later. "Tip off anybody you can to get out in the lead."

Generally this meant I would have to write a speech for some member of Congress, and even worse, that I would have to listen to him deliver it. To me, at least, there is no torture like listening to a speech you have written for someone else, because it is generally mangled in delivery.

McCormick was engagingly frank about his radio talks. Now and then he would have someone, generally Francis Coughlin, or myself write a talk for him, but he never passed such talks off as his own. If complimented on such a talk he would immediately identify the writer. Once he wired me: "Response to your Truman scandals broadcast the greatest I ever had."

During a pretrial examination in a suit involving the *Times Herald*, William Roberts, attorney for the plaintiffs, pressed McCormick on these broadcasts. The lawyer led up to his big question: "Colonel, why do you make these broadcasts?" The Colonel looked up at the ceiling and then at Roberts: "Vanity, I guess," which answer destroyed the point the lawyer was trying to force as a grudging admission.

When the *Tribune* acquired the Washington paper, McCormick was feted at a sumptuous lawn party near Baltimore. On being called on for a speech outlining his plans and proposals, he pleased me so that I could have kissed him. As it was I was proud to be associated with him when he said simply that he had despaired of bringing Washington officials to America, so he was bringing America to Washington. To him the paper was Fort Necessity on a wild frontier of despoilers of traditional domestic and international policy.

The acquisition of the paper added greatly to my duties. I had to meet every plane or train when he came to town. I had to get in waiting cars first, like a military aide, so that he would not have to move over for me to get in. I had to drive him to the ramp of his private plane; generally this involved fending off irate airport police, who had to be convinced I had made prior arrangements with airport authorities. I had to lunch with him almost every day he was in town, and Carol and I dined regularly with the McCormicks. Now and then we would find him eating when we arrived because he had become hungry and was always on the impatient side.

He made my home his own, dropping in whenever the spirit or spirits moved him. After one dinner given by Senator Brewster of Maine, a confirmed dry, I found him on the doorstep of my home, which was about halfway between the Sulgrave Club, where he and Maryland had dined, and his own home in Washington.

"Walter, give me a drink," he begged. "You were smart not to go. All Brewster had was speeches and dull ones at that."

Over the five years he controlled the paper, I was forced to add a new occupation to my growing list of operations—I became an expert on Washington real estate and house alterations. I arranged for suites in three hotels, the purchase of two houses and the renting of an apartment, seeing to the installation of an elevator in one home and the rearrangement of rooms in others. In the process I toured almost every available large home in the city.

He was a restless home owner. Hardly had he been settled in a house on Kalorama Circle when he had me switch him to the former home of Senator Guffey of Pennsylvania, which was off Rock Creek Park, near Massachusetts Avenue, because he wanted more ground for his dogs. While he still owned both houses I got a call one morning, ordering me to his bedside. Before I could ring off he told me I didn't know where he was. I assured him I knew the location of the Guffey home. To my astonishment he told me he wasn't there but in a suite in the Alban Towers Hotel on Wisconsin Avenue.

When I got to the suite I found him stretched on a bed, obviously not in the best of health. He told me he had been forced to leave both homes because of Washington's heat. Since the room in which he was lying was quite warm, I went over to the air conditioner and found that it was belching hot air and told the colonel so.

"Get out!" in a rare mood of petulance, as far as I was concerned, "and don't come back until you acquire some sense."

I went out for about five minutes and then came back, asking him if he didn't want a blanket, against the chill of the air conditioner. He had to laugh at himself and grumbled that I was learning how to get along with him anyway. That night he returned to the cooler Rock Creek home.

All in all, I was for many years the highest paid military aide in the capital, without rank or status, but following military protocol without a uniform and without gold *fourragères*. It was very trying at times, but never dull.

Once he called me to his hotel suite, complaining that he couldn't get breakfast. When I raced to the room, I found three breakfast trays, with food, outside his door and entered to find the colonel eating from a fourth. In his impatience he repeated his order four times and would not listen to any suggestions that earlier orders were under way.

Another time an Arabian stallion became my personal problem.

The colonel had been offered the horse on one of his world trips by Ibn Saud. When his niece, Bazy McCormick Miller, who was then running the Washington paper with her husband, Peter, heard about it, she reminded McCormick that she was interested in raising Arabians and would like one from the king's stables. I was told to get it for her.

This necessitated negotiations with the embassy of Saudi Arabia, the King, steamship lines, railroads, the Department of Agriculture and the Bureau of Customs. Matters got critical when the animal balked at going below deck on the ship and refused to eat aboard ship or on the train which brought him from the West Coast. He arrived in the capital more scarecrow than steed. It might have been better had I looked the gift horse in the mouth before he undertook the journey because he turned out to be more goat than horse and was no asset at Al Marah, Bazy's horse farm.

He commanded me to have the State Department translate and send around the world the various great American documents of independence. When he found this was being done, he kept expanding his list until he found documents the State Department wasn't sending, like the Otis writs of assistance. He regarded the granting of independence to the Philippines as the greatest American action since the signing of our own Declaration of Independence and couldn't understand why it was not being trumpeted all over the world as glowing evidence that the United States was not imperialistic, as Russia was charging. He had no patience with the explanation that other countries were trying to hang on to their colonies and feared such trumpeting would only encourage revolt.

About the same time he got interested in having monuments erected at Tripoli to commemorate the daring exploit of Stephen Decatur against the Barbary pirates; off Spithead, England, to mark the brilliant revolutionary sea raiding of John Paul Jones, and off Cherbourg, France, to commemorate the duel between the USS *Kearsarge* and the Confederate raider *Alabama*.

"I forget the name of the captain of the *Kearsarge* [John A. Winslow], but Farragut's admiration of him was so enormous as to warrant a monument to him," he wrote.

The French were uninterested in marking an American engagement, the Libyans were not anxious to rake up an unfavorable episode in the lives of their pirate ancestors, and the British did not want to recall a dark page in their history. The State Department was not enthusiastic, but the *Tribune* kept plugging away from time to time, which satisfied the colonel he was well in advance of "the café society boys" he assumed were in the saddle.

McCormick was more successful, and so was I, when he commanded me to bring a historic World War II submarine to Chicago's lake front, but the spadework on that project had already been done by Admiral Daniel V. Gallery. Dan enlisted the colonel in his project and I went along with the package.

The colonel was forever waging a personal vendetta with the State Department. He was always drawing his "vorpal blade," as Lewis Carroll put it, and my typewriter, in such assignments as "The State Department explanations would carry more weight if the department were not full of Reds," or "Why is the State Department dead from the neck up?" or "What about the society boys in the State Department?" or "Have a story on the colleges of the diplomats."

He seemed to think the department was the property of interested Harvard, Yale and Princeton graduates, with a heavy influx of Rhodes scholars. He would froth at the mouth over any suggestion of union with Britain, sending me such messages as: "What makes Kefauver so un-American?" and "What do Kefauver and the Atlantic Union people propose to do with the kings and nobility in European countries?"

While he seemed to enjoy and even court the company of foreign diplomats, he waged a long and unsuccessful campaign against abuses of diplomatic immunity, especially when traffic deaths and violations of traffic laws were involved.

McCormick never seemed to tire of running the names of American holders of foreign decorations, particularly those that carried knighthood in Britain. Often I got orders to "Send the full list of American knights" or "Send a complete list of American Rhodes scholars."

Yet he never turned down any foreign decorations offered him, and even accepted one from Argentine dictator Juan Perón. Near the end of the war, Syngman Rhee, an old and treasured friend, offered me the Order of Teigok, in appreciation of my efforts to help his country win independence. I dodged the saintly fellow by suggesting he offer it to McCormick. It did surprise me, but only mildly, when the colonel made a special trip to the capital to accept the oldest of decorations, saying Korea was a small country so he could take it.

McCormick did not comment on the fact that the order was given, in part, because he had assigned me to Washington. After the war, the colonel made a second trip to accept the Medal of the Republic of Korea, also partly awarded because he had assigned me to Washington. Needless to say, I didn't mention either of these sections of the citation in my stories of the awards. After the colonel's death I found that he was a Chevalier of the French Legion d'Honneur, one of those decorations he seemed to regard as subversive on the breasts of others, but I must say I never saw him wear the insignia of any decoration.

Almost anything could come by mail, phone or wire. Out of the blue he called on me for the name of his London hatter. He had named his first private plane, the "'Unting Bowler," because his hatter told him he could fall from his horse, while wearing such a derby and not crack his skull. My reply was that I didn't know but presumed it was Locke, the only London hatter known to me. A few days later he wrote:

"I thought you had the wrong name for my hatter. He was A. J. White. My haberdasher was Mulenkamp; my shoemaker was John Lobb; my tailor was Hills brothers, who have since joined with Peale. I might say they were my father's before me."

Another time he phoned to ask who had licked James J. Corbett. I told him it was Robert Fitzsimmons. He argued but was convinced when I told him I had met Corbett's widow and we had talked of the fight.

"Your memory is better than mine," he wrote the next day. "I thought it was Joe Wolcott."

Wolcott was a welterweight, not a heavyweight, but the colonel's knowledge of sports was dated at best. I sat with him through an All Star football game in Soldiers Field in Chicago and bet a quarter with him on the collegiates. When they lost to the pros, he said I should have won because the All Stars had the best punter, not recognizing that the pros didn't have to punt as often and that punting was more important before the development of the passing game.

I became something of an expert in decoding the colonel's cryptic and ambiguous messages. This task was complicated by the fact that his secretaries had little knowledge of current events or political personalities, so that Syngman Rhee would, as likely as not, come out Seaman Reed, or Chief Justice Fred Vinson as Red Vincent. The editors often consulted me on the meaning of messages they got from the colonel and once I got a wire from McCormick himself, which read: "This is a paragraph from my radio broadcast. What did I mean?"

When he was in Washington I had to act as a guide at various Civil War battlefields in the area or such sights as the Tomb of the Unknown Stranger, a young unidentified woman who died suddenly in an Alexandria inn in the eighteenth century, or the statue Charles Francis Adams erected over the grave of his wife, in Rock Creek Cemetery. The brooding figure by Augustus Saint-Gaudens was fittingly designated "Grief," by Mark Twain, although the sculptor and the husband left it unnamed.

Little escaped his eye. One winter I daubed some Mercurochrome on my lip to doctor a cold sore, as McCormick and I were about to set out on a short journey. I overheard him say to Maryland: "Walter's got lipstick on his mouth; I suppose it's Carol's."

Most of my assignments concerned the colonel's feud with Truman and his Administration. McCormick continued to hammer as though the 1948 campaign was still under way. I must confess I relished my role. I knew Truman read me, as did all Democrats. Some, like Bertha Joseph, former secretary of Senator Robert F. Wagner, said that reading me at breakfast was like "sucking a lemon." Truman's critics, opposition and enemies poured in a steady flow of tips.

There were many stories the President didn't like, but he held his anger. He never wrote me an angry letter. I think it was more because he had a sneaking admiration for a fighter than because he knew I would print such a letter and because he considered the *Tribune*'s opposition part of the game of politics. I say this because after Mrs. Patterson died, he told me that her editor had come to him with an olive branch.

"He came crawling in here on his big fat belly," Truman said. "I'd have more respect for him if he'd stand and fight like you do."

It was the fighting spirit, I believe, that made Truman enjoy his press conferences. Certainly he did better with them than his predecessor and better than most of his successors. He removed the ban on direct quotation, imposed by FDR and Hoover and Coolidge. He made edited transcripts quickly available.

He was quick to recognize that the conference format favors the Chief Executive because he cannot be cross-examined and that it is invaluable in building the affection of the people and in selling administration programs. Conferences require a good deal of work on the part of the President. While he knows pretty well what will be asked, he must be prepared for surprises. He must study a considerable amount of material submitted by various departments. Truman never shirked this responsibility and he was careful in the delivery of his answers. His expression was good and his intent unmistakable.

Presidents frequently take dislikes to some of their questioners. Truman's particular bête noire was May Craig, although I am not sure that she ever knew it, nor did many in the conference. HST often clenched his hands under his desk when her voice edged through the air, like a knife, with a sharp question, as though he would have liked to have wrapped his fingers around her throat. He did put an edge in his answers but no more. I don't think it was her questions so much, although they were pointed, as the fact that her voice to him was like the scraping of a faulty grain of chalk on a slate blackboard.

In 1952, when Truman decided not to run for re-election after a slate of delegates, pledged to him, was defeated in New Hampshire by a Kefauver group, McCormick saw it as a confession of defeat. Truman had not entered the slate or approved its entry, but that didn't stop the colonel, who rejoiced in a *Tribune* victory. McCormick laid it to recognition that corruption at home and failures abroad would bring him defeat. The limitation to two terms, adopted by constitutional amendment in his Administration, did not apply to Truman, so that he might have run.

McCormick had blamed the war in Korea on Truman's bungling and continued to do so after the decision not to seek re-election. Acheson had drawn a line in the Pacific, which placed Korea outside America's sphere of influence, of which Moscow was certainly aware. This was later repudiated and corrected, but there were other Administration mistakes in evaluating intelligence. McCormick argued that Truman had declared war without consent of Congress on the excuse that the war was a UN venture. Significantly, Russia stayed away from the UN session that launched the conflict, when she might have exercised a veto, which gave rise to belief that the Kremlin wanted the United States in the conflict so that this country might further deplete its resources and to see how far this country would act against aggression.

I disagreed at the time on McCormick's assessment of the reasons for Truman's withdrawal from politics and still do. I am and was satisfied that Truman was aware that FDR's defiance of tradition had hurt the country and the party by holding back younger men, and that he had resolved not to do so himself. Truman did have a fine regard for tradition, especially if it were Democratic tradition, and the constitutional processes.

And the presidency is a lonely job for all its sycophants. I have been in the White House with Presidents for hours at a time and the one thing that has struck me most of all is the silence. It seems to be silent as the tomb even though one knows the Secret Service and the staff are within call. The telephone seldom rings, mostly because the President is not disturbed except for the most important developments but also because few dare to phone for nothing more than a chat.

This doesn't mean that the Chief Executive isn't beset by advice —on the air, in the press, from leaders of his party and from the opposition. At times the advice is rather silly as when Senator William Fulbright of Arkansas suggested Truman resign and let the Republicans take over after the Democratic loss of Congress in 1946.

"He's an overeducated son of a bitch," was Truman's delicious comment.

Truman's conduct out of office was in keeping with his quiet determination and dedication. He did not second guess any of his successors, Republican or Democrat, but made himself available to leaders of both parties for consultation. He patched up his feuds including that with Nixon, which began when Truman regarded the

California congressman as the embodiment of the efforts to pin a Communist tag on the Fair Deal administration.

At the only Gridiron dinner he attended after he left the White House, Truman accepted a drink of bourbon from the defeated Republican presidential candidate, when John F. Kennedy was the guest of honor. This acceptance enabled Nixon to bring down the house when, as the speaker for the Republican party, he noted that it was a great dinner and a greater country, when a fighting Democrat could accept a drink from a stanch Republican.

Truman busied himself with memoirs and making speeches before various groups across the country. Because he had played an important part in the establishment of Israel he had more invitations from Zionist groups than he could fill. In early retirement he drove Mrs. Truman across the country to New York to visit his daughter and her growing family.

In his last years he retired further and further into his family, recognizing, as all men must, that their most important possessions are their children and grandchildren. His health declined, as it does for the aging, but not so much that he didn't know the end was near and that he must prepare for it. In his final instructions, he directed that his funeral be simple and as much of a family rite as possible. He barred any lying in state in Washington and discouraged any national mourning. Having been wedded to simplicity throughout his life, he demanded and was accorded it in death.

When he retired to Kansas City, the *Tribune* did not pursue him, even though McCormick had once called for his impeachment. The colonel was not given to lashing old foes, because he was generally busy acquiring new ones. McCormick believed in thrusting aside old enemies, because there were always plenty of new men seeking and reaching power.

Truman became ill in 1954. McCormick promptly wished him a speedy recovery and expressed the hope that the former President would remain among the living for a long time to come.

"There are a lot of things wrong with Harry Truman," the *Tribune* said, "but there was always more candor, less hypocrisy and more natural man in his words and behavior than most politicians would dare to display."

That might very well serve as an epitaph.

EISENHOWER AND TAFT

H ISTORY, it might be argued, is the story of the right man in the right place at the right time. So it was with Dwight David Eisenhower, the soldier who waged a victorious war and who became the thirty-fourth President of the United States to wage a less successful peace.

I would like to be able to report that I recognized him as a man of destiny or even as a man of remarkable charm on our first meeting in 1934, when he was a major just turned forty-four, and I had recently celebrated my thirty-first birthday. My battered personal phone book of unlisted and frequently called numbers lists him on extension 1278 of the old War Department exchange of National 2520, a number he told me he had forgotten when I reminded him of it in the White House.

Our meeting was a must for me, because of McCormick's interest in the military. The colonel's personal cure for the Depression—and it must be acknowledged that it was not the worst of panaceas—was to build a modern army and a strong navy. These, he said, would not only be a mighty instrument in the attainment of world peace, but would put many to work building ships and guns and tanks and create other jobs in a variety of industries in the maintenance of the armed forces.

Boettiger brought Ike and me together on my arrival in the capital. I found the major pleasant and co-operative, but a bit slow, when my editor was impatient. Never did he give me an immediate answer, but always had me come back while, he said, he investigated and cleared my question. One day after I asked him for the tables of organization for a modern infantry division, with a special emphasis on changes in artillery components since World War I, I left his office empty-handed as usual. Not far away, I passed the door of Major Willis Crittenberger, who called out to me, demanding to know what I was doing in the old army munitions building on Constitution Avenue. When I explained, he picked up a tablet and rapidly set down what I wanted. Two days later Ike gave me exactly the same thing, but by that time I had Crittenberger's data in the paper. Naturally I shifted to Crittenberger as a favored source. I cite this as another evidence of my frequent fallibility, although I didn't do too badly. Crittenberger became a four-star general. It never occurred to me until now to wonder what manner of President Willis might have made.

In 1935, Ike left for the Philippines, so he was lost to me for years. MacArthur asked for Ike when the former chief of staff became military adviser to the Philippines. He also asked for Major James Ord. Both majors were carried on the active military service list of the U. S. Army, although assigned to the Philippine military mission, which was established when the islands were granted independence.

Ike had attracted MacArthur's attention in 1932, when, as a captain, Eisenhower had donned his uniform and helped the booted and spurred chief of staff clear out the bonus marchers, who had camped on the capital grounds near the Potomac. George S. Patton, then a major, took part in clearing out the World War I veterans, who were demanding a bonus and proposing to camp in Washington until they got it. This was not a Communist or a political demonstration, although Communists and politicians promoted it for profit, which I knew because I interviewed many of the marchers.

In the Philippines, Ike was MacArthur's chief of staff with the rank of lieutenant colonel. However, the cordial relations between Ike and his commander were to be shattered permanently in the Far East. As usual, there are two versions of the rupture. In *At Ease,* a volume of military reminiscences, which was not published until after MacArthur's death, Eisenhower said the break came because he opposed MacArthur's plan to increase spending on the island's military, although President Manuel Quezon had pledged himself to live within his budget.

The MacArthur version, which can now be told here, is that Ike and Ord, who was fluent in Spanish, tried to get Quezon to increase the budget. What infuriated MacArthur was that they undertook to work behind his back to do so. The general suspected both officers were trying to succeed him as chief of mission, which paid far better than the Army, but did not fault them for such ambition.

Whichever version one accepts, it must be borne in mind that MacArthur was not the most placid of men. He summoned Ord and Ike into his office and gave them a tongue-lashing in the presence of a third officer, Bonner Fellers, who died in the fall of 1973. Mac-Arthur accused them of disloyalty and of furthering unsound policy. Among other things, he said that he would like to have sent both officers home, except that such action would reveal that he had committed a grievous error in asking for them in the first place.

The sending of the two officers home under a cloud could have injured Ike's career irreparably, but it might have saved Ord's life, because he was killed in the crash of a training plane in the islands shortly after this incident.

MacArthur's cold rage left wounds that could never be healed, partly because he chose to deliver the dressing down in front of Fellers, who was informed by Quezon of the machinations of Ike and Ord. Ike sought and obtained a transfer to the mainland. Mac-Arthur did not put his reprimand on the Eisenhower record.

Fellers, the unwilling witness, was assigned to Egypt in the early days of the war and then joined MacArthur, at the latter's request, for the island-hopping campaign against Japan.

Aware that Eisenhower had a long memory, Fellers resigned from the Army as a brigadier general when Ike became chief of staff. Later he resigned as director of veterans' affairs for the Republican National Committee, the moment Ike was nominated for President in Chicago in 1952.

In the United States Ike was assigned to the Northwest, where he resumed his acquaintance with Boettiger and the latter's wife, Anna, FDR's daughter. This friendship may have paved the way to five-star rank, because it certainly didn't hurt to have the President's vibrant daughter mention him to her father, nor were his chances hurt by the fact that Ike's brother Milton had helped Wallace kill piglets in the Department of Agriculture and then moved on to the State Department.

However, the official version of the promotion is that Ike, then a brigadier general, made a great name for himself in the Louisiana war maneuvers of 1941 by winning a mock war exercise. Such games, and I have seen many, have their ridiculous side, although they count heavily with the military in peacetime. Naturally, there can be no shooting or prolonged campaigning, so victory is determined by arrival at a designated strategic area.

Ike threw kitchens and all other extraneous baggage off every vehicle he had in order to bring men and material, largely synthetic, to the designated area. Ike's forces got "thar fustest with the mostest," in the less than erudite but accurate language of General Nathan Bedford Forrest, the Confederate cavalry commander, so Eisenhower unblushingly accepted the palm of victory.

This is not said in detraction of the general's ability, which he certainly demonstrated in Europe, nor as any reflection on his character. The name of the game of war—hot or cold—is to win, by any means. Following Louisiana, Ike returned to Washington, where we renewed our acquaintance, although we were both very busy, to become the head of the war plans division and then assistant chief of staff under Marshall, which brought him into contact with FDR.

He had become the right man and was in the right place at the right time.

It is now possible for me to reveal an unknown facet of history. With America in the war, the British wanted Marshall to head the American forces in Europe. They wanted him to direct the landing in Africa and the American landing in France, but not necessarily as the supreme allied commander, a post London was convinced should go to a Britisher as it had in the past. No doubt they considered Marshall malleable to their purposes, even to subordinate service.

I do know that Marshall didn't want the command and, although we had our differences and he knew I was not popular at the White House, he enlisted my aid, because the *Tribune* had the family relationship with Cissie Patterson's morning and afternoon papers, which she subsequently combined into the Washington *Times*

Herald to operate an around-the-clock paper. I was appearing regularly in the morning paper.

I doubt that Marshall discovered for himself that news stories could move Congress to demand that he be retained as chief of staff on the ground that he was irreplaceable. However, he had many able former newsmen in the army's public relations sector and there was Early, in the White House, who had helped to make him chief of staff, available for consultation.

At any rate I was fed various stories that the American war effort would be hamstrung if Marshall were to leave. In so doing I learned that Bill Hutchinson of INS was being fed similar stories for Cissie's afternoon paper. I suppose we were enlisted because the two papers were anti-Administration and would criticize Administration plans more freely than the other Washington papers.

I enlisted in this campaign joyously, because I knew that Marshall had never been a success with troops. When he was destined for a general's stars, earlier in his career, he was given command of the army's finest regiment, the Eighth Infantry, and took first rank away from it in a matter of a few months. I also knew that he owed his selection over Major General Hugh Drum, considered a better soldier, to army politics. He became the first non-West Pointer to head the Army in modern times, having been graduated from VMI, and went on to become Secretary of State and Secretary of Defense under Truman, who considered him the greatest soldier and statesman of our time.

In this campaign Sir John Dill, chief of the British liaison with the Pentagon, worked with Marshall in the campaign to keep him in Washington. Dill worked quietly because he was working against London, which might have been fatal to his career had it become known. When Dill died in Washington, Marshall had him interred in Arlington National Cemetery with a large equestrian statue marking his grave, a plot which would have accommodated a number of American war dead. This was a mark of Marshall's gratitude. I got no reward beyond a grudging thanks, although there were times, I am sure, when Marshall would gladly have dug my grave in Arlington himself, had I been eligible for a plot, especially when I began nosing around Washington for responsibility of Pearl Harbor.

Marshall pushed Ike forward as the logical man for European

command. The British generally accepted, although there were exceptions, like Alan Brooke, an extremely competent officer, who no doubt wanted the post for himself. Ike was picked because he got along easily with people and because his first function would be to see that the Allies got along well together. This Ike did very well, even to relieving some officers who could not get along with their British cousins, like Theodore Roosevelt, Jr.

I didn't see Ike again until after the war, when he became chief of staff when Marshall went to the State Department. Although by that time he had reached Olympian heights, he was his pleasant, affable and uncommunicative self.

After two years as chief of staff, Ike became president of Columbia University in New York. He was not selected for his scholarship, but because it was believed he would stimulate contributions and endowments. He was not a favorite of the university's academic set, since he wasn't interested in their problems. Nor was he popular with its trustees because he did not go out of his way to collect the money they expected. When Carl Ackerman, dean of the institution's famed School of Journalism, undertook to write a history of the university, he was moved to make it somewhat top-heavy with criticism of the Eisenhower regime. It was so in the first draft he showed me, which the authorities did not like as much as they agreed with his evaluation.

Two years later he took a leave of absence to become supreme allied commander in Europe, during the cold war. This was an excellent choice, but I had a quarrel with it because Ike took my good friend Major General Wilton B. Persons from the presidency of Staunton Military Academy to Europe with him and later into the White House. Persons would often tell Ike that he should have heeded my advice and remained at Staunton. Such complaints invariably were begun with the sentence: "Walter was right," so that Ike always knew what was coming.

It was during the Paris service that the presidential draft for Eisenhower began gathering its head of steam, and at McCormick's orders I began building a dossier against the general's political hopes. This was quite a dossier. Much of it was used, including his youthful Democratic campaign speech, but quite a bit was not. This concerned his love life, from his days at West Point to his service in Europe.

The far-right opposition to Ike made much of the fact that the West Point yearbook referred to him as "the Swedish Jew," beating the gongs of anti-Semitism against him. What they failed to see was a reference to Ike's pursuit, with considerable success, of the wife of a member of the institution's staff. I had the story from classmates.

Far more widely circulated were stories of Ike's relations with his British WAAC chauffeur, Kay Summersby. I gathered statements and affidavits from various officers. Also I was seeking access to Patton's diary, after the flamboyant but magnetic general died in an accident in Europe. During my negotiations, the lawyer for Patton's widow got a political appointment through Senator Henry Cabot Lodge, who was a leader in the draft-Eisenhower movement. The diary was denied me.

The story, widely circulated in Washington, was that Ike and Harry Butcher, a Washington radio executive, who became the general's naval aide, had agreed to divorce their wives and marry their WAAC drivers. After the war, Butcher did, but Ike did not.

Kay got the news, according to a colonel I knew in Patton's headquarters, after Eisenhower's return to Washington. Ike's message to Kay went in code to Patton, who was asked to deliver it. Patton read her the message, but reportedly copied it in his diary.

The message said simply, I was told, that all marriage plans were off because Ike was going to be named chief of staff and knew not what would come after that. My colonel friend reported that Kay came dashing out of Patton's headquarters, shouting: "He's running out on me."

Whether Ike ever thought seriously of divorce is debatable. There is little doubt, however, that Kay was convinced he was going to take the step. Many of the military around Ike thought so as well, but they may have wanted it to happen because power doesn't always generate love. Kay did publish her memoirs. Her mother appeared in the States in 1956 talking of the memoirs, which would contain a chapter unfavorable to Ike, but Kay was induced to change her mind, possibly for a price. Of such activities are many campaigns, even presidential, spiced.

During the war Mrs. Mamie Doud Eisenhower remained in Washington tending the home fires. She was ever a charming and gracious lady. She had a genius for making guests feel, when she greeted them, that the only reason she was holding or attending a function was in order to see them.

But she could not escape calumny. It was said that she had taken to drinking heavily with Ruth Butcher, the wife of her husband's naval aide, in sorrow over their threatened divorces. These stories followed her to the White House.

It has never ceased to amaze me how people who had never been in the White House, except possibly on a public tour, could look one in the eye and swear to eyewitness knowledge of accusations I knew to be false. The only explanation is that gossip is a thousand-headed hydra. Mrs. Eisenhower stood by her friend Ruth Butcher after the latter's divorce and did not drop her when she became First Lady.

There was a hint in the reported message that Patton relayed that what might happen was the presidency and that Ike was dreaming of it as early as 1945. He was to deny such ambition many times before he openly began his quest in 1952. The first to plant the idea in his mind, as far as I know, was Ray Clapper, the Scripps-Howard columnist who visited the African front in 1942.

Clapper was a highly competent newsman, but not one who could resist the temptation of trying to be a kingmaker. In talking with Eisenhower, Clapper told him that as a successful warrior he would automatically become a presidential contender. Ike waived him off, Ray told me, saying that seeking the White House would mean that he would have to go to church and all that sort of thing. The idea was planted and it was to grow.

The general was at Columbia when the effort was made to swing the Democratic nomination to him in 1948. He was in Paris when desperate Republicans, looking for coattails to ride into office, began pressing him to compete for the GOP nomination. Ike at first denied any such ambition. Later he said he would not come home to seek the nomination. He was to change his mind on both counts, allowing his name to be entered in primaries and then came home to bid for support.

McCormick had called on Eisenhower at Columbia, when the general was denying any presidential ambitions in 1949.

"He talked very reasonably," the colonel wrote me. "Said there was a limit to the amount of money we could spend on defense, and that the three services ought to be less pigheaded and work together."

When Ike was growing as a candidate in 1950, the colonel wrote:

"You may have noted the very catchy song in Ethel Merman's play —'They [I] Like Ike.' It is obviously political propaganda.

"I don't know anything about Berlin's [Irving Berlin, the composer] connections or whether he is mixed up in subversive activities."

I promptly reported Berlin was not.

A short time later, McCormick wrote: "Ike is now a candidate for President although he wasn't some years ago. This is certainly not the time to campaign against him, but you might collect arguments that could be used against him if he were nominated."

In 1951, the colonel and Maryland met with Eisenhower in his SHAPE headquarters outside Paris. They had a frank talk on politics for which McCormick was grateful, although he made it clear that he didn't agree with the general and would not support him.

As they left the office, Maryland pulled back the lapel of her fur coat to display an "I Like Ike" button to Persons, who gleefully reported the amusing episode to me. I was not so sure that she liked Ike so much as I was certain she didn't like Taft.

McCormick was ever mindful that his grandfather Joseph Medill had played a major role in the founding of the Republican party and in the nomination and election of Lincoln, so that it was only natural he should aspire to be a President-maker himself. Also he was aware that Horace Greeley, editor of the New York *Tribune*, had maneuvered a presidential nomination for himself, so I am sure he would never have discouraged any effort to gain one.

About this time he wired me jubilantly: "I have found my Fremont; it's Wedemeyer."

I knew, of course, that General John C. Fremont was the first Republican presidential candidate against James Buchanan in 1856, but I didn't want my friend General Albert C. Wedemeyer to lay his head on the political block as the colonel's sacrificial lamb. Al would have made a good President, I am sure, but had not attracted wide political notice outside his native Nebraska.

As a young lieutenant on the staff of the White House military aide in the administration of Herbert Hoover, Al gave indication that he was destined for greatness. One Armistice Day the aide was in a tizzy, because the wreath which President Hoover was to place at the Tomb of the Unknown Soldier in Arlington had not arrived at the White House. A phone call disclosed that the White House greenhouse was closed for the holiday.

The aide was at the point of suicide. Wedemeyer told him to go ahead with the ceremony as planned, that he would provide a wreath. Al went to the office of the cemetery and asked what funerals they had had the day before. He found that of a colonel, a high rank in those days, and raced to the graveside. There he selected the largest wreath and went with it to the site of the ceremony.

When the President and his party arrived, Al handed the wreath over to the military aide, who gave it to Hoover. The President placed it on the tomb of the soldier who "rests in honored glory," and left for the amphitheater to make a brief address. Al waited until all the party had left, recovered the wreath and returned it to the grave of the colonel. Later, Wedemeyer got the President's wreath from the greenhouse and put it where it belonged. It was not surprising that Wedemeyer should become the supreme allied commander in China or that McCormick, to whom I had told the story, should pick him for a possible Republican nomination.

It was at this time that McCormick phoned from his home at Boynton Beach, Florida, to inform Maxwell that his managing editor had "lost a star in his crown," by failing to report a speech Wedemeyer had given the night before in a Palm Beach club. Maxwell had printed a paragraph or two that the AP had carried, but that wasn't enough for the colonel, who was quite brisk with Maxwell. Being fearful that he might be crossed out of succession to the editorship in the colonel's will or even that he might lose his job, Maxwell appealed to me for help. I found Wedemeyer in his home, Friend's Advice, outside the capital. I learned that his speech was one I had in my files and had written. The *Tribune* had carried the speech a couple of months earlier. The general also told me that McCormick, suffering from his ailing bladder, hadn't heard any more than the first paragraphs of the talk, paragraphs which harkened back to the military situation in the Peloponnesian War. Wedemeyer didn't consider the speech one of his better efforts. When all this was reported to the colonel, his verdict was: "Wedemeyer didn't realize the importance of his own speech." Later he added: "It wasn't too good a speech anyway," although I knew he hadn't heard it and that we had carried it earlier without an editorial reaction from him.

One of my greatest problems with McCormick, over the years, was that I could never get him to wait for a story before he ran an editorial. Time after time I was ordered to write the story after the editorial appeared.

It wasn't long before McCormick was to forget Wedemeyer and was back supporting Taft, who had twice been denied his party's nomination. Taft was considered the logical candidate, but there were hungry Republicans who agreed the senator was "Mr. Republican," but honestly thought he lacked voter appeal and could not win. It wasn't so much that they disliked Taft as they craved power. After all they had been out in the cold for twenty years.

I was devoted to Taft and knew him more intimately than any other Washington reporter. I regarded him as the last hope for curbing the excesses and abuses of the New Deal and Fair Deal and I still think I was right. Because they feared that Taft might discredit their beloved welfare state and planned economy and promote a return to government by reason instead of government by handout, the New Deal sympathizers in the press joined in building up Ike, although they did not want the general elected. They were interested in stopping Taft.

I was confident that Taft would make a valiant fight to end class strife and that he would work to return to constitutional processes. This doesn't mean that I thought the senator would go back to William McKinley or even to his father, because Taft was no more of a hidebound reactionary than I. He was one who would work to apply the lessons of the past to the problems of the day.

While I still regret Taft, it does not mean that I am at all in sympathy with those liberals who would classify Ike as a failure in the presidency, as insignificant in performance as Harding. Ike was a much stronger President than I ever thought he could be and his Administration was marked by considerable accomplishment, which is more than anyone can say of that of Kennedy, a reactionary turned liberal, possibly out of conviction but certainly for political advancement.

This is my considered judgment as the reporter who hit Ike the hardest and most often in the preconvention campaign of 1952, when the general was the darling of liberals. They did not hesitate to pick the GOP ticket, although they never had any intention of voting for it or supporting it. It is also the conviction of a reporter who was as far out of favor when the Eisenhower administration went in as he ever was under FDR and HST. That was to change.

In 1952, Taft told me in the presence of his administrative assistant, I. Jack Martin, that he was going to make me press secretary when he got into the White House. The senator was that confident of victory at the turn of the year. I was horrified and said I wouldn't take it, not only for myself but for his best interests. I do not think that newsmen always make the best public relations men.

"Oh yes, you will, Walter," Taft said: "I'll tell the colonel that I just can't operate without you."

My answer was that the colonel considered the role of the *Tribune*'s Washington bureau chief as high as the Cabinet, if not higher. Taft knew that not long before I had been offered the post of publicity director of the Republican National Committee at $25,000 a year with another $25,000 from Joseph Pew of Philadelphia, in the belief that I would be a Republican Charley Michaelson. Charley was a very nasty fellow with a typewriter and I had demonstrated I could be no less courageous. I declined with the full support and blessing of McCormick.

Taft was an amazing politician to work with, because he was quick to confess error. Once I was in his office urging him to make an issue of rising prices. He told me I was wrong. I told him I had been shopping with Carol and knew I wasn't. He turned abruptly, dug into his desk for price indices. After leafing through them he looked up at me with an embarrassed smile and said:

"Walter, you're right."

He was great to work with because when he reposed confidence he meant it. Now and then he would send me a proposed magazine article, with the request: "Please take the Taft curse off of this." I wouldn't change the thought much or the style, but I would break up his sentences and suggest revisions, additions or cuts. I never got any acknowledgment, but when the article appeared, I found all my suggestions had been accepted. Unlike others he didn't submit his article to a circle but to one man in whom he had confidence.

Herbert Hoover used to send me some of his speeches in galley form with a request for comments and suggestions. He wrote his speeches on ruled legal paper, had them typed and then sent them to a printer. Instead of working on typed pages, he liked to work with galley proofs. This is an expensive method, but it worked for him.

Taft called on me to help him with a speech he was to make as the Republican spokesman at the Gridiron Club. He explained that he had made a botch of an earlier speech before the club, because he worked it out on a train trip from a visit to his alma mater, Yale, from New Haven to New York City.

Taft's draft had an excellent idea, which was that he was speaking as the representative of the loyal opposition, about the only thing loyal about Truman at that time. I reworked the draft, sprinkling it generously with quips such as having Taft say he loved the White House because he had been raised there and nothing would please him more than a return to the Old Homestead. The second speech brought Taft a standing ovation. "All the best laughs were yours," he grudgingly acknowledged in a note of thanks.

On one of his strength-testing trips, the Ohioan was scheduled to speak before the student body of the University of Oregon at Eugene. The Saturday before his address, the school's football team had defeated its arch rival, California, for the first time in years. I told Taft that he should begin his speech with a mention of the victory.

When he hesitated, saying it wasn't like him, I typed out a couple of lines for him to deliver. He grumbled that the words didn't sound like him. I threatened to leave his cause if he didn't read the lines. I was below him when he reached the podium. I could see that he was hesitating, so I shook my fist at him. He took a deep breath and delivered my lines; the students almost cheered the roof off the hall.

"As usual," he said, when we were leaving, "you got the biggest hand."

He could be startlingly honest for a politician. When he was trying to pick up votes against Ike he went to the Dakotas, where some were hoping for a raise in the price of gold as the best means of reviving gold mining in that area. At a meeting with the citizens of a mining town, he was asked what he thought of increasing the price of gold. "I think it's silly," he snapped.

Victor Johnston, a Wisconsin political operator, who had joined the Taft team with Thomas Coleman, one of the most charming and skillful businessmen interested in politics I have ever known, saw faces in the group drop. He sought to assure them Taft had delivered an offhand judgment and if someone would ask him the question at a luncheon the next day, Johnston said he was sure they would get a more favorable exposition of position.

Johnston went to Taft and told him what he had done, stressing the importance of the state's delegation, which although small would help. Taft nodded. The next day at luncheon the town banker asked Taft if he had had time to think over his statement on the price of gold and whether he might have something to add to it. "Yes, I have," said Taft. "I think it's damned silly."

When Coleman came to see Taft in Washington after joining the senator's preconvention team, Tom pulled a worn telegram from his pocket and said he wanted to thank Taft for the kind words and the warm sentiment. Taft asked if he could see it. The telegram signed "Bob Taft" thanked Coleman warmly and gracefully for joining the team and expressed confidence that victory would result. "That's Jack Martin's work," Taft said, handing the telegram back. "I didn't send it but wish I had."

This honesty made Coleman a more devoted follower.

Taft differed from his fellow politicians in many ways, mostly for the better. In any debate he would present what he considered the essentials and what he and his party wanted. When the opposition presented its case, he assumed their proposals were offered in the same good faith, so he would immediately stress the points of agreement and undertake to resolve differences.

Many politicians like to pose as unyielding men of principle, who nail their flags to the mast and go down with the ship, but never do. Taft was no poseur, but a believer in action. Because of his readiness to meet the opposition at least halfway, Taft was called "the great compromiser," by those who sought to belittle him. Yet, without this attitude, which I did not share very often, Congress would have gotten through far less work than it did.

Also he had a greater awareness of his own shortcomings than many ever credited him with and a greater forgiveness of associates than most men in public life. Too many seek to blame their own mistakes on those about them.

I was with Taft in Dallas early in 1952 when he got word that his cousin David Ingalls, who had joined his strategy team, had told reporters that if Taft lost New Hampshire, the senator would have to fold up his campaign. This was a colossal blunder that shook the faith of many a Taft supporter. Coleman wanted Taft to repudiate Ingalls, but the senator would not, saying that the poor fellow didn't know politics very well but meant to be helpful.

A few days later I was in the senator's suite in El Paso, Texas, when votes were being counted in New Hampshire. I was getting the results by phone from the *Tribune*. The news became worse and worse as Ike votes mounted.

"It will be all right by morning," said Taft and went to bed.

He was asleep when we learned that he had lost the nation's first primary. Martin, Carol and I walked the streets of Juarez, across the Rio Grande. Jack was the picture of utter rout. Never had I seen anyone take results of an election so hard.

The next morning Taft dismissed the loss with a grin, saying that all it meant was that his forces would have to work that much harder.

Unfortunately, Taft had no great personal magic. One had to know him to like him and the more one knew him the greater the liking grew. What he lacked in charisma, he made up by impressive honesty and remarkable ability that stood out from him like a nimbus to those who knew him. I can never forget a young Ohio college girl, who broke into tears when I introduced her to Taft in my home. He was the idol of her family and she was overwhelmed by his obvious dedication to public service.

Taft wasn't a quipster or a joke teller, but he enjoyed a laugh as well as anyone, which was one of the reasons he liked me as he did. There wasn't a fiber of demagoguery in him. Perhaps, if he had had any lacing of this political standby in his system, he would have been better able to project himself before the American people.

When his alert and gifted wife, Martha, who could make a much better speech than her husband, suffered a stroke and was confined to a wheel chair, Taft came home every afternoon to read to her despite the press of duties and the strains of his campaigning. Usually she favored an Agatha Christie mystery, but actually what served her best was his presence and his voice, because it was not always clear that she was following the plot.

Senator Harry Flood Byrd, the elder, did the same thing for his wife in her last days and as quietly and unobtrusively as Taft had. Neither sought to make political capital from their labors of love. As so often happens, Mrs. Taft, whom all expected him to survive, was to survive her husband. We often visited her and her faithful friend, Mrs. Darrah Wunder, in their apartment not far from our home.

I knew Taft in his most trying moments, including occasions when he tried me most. I knew him when he was tried most as well. Also I knew him in the bosom of his family and in the company of his closest friends. In fact, I almost became a member of the family and I was certainly among his closest friends.

To me, Taft was unique. I know, because of my rapid advance toward winter years, that I shall not see his like again, but devoutly hope that the country will. He was a rare combination of ability, courage, courtesy and integrity seldom encountered in politics or anywhere else for that matter.

Yet aware of all this, the Eisenhower strategy forces branded Taft as a "thief," something the senator's Democratic opposition had never done. They charged him personally with responsibility for vote maneuvers by his overzealous Texas supporters, which gained Taft a solid Texas delegation. When the cry of vote theft was raised, Taft generously offered to split the Texas delegation.

I was breakfasting in the Blackstone Hotel grill alongside of Ike's strategy team, when they were discussing Taft's offer to split the delegation. One of the group, Arthur E. Summerfield, later to be GOP national chairman and Postmaster General, described Taft's offer to be a fair one. He was promptly squelched by Herbert Brownell, who had guided Dewey's ill-conducted 1948 campaign and was to become Attorney General.

"My God," Brownell exclaimed. "Don't you see we can't accept it? We'd lose our only issue."

The issue did help Eisenhower capture the nomination, although it was none of the general's making.

The convention was a sad one for me and a sadder one for Taft. Early in the proceedings Taft came to me in the *Tribune* workroom in the basement of the Stevens Hotel to suggest that I have the colonel soft-pedal his militant support of the senator's drive, saying he feared it might drive away some of the wavering liberal delegates. This hurt and angered me. At the time Taft needed every bit of support he could get.

The Eisenhower forces chipped away steadily at Taft's strength. The senator could see this when we went over tables of delegate support. When he arrived he was counting on a first-ballot nomination, but as the days went on, estimates of Eisenhower delegates rose, so that just before the balloting it was clear the soldier would win.

Herbert Hoover called me to his hotel suite and asked me to prevail on Taft to withdraw in favor of General Douglas MacArthur. I refused, saying I couldn't bring myself to do it and I could not see Taft running up the white flag. One year before MacArthur might have been nominated by acclamation if he had allowed his name to be submitted. At that time he was making a triumphal tour of the country after being removed by Truman. One of the saddest things I have seen in any convention was the motley crew of skid-row demonstrators, who were recruited by a Wisconsin man to place MacArthur's name in the running without the general's permission. It was a sad note in a brilliant career.

About this time Maryland McCormick came to Taft's headquarters and urged him to withdraw. Thinking that she might be reflecting the colonel's opinion, Taft called me to ask what he should do. I told him to go down with his flags flying, as the colonel had earlier advised, adding that McCormick was not one to be swayed easily even by an adviser wearing skirts.

Mrs. McCormick told the story, which I never believed, that Taft mistook her for the wife of Representative John W. McCormack, from Massachusetts, later Speaker of the House, asking after the Democratic leader, when the colonel's wife entered the office. Even a man so blind to women's dress as Taft knew that Mrs. McCormack was given to wearing horrors she called hats and clothes to match.

Ike made one of the most gracious gestures I have ever seen in politics when he was nominated in Chicago. As soon as the winning vote was flashed on TV screens, Ike walked across the street from his suite in the Blackstone Hotel to the headquarters of his defeated rival in the Stevens Hotel. I presume he was schooled in this courtesy by the military tradition that a victorious general should have his defeated enemy to dinner.

Ike was to tarnish this fine gesture, somewhat, after saying that he was sorry that his victory had come at the expense of so fine an American and so faithful a public servant. "I want you to know," Ike added, "that I don't hold all those dirty things your crowd said about me against you."

I was sure this was a reference to me, in part, because I had been saying the dirty things ordered by McCormick.

Nixon was nominated for second place and the convention closed. I went to Taft's living suite in the Congress Hotel to bid him farewell. He was not as depressed as I had expected, but somewhat relieved.

"In a way, I am glad it's all over," he said. "I won't ever have to try for a nomination again."

Then, with a sad smile, he added: "I suppose that I was driven, in part, by the desire to make amends for my father's defeat in 1912 as much as by the fact that my choice of public service dictated that I should seek to gain the highest level, or by ambition if you would choose to call it that.

"I am sorry I let down my friends, like yourself, but I am not entirely unhappy that it is now done."

Taft did not have a high opinion of Ike's political potential. He left Chicago for Murray Bay, Canada, where the family had long had a summer home. During his stay, he wrote me that he was going to Morningside Heights in New York City, the seat of Columbia University, to confer with the candidate on the issues. There, he said, his greatest problem would be to put them in language simple enough so that Eisenhower could understand them.

I did not publish the letter at the time, not so much because it could not help but injure Ike as because I knew Taft regarded it as confidential. Taft was not one to nurse grudges or weep over defeat, as I well knew from the loss of his nomination in 1948, but he would have had to be more than human if he had not been somewhat resentful. However, he came to reverse his judgment and to forgive and admire Ike, which I cannot say he did for Dewey.

The Democrats nominated Governor Adlai E. Stevenson of Illinois, who was a reluctant dragon. Truman favored Adlai over the field, which included Senator Kefauver, then the hero of the investigation into organized crime, and W. Averell Harriman, the international banker who became a Democratic expert on international affairs. Truman was to regret his choice during the campaign, when Stevenson made a casual, but unhappy, reference to "the mess in Washington," in a campaign speech in the Northwest.

I met Adlai when he was serving in the Department of Agriculture during my earliest days in Washington. Now and then we picnicked on Civil War battlefields with sandwiches and a bottle of wine, occasionally accompanied by our sons and with a friend or two. The war cut this short when he moved on to other departments, finally becoming Assistant Secretary of State and undertaking a number of missions abroad.

Adlai was pleasant company, being literate and learned, but he never was at ease with the common man. This doesn't mean that he was a snob, but that he was uncomfortable in the presence of those with whom he had no small talk or common ground of humor. When I first knew him, he was not much of a speaker. He became one, when he returned to the Chicago area after the war and presided over sessions of the English-Speaking Union.

His humor was of the British pattern, which his social equals admired, as I do, and his delivery was more intellectual than political. It was not without effect, but was hardly calculated to inspire frenzy among the electorate. In 1948, he was elected governor and had an administration relatively free of corruption and influence. He never failed to call me on visits to Washington.

In his campaign his followers tried to make him a champion of the people by making much of a photograph which revealed a hole in the sole of one of his shoes. They made this shoe a campaign badge, but his urbanity led to his characterization as "an egghead." This stuck deeper and drove votes away, especially after Stevenson tried to make it a badge of honor, by asserting: "Arise ye eggheads, you have nothing to lose but your yokes," in a paraphrase of the battle cry of Karl Marx, calling on workers to arise because they had nothing to lose but their chains.

Stevenson's speeches had more appeal abroad than at home. The election was a foregone conclusion when Eisenhower promised to go to Korea and end the war there.

In Stevenson's days in government service, he once undertook a journey by plane to South America. Aware that he had stopped overnight in Belem, capital of the Brazilian state of Para, I went to Bill McAvoy of Pan-American Airways and begged of him one of the blank bills of a Belem brothel, Madame Zeze's, which was widely known as the American Club. Bill had been intrigued by the fact that such institutions invited charge accounts, so he secured a block of blank bills.

I filled one out laboriously, with what I am sure were innocent Portuguese words, but which might have been assumed to carry double entendres. In those days the currency of Brazil was the reis and one milreis was written 1$000, so that the long list of items I drew up ended in a total of what appeared to be thousands of dollars.

I had an obliging secretary place the bill on the top of his mail. Naturally he exploded and she had to disclose me as the author of the statement, which he promptly returned to me with the notation: "What do you think I am, a bull?"

Stevenson ran as a divorced man. How many votes, if any, this cost him no one can say. He was injured by a whispering campaign, encouraged by his angry former wife, who told one and all that she wouldn't have minded if he had left her for a woman, but could not tolerate his leaving her for a man. I am sure this was no more than a woman's vicious wrath. I must say he bore it well.

The *Tribune* supported Ike in the campaign, firmly enough but hardly enthusiastically. Neither the paper nor the colonel claimed any responsibility for his victory. The colonel interested himself in foreign travel before and after the campaign. A number of times he invited me to accompany him on his world tours, but I invariably refused. I told him, frankly, that my idea of travel wasn't a look out of a plane window and a ride from an airport to a hotel and back. I preferred days of prowling about on foot.

Perhaps the most amazing personal assignment I ever got from McCormick came out of Entebbe, Uganda, on February 29, 1952, as I was preparing to leave for Oaxaca, Mexico. I found it wise to take my vacations when the colonel was making one of his tours. This assignment came by cable and read:

"MUST HAVE ACCOMMODATIONS FOR FIVE TRIPOLI MARCH 1 OR 2 AT MY CONVENIENCE STOP ABSOLUTE MUST"

This order, I recognized, moved the colonel's schedule up three days. The same message went to Maxwell. The message reached me at 7 P.M. Entebbe time, the eve of his March 1 deadline. I had to act and act fast.

My first call was to the State Department where I learned that the American foreign service officer in Tripoli was John Stewart Service, whose loyalty the *Tribune* had questioned in news stories and editorials. These were partly responsible for Service's exile to his African post. Nonetheless, any port in a hurricane, so I had the department cable him to exert every possible assistance.

Then I went to General Hoyt Vandenberg, a nephew of the senator and chief of staff of the Air Force. He radioed Colonel F. O. Easley, commander of the Tripolitan air base. I cabled the hotel, although I was sure this had been done, merely to add the weight of a message from far-off America. Also I went to my friend Frank Mitchell in the British Information Service and another friend in British Overseas Airways.

Maxwell didn't have any potent avenues in Chicago, but he petitioned help from the AP, Reuter's news agency and Pan-American Airways. He reported our joint efforts by cable, signing the messages, Maxwell-Trohan, being frank enough to confirm my suspicion that if the efforts failed he would have company on the sinking ship.

I went off to Oaxaca, not sure that I would have a job on my return. Two days later I got a cable from McCormick which read:

"MAXWELL-TROHAN COMPLETE SUCCESS STOP EXPRESS APPRECIATION EVERYBODY."

Later, Vandenberg reported Colonel Easley had a military guard with a band to blare welcome to the colonel and his party. Cars were provided for transport through the efforts of the despised Service, but his work didn't ease the *Tribune*'s abuse in the slightest.

The hotel manager had the staff standing by with thermometers in drawn baths.

The next time I saw the colonel I asked him why he had changed his schedule to cause so much trouble. He laughed and said: "Veysey [Arthur Veysey, the *Tribune*'s London correspondent, who was one of the party with his writing wife, Gwen Morgan] said we couldn't change our reservations and I wanted to show him what *Tribune* people can do."

I also learned from Howard West, the colonel's pilot, that McCormick became so annoyed over Veysey's sending postcards to his daughter from every plane stop that he ordered his craft to take off without the reporter. This would have stranded Veysey in darkest Africa almost as deeply as Dr. David Livingstone. Fortunately for me, perhaps, West found a minor engine fault as an excuse for delay until Arthur got aboard, or I might have been assigned to footslog over Africa in search of my colleague and I didn't have a great line to compete with Henry M. Stanley's "Dr. Livingstone, I presume." I mused on this when I was at the ruins of Persepolis in Iran with Vice President Spiro Agnew in 1971 and came upon the explorer's name and "N. Y. Herald" carved between the legs of the huge stone horses among remaining fragments. As a reporter for that paper Stanley had been ordered to find the missionary by James Gordon Bennett, the younger, who must have been something of a McCormick in his day.

After the 1952 election he was off again. Before the inauguration, the colonel ordered me to give the new President every chance, which was hardly surprising.

REPUBLICANS RETURN
TO THE WHITE HOUSE

THE ADVENT of Eisenhower in the White House did not change my life markedly. I aroused considerable suspicion in those around him because of the *Tribune*'s known preference for Taft. To many Republicans as well as many Democrats I was something of a whited sepulcher. Nor did I find myself endeared to liberal reporters, because their differences with the new Administration were not mine.

Almost two decades had wrought a great change in the capital, so that it was difficult to gain access to top figures. Although the Eisenhower campaign had been carried on the theme of his second crusade, the first being victory in Europe, there was no joyous influx of victorious Republicans and their coterie of angels and saints. There were few jobs to fill.

This was a far cry from the 125,000 jobs FDR had when he came to Washington in 1933. In those days Senator McKellar was the author of one of the government printing office's all-time best sellers, under the unattractive title *A List of Non-Civil Service Positions in the Federal Government and the District of Columbia*. It was published during the 1932 campaign year in anticipation of victory. Every office seeker and potential office seeker came to the capital with a copy of the book in his hand with the positions he coveted clearly marked for presentation to possible sponsors. Many more studied the book in their homes and wrote to Washington sponsors.

It is no wonder then that Farley became the greatest Democratic chairman ever, because every one of the 125,000 jobs was filled through him. There were more than a million job seekers in the early days of the New Deal. As time went on, virtually every one of these 125,000 jobs was wired into the civil service, so that today no new administration has more than about 2,000 jobs to fill. This made Nixon's call to supporters and contributors after his election in 1968 for the recommendations of persons to serve in his government entirely ridiculous. The call resulted in a flood of letters so great they were never opened, because it was known jobs were few.

There was dancing at three inaugural balls around the capital after the inauguration, but no dancing in the streets. There were no descents of miracle workers, planners, programmers and idea men as there had been when Roosevelt came to town.

I was on the Hill for Ike's inaugural address and prayer. He had joined his wife's church, the Presbyterian, a short time before, because his parents were of the River Brethren, an offshoot of the Mennonites. He gave Mamie a hearty buss to mark his great day.

After writing my story, I went to Taft's home, delighting him and his wife by saying I was sticking by my real leader. The Republicans had also regained Congress and the senator, to the surprise of many, consented to be the majority leader for the man who had bested him in Chicago. This was not surprising, however, to those who knew Taft's dedication to service.

Rather soberly, the new arrivals in Washington set about the business of running the government instead of reforming it. Although Taft and his men were accepted on the team, Governor Sherman Adams of New Hampshire, who became top White House aide, Attorney General Brownell and their ilk didn't throw open their arms to welcome me. This was just as well with me because I didn't want to be considered part of any establishment—Republican or Democratic.

Fashions in reporting had changed as well over the twenty years. TV was becoming more important to politicians than radio had been. Members of the press were not the favored darlings they had been in 1933. First they lost ground to radio reporters and then to TV commentators. The decline in favor and influence has been steady, I am sorry to report.

I still believed in personal contacts, rather than press conferences as the best source of news. I had to sell myself to new men, which was not too difficult, but after all I was twenty years older and had lost my brimming cup of enthusiasm. I began relying more and more on lunches with various figures, late afternoon meetings in their offices after busy days and on dinners in my home.

Fortunately, I maintained my contacts on the Hill in both parties, but I found the number of senators and representatives informed on operations of the government had dwindled. Of course, many in top civil-service posts remained around. I could still do a great deal by phone because of my friendships.

Yet the pattern of news had changed no less markedly than reporting. The world was the field of operations rather than the nation. What was happening abroad became more important than digging for scoops at home.

One of my regular luncheon guests was my old friend, General Persons, then No. 2 and soon to become No. 1 man in the White House. In time Robert Richards of the Copley Press persuaded me to combine and broaden our luncheons, because he was also seeing Persons regularly. We met once a week with such top White House men as Bryce Harlow, Jerry Morgan, David Kendall and Jack Martin, who had joined Ike's team and was to become judge of the Court of Customs and Patent Appeals. Lyle Wilson of UPI was almost always on hand.

These sessions didn't produce news so much, but served to keep us informed on Administration thinking. Actually, the luncheons were of greater assistance to the White House aides than to us, because it gave them a chance to sound out press thinking on emphasis and timing of the programs and problems in their domain.

The Administration began well by ending the war in Korea, as Ike had pledged in his campaign, although the peace was uneasy and has necessitated the continuance of some American forces in the area. The Administration maintained peace abroad, although by delicate manipulation, through the operations of the John Foster Dulles policy of going to the brink of war and brandishing the doctrine of massive retaliation.

In 1952, a friend of Dulles had sought to get McCormick to support Dulles for the presidency. The colonel confided to me that he told the man that he would "just as soon support Judas Iscariot."

Also to the credit of the Administration, Chinese Communists were kept out of Formosa and the Russians from making a Red pond out of the Mediterranean. Eisenhower tried to save the French in Indochina, but without spilling American blood; abruptly pulling Dulles back from the brink of that conflict. Dulles favored intervention with men and guns.

The record wasn't an entirely happy one, however, because Dulles alienated Gamal Abdul Nasser and thrust the Egyptian into the Red sphere of influence. Whether the Middle East problem could have been solved by the maintenance of better relations with Nasser is highly debatable. Some argued that the Administration should have supported Israel's demand to make the Suez Canal an international waterway, but this might only have deepened hates.

The Administration did create the hemisphere's No. 1 problem, Fidel Castro, in its anxiety to end the dictatorship of Fulgencio Bastista. The State Department helped bring Castro into power, although its intelligence files and those of Colombia and Cuba identified the bearded rebel as a Marxist and one who preferred Moscow to Washington. These files were made available to me and I disclosed their contents in a story, which clearly identified Castro as a Red when many were hailing him as a Robin Hood.

Shortly after Castro came to power, Maxwell asked me to persuade Ike to speak before the American Society of Newspaper Editors at their annual meeting in Washington. I got Ike's grudging consent. Then Maxwell got Jules Dubois, our remarkable Latin-American correspondent, who was the last of the Richard Harding Davis school of foreign reporters, to produce Castro. When Jules was successful, I had to advise Ike because I could not confront him with a situation that could prove embarrassing.

Ike hurriedly declined the ASNE invitation, arranging to be out of town, playing golf at Augusta. I was sworn to secrecy and told that even then American planes and warships were following a Cuban flotilla, apparently headed for Panama and its canal. The President did not want to be caught sitting with Castro at the moment his forces might be striking at the canal. The flotilla never attacked, evidently because it discovered that it was under the eyes of superior forces, but possibly because the American President would not be trapped dining with the Communist President.

The dinner produced one of my most enjoyable laughs. The Sunday after the banquet, Maxwell joined Turner Catledge, editor of the New York *Times* on a plane trip to New York City. At the National Airport, they were seized by overpowering thirst, although they had both drunk deeply and well. They had a bottle but no glasses, so they repaired to a men's room, squeezed into a booth and tilted the bottle between them.

They came out into the arms of a waiting policeman, who demanded an explanation. When each identified himself as an editor, the cop was certain he had nabbed two sex offenders. He took them to a detention room where they sent out frantic calls to avoid being tossed into the pokey. Of course, these stalwart defenders of freedom of the press and the public's right to know suppressed this story as something the people had no right to know.

The Eisenhower administration didn't support the freedom fighters in Hungary. It was feared such support might provoke a general war. I might as easily have promoted freedom, because the masters of the Kremlin were reeling under adverse world opinion. It is more than likely they would have called off or eased the flow of Red planes, tanks and guns into Budapest.

American intervention in Egypt might have turned the tide in favor of the British and French and against Nasser, which could have been a stabilizing influence in the Middle East. America would have had to bear the brunt of such action because the British and the French didn't have the financial resources or the manpower to maintain a sustained campaign. America's standing aloof did preserve the peace of that time, but whether the action was good for all time is another decision history must make.

In a large part the British were totally responsible for Ike's refusal to join them against Nasser. Intervention was determined upon by Sir Anthony Eden. He had succeeded to the premiership, for which he was considered the best-trained and best-equipped man in England, after a long apprenticeship under Churchill. Unhappily he was ailing when he made his ploy and did not consult with his Washington ally.

The British Ambassador Roger Makin announced the Egyptian venture to a startled Under Secretary of State Herbert Hoover, Jr. Makin apologized for confronting the American Government with a fait accompli, Herb told me, but Makin added that he knew nothing of the plan until he was instructed to report the move. It followed that the American reaction to the British and French thrust was one of anger rather than of sympathy.

The keeping of the peace was largely the task of Dulles. Ike ran the presidency as he had run the war. He left all details to his staff, but demanded that any program be brought to him for approval before it was launched. Generally he went along with his staff. Also Ike almost invariably went along with Dulles although he did overrule the Secretary when the latter wanted to send fighting troops to Vietnam, a course Ike's Democratic successors would have been wise to follow.

Dulles was a dedicated man for whom I had considerable respect and not a little sympathy. The Secretary, unhappily, could not entrust the carrying out of policy to others, but was impelled to fly around the world from one troubled spot to another, interviewing leaders himself rather than trusting ambassadors or departmental assistants. He was never at rest and, in my opinion, helped to burn himself out before his time.

He had no small talk, everything was grim and earnest to him. He had no relaxation other than his work. If he had had but a small measure of the humor of his brother, Allen, who was head of the Central Intelligence Agency, he might have developed a better and more flexible policy. And he might have lived longer.

In a burst of confidence, Dulles once confided to me that he had never been asked to stay to a family dinner in the White House, although he had often worked with the President well into the dinner hour on major problems. He acknowledged that this hurt him a bit. I was mildly surprised that he didn't understand why this was so. He said he did not, so I gave him the explanation, which he immediately recognized as correct.

I told Dulles that as a top military man, Ike had been schooled in the compartmentalization of his life so as to divide duty from relaxation. I told Dulles he belonged to the business side of Ike's life, so that when the President was through with business he was also through with his Secretary. From business, I said, Ike turned to the dinner and bridge and golf side of his life. Ike, I said, was determined that never the twain should meet. Dulles was grateful to me for relieving his mind of this simple burden.

I sat beside Dulles at a dinner on his return from the opening of the Vienna Opera House. When I asked him about the function, he launched into a lengthy description of most of the boxes in the house and their seating, which illustrated the relative importance of each country's dignitaries in the gathering. I cut him short, saying I wasn't the least interested in the politics of the situation, but the performance of Beethoven's *Fidelio*. It had been chosen as the production for the première performance of the new structure American money had rebuilt, because of its message of freedom and the fact that it was written in Vienna.

"Oh," he said, "it was all right, I guess."

Dulles did not remember the name of a single performer. From then on, Dulles invariably addressed me as: "My music-loving friend."

The time has come to note that the first Eisenhower administration was most memorable to me for three events that deeply touched my personal life—the death of Robert A. Taft, the sale of the Washington *Times Herald* and the death of Colonel McCormick.

The Ohio senator worked wholeheartedly for Eisenhower, taking over the arduous and exacting role of Senate leadership. Neither of them knew, and neither did I, that death was even then gnawing at Taft's vitals. How much this was due to his bitter disappointments no one can say, at least in this life.

Eisenhower came to hold his rival in high esteem, so much so that he once rebuked an aide, who spoke slightingly of Taft in the presidential presence, hoping no doubt to advance himself in presidential estimation. Ike said Taft was his friend and a great man and that he wanted to hear no more slurs against the senator.

Taft's was one of the few private homes Ike visited in the capital during his presidency. Also he played golf with Taft, who shot in the low eighties but never tarried for the drinking at the nineteenth hole. After the first of these games, Taft told me:

"Walter, you think I'm crazy about the game. You should play with him. I've never seen anyone who loves the game more or takes it more seriously. I really think he should have been a golf pro."

Ike didn't play with setups. He chose the best Burning Tree

Country Club had to offer and regularly played with pros who came to town.

The last time I saw Taft was in his final days when he invited me to lunch in the Senate dining room, along with his eldest son, Robert, and Jack Martin. Taft talked lightly of his last stay in the hospital and his impending return for further treatment, saying:

"Walter, you'll never guess who came to dinner in the hospital but didn't eat."

I said I could not.

"Tom Dewey," he announced with a laugh, largely at my astonishment.

While we ate, several senators came over to introduce members of their families or constituents to the Ohioan, including Stuart Symington and Wayne Morse of Oregon. At one point Taft inquired about the health of the colonel. When I reported that I was quite worried, Taft really shook me, because I knew his own condition was most grave, by expressing concern over the loss of McCormick and wondering, "How we will get along without him."

When we finished lunch and made our way out into the hall, Taft rested on his crutches and asked: "Walter, do you want to see me alone in the office?"

I am no easy weeper, or at least wasn't at that time, but I must confess I was near to tears. I had to cover up with an assumed brusqueness; I just couldn't trust myself alone with him.

"Now what would I want to see you alone for?" I asked. "I know everything you know better than you know it yourself."

Taft turned and went down the corridor on his crutches between Bob and Jack. I watched him go, wondering if it were for the last time. I could not see his companions; all I saw was his familiar spare figure making his way in pain down the lonely corridor.

Taft died in the summer of 1953.

Colonel McCormick's acquisition of the Washington *Times Herald* was ever a source of trouble for me, not reportorial as much as human problems. From the very beginning the paper was to pose a major personal question. It was suggested I be named editor, the post I had rejected for years when offered by Mrs. Patterson. All my newspaper training had been as a reporter and the trade was suited to my gregarious nature and inquisitive disposition.

It required some fancy footwork on my part to get out of that bind. I did it by consenting to become editor on one condition, which was that I could announce in a page-one box on my first day that the *Tribune*'s law firm of Kirkland, Fleming, Green and Ellis would no longer represent the *Times Herald*. I had long resented some of the things I had been required to do for the firm, but I was grateful when its leaders persuaded the colonel that I was much too valuable a man where I was, after I made my threat to shift lawyers.

I am not sure that the colonel didn't make the offer merely because he knew I would refuse it and that he wanted to give me the pleasure of being considered for the post. He named his niece, Bazy, and her husband, Peter Miller, who were running a paper in La Salle-Peru, Illinois, and doing quite well. I knew them only slightly, but grew quite fond of them both and their young daughter and younger son. I was distressed, therefore, when the niece decided to change husbands, by replacing Peter with her managing editor, Garvin E. Tankersley, a couple of years later.

Washington being the sort of town it is, the split was rumored almost as soon as it occurred. The colonel did not approve of divorce although he was proud of the fact that two women had divorced their husbands to marry him. McCormick did not act until he became absolutely certain of her intentions. Then he ordered Perry Patterson of the Washington office of the *Tribune* law firm to his hotel suite at 10 A.M. and told me to pick him up in his car at 10:30 for a private showdown with his niece.

No sooner had his limousine got under way than McCormick said: "I want to get a pair of red slippers." For a minute I thought he had flipped his lid—slippers and the marital crisis didn't seem to have any relationship whatsoever. I directed the chauffeur to Lewis and Thomas Saltz, where the slippers were not red enough. Looking at his watch, he said he would have to go to Bazy's office and leave me to find the slippers.

When I picked the colonel up again, his first words were: "Did you find the slippers?" I reported I had and we went to Hahn's to pick them up. Back in his car, the colonel explained:

"All my slippers are brown and I can't find them when I reach into my brown-lined bag, especially aboard the plane. These will do the trick, I'm sure."

Then he did an abrupt switch.

"I suppose you want to know what happened with Bazy," he said. "She admitted she is going to marry the fellow. She cried and I cried, but I told her she'll lose the paper."

Curiously enough the colonel was given to forgiving peccadilloes among his men, even to a city editor, later a managing editor, Robert M. Lee, who was playing house with an opera singer and employed the colonel as his cover, without McCormick's consent. Lee spread the word that the singer was the colonel's lady, a tale which persists to this day.

At a luncheon, about this time, the colonel offered to make Mrs. McCormick the vice president of the Washington paper. Maryland promptly refused, insisting that she knew nothing whatsoever about the newspaper business. Later, the law firm was to fan fears of the prospective trustees of the *Tribune* that she was trying to get control of the entire Tribune empire, including the paper, but I never saw the slightest evidence of such ambition. Certainly, in sharing his bed, she was in a powerful position to move in that direction had she been so minded. Today I can't help but wonder whether such a move might not have been better for the *Tribune*.

At another of these Washington luncheons, Maxwell, one of the designated trustees, came as close to being fired as I have ever known anyone at the *Tribune*'s top level to be. I was called from a luncheon table in the Carlton Hotel to a phone. An excited Maxwell said he was planning to go to press with an eight-column line announcing the *Tribune* was offering a reward of $500,000 for the arrest and conviction of the killer or killers of a mother and daughter in Chicago's Drake Hotel. Maxwell said he had a penciled note from McCormick authorizing the outlay.

I accused him for reaching for the brass ring on the news merry-go-round, which was not an infrequent trait on his part. He countered that McCormick was given to grand gestures, but acknowledged that I might be right, which is why he wanted confirmation. I put down the phone and went back to the table and relayed the inquiry.

"The God-damned fool!" McCormick exploded. "He's crazy."

I didn't wait for any more but went back to the phone and told Maxwell he better find smaller type for his line, which would have to be for $50,000. I added that he might have to begin packing. Maxwell became really excited.

Back at the table, I undertook to defend Maxwell as best I could. McCormick insisted that he should be fired. The day was saved for Maxwell, not by me so much as Maryland, who reminded the colonel that his handwriting was as bad as her own, so that no one should be blamed for misreading it. The fault, if any, was with the colonel's secretaries, who should have typed the penciled note, under his scrawl, which was customary. The $50,000 reward didn't solve the murders, but there is no reason to believe that $500,000 would have done any better.

Early in 1954, I was saved from an editor's fate by the sale of the paper. In Taxco, Mexico, where we were vacationing together with our wives, Maxwell talked far into the night in persuading me to accept the post of city editor of the *Tribune*, a job which would eventually lead to that of managing editor. I protested without avail, that I had been away from Chicago too long—by then thirty years—and that I was too old a dog to learn new tricks. However, I gave in on his representation that he needed me and no doubt on the mellowing influence of tequilla.

When I came to our bedroom in El Chorrillo after two o'clock that morning, Carol awoke and said, laughing: "Walter, you're drunk."

"You don't know how drunk I am," I muttered, "I just consented to be city editor of the *Tribune*."

"You're not drunk, you're crazy."

Happily for me, but sadly for others and the newspaper business generally, the sale of the *Times Herald* got me off that hook. Maxwell's offer was withdrawn without any consultation with me, in order to make room for Thomas R. Furlong, managing editor of the Washington paper and former financial editor of the *Tribune*. He had saved Maxwell from being sent to Washington as editor.

I knew nothing about the sale until it was an accomplished fact on March 17, 1954. I knew something was up and should have realized what it was, because I was at a party the colonel gave in the 1925 F Street Club, the night before, but St. Patrick's Day would mark our twenty-fifth wedding anniversary and we had planned a dinner party for twenty-four, so I was occupied and anxious to get the colonel, his lady and top *Tribune* executives out of town. Still, I was stupid.

I saw that Bazy and her new husband, Tank, were most unhappy. I could see that Maxwell, Chesser M. Campbell, second in command on the *Tribune,* and J. Howard Wood, the paper's auditor, were sharing a secret. I thought it was because the party was signaling the retirement of Elbert Antrim as business manager of the paper and his replacement by Wood, who thus joined the elect circle of designated trustees. Not until I got a call the next morning from Benjamin M. McKelway, editor of the Washington *Star,* did I learn that the paper had been sold, almost from under me, to the Washington *Post.*

That afternoon, the colonel called me from Chicago to say that he wanted to tell me about the sale, but Campbell wouldn't let him. I took this for what it was worth—very little—because I knew that Campbell didn't dictate to McCormick any more than I did. The same afternoon Campbell called to assure me the decision not to tell me wasn't his, as I suspected. The colonel just didn't want to tell me because he knew that I would argue that he was betraying all he pretended to fight for.

Strangely enough, I was to learn later, the sale was inspired by Kent Cooper, former head of the Associated Press, who should not have allowed himself to be involved in the dissolution of any paper, even for profit. The deal was, of course, the making of the Washington *Post,* giving it a monopoly in the morning field at a time when the influence of morning papers was growing and that of afternoon papers, declining. The conservatives were left without a voice. The liberal *Post* grew into a paper of tremendous national and world influence.

I consider the sale of the *Times Herald* the colonel's greatest mistake, even to his support of Captain Patterson in launching the weekly magazine *Liberty,* which cost some fourteen millions. The sale of the *Times Herald* made almost that much, but it was not unlike Napoleon's retreat from Moscow as far as the colonel was concerned.

Of course, it must be acknowledged that McCormick was a tired and ailing man. He had tried to take over a property beset by the internal feuds of its Hearst beginnings and marked by men of less than average ability. He hoped the staff would catch fire from his presence among them some three days a week, but he was aging and petulant and hardly given to making new friends, to say nothing of picking up the pieces of an unhappy bargain to forge another *Tribune*.

Another not inconsiderable McCormick mistake was born of the war. When *Tribune* men went to war, the colonel hired men to take their places who were exempt or a bit older. The understanding was that the jobs were temporary and that the newcomers would be replaced when the war ended. Meanwhile, McCormick paid the *Tribune* men who went to war up to 70 per cent of their pay, depending on their service and family status.

However, by the end of the war, many of the new men had served on the paper for four years, so McCormick decreed that they had earned the right to stay. The result was that the *Tribune* didn't have as many young men coming up as it should have had, so there was no great talent reserve to draw upon when the returned veterans and the wartime employees reached the retirement age about the same time. There has been a concerted effort to push out older men and an emphasis on youth for youth's sake, but it has not been entirely successful as circulation, advertising and profits show.

In his last years, the colonel was tortured by bladder trouble, which was complicated by his mixing whiskey and sleeping pills. He was a most impatient patient, even when ministering to himself. The sleeping pills never acted quickly enough to suit him, although he sometimes took them as though they were peanuts.

Once when he was in Chicago's Passavant Hospital, he called the city desk in the middle of the night and demanded to be taken out. While the panic-stricken editor debated a course of action, McCormick got out of bed, put on his bathrobe and started down the hall with a terrified nurse following him and clutching a flask attached to the patient's urethra by a rubber tube.

In the middle of 1950 I was called at midnight by a distressed Mrs. McCormick, who said the colonel had fallen in his room and cut himself on the face. I had prepared myself against such an emergency call by having medical friends get me in touch with the biggest doctor, physically, in Washington. The colonel didn't like doctors generally and wasn't impressed by small men. He was given to calling his own doctor, Theodore R. Van Dellen, who was about my height, "the boy scout." I suppose if we had both been six inches taller, Ted would be the greatest doctor in the world and I would have an assortment of younger men praying for me to retire as editor and publisher of the *Tribune*.

The doctor I found was a Dutch refugee of impressive height and breadth. When the medico entered McCormick's bedroom, the colonel cocked a rather bleary eye and said: "Who in hell are you?"

Having been warned, the doctor told his patient to shut up and went about his examination.

"You're a big son of a bitch, whoever you are," the colonel said and meekly followed orders, which included a short hospital stay.

It has been written that the colonel feared death and tried to ban any mention of the Dark Angel in his presence. This was not so, because that just wasn't the colonel's way. Rather, he would have ordered Death not to stand in his two eyes or call him until McCormick was ready.

He was in no hurry to take the leap into the dark, being not unlike the roué who prayed for chastity and continence, but not just yet. However, he insisted he did not want to be held beyond his time by doctors who proposed to draw out his soul in great agony. He told me he had prevented doctors from prolonging the death throes of his own father. This I could believe.

McCormick also told me that he had killed a man in gunplay in Texas, while he was counting the last hours of his grandfather Joseph Medill, and that he had hidden the revolver in the latter's coffin. I didn't accept this story entirely, any more than I did his confidence that his brother, Medill, committed suicide in his disappointment over his defeat for re-election to the Senate.

The only time McCormick ever knocked me speechless was in his last days. To leave me without words is quite a feat, my friends will agree. Carol and I were house guests in his Boynton Beach home in early February 1955. One evening the colonel and I talked at length of Philip Sheridan's highly important Shenandoah Valley campaign in the Civil War. General Grant had made his way to Harper's Ferry, West Virginia, to order the campaign and then, with characteristic modesty, had returned to the capital, so that Sheridan would get full credit for raiding Robert E. Lee's provision base. Also we traced the campaign of the British cavalry leader Banastre Tarleton from Charleston, South Carolina, in the Revolutionary War to his defeat at the Battle of Cowpens in the same state.

After breakfast the next morning, the colonel repaired to the enclosed porch of his winter home. There he asked Maryland and Carol to leave us for a few moments. When they disappeared, he turned to me and asked with his characteristic directness:

"Walter, what do you hear about my being senile?"

I was stunned. Fortunately, he was given to long silences himself, so that I had time to collect my thoughts. I pursed my lips to keep from gaping in surprise. I couldn't tell him I had heard it most often from Campbell, Wood and Maxwell, whom I knew he was making his trustees, and from his wife. So I countered by saying that anyone who could ride every mile with Sheridan down the valley and up through South Carolina with Tarleton wasn't senile.

That apparently satisfied him, but I couldn't be too sure. Then he continued by saying he didn't like his will. He said Campbell was a dying man, that Maxwell was a "boob," and that there wouldn't be a woman safe on the North Shore, where the *Tribune* had timberlands in Canada, if Wood were let loose. He recalled that he had wanted Paul Miller of the Associated Press to succeed him as editor-publisher, but had been beaten to the draw by Frank Gannett of the chain of newspapers bearing his name, who had hired the able and personable newsman first.

I tried to comfort the colonel by reminding him that all three of his selected trustees were loyal to him and his ideals and fully qualified to carry on his aims and goals. I do not pretend my plea influenced him to stand by the will, but it certainly did not hurt.

Amusingly enough, I did not know until later that the three trustees designate were even at that moment meeting in Chicago, wondering whether they had overlooked me as a contender for the McCormick torch. A day or two before, the colonel had ordered Campbell and Wood to leave his home, because "Walter and Carol are coming." Wisely, the three decided I was not being disloyal to them.

Abruptly, as one would push in a desk drawer, McCormick ended the discussion by asking me to "call the girls back." When they returned he told Carol he was going to make good on his promise to walk arm in arm with her down Worth Boulevard in Palm Beach. He made himself ready and we packed our bags for another vacation in Taxco.

McCormick did get to Worth Boulevard and he did walk a few steps with Carol, but he almost collapsed. I ran and got him a suite in a small hotel nearby, so he could regain his strength. When he had recovered somewhat, we went in to say good-by. We never saw him alive again.

When we got word of his death, in an early-morning phone call from Maxwell, Carol and I lay in bed talking of the good fortune we had had in knowing him as intimately as we did. I recalled that he was difficult and even impossible, but all the greater for being human. Many wondered why I remained with him, but I was young, although not quite young enough to know everything, and I was completely convinced that I was helping to save my country. With all his faults he was a better editor and a better man than those who mocked him and derided him. And, most unfortunately for the *Tribune*, he was a better man than those who pretended to love and admire him.

The miracle was not that I stayed with McCormick when I had many offers elsewhere, but that I stayed on after his death. In considering the future, the morning of his death, I thought that my days as civilian aide were over, but I was soon to learn that I had exchanged one leader for three, each demanding all the prerequisites the colonel commanded of me and more. I never thought I would miss the flow of McCormick messages, but the day came that I did.

I missed the colonel's consistency. After he died I never knew quite what was wanted. If I didn't send a story, I was told McCormick had always favored that type of story. If I sent a story which had been a bell ringer with the colonel, I was told that a new day had dawned and such stories were out. Over the years I was told that while new leaders were faithful, in their own fashion, to the McCormick creed, changes were being made to promote circulation and advertising. I was assured that McCormick would approve every one of the changes that were being made. Just how they got their approval from beyond the grave was never explained.

It became quite clear that I would have to give up my proficiency at walking the tightrope, developed under McCormick, for a new trade of walking on eggs. It wasn't that the trustees were arrogant or exacting so much as that they were extremely sensitive on the deference due them in their exalted positions. They were not mean or cruel, but extremely self-conscious and not a little unsure.

However, let me be frank and acknowledge that I was something of a trial. I have always resisted authority and been something of a rebel. I consider myself a true liberal, not one who binds himself by his emotions to any faction. And I have at all times been quite impatient with stupidity, even my own.

I knew the trustees as fellow toilers in the McCormick vineyard. I knew them to be dependent on the colonel's bounty, even more than I was because they were hungry for power. I watched with sympathy when they fawned, while I stood up in dealings with McCormick. But then I didn't want anything.

Wood and I had covered police stories together in his reportorial days. Maxwell I knew best of all because we were associated in news, but I was aware he owed his good fortune to the fact that he was the nephew of Teddy Beck, the colonel's favorite managing editor, as much as to native ability. Campbell, as an advertising man, was considered no more than a peddler by me, a reporter. Yet, he was to prove more concerned about his trusteeship, working to improve pay and pensions. Unhappily he died, as the colonel feared he would, within five years, leaving his work undone.

Quite frankly, I didn't think the colonel's committee system would work, because I thought one of the three would emerge as dominant over news as well as financial operations. I was wrong; they worked together quite well, although they were never privately enthusiastic about one another.

One of the first things the trustees did on reaching power was to force retirement at the age of sixty-five, which rule had its merits. The next thing the surviving trustees knew was that they were sixty-five. Age didn't seem as old as it had ten years before, so they continued for a time and then began creating new posts, such as chairman of the Board, chairman of the Finance Committee and editorial consultant. Maxwell never learned that the first function of a retired consultant is to keep his mouth shut, so he has been unhappy because he hasn't been able to exercise the power he had hoped he would retain.

I was put in my place in a hurry by the trustees. Carol and I went to Chicago for the colonel's funeral rites. We were in the widow's apartment, when the three trustees entered single file in order of rank. Each kissed Maryland—something they had never presumed to do before—and each came around to me to ask why I had presumed to visit her before they did. I explained she had phoned us and asked us to bring a black coat from her Washington apartment, but this didn't satisfy what they considered a break with protocol.

At the services in the library of the Wheaton estate, I was pressed, at the last minute, to lead Governor William G. Stratton of Illinois into a row in front of the trustees. At the memorial services in Chicago's Fourth Presbyterian Church, the next day, we were taken to a pew in front of the trustees. I was reminded these seatings constituted a further breach of protocol, although I insisted both of them were beyond my control. Maxwell told me he thought his future as editor dictated that he remain in the local room as managing editor in fact, although not in title. Assuming our old pattern of camaraderie still held, I told him that I thought he was nuts. I insisted that he must sever the umbilical cord of the local room in which he could only plan tomorrow's paper, and climb into the colonel's ivory tower to the *Tribune* of next month, next year and the next decade.

I was reminded sharply that I was presuming to dictate to the editor. A few days later, on his first visit to Washington, he changed trains without notifying me. I missed his arrival, and he ignored my outstretched hand of greeting in his hotel room and charged:

"You didn't meet THE editor!"

Fortunately I had had a lot of practice in keeping my temper, but I didn't extend my hand when I left. There were times when I exploded and quit, but was prevailed upon to remain. I have always known that a quarrel has two sides and that the right is seldom entirely on one side. For the most part we got along, continued to be friends, but only so long as I knew my place.

Some months after the colonel's death, Maxwell told me that his nightmares frequently concerned imaginary phone calls from the colonel, disapproving some action or other. He said the voice seemed as real as life.

"I wake up in a cold sweat," he confided.

My only observation was that such a call, if real, would sure make "one hell of a story."

When my new leaders came into power, they became interested in meeting top people. They particularly wanted to get a White House invitation, but never asked me to arrange it. They worked through former Senator Brooks, so I put in a block through General Persons, just to teach them a lesson. It was petty on my part, but they never made it.

I did fix a dinner with Vice President Nixon when I was asked. My leaders brought their counterparts on the New York *Daily News* to the dinner, not so much out of affection as to impress them with their pull. It is worthy of mention only for one phase of a rather dull evening. The leaders soon ran out of questions, none of them being overly familiar with national and international affairs, so I was urged to take over. I didn't want to sing for my supper as well as provide the guest of honor and arrange the menu, so I played a bit dirty. I asked Nixon to explain the difference between the Republican and Democratic parties.

The Vice President launched into a half-hour speech. It left my leaders dazed and puzzled. Over the years I have asked this question of various Presidents and many leaders, but have never gotten a clear or honest answer. There is a lot of mumbo jumbo about a party with a heart and a conscience from the Democrats, and a party with responsibility and genuine concern for the people from the Republicans. It is no wonder, then, that politicians have little trouble in switching parties. As nearly as I could determine from my explorations of this question, the party that gives office to the speaker is best for the country, because it is supporting him and giving him power.

My leaders didn't stop at bagging American lions, although they asked me to produce President Eisenhower at a private luncheon, when he came to Chicago to accept his second nomination in 1956. I was ordered to produce Queen Elizabeth II in the lobby of Tribune Tower, when she came to Chicago on her American visit. The only purpose of the stop was to give her an opportunity to shake hands with my leaders. I got out of that one by producing Clement E.

Conger, State Department protocol man, who was in charge of American details of the visit. I never knew what happened but I do know the Queen did not visit the tower, any more than Ike drove sixty miles to lunch with the trustees in the colonel's old home.

I was covering news all this time, as well as engaging in social maneuvers which would enable my leaders to drop names. I was at the first summit meeting in Geneva in the summer of 1955, the second summit that failed in Paris in 1960 and the President's trip halfway around the world to India in 1959, as well as lesser travels. These journeys never impressed me very much, but I could not get out of them. It has often amused me that such tours are presented as great triumphs of diplomacy or great steps toward world peace, but time judges them as without accomplishment or loaded with more defeat than victory. At best, they serve largely to flatter the ego of the makers, including Presidents.

Ever since the Field of the Cloth of Gold, near Guines, France, where the young and vigorous Henry VIII of England met the young and agile Francis I of France in 1520 to consider an alliance with each other on the death of Maximilian I (1519), such meetings have been held under trumpetings of great promise. Altogether too many are held today. There was a great display of splendor and magnificence in France, but nothing was accomplished and inclement weather spoiled many of the feats. Yet, the history of the world might have been changed if Henry had not contracted syphilis, and if FDR had not been a dying man at Yalta.

At the first summit meeting in Geneva, I was at the airport with Eddie Gilmore, the AP Russian expert, when the plane bearing the Russian delegation landed. Nikolai Bulganin started to descend but he was pushed aside by a chunky figure I didn't recognize.

"Who's the boss man?" I asked Eddie, being aware that one must be boss if he pushed the Premier about.

"Khrushchev, and believe me, he seems to be the boss man," Eddie replied.

Not until 1959 did Ike tell me in the White House that when he gave a party for his fellow summiteers in his villa, Bulganin expressed himself on a subject under discussion. Later, Ike recalled, Khrushchev came to him and said: "I don't agree with our chairman."

I could only tell the President that I wished he had reported the incident at the time, because it would have proved the correctness of suspicions that Bulganin was a mere facade for the chubby Russian. I didn't meet Nikita at the time, but did on his visit to America in 1959, when the truculent and troublesome Red talked to Ike at Camp David. There was a great deal of nonsense written at the time about "the spirit of Camp David," but it was no more than a glittering phrase which was as attractive as a soap bubble but no more lasting.

In Washington I took Khrushchev by the hand and found it soft and flabby. The great blusterer couldn't have punched his way out of a wet paper bag for all his belligerency, it seemed to me.

During the Geneva conference I ran into an amusing sidelight. The Swiss police, who take a very dim view of destroying property, arrested a couple of CIA men. They had been drilling into the lead roof of the Metropole Hotel where the Russians had their headquarters. The American agents, Secret Service men told me, were forced to confess that they were seeking to bug the Russian headquarters. The Swiss police told them that there was no necessity for destroying property; that the CIA men should have come to the Swiss and they would gladly have turned over copies of their tapes. This would indicate the Swiss were monitoring all headquarters, which was their right.

On Khrushchev's visit to America, he stopped at the farm of Roswell Garst, an Iowan, who had made himself something of a patron of Soviet agriculture by producing a hardy variety of hybrid corn. Garst's neighbors resented the concentration of Russian and American protection. "I don't understand the great concentration," an Iowa farmer observed. "Nobody here wants to shoot Khrushchev, but if they're protecting Garst, that's another matter."

At the abortive summit planned for Paris in 1960, Khrushchev figuratively spat in Ike's eye and torpedoed the meeting by refusing to sit at the conference table with his host of the spirit of Camp David. The Russian leader seized on the shooting down of the U-2 reconnaissance plane in Russia as his excuse for refusing to join the meeting and for withdrawing his invitation to Ike for a return meeting to Russia.

The wily Muscovite was at his demagogic wiliest when he explained his action at a news conference in a sagging chamber of the Palais de Chaillot, across from the Eiffel Tower. Inclement weather disrupted the power service, an interruption Nikita laid at the door of America, but he went on speaking in the dark, punctuated by flashes of lightning. He postured, ranted and raved so that some of the newsmen joined in booing the Red leader. That made him all the more angry, although no one could be sure whether he was in earnest or putting on an act.

There was much act to it, some of us knew, because a dozen American newsmen joined in submitting several dozen copies of the same question to Khrushchev. Conference rules required that all questions be written and signed by the interrogator. An aide apparently picked the questions at random, but he never read a copy of the one in which Khrushchev was asked if he had not seized upon the U-2 incident as an excuse for canceling the visit by the American President, who was also a victorious general. If the questions were not planted, they were certainly selected.

Khrushchev was not one to underestimate his own importance or to spare the feelings of a subordinate. A Swedish newsman once asked Nikita what Gromyko thought of an international situation. Khrushchev snapped that Gromyko would think and do what he was told "even to sitting on a cake of ice—with his pants down." At least one Russian didn't weep when Nikita went to his relatively obscure grave.

Ike's most spectacular, if fruitless, tour was his 18,500-mile journey to Rome, Ankara, Karachi, Kabul, New Delhi, Agra, Teheran, Athens, Tunis, Paris, Madrid and Casablanca in December 1959. This was designed in part to offset the earlier visit of Bulganin and Khrushchev to India.

If it was crowds that Ike craved, he certainly got them—doubled and in spades. Everywhere there were huge and enthusiastic turnouts for the soldier President. Everywhere there were cheering, joyous, flower-pelting and even hysterical crowds. In New Delhi people buried him under blossoms and massed so that his car had to stop. Premier Jawaharlal Nehru was forced to get out of the car and plead with his people to make way for the guest. The reception far surpassed that given to the Red leaders and anything I have ever seen in my life. The most impressive thing of its kind I have ever seen was the massing of one million people who gathered to hear Ike speak. This was not a sea, but a continent of humanity, which threatened at times to break through police lines and engulf everything in its path, including the idol of the moment. I am not easily impressed by crowds, but I was awed by the vast assemblage, which brought to mind what is to come on the Day of Judgment.

In approaching Kabul, the capital of Afghanistan, where Alexander the Great ranged twenty centuries before, there was a suspenseful period. Two squadrons of MIG jets came out to meet Air Force One.

We breathed easier when we were informed that they were Afghan, not Russian, and constituted an escort of honor. Ike flew from the airport to the capital in an American helicopter. The press had a more difficult journey over miles of sheer mountain roads.

There were about twenty in our bus, but we were later fabled to have more than a hundred because of our adventurous journey. Our driver fell asleep at the wheel. He was awakened in time to avoid plunging into the valley some three thousand feet below, but still high in the Hindu Kush ranges some fifteen thousand to twenty-four thousand feet up. Someone suggested the driver be given a cigarette and a half dozen were jammed in his mouth because he nodded again. Someone else suggested the heat was putting him to sleep. Windows were opened so that for the rest of the journey it was a tossup as to whether we would go over a precipice or freeze to death. As we hit the paved road the Russians had built in the Afghan capital, I shouted to Robert Richards of the Copley Press:

"Never mind the palace, Bob, just drive to the nearest laundry."

What I didn't know was that a radioman had his tape recorder running and the witticism, which I thought was restricted to our party, went over the airwaves that night in America, with full credit. Riders in other buses came to ask if we would mind if they said they had been on the famous ride. We didn't mind; in fact, I wished that they had been.

A myth that grew out of that trip must here be spiked for all time. I regret doing so, because I like a good faked story and there is no better place for faking than remote Kabul. The myth was that Ike suffered a heart attack in the mile-high city and was saved by the prompt action of his chauffeur, Dick Flore. My old friend Dick was said by the chief of the Secret Service, in his memoirs, to have produced an oxygen tank kept in the presidential limousine at the opportune moment.

I was the press poolman on that trip and was with Eisenhower every minute of his stay, representing and reporting to my colleagues. King Mohammed Zahir Shah gave a luncheon for his guest, which I attended. I watched Ike get into his car and followed in the car behind. I flew back to Air Force One in a helicopter, which I can recommend over bus travel on that road any day. No oxygen tank was produced because it was not needed.

When we landed beside the presidential plane, I accompanied Ike when he shook hands with the pilots of the escorting MIGs after the exchange of farewells and national anthems. I exchanged a few words with the President as we boarded his plane, so I know he was fit. He did snatch a rest aboard the plane, but he knew it had been a long day and that he had a trying reception ahead in New Delhi.

In Rome, Ike had called on Pope John XXIII. There he congratulated the Pontiff on his English, because he knew the churchman had learned a few phrases in order to greet his guest. "When I hear myself talking English," the Pope sighed, "I begin to doubt the infallibility of the papacy."

In Morocco, while Ike lunched with King Mohammed V, I headed for the harem, which I found was not guarded by two eunuchs with drawn scimitars, as I had expected, but a pair of Medusas for all the world as tough and hardened as any madam in any brothel around the world.

Still this great mission, although the most extensive ever attempted by a Chief Executive up to that time, accomplished nothing. I was reminded of this when Ike told a small group of reporters, after a White House dinner, that on returning to private life he was going to "use my name, if it has any value and I am told it has," to advance world peace.

I opened my mouth to speak but snapped it shut. Later Persons came to me, saying he saw I was going to offer something, and asked what it was.

"I was going to say that when he leaves the presidency, he will find that his name will have lost much of its magic, Slick," I said, "but he'll learn it soon enough without my telling him."

"I am afraid so," he agreed.

Ike sighed for the "lovely title, ex-President." Yet when he watched the stands being erected in front of the White House for the inauguration of his successor, he said: "I feel like the fellow in jail who is watching his own scaffold being built."

The shift from the presidency to private life must be one of the most abrupt that man is heir to. One moment the holder of the office is one of the most powerful men in the world—a commander of men, resources and destiny—and the next he has nothing but the power of his voice and it behooves him to be sparing in the exercise of that. Nothing brought this home to me as much as the departure of Harry S Truman.

On January 20, 1953, after accompanying Eisenhower on the ride to the Capitol for the swearing in, HST climbed aboard the *Magellan* in Washington's Union Station. The private car, from the back of which he had won his surprising re-election, was no longer his but Ike's. He was riding it by the courtesy of his successor. The car was not part of a presidential special, as it generally was, but was attached to the crack Capital Limited of the Baltimore & Ohio Railroad. After settling himself, Truman rang for Sam Mitchell, who had also been loaned to him by the President, and ordered him to get the train under way. "Yes, sir," said the imperturbable Sam, as he left to carry the word to Daniel L. Moorman, the passenger agent of the railroad, who was clocking the departure as a courtesy to the former President.

"You go back and tell him he ain't President any more," said Dan.

"No, sir," Mitchell declared. "I aim to let him find that out for himself and this is as good a beginning as any."

The transition is difficult but not near so steep for members of Congress who meet defeat. Wheeler told me that the hardest thing for him to get used to, after he left the Senate in 1947, was that he was no longer called upon to comment on major national and international developments. It took some time for him to realize that the world could and did get along very well without his opinions.

On the other hand, many wives found it far easier. Dorothy Danaher confided that the defeat of her husband for the Senate in Connecticut was not without compensations because she could go home and "not be nice to people I don't like."

On the domestic side of the coin, Ike did bring down deficits and even fulfilled his promise to balance the budget. The balance was thrown out of kilter by the mild recession of 1957, which saw a considerable slump in the market.

Eisenhower did more for the Negro than either of his predecessors, whose chief contributions were mouth honor and an occasional handshake. Having seen Negro troops in action, Ike was for extension of civil rights and opportunities, not for votes, which he didn't need, but on a firm basis of education and qualification. He did take a strong stand for improving education of blacks when he sent troops into Little Rock, Arkansas, to see that Negro children got into a high school.

Once we discussed something I had seen many times and invariably found cause for reflection. In my reportorial travels, largely in the South but also in the North, I often saw Negro veterans relegated to the tail end of various memorial and patriotic parades. Yet they carried the flag as high and as proudly as white units, even though that flag was not doing all it should by them. Ike felt much the same, which was one reason why he called out the troops in Arkansas, he said.

The Eisenhower administration, like most others, was not without its scandals. I got my first tip on the first of these from McCormick, who wired me to tell the President, "Talbott is a crook." Talbott was fired soon after, but not by my efforts or the colonel's. Ike threw him out when he learned that Air Force Secretary Harold E. Talbott had promoted a firm of efficiency engineers, with whom he had been associated, by writing on air force stationery to various corporations urging the employment of his former associates. These letters were not what the colonel had in mind, however, because he was concerned over the fact Talbott was able to get the government to dredge a channel in Florida in order to enhance the value of property in which the Air Secretary was interested.

The most publicized scandal was that involving Sherman Adams, the top presidential assistant. Adams was not a popular figure. By virtue of his job he was forced to say, "No," to many people seeking jobs and favors. Unfortunately he enjoyed saying "No" and made no secret of it, so he was hated. Persons, who succeeded him, said the word just as often and to just as many, but slowly and sorrowfully, so that he was loved.

So, when it was disclosed that Adams had accepted payment of some hotel bills and some moth-eaten rugs from one Bernard Goldfine, a textile manufacturer, who fancied himself as an influence operator, there were a host in Congress and the press who joyously poured verbal heat on the cold and reticent New Englander. The Goldfine affair was built into a major scandal, which hurt Ike deeply, although it was actually petty. The sums and gifts involved were small and accepted only because Adams was supremely confident of his own incorruptibility. Goldfine and Adams were the losers, the former going to jail and the latter forfeiting his most cherished ambition, which was to crown his career by becoming the president of his alma mater, Dartmouth College. I could not help but be sorry for him, because he paid a high price for a casual friendship.

Of far deeper concern was the failure to clean out the Department of Justice and turn the Supreme Court from legislating by decision. Ike made no secret over his annoyance with Brownell and William L. Rogers, who succeeded him, for their failure to initiate the house cleaning he expected. He blamed them for not picking stronger men for the High Court. When Ike learned Nixon had picked Rogers for his Secretary of State in 1968, the former President said that was the end of the promised house cleaning in that department, noting Rogers had failed to clean out Justice for him.

Time after time, Ike expressed his exasperation over the libertarian decisions, guided by his Chief Justice, Earl Warren, and supported by William Brennan, another of his appointees. Both of these appointments were engineered by Dewey and Brownell. I had occasion to tax them for their responsibility at a small black-tie dinner given by Nixon in the White House, shortly after his inaugural, for a former Australian premier. The guest of honor had entertained Nixon on his visit to that continent as Vice President. Dewey and Brownell both acknowledged their culpability.

"You know Warren ran with me in 1952," Dewey explained from Nixon's left.

I told him that I was aware of that and offered to give him the name of his first running mate, John W. Bricker, in case he had forgotten it.

"And Brennan was recommended strongly by Chief Justice Arthur Vanderbilt of New Jersey, a former head of the American Bar Association," said Brownell.

I said I was aware of that, too, but reminded him that he should have read some of Brennan's opinions before recommending him to the High Court.

Nixon, who was even then contemplating Warren E. Berger as Warren's successor, said nothing in this discussion, but he did credit Dewey and Brownell with helping him pick his Cabinet.

"That's another thing I have against them," I declared, being ever ready to speak my mind.

"Why, Walter," Nixon said mockingly, "do you mean that you don't like my Cabinet?"

I made it clear I didn't. I would like to claim some measure of omniscience for the fact that Nixon was the architect of his own Pandora's box of troubles in naming his Cabinet, but I can't. I just didn't consider the Cabinet a collection of strong and experienced men, except for Defense Secretary Melvin E. Laird.

I have maintained most cordial personal relations with both Warren and Brennan, although they often found me publicly and privately critical of their decisions. In 1967, Warren phoned me to ask that I write a humorous speech for him for delivery at a Gridiron dinner.

"You know, I can't be very funny, Walter," he said.

"Have you reread any of your decisions lately?" I asked with mock innocence.

But Warren is by no means without humor. Not long ago we greeted each other, after our retirements, at a Washington dinner, where I observed he was looking very well indeed, while Brennan looked on.

"You're looking great yourself," Warren observed. "I guess it did us both good to get away from the *Tribune*."

From beside Patrick Cardinal O'Boyle, Brennan quipped that I was doubtless enjoying good health because I was evidently relaxing in good liberal company.

"I am not," I answered, to the cardinal's great enjoyment. "I have the same regard for liberals that I have for marrying priests."

Not all of Ike's Court appointments gave him cause for concern. He had kind words for Justice Charles Whittaker and Potter Stewart and rejoiced that John M. Harlan had swung away from the influence of Warren and Brennan. Whenever he talked of the Court, Ike seemed to sigh over lack of opportunities to change that body before he left the presidency.

The outcome of the 1956 re-election campaign was a foregone conclusion. So much so, that it has now faded from mind. There was some effort in the liberal press to dissuade Ike from running by pretending to believe he would not because of his heart attack suffered in Denver in the summer of 1955. This did not get anywhere. It was no less obvious, at least to me, that Stevenson would run again and that his probable running mate would be Kefauver. At least, I was one of six reporters in Washington to pick both tickets correctly, which didn't seem to me much of a feat then or now. The campaign was something of a replay of that four years earlier.

I have always felt that not the least of Ike's contributions to the presidency was the farewell address in which he warned the nation of the dangers of reliance on the industrial-military complex. This warning, all the more compelling in coming from the mouth of a lifelong soldier, went pretty much unheeded. Politicians know that the one way they can stimulate industry is by going to war and putting many people to work maintaining troops at the front, or by building strong defense establishments which also put people to work maintaining those in uniform and in supplying them.

Ike and I got on our prewar footing long before he left the White House. After his retirement, I was consulted occasionally on matters relating to the press. On one of my trips to the Eisenhower farm I was going about that portion of the field which had been a part of the battleground, when a flicking branch cut my left eye, so that I have since been able to say I was wounded on the battlefield of Gettysburg. There are those, including some of my later editors, who believe I was old enough to have served in that engagement.

Ike took retirement gracefully. After all, retirement has long been a desired goal among the military, probably more so than among persons engaged in other fields. Of course, many military men go into other fields on retirement and do well, but few choose politics.

Ike was always proud of the fact that he was the oldest man ever elected to the presidency, saying humorously that he would live in history for that, if for nothing else.

During his final illness in Walter Reed Hospital, where he was wired up like a Christmas tree with an array of heart-monitoring equipment, he asked Kevin McCann, his college president speech writer, why he was leaving. McCann explained he was lunching with me.

"With Walter!" Ike exclaimed. "That's great! Give him my very best regards."

Then he paused and reflected a moment, and added: "Of course, Walter wasn't with me in the beginning, but he came around."

This was accepted by me, as putting me in the favored classification of a reportorial Justice Harlan.

KENNEDY

To me the advent of the Kennedy administration was something of a replay of the New Deal, not an instant replay so much as a replay of enthusiasm. There was much the same snake dance of great minds, deep thinkers, youthful geniuses and gay enthusiasts—all across a rainbow of visionary schemes and plans.

FDR began by saying: "We have nothing to fear but fear itself." And Kennedy said: "Ask not what your country can do for you, but what you can do for your country." Both FDR and JFK had charisma to the nth degree, being able to send their followers into ecstasies of adoration and jubilation by the wave of a hand.

Of course, there were differences. What was Washington became Camelot. The Brain Trust became the Irish Mafia, although the best of its brains were not Gaelic. There was the same concern about family but with a different accent. With FDR the family was important, but he was its embodiment. With the new Administration, the family was all important, but JFK was merely the beginning.

The Kennedy family made no secret of their divine faith that the White House was their thing and talked openly of family succession and planned for it. The one-man rule of JFK was to launch a dynasty. Unhappily, this dream had to be shattered by tragedy, but it is not yet dead, persisting in Senator Edward M. (Teddy) Kennedy, the last of four charmer brothers.

The campaign had an overtone of sadness for me from its inception.

For the first time, in my career, both the men running for President were far younger than I. This served to remind me my course was being run and the end, welcome though it was sure to be, was not far away.

Strangely enough, the final summons seems further away now than it did then, because man's optimism seems to rise as the inevitable nears. However, some of the sadness may have been due to the fact I could not help but feel I was watching an old movie, while in retirement I have begun a new life among a friendly and delightful people.

At any length, I was moved to forgo any campaigning whatsoever, having had more than my share, and because I wanted to give experience to younger men. I was, however, in New York, on another story, for the famous first TV debate between Kennedy and Nixon. I firmly believe the encounter cost Nixon the election, along with some adept vote counting by the Democratic machine in Chicago and wholesale rejection of Republican ballots in Texas by the state's Democratic machine. I looked in on the debate.

I knew of the debate long before it was set. I did my very best to have Nixon refuse to participate, but I was only one among many whose advice he took and ignored. Leonard Hall, the Republican chairman, agreed with me, when I sought to prevent the confrontation, but he also lost out.

My argument was that Nixon was lending his audience to Kennedy for conversion, where he could not expect to meet with any success in proselytizing among dedicated Democrats. Nixon then, as now, had sublime faith that he could capture and maintain loyalty. I tried to point out that it was the Douglas-Lincoln debates when the relatively unknown lawyer began arguing with the great senator, but they became the Lincoln-Douglas debates in history.

Victory in the first of the debates was clear for Kennedy. He played the game rough, having friends turn up the heat in the TV studio, because he knew that Nixon is given to easy perspiration, and JFK wanted to make it appear Nixon was sweating because he was on the ropes. Nixon did better in the remaining debates, but never regained the ground he lost.

Rather early in the campaign it seemed to me that JFK was going to win, so I wrote to Father Joe and said so. Joe was delighted over my prediction. He wrote promising that if he could do anything about it, he would see to it that I would be "persona grata" in the White House with the new Administration. I could not resist replying:

"If I am, it will be the first time."

I did not expect the eyelash victory, nor that it would be rooted in fraud. Also it was no surprise to me that my liberal colleagues in the press could find nothing reprehensible in the frauds that brought victory to their darling.

Not long after the election I did approach Mayor Richard J. Daley of Chicago and Cook County Board President Dan Ryan at a dinner in Chicago and charge them with manipulation.

"How is it?" I asked mockingly, "that we are all three products of Chicago schools, but I learned how to count and neither of you did?"

"You should have seen what the Republicans did to us downstate," they chorused, not denying my allegation.

In that campaign an enthusiastic young female Kennedy worker confronted me at a Washington party. She waited until she was sure she would command attention and then shouted:

"I know why you're against Kennedy!"

"Why?" I responded.

"Because he's a Catholic."

"No," was my answer, "because I am."

At the Los Angeles convention Chalmers M. Roberts of the Washington *Post* was disturbed by Kennedy's religion. Roberts approached his editor, J. Russell Wiggins, while we were talking, and broke in to say:

"Kennedy's a Catholic, but I guess that's all right, because he's not a good one."

"Does that mean that a bad Christian makes a good liberal?" I asked Wiggins.

I first met JFK when he was a young boy, but didn't get to know him as well as I knew his older brother, Joseph, Jr. While the elder Kennedy spent much time in the capital, the family preferred Boston. Young Joe was around the capital more than the others.

In the 1940 convention, Joe, Jr., was an elected Massachusetts delegate pledged to Farley. Great pressure was brought on him to shift to FDR. One of those applying the pressure was Representative McCormack, later to be Speaker, who screamed in indignation when comparable pressure was brought against his nephew when he was running for the Democratic senatorial nomination against Teddy in 1962.

I had told Joe that if I could help his boys in any way, I would do so. The father sent young Joe to me in Chicago for advice on the importunings to desert Farley. My advice was that a politician has but one thing he can give and that is his word, so when it is given he should stand by it. I told him no one could fault him if he did. He confided that Arthur Krock had given the same advice, but no doubt much more learnedly and sprinkled with historical evidence. At any length the young man stood by his pledge and helped to make a fiction of the carefully stoked draft movement. I regard him as the ablest and most promising of the Kennedys and often wonder how he might have changed history had he not died in the war, because he would doubtless have been elected President in 1960.

JFK didn't come to Washington to live until he was elected to the Eightieth Congress, along with Nixon. This Congress could have been as bad as Truman was to represent it, because it gave the country two Presidents. In those days Kennedy was to the right of me and Louis XIV, for that matter. He was critical of labor and was to support Joe McCarthy.

During Jack's campaign for the Senate, I ran into Father Joe aboard a train to New York. When he learned I was writing a series of stories on the political situation in various states, he invited me to Boston where he proudly showed me an entire floor of one of the town's leading hotels which was given over to Jack's campaign. It was bustling with workers turning out speeches, releases, propaganda and insignia. I couldn't help but smile some months later when the Senate published a report of campaign expenditures, because Jack listed his total personal expenditures at some 30 cents for a few stamps.

Let me have it clearly understood that I do not pretend to any great intimacy with JFK, as so many others have, that influenced any international or domestic policy. There was something of a generation gap, although I could get him on the phone in the White House. My relations were closest to the patriarch of the family. I didn't get to know Robert F. until he came to Washington as Attorney General, and I first met Teddy when he came to get primary returns in the offices of the Boston *Herald* and *Traveler*, where I was covering the 1962 election returns.

Joe was one of the more interesting men I have met in politics. This tall redhead possessed tremendous drive, amazing vitality, enormous ability and elastic morals, which he displayed in a wide variety of activities from banking to motion pictures, from market operations to the liquor business, but especially in government service.

He served with distinction as chairman of the Securities and Exchange Commission, although he had amassed a huge fortune in selling short that helped deepen the 1929 market crash. He was no less effective in promoting the American merchant marine as chairman of the U. S. Maritime Commission. He was the first Roman Catholic ambassador to Great Britain. Joe did his best to discourage the British from going to war and to keep the United States out of the conflict. Yet, he could allow a young American code clerk, Tyler Kent, to be sent to a British prison for allegedly leaking information on the exchange of intervention messages between Roosevelt and Churchill which were promoting the war Kennedy didn't want.

I talked with Kennedy in the embassy in London in 1939 before the war and again in 1940 after it had started, but before the United States was in. He was highly critical of British leaders in our first talk, saying Britain was not ready for conflict and couldn't win a war without America. He also emphasized that British leaders didn't have the slightest idea of what they wanted from any struggle. Looking at Britain today, its leaders might have done better had they heeded his advice.

Early in 1940, Kennedy was frank to say FDR was headed pell-mell for war, but had no idea what he wanted either. Kennedy was convinced that American entry would be a tragic folly, so much so that he was later to be accused of befriending Hitler, which was not true.

For all his Harvard upbringing, Joe's language was salty but left no doubt about his opinions or sincerity. During the war, I lunched with him in Washington's Carlton Hotel, after he had lost his first son in an air action over the North Sea and his second, Jack, was missing in action.

"For a guy who did his God-damnedest to keep out of war," he told me, "I have sure had more than my share of the crowns of suffering on my soul."

I have had numerous occasions to think of his "crowns of suffering." Angels no doubt have pleaded trumpet tongued against the deep damnation of the taking off of two sons by assassins' bullets, the heroic death of the eldest in war, the plane crash that took the life of the eldest daughter, and the sad deaths of grandchildren in infancy.

There is sadness, too, in the lingering incapacity of the patriarch for years before his final summons. It is hard to write objectively of a family so strewn with tragedy—as deep and as dark as the royal family of Denmark in the great hall of the castle at Elsinore in the final scene of *Hamlet*. It is time for Heaven to cry: "Hold enough!" but we cannot escape foreboding when the last of the sons is eying the Executive Mansion.

Others, far more able and more intimately associated with the President and the New York senator, have written the tale of their lives. I can only add a few footnotes.

The founding father was quick to recognize the value of newsmen and to cultivate them across a wide spectrum of ideologies as sources of information. He was quick to pick them up and just as quick to drop them, when they had been squeezed of their value and he thought he and his boys could get more from others. I had my uses because the *Tribune* was a leading voice against FDR, HST and not too enthusiastic about Ike. Besides, Joe was a great friend and near neighbor of McCormick's in Florida. After the war Joe used to call his man in Washington, Timothy A. McInerny, a former newspaperman and publicist, to ask what was going on in the capital and never failed to ask what I was writing or thinking.

Although he fought the Boston Brahmins, as "them snobbish bastards," all his life, he was no less of a Bourbon in his own way. If anything, Joe was more against the liberal establishment than McCormick. After he came home from the Court of St. James's, Kennedy consulted me—and God alone knows how many others—on a speech he was asked to deliver at Oglethorpe University in Atlanta, Georgia, on May 24, 1941.

"For example," he declared, in counseling graduates against adopting shibboleths of the day, "the word 'liberal' has become entirely suspect because of the grossest sins committed in its name. Today many so-called leaders are professional liberals. They would rather be known as liberal than be right. They have tortured a great word to cover a false philosophy, to wit, that the end justifies the means.

"Liberalism, your studies here at Oglethorpe have taught you, has never meant slavish devotion to a program, but rather did liberalism connote a state of spirit, a tolerance for the views of others, no less in social fields than the physical sciences. Basically, liberalism predicates that man is spirit and out of Godlike qualities can come the triumph over the basic instincts that have made him many times so 'vile.'"

I often wonder whether JFK ever read the speech after his conversion to liberalism.

The father was to live and die in his belief. Perhaps he didn't conquer "the basic instincts," as much as he may have aimed to, parading his affair with Gloria Swanson, the famous screen actress. But the father didn't like Jack's joining "the professional liberals," although Joe wanted Jack to win and win in any way—there was no substitute for victory among the Kennedys.

If Joe lost at golf or tennis, he came back until he won. When Bobby and Jack were in a boat race, they headed for shore, pulled their craft across a spit of land in order to shorten the course and come in first. It may not have been sporting to miscount the votes in Illinois and throw out legal ballots in Texas, but it was victory. Joe would have held, in the case of his son, that the end justified the means. He might have been right.

Although he was accused of being more ruthless, meaner and a far dirtier fighter than Jack, Bobby was more affectionate, even to the point of shyness. With him no one could be entirely bad who was kind to his father, even though he realized there were many who courted his father and himself for their influence and power. Father Joe knew politics and how to apply his money in his son's behalf. In the spring of 1960, John L. Lewis invited me to his office. I found the bluff labor leader chuckling in amusement. He said Joe had called him the night before from Arizona to make an appointment and flew through much of the night to keep it.

On his arrival in Lewis' office, Kennedy wasted no time in asking for the mine leader's help in the critical West Virginia primary. "I informed him," said Lewis, "that he didn't need my help. I told him he already had the state in his pocket and that he knew it and I knew it.

Kennedy said he was glad to know that I considered the state safe, thanked me and left as happy as any cat with a canary singing loud in its stomach."

I told Lewis I could understand how he knew what would happen in West Virginia, but was puzzled as to how he knew Kennedy knew.

"Joe's men have contacted each and every county chairman in the state," Lewis said. "The chairmen have been asked what they wanted in the election and how much it would cost. Some wanted an assessor, others a county judge and still others the county treasurer.

"In each case, the costs were comparatively modest. A few thousand here, a few there and perhaps more elsewhere. Never was the name of Jack Kennedy mentioned, but the chairmen got the message and you can be sure, Kennedy will carry the state."

Jack won handily. The victory torpedoed the hope of Senator Hubert H. Humphrey for the nomination and was a severe setback for Lyndon B. Johnson, who was working for the nomination, but had not entered the primaries.

After the West Virginia primary, John B. Connally, then a Johnson aide, was trying to sell the story in Washington that Kennedy had stolen the election. I wouldn't buy it, particularly because proof was being offered after the story was printed. One paper did print it and the proof never came.

It was ironic that Connally, who became governor of Texas, should be shot when he was riding beside the President on that fatal day in Dallas. The man who had tried to brand Kennedy as a reprehensive practitioner was destined to share a measure of sympathy with the dead President. There are many strange things on earth, but few stranger than what goes on in politics. Connally was to serve the man Kennedy defeated for the presidency as Secretary of the Treasury and to join the Republican party.

Father Joe used politicians as he did newspapermen—for his own purposes—covering both sides of the street and all the alleys. He had helped elect Lodge in his early senatorial races, but turned on him when Jack ran. While he distrusted many FDR policies and knew Roosevelt wanted to go to war, he wrote a book, *Why I'm for Roosevelt*, which called for the President's third-term election. It was whispered in Washington that the book was written in response to arm twisting on income taxes, but no one could ever prove it. Joe also made a speech in FDR's behalf.

In the 1924 presidential campaign, which was a three-way race, Kennedy loaned his car and chauffeur to Burton K. Wheeler, a native of Massachusetts, who was running on the Progressive ticket for Vice President along with the elder Robert La Follette. Wheeler denounced Wall Streeters all over the state from the rear seat of the car, which must have amused Joe. This was the campaign in which Calvin Coolidge won over John W. Davis.

Kennedy had a genius for making money. He was one of the big winners in the market crash. He was one of the first to see the potential for fortune in repeal. When FDR was a sure winner, Joe took Roosevelt's eldest son, James, to London with him where he negotiated exclusive rights for sale of Haig & Haig whiskey in America. Kennedy paid Jimmy $25,000, which the latter thought was all the money in the world, but Joe made millions.

Curiously enough, the father never trusted any of his boys with the control of family money or property, but did place confidence in two of his sons-in-law, Stephen Smith and Sargent Shriver. The latter managed Chicago's vast Merchandise Mart, a thirty-million-dollar structure, which Kennedy acquired for less than twenty million, with the seller making a tax profit and Kennedy acquiring a valuable property at a bargain. Of such operations is the kingdom of finance.

Joe was an indulgent father as far as the romances of his sons went, being concerned not with their morals but that they might be trapped into an undesirable marriage by some nubile and accommodating schemer eying Joe's money.

The father's advice, so he said, was to play divorced women as easy to get and easier to discard. I can't say, because my own personal FBI is rigidly intolerant in this respect and does not believe in sharing wealth. Also I am something of a verbal Lothario, but run to her for protection when the going becomes sticky.

The following of parental advice on divorced women led me and many another newspaperman on one of the strangest wild-goose chases ever to involve a President. Hardly had Kennedy entered the White House than a dowager of the Daughters of the American Revolution came into my office bearing a heavy tome, which was the genealogy of the Blauvelt family in America.

Triumphantly she pointed to a listing which gave Representative John F. Kennedy as the fourth husband of one of the family's descendants. This was sensational stuff, indeed, if true. After all, Kennedy was the first Roman Catholic in the White House and the Church, at least in those days, didn't encourage multiple marriages. However, I found the story hard to believe, especially since I was quite aware of some of Jack's amorous activities.

Nonetheless, the story had to be run down. It cost me some six months of effort, although my days were not entirely devoted to the reported marriage. The compiler of the volume had died and left his records in a mess. Many had disappeared, among them that reporting the fourth marriage of the lady in question. I did learn she had not supplied the information.

It was not long before I was completely satisfied that the entry was an error but this had to be established. I enlisted the aid of friends of the woman in question, who had remarried and still is, as far as I know. Naturally she didn't want publicity. The more I dug, the more the story persisted.

There was a report that a Texas millionaire had a copy of the marriage certificate and was using it for blackmail purposes to keep the Administration from cutting the oil depletion allowance; that the marriage had taken place in London and records might be found there, and that Fidel Castro discovered the marriage had taken place in Cuba and was using the knowledge to prevent American intervention in the island. All these had to be run down.

Finally, the White House recognized that the rumor was growing and would not die away. *Parade* magazine, a feature of many Sunday papers, broke the story of the genealogy in a question-and-answer column. There followed an official denial of the marriage story in *Newsweek*, which is one of the properties of the Washington *Post*, whose editor-publisher Philip Graham was a Kennedy intimate. In the *Newsweek* report, Kennedy admitted knowing the woman in question, acknowledging that he had once taken her to a football game.

It would seem likely that some elderly relative of the Blauvelt blood spotted Jack and the girl at a football game or elsewhere. The descendant might casually have introduced Jack as her husband in order to put her off. The elderly relative may have sat down and re-

ported the marriage to the man she knew was compiling the genealogy, because many become involved in building family trees. Despite
the denials, many people still persist in believing JFK was married
before he wedded the socialite Jacqueline Bouvier.

A more factual tale of JFK, which still could not be published,
concerned a Georgetown woman, who was annoyed over the President-elect's trysts with a young woman neighbor. She took a flash-
light photo of Jack leaving the neighbor's door at an early morning
hour and threatened to publish it. I was approached and offered a
copy of the photo, which was an interesting one, I must say. The
Tribune was not interested in my report of the affair. The offer was
withdrawn before I could turn it down, however. Later I learned
that Joe had called on the woman who took the photo and bought a
rather ordinary painting off her wall for a sum well into five figures.
She got the message and he got the photo.

After Kennedy entered the White House, I received a call from a
friend who had married an attractive widow. She had a pretty unmarried daughter. I was puzzled by his call because he asked me to pick
some place for our lunch where neither of us would be recognized.

When we met, he confided that his stepdaughter was playing house
with the President. His problem, he said, was whether he should tell
his wife. I demanded to know if he were sure. He said the young
lady had admitted it; in fact, she was rather proud of it, although not
enough so to tell her mother.

My advice was that my friend should forget it, because he could
only destroy his own marriage, since the mother would never believe
it, not only of her daughter but of her political hero. He took the
advice and never regretted doing so.

As President, Kennedy maintained an apartment in a hotel near my
home, I often knew when he was there, as I passed, because of the
presence of Secret Service men trying to look unobtrusive. I frequently twitted them about how far their protection extended to the
Chief Executive in his hotel suite, whether to a closet or under a bed.
They did not consider me amusing.

There were stories that Jacqueline threatened divorce and was
bought off by a million-dollar gift from her father-in-law. This Joe
denied in a scatological outburst. All the Kennedy men were given to
ripe language. Under the New Frontier, the use of four-letter words

mushroomed among women in the capital, but I would not put the responsibility on the Kennedys as others have. The family and free language arrived about the same time. I am not squeamish, but I am not fond of the words myself and hardly consider them as pearls gushing from milady's lips.

Bobby gave his father less trouble. I never heard of his leaving the trail, except for one report, supported by a diplomat eyewitness, that he accompanied a Japanese entertainer to her apartment in the interests of determining for himself whether Orientals are fashioned differently. I couldn't take this too seriously, any more than I could reports that Marilyn Monroe was a great love. No doubt she called Bobby, but I am sure for advice rather than assignation.

Teddy was something else again. In Panama and in Rio de Janeiro, I encountered a couple of his crops of wild oats. Joseph P. Farland, then American ambassador to Panama, who said, in response to my query, "I can tell you what I told Teddy the next morning. 'The harm that you have done in six hours will take me six months to undo.'"

In Rio, I was told at the American embassy that Teddy sought to bring women into the nation's guesthouse. When he was denied this wish, he moved to a hotel with his entourage.

When he was running for the Democratic senatorial nomination against Edward J. McCormack, a TV debate was arranged between the two candidates. The nephew called me to ask if I would mind telling him the story that he had heard I knew about Teddy's activities in South America. I said I had no compunctions, but warned him he could not use what I knew in the debate. However, McCormack made an early reference to the real nature of Teddy's Latin-American fact-finding tour, which left no doubt that he was armed with facts. Teddy became so flustered that he lost the debate, but he won the nomination in the primary and the election in the fall.

Jack Kennedy's service in the House and the Senate were not exceptionally distinctive. He was seldom on the floor unless he had something to say for himself. Because of the war injuries to his back, his absences were excused by his colleagues. He did have his bursts of energy, but for the most part he was lazy, a trait I envied because I had never been able to afford laziness myself.

In his bachelor days, Jack lived with his sister Eunice, then unmarried and working on children's problems in the Department of Justice. They entertained regularly and well, but rather casually. I shall never forget one evening we arrived for dinner to find the house deserted, except for servants. As we entered, the record player was endlessly grinding out "So in Love Am I," from the then-current musical, *Kiss Me, Kate*. How long it had been playing, I don't know, but it continued while we waited.

Eunice arrived like a welcome breeze. With her was the sister of the Marquess of Hartington, whom Kathleen had married. (He died in battle in World War II; Kathleen died in a plane crash over the Alps in 1948.) Other guests trailed in, including Representative George Smathers of Florida. But there was no Jack. Cocktails were brought in and replenished, but he did not arrive. Finally, we sat down to dinner. There was one vacant chair until dessert, when Jack came in and sat down without any explanation or apology. Smathers and I knew there was nothing to keep him on the Hill.

When the women retired to the living room, leaving the men to brandy and cigars, Jack launched into a blow-by-blow description of an enjoyable amour. Because of his back injury, I listened politely and excused him, as I did FDR because of his affliction, feeling both felt they had to prove themselves whole men. Tales of sex exploits are more often boring than not.

Next we discussed the course of the Truman administration in the new Eighty-second Congress. Of more interest to me was whether Jack and Smathers were going to seek Senate seats. They were exploring their situation, they acknowledged, but not committed. I remember JFK saying he was not sure whether he might not have to carry the weight of discontent with the Truman administration on his shoulders, rather than be carried by it to the Senate. The White House was not mentioned as within the grasp of either of the two congressmen. The two were buddies.

It is the considered judgment of many newsmen that JFK never dreamed of the White House until that night in 1956 in Chicago, when Adlai Stevenson tossed the vice-presidential nomination up to the convention for grabs. Jack was almost swept in by an enthusiastic ground swell that began with discontent toward Kefauver, the ultimate victor.

I am sure that the idea of the White House was firmly implanted in

Kennedy's mind when he first ran for Congress in 1946. The father pushed him into politics for the purpose of capturing the Executive Mansion and no one in the family ever took their eyes off it. Jack stepped into the role the father had hoped to carve for his eldest son. In fact, the father dreamed of the White House himself, but that was not to be.

I know the father disapproved of Jack's try for the vice-presidential nomination, because he considered second place a political cul-de-sac. Jack would have won the nomination, I felt sure then and still do, had Sam Rayburn of Texas, who was presiding, recognized a delegate who was about to announce a shift that would probably have brought Kennedy victory. However, Speaker Sam, as much as he distrusted Kefauver, didn't like Jack because he didn't regard him as a team player, but a lone wolf.

In that floor battle Jack rode the crest of distrust for Kefauver. Many of those who voted for Kennedy didn't have any idea of what he stood for, but were trying their best to keep Kefauver, who had been unsuccessful in his quest for the first-place nomination, off the ticket.

The Southerners gave Kennedy some of his strongest support. This came in line with a great American political truism—voters do not cast their ballots for a candidate so much as they vote against his opponent. At any rate, when I saw Kennedy after the race, he was jubilant rather than depressed in defeat, because of the heavy vote he as a Roman Catholic had polled among states that had voted against Al Smith, less than a generation before.

From that convention Kennedy began acting like a candidate. Strangely enough, the political decision Jack made and was the making of Jack was never accepted by his father. Papa Joe couldn't understand how a son of his could run for anything but first place in a presidential convention. Yet, if JFK had not tried the water and if he had not gathered much sympathy and support in defeat, I don't believe he could have been successful in 1960. But if he had been nominated he would have gone down to defeat with Adlai, so that it is doubtful he could have gained the presidential nomination in 1960, but he might have been able to run in 1968 or 1972, as FDR did in 1932 after his 1924 defeat with Cox.

Kennedy undertook to build up a public image. He began making speeches on the plight of the French in Indochina and in Algeria. I told him I thought he was going a long way off to light a political boom, but I was wrong because he was establishing himself as a deep thinker on international affairs. Strangely enough, in these early speeches, he warned strongly against American intervention, which he was to launch in Vietnam and his successor was to extend.

It was not long before Kennedy was following the old traditional method of igniting a presidential boom—by rubbing denials together. The founding father rushed to his support, pledging the full weight of the family fortune. I must acknowledge I did not expect Jack to capture the nomination in the beginning, although I did write stories on his speeches. He asked me to, being interested in winning the Illinois delegation.

I thought the Democratic nomination would go to Lyndon B. Johnson who was better known in the country and more popular in the South, where Kennedy and any other Democrat had to make good in order to win the White House. Johnson played his cards too cagily with the result that he defeated himself. He and Rayburn believed that senators and representatives would dominate the convention and counted on them to swing the prize to Lyndon.

However, by the time the delegates had gathered at Los Angeles, it was all over but the shouting. Kennedy stepped out in front when he won in West Virginia and never faltered. There was nothing for Lyndon to do in the City of Angels but swallow his pride and take second place on a political platform abhorrent to his stands in Texas campaigns and to his leadership policies in the Senate.

In the spring of 1960, LBJ came with Lady Bird to Maxwell's suite in Washington's Statler Hilton Hotel after an ASNE banquet, which he had addressed. At that time the Democratic convention site had not been picked and LBJ thought it might go to Chicago. He didn't ask for *Tribune* support, but it was obvious he was hoping for sympathetic treatment. He remained a couple of hours and then excused himself, saying he had had a busy day. A short time later we came upon him in the dining room dancing with Lady Bird. He grinned sheepishly, but was quick to add:

"I have to make excuses to get off with my wife now and then."

Johnson was moved to accept the vice-presidential nomination only on representations from Kennedy forces that JFK could not possibly win without him. The South wasn't hostile to Kennedy but needed assurance of his acceptability. Johnson didn't want second place, but knew he could help. Democrats wanted to regain the White House, so Rayburn, who had been against Johnson's taking second place, changed his mind. There is no question but that Johnson did help far more than most vice-presidential running mates.

I was amused to learn that the founding father had placed a goodly stock of his scotch whiskey at the disposal of Democratic National Chairman Paul Butler, who was reputedly neutral in the nomination battle, but was distributing the liquor among members of the press helpful to Kennedy. Some went to me, because of my long friendship with Joe and Paul, although I tried to decline it because I was not drinking.

I was somewhat surprised when I learned that Kennedy chose to relax in the company of a pretty and talented popular singer after his nomination. I had expected greater exercise of caution, but there evidently was not much interest in such antics.

Kennedy made no serious mistakes in his campaign. The momentum of his primary victories continued. Much of this was attributed to the smooth-running operations of a great team, but then all teams that win are great, with the possible exception of Nixon's 1972 group of slap-happy spies.

The Democratic candidate charmed the people with his ready smile and engaging manner. His Boston twang, which had become familiar under FDR, who had the more polished Harvard accent, helped rather than hurt. He beat drums on his religion to attract sympathy, although his opponent, Nixon, had and has less religious bias than any man I have ever known in politics with the possible exception of another Quaker, Herbert Hoover.

Most important of all in the campaign, Papa Joe cultivated the bosses of the city machines. After he won, JFK was able to joke about the narrowness of his victory. He told a Gridiron Club audience that the morning after his victory he received a telegram from his father saying that, after all, he had refused to pay for a landslide. Kennedy hadn't thrown his diaper into the ring, as some cartoonists quipped, but Papa sure threw in the marbles.

Of the Kennedy administration, little is remembered. Its only boasted accomplishment, the Russian missile crisis in Cuba, has still to be resolved by history. It would seem that Kennedy pushed the withdrawal of Red attack missiles pointed at the United States ninety miles away because Khrushchev was ultimately forced to walk the plank over this crisis by his colleagues in the Comintern. But there are those who view the Kennedy settlement as a defeat, since it entailed an American promise not to invade the island a second time in any attempt to set it free.

Another major development in Cuba in his Administration was the tragic Bay of Pigs invasion, launched from the United States. This invasion, according to a Kennedy in-law, was planned in the living room of the father's Palm Beach home by younger members of the family without experience in strategy or logistics. This informant was horrified by the parlor game of human lives being played by the family and New Frontiersmen.

The invasion was doomed to failure before it was launched, because it was denied necessary air support. However, history is full of similar catastrophes in the playing of the patriot game. The Administration had more than its share of warnings about the Soviet missile build-up. Charles C. Keely, Jr., of the Copley Press, told the story months before the White House acted. Jerry Greene developed the story in the New York *News*. Senator Kenneth Keating of New York disclosed the story on the Senate floor.

Yet the Administration did not act. Nor did it move when U-2 reconnaissance flights showed missile installations. No one can charge that the crisis was deliberately held up in order to influence the 1962 congressional elections, but the development did help to maintain and continue a Democratic Congress when JFK broke it shortly before the election.

Kennedy had promised to be a stay-at-home President, but he set out on world travel in his first six months in the White House. No doubt he precipitated the building of the Berlin Wall, because the Reds decided on sealing off the city's demarcation line between the East and the West, shortly after Kennedy met with Khrushchev in Vienna, where the wily Red leader took his measure of the new American President. Nikita's assessment was not in the least favorable. Kennedy knew he had failed to impress or win Khrushchev and was deeply concerned and even fearful over the future.

The joint communiqué, released at the end of the conference, described the Kennedy-Khrushchev talks as frank, courteous and useful. Those who watched its release were not as enthusiastic or sanguine, at least not all of us. Charles E. Bohlen, State Department careerman and former ambassador to Russia, was sharply questioned by those of us who could see or feel a Red glow over that summit. While Bohlen did not lift the curtain on the communiqué, it was evident that the confrontation was more of a setback than an advance in Russo-American relations.

Like so many before him, Kennedy undertook to approach Nikita as a reasonable man who could be charmed and influenced by the proper approach. Instead, he found Nikita adamant on his stands on Germany, nuclear testing, the Far East, Cuba and the United Nations. Kennedy summed up the Vienna talks by confiding: "It's going to be a long, cold winter."

On his part, Khrushchev told associates; "I think I have taught that young man what fear is." This story was first told to me by Willy Brandt, then mayor of Berlin, in his office shortly before the anniversary of the June 17 East Berlin uprising.

When I returned home, I learned from friends high in the military that Kennedy called for an estimate of the number of Americans who might be expected to be killed in a nuclear war, immediately after his arrival from Vienna. The number was a frightening 70 million. So, when Nikita gave the Russian answer on Vienna by sealing off East Berlin, the Kennedy administration temporized and finally gave in.

I must tell one sidelight of Vienna, which passed relatively unnoticed in the press. At the airport, I saw Khrushchev brush past the once powerful Foreign Minister V. I. Molotov, who was in the rank of Russian officials greeting the party chairman. Nikita didn't even condescend to nod to the man who was such a symbol of resistance to Nazi legions that the fiery Molotov cocktail, used against tanks, was named after him.

A few hours later I was lunching with Larry Rue, Chicago *Tribune* correspondent in Germany, Marcel Wallenstein of the Kansas City *Star* and Waldo Drake of the Los Angeles *Times* in a hilltop restaurant above the Vienna Woods, from which one could see Red Hungary. At the next table was Molotov with his wife and two granddaughters. He was representing Russia on a commission developing peaceful uses for atomic energy, but had not been invited to join the luncheon attended by Kennedy and Khrushchev. There was never a more solicitous grandfather, but I could not help but wonder whether he would not have preferred to hurl one of the war cocktails at Khrushchev.

But if Kennedy's first European tour was a diplomatic failure, it was a political triumph. The trip was hailed in rapturous headlines as a great journey for understanding. So, if he got the back of Nikita's hand, he captured the front pages at home. Before going to France, he did his homework on Charles de Gaulle's memoirs and did charm the old soldier, who had been speaking of him disparagingly as the "young boy."

If Kennedy did well, his wife did even better. There were reams of copy on her clothes, her hair styles, her manner and her mastery of French, which was not without its garbled syntax. So great was her return to France, where she had attended school, that JFK was to refer to himself jestingly as the man who came to Europe with Jacqueline Kennedy.

After the erection of the Berlin Wall, doubts began to gnaw at his image, but political services were to be well served by this and other trips to the Old World, including Germany and Ireland. The idolaters said Kennedy had returned Camelot to Europe. They pointed to photographs of the youthful President and his even younger wife beside the stubby Khrushchev and his dowdy wife, and beside the quixotic de Gaulle and his aging wife, asking who could doubt the triumph of the American dream over worn-out European diplomacy.

But rumblings and grumblings grew louder. The Asian situation became confusion worse confounded. Kennedy abandoned his own policy of noninterference and Eisenhower's limitation of Americans to advisory roles. Kennedy not only sent Americans into combat but he and his successor were to do so by geometric proportion. Furthermore, he undertook to interfere in South Vietnamese internal affairs. The interference led to the assassination of President Ngo Dinh Diem, who had been elected after all, and his cabinet minister brother.

On the domestic side, JFK was unable to push any program through Congress. There is reason to doubt that he wanted to do so. The Democratic platform at Los Angeles had outliberaled FDR and HST in pie-in-the-sky promises. Southerners were alarmed over the extension of civil rights, but aware of the narrowness of his victory in 1960, JFK determined to extend the votes to blacks everywhere.

The platform contemplated full government control over the economy and envisioned a full welfare state. The only legislative proposal Kennedy gained was a trade act predicated on Britain's joining the Common Market, but de Gaulle blocked Britain's entry so the act was of no immediate value.

In fact, Kennedy seemed to throw the platform out the White House window in his famous inaugural address. The platform promised something for all segments of the body politics, but when Kennedy spoke he asked the people not to think of what the government could do for them but what they could do for the government.

These were nothing but words and borrowed words at that, because Grover Cleveland had said that it was not for the government to support the people but for people to support the government. No one has taken them seriously; governments are handing out doles and subsidies and people are holding out their hands for all they can get. As most employers know, young people seeking jobs invariably ask what the company will do for them, not what they can do for the company.

Yet, after more than twelve years it is for this line that JFK and his Administration are best remembered. He kept no promises and realized only questionable achievements. He did slap down industry when he lashed at steel executives for raising the price of steel.

"My father always told me they were sons of bitches," he said, "but I never really believed him until now."

This was the old Democratic game of dividing classes. But he went even further in division, by going back on his promise to keep America out of war and split the people on the issue of Vietnam as they had never been divided before.

Sober analysis of the JFK inaugural will reveal it was not only a borrowing from Cleveland, but there was much borrowing and rephrasing from Abraham Lincoln. It was a skillful blend of tried-and-true political incantations with a poetic beat. Of such borrowings are many great political documents compounded. If history doesn't repeat itself, politicians certainly repeat one another.

Jack was blessed with the greatest of political gifts, as was FDR— both were political opportunists but did not look the part. They ap-

peared to be men of dedication and vision—Kennedy, a young Galahad, and FDR, the noblest Roman of them all. At the other end of
the political spectrum were Johnson and Nixon, who looked like
opportunists whether they were or not.

I always appreciated the fact that JFK never tried to charm me
into joining the rat pack. It may be that he really didn't care, but I
like to think it was because he knew me well enough to know I had
my own code and was determined to live by it.

Both JFK and FDR seemed to be saying something new and startling when they were at their most banal. Also they seemed to be
forthright when they were devious. Both had the happy faculty of
announcing that it was a beautiful day, in such a manner as to make
their auditors recognize the statement as a great truth, although they
had known it all along, but didn't come to realize it until they heard
the mellifluous accents of their leaders.

The inaugural was the high moment in Jack's life, but I am sure
that it would not have remained so, had he survived the senseless
tragedy of Dallas. There is no question in my mind but that he would
have been renominated and re-elected in 1964. No doubt his second
term would have been marked by accomplishment, because he would
have been more firmly entrenched in the White House by a clear
victory. I like to think that he would have been a good, if not a great
President in his second term; certainly he had the potential despite his
illness.

Kennedy was not the first youthful President to be stricken down
in office, before realizing his potential, nor the first to precipitate an
orgy of national mourning, breast beating and penance. All Americans seemed to claim a share of blame for his death even though it
came on a journey undertaken to mend political fences rather than
to advance the national welfare.

On July 2, 1881, the forty-nine-year-old James A. Garfield was
shot in the capital railroad station by an unbalanced office seeker,
Charles J. Guiteau. The President lingered until the following September 19, when his death provoked a national flood of tears not
unlike those shed for Kennedy. In fact, the language of the news
stories and editorials of that day matched the overtones of those on
the death and promise of Kennedy eighty-two years later.

Yet nothing remains to mark the memory of Garfield in the capital. There was an extensive hospital but it was razed, having out-lived its usefulness. Nor is there anything, as yet, to mark the admin-istrations of Roosevelt, who turned the American way of life upside down and it has not yet been set rightside up if it ever will be. But what can he do for politicians now?

I knew Jacqueline Bouvier Kennedy before her marriage, but only casually, because she worked on the Washington *Times Herald* as an inquiring reporter with camera. She was full of energy and purpose, yet I often wondered if she knew what that purpose was. She frequently charged around my Kalorama Heights neighborhood, probably because it was loaded with embassies.

I found her a refreshing change from most of the female press corps, some of whom resemble nothing so much as fruitless, spavined mares with twice the ill temper of those beasts. I have known many women reporters, who were every bit as competent and informed as any men, but too many were failures as wives or frustrated old maids. The women in the Washington press corps gave Jackie the short end of the stick in her reportorial days, because those who fancied themselves as deep thinkers considered the inquiring pho-tographer as little more than a journalistic navvy.

During Ike's inaugural festivities, she did a gem on the family of the in-laws of the new Chief Executive, Colonel and Mrs. George Gordon Moore. I was moved to compliment her on a job well done, which she accepted woodenly and with a slight quizzical expression, as though I were spoofing her. This puzzled me, so when I learned she was going on a date with Eugene R. Black, Jr., son of the head of the World Bank, I made a point of getting an appraisal from one of her own generation.

Young Black described her as the most cold and calculating young lady he had ever dated and predicted that she would marry power or money. Thus her marriage to Kennedy was no surprise to me, nor her marriage to Aristotle Onassis. The only surprise remaining to me is that such a discerning young man as Black hasn't been named the head of the FBI or the CIA.

When Jack died, Jackie said there would never be another Camelot. She also said she would never live in Europe. She did much to strip the tinsel that was Camelot by her remarriage. Certainly it proved she had no political dedication to what her first husband preached in order to win the White House and made it doubtful that he did. One of the great regrets of my life is that I shall not see her an old woman, because in her early forties she is as imperious as any grand duchess and can only be expected to become more so as time goes on.

After Kennedy's death, there was a spate of wild rumors about his assassination. I was aware of the strange tales that had followed in the wake of Lincoln's murder, so I did not take the wild Kennedy reports at all seriously. Still, I did go to Dallas and went over every inch of the fatal parade route, the assassination scene and Harvey Oswald's flight.

I leveled an imaginery rifle at the window of the book depository from which the fatal shots were fired. I visited the room in which Oswald had first plotted to kill General Edwin Walker, the stern anti-Communist, then Richard M. Nixon and finally the young President. I went to the theater in which he hid for a time after the shooting and to the street in which he shot a policeman, who was on his trail. Also I went to the garage in which Oswald was shot in turn by the punch-drunk former boxer Jack Ruby, then the owner of a Dallas strip-tease emporium.

All that I saw and all to whom I spoke supported the findings of the Warren Commission, which investigated the crime. However, I did not approve of the commissioner's star-chamber sessions, nor could I favor the stepping down of the Chief Justice of the United States Supreme Court to preside at what amounted to an inquest.

I know far less of the second and equally incredible Kennedy assassination, that of Robert Francis Kennedy, one of America's most remarkable young men whether one likes him or not. Many hated him in his lifetime, even some who admired his brother. I did like him and admire him, although I often did not approve of his methods or his policies.

Bobby Kennedy was the closest official America has had to a prime minister. When his brother was in the White House, even fellow Cabinet members cleared through him. The one sure and quick way to get a matter brought before the President was through his brother Bobby. And if Bobby asked for something, he almost invariably got it, probably because it was generally thought he was making the request for his brother.

After Jack died and Bobby lingered on in the Department of

Justice for a while, I wrote an ironic piece which said that the lonesomest telephone in town belonged to Bobby Kennedy. Where it had rung almost constantly for three years, I continued, it was now almost silent. As soon as planes could fly my column to Washington, I got a call from the lonesome phone thanking me for my most understanding and sympathetic piece.

I have little doubt that Bobby would have succeeded his brother had the latter lived or that Bobby would probably have become President had he lived. It is entirely likely that he would have succeeded Johnson, because he was well on his way toward capturing the Democratic nomination when he was struck down by Sirhan Sirhan, the Middle East fanatic in a Los Angeles hotel.

Before he embarked on that effort, Bobby asked my opinion of such an attempt. I was as wrong as a political observer can be. Bobby asked my opinion weeks before LBJ announced he was not going to seek re-election. I had no idea that he would turn down a nomination that was his for the asking, so I told Bobby that it would be impossible to deny the nomination to an incumbent Chief Executive if he wanted it. Bobby was politically wise in ignoring my advice, but he might be alive and in the White House had he taken it.

Many said Bobby was arrogant. I found him shy. I think the charge of arrogance stemmed from his impatience. There were complaints that he didn't answer his mail. He always answered me—in long hand—which meant that he labored over the letters personally, a fact he knew would not be lost on me. However, I must confess when the Kennedys set out to woo a person, they never overlook a bet. Also, they have no compunction about throwing away such a person, when through with him, like a squeezed lemon.

While no man can speak with any authority in predicting, I am firmly convinced that Bobby was better equipped mentally and physically to be President than either of his brothers. Sure he was ruthless, unforgiving and vindictive, but of such stuff are strong Presidents made. He wore no man's collar; he could not be tied to bosses by gratitude. Yet, he was as dedicated to the family as his father. Several members told me, in disclosing Jackie's impending remarriage before it was announced, that they were sure that Jackie would never have married Onassis had Bobby lived.

Bobby didn't hesitate to order the FBI to tap the wires of James

Hoffa, teamster union boss, whom he had made the target of a personal vendetta, any more than he hesitated to convict him on information secured from the taps. But he didn't waste any time excusing wire tapping by Hoffa on union enemies. Nor did it prevent him from publicly decrying wire tapping in working to replace the FBI with a national police academy, which would be more amenable to liberal control than J. Edgar Hoover.

I broke the story of the Kennedy-ordered wire taps on Hoffa. This didn't anger Bobby or, if it did, he didn't let me know it. He knew I was not violently opposed to wire tapping, but certainly didn't like a dual standard on bugging. Bobby also ordered taps on the phones of the Reverend Martin Luther King, although the Attorney General and the President were posing as the best friends of all black men. Bobby left the name of his law school—the University of Virginia—off the jacket of one of his books because it didn't fit the image of black champion.

Almost from the beginning of his brother's administration, Bobby was working to have LBJ dumped as Jack's running mate in 1964. He encouraged the investigation into the influence operations of Bobby Baker, the Senate secretary, who was a Johnson protégé. It is entirely possible, as some suspect, that he inspired the investigation into the war in Vietnam, which culminated in the controversial Pentagon papers. This didn't keep Bobby from remaining in the Department of Justice, under Johnson, as long as it suited his purposes, until he decided to run for the Senate in New York, before he was eligible to vote in the Empire State.

I believe he could have been elected President. But I also believe that he could have been shot in the job for arousing more ill will than his brother ever generated.

JOHNSON

I LIKED Lyndon Baines Johnson.

Not that I would expect an angel to inscribe this statement in a book of gold, or to find my name leading a list of those whom the love of God had blessed because of my proclamation. Rather it is because of what I once told him privately:

"Mr. President, your enemies are making me like you in spite of my own better judgment."

He laughed, but not too loudly.

All politicians crave to be loved by everybody. It is hard for them to understand why their harshest critics don't see them as they see themselves, dedicated toilers for the best interests of all. But politicians generally get confused so that they measure the common good by what is best for themselves personally and their pocketbooks.

God knows LBJ had his faults. He was vain, conceited, stubborn, ruthless, unforgiving and not overly concerned about ethical practices in politics. But he had no corner on any of these things. He was a devoted husband, an indulgent father, a warm friend and—in his own lights—an honest man.

No one in my time was better trained for the presidency, having served as a federal official, a congressman, a senator, Senate majority leader and Vice President. Few knew the operations of government any better. When she wanted things done, Jackie Kennedy came to him and not to her husband. She got what she wanted.

As majority leader he prided himself on the number of unanimous votes he was able to maneuver. He boasted of these at regular Saturday sessions with intimates in the press.

Johnson had the highest regard for the presidency as an office of any of the seven men I knew in that office. He gave his support to the occupant of that office whenever he could, as in the Eisenhower administration, without regard to partisanship.

LBJ had the reputation of being a wheeler dealer. This was so but within limits. Even he did not know—or hesitated to employ—the full power of the presidency. Once he confessed to me that he was weighed down by the barrage of newscasts that were his nightly lot on four TV sets he often operated simultaneously in his private quarters. He asked me what he could do to change the unfair presentation.

"Mr. President," I answered, with tongue in cheek, "I suppose that I am, at heart, a much meaner man than you. I would manage to send word to broadcast executives that the airwaves belong to the people and that some of your people wanted to introduce legislation to prevent them from selling channels among themselves and to provide for periodic examination of licenses and operational practices. They would get the message and present the news more fairly and objectively."

"I couldn't do that," he exclaimed without a moment's hesitation and with some horror. "It would be an unwarranted infringement of freedom of the press."

Much of LBJ's wheeling and dealing was persuasion. Few men could be more compelling than he was when he bent his mind to it. He could pull out all the stops on love of the flag, love of country, love of home and love of mother, when they served his purposes.

I was among the more surprised Washington reporters when LBJ got Chief Justice Warren and Senator Richard Russell of Georgia to serve on the commission to investigate the Kennedy assassination. I knew Russell couldn't abide Warren for his pattern of liberal decisions, especially on civil rights, and I knew Warren, as a result, was uneasy in Russell's company. Also I knew Warren was not eager to step down from the High Court to act as a coroner.

So, I had to find out how this was accomplished. LBJ reminded Warren that the country had been good to him, I learned, because he had been attorney general and governor of California, a candidate for Vice President and Chief Justice. Now it was time he bury petty irritations, Johnson argued, and repay part of that debt by resolving doubts that were perplexing the American people over the foul murder. LBJ said Warren could do that by gathering together and presenting all the facts without fear or favor. LBJ insisted the people would not be satisfied with a report from a lesser figure than their Chief Justice. Warren accepted.

Russell proved a harder nut to crack. He was first approached by phone and turned down a place on the commission, Russell told me. Johnson then invited the senator to the White House, where he talked for two hours of the debt Russell owed the country and the Democratic party. LBJ brushed aside objection after objection, Russell confided, so that there was nothing for him to do but give his grudging consent.

Much of LBJ's wheeling and dealing was of this pattern. It wasn't that LBJ was a purist in politics, because he most certainly wasn't. He was first elected to the Senate by a majority of 87 votes, after a campaign in which some members of his opposition were brutally done to death in gangland fashion. When LBJ first took his seat in the Senate, he was twitted over being "Landslide Johnson." But he was capable of telling a joke on himself even on so touchy and bloody a matter. He liked to tell of a man coming upon a crying Mexican child in a Texas village the day after Johnson's election to the Senate:

"What are you crying about, Pepe?" the man asked.

"My father came to town yesterday but didn't come to see me."

"But, Pepe, you know your father has been dead for two years."

"Yes, but my father came to town yesterday to vote for Lyndon Johnson; why didn't he come to see me?"

Nor did the throwing out of thousands of Nixon ballots in the 1960 election cause LBJ to lose any sleep. Of such things are elections made and power goes only to the winner.

Few relationships in public life were as genuine and warm as that of LBJ and Lady Bird. Sure he put the LBJ brand on Claudia Alta

Taylor, renaming her Lady Bird, and he gave their daughters initials matching his own.

Mrs. Johnson is a lady. I don't know anyone who would say LBJ was a gentleman in the highest sense of the word, but he was the finest of gentlemen to his wife. He shared all decisions with her and respected her judgment above that of his most intimate male associates.

Someday I hope she makes his and her love letters public. They are letters that are loving and friendly but also interesting. I had thought the Johnsons were going to make them public during the 1968 campaign, but he didn't make the race. Later he said he would not leave such tender missives to the savagery of the political lists or open such tenderness to the public gaze.

LBJ had a natural gift for a fine turn of phrase. His correspondence was better reading than that of any President of our time, except Herbert Hoover. Both did their own letters in their own words. LBJ was quick to give thanks for what he regarded as favors, slow to anger and even forgiving in his letters, where Truman was often violent.

Before Johnson left the Executive Mansion I had a glowing letter from him, thanking me for my advice and counsel over the years. It was so warm, I sent photostats to my leaders on the *Tribune*, observing that I had never received anything approaching LBJ's generous words from them. But I couldn't resist writing the President to ask why, if my advice and counsel were so good, he didn't ever take it.

It has been written that LBJ couldn't take criticism from those who disagreed with him. I never found it so. "You have done more for me than you know," he wrote in 1969. "I have always treasured your confidence and friendship, and most of all your candor and frankness. I'm so glad I've had a personal friend as genuine as you, although I would not expect you to subscribe to all my political philosophies, nor I to yours."

He was among the number who urged me to write this story, saying he hoped I was "taking a few minutes each day to record . . . your recollections from your reporting days." In another letter, he wrote: "Everyone sees his experience in Washington from his own perspective, and we must leave it to time and several generations of historians gradually to sort it out."

It has also been reported that while LBJ could tell a joke, he really had no wit. This is not true. I sat beside him at a Gridiron dinner in colonial Williamsburg, where I watched him rework his speech, adding quips that were among his best and striking out others that did not please him.

At that dinner, the first in a half century to have women guests, and at my insistence, Governor Winthrop Rockefeller of Arkansas spoke for the Republican opposition. The governor got so carried away with the sound of his own voice that, when he came to the end of his prepared remarks, he fell back on some of his campaign speeches and droned on and on.

"Somehow, Walter," LBJ whispered, "I get the feeling that the war in Vietnam [he invariably pronounced it Veetnam] is going to end before his speech."

The next day, while sitting in George Washington's pew in Bruton Parish Church, LBJ became a target of criticism for the conduct of that war from its pastor. This abuse of clerical privilege was characterized by Carlisle Humelsine, president of the Williamsburg Foundation, as "in exquisite bad taste."

LBJ enjoyed the role of White House host more than any other recent Chief Executive. He broke away from the traditional and more formal U-shaped table, with its rigid protocol, introducing a series of round tables in the dining and Cabinet rooms. He did the seating at the principal tables himself, so he could look up from time to time and catch the eyes of friends and others he wanted to impress. It was somewhat disconcerting to find a dinner partner, jabbing one's ribs to say: "The President wants you." All LBJ wanted was to exchange nods and flash a grin, which seemed to ask: "How am I doin'?"

After a formal state dinner to President Marcos of the Philippines, he once stood up in the front row of the East Room, looked over the assemblage until he spotted me, well to the rear, marched down a side aisle and came to ask Carol and myself what we thought of the entertainment. I must say he impressed the guests, especially those from out of town, who had no idea who I was. They became most polite and interested, mistaking me for an unknown high Administration official or White House intimate.

LBJ was also given to entertaining at luncheons in the living quarters of the White House. Here he gathered relatively small groups of no more than ten. The informality matched his eating habits.

I have seen him pick up triangles of toast and melted cheese, throw back his head and drop them into his mouth as though he were a small boy eating cherries. And he would lift up a dish of his favored tapioca pudding and scrape it off the edge of the dish into his mouth.

Once, when he found I hadn't met his new son-in-law, Patrick Nugent, he summoned the young man and his daughter Luci to his side for introductions. Noting that Nugent was a Chicagoan, LBJ said he hoped I wasn't going to try to make his daughter a Republican.

"No, Mr. President," I responded solemnly. "I am not interested in her any more. We got her into the Catholic Church and now I am aiming for other game."

"You mean me?" he asked in surprise.

"No, sir," I continued, pointing to his aide, William Moyers. "I'm interested in getting him. It would be a great thing for us to capture a former Baptist preacher."

Another unusual feature of the Johnson household was to get a Sunday phone summons from the President himself, suggesting that a couple drop by for hamburgers. It was startling to learn that there was nothing general about the invitation, but that it would be a foursome with Lady Bird and himself or a threesome, if she were not around.

When Johnson succeeded to the presidency, it fell upon me to check any extracurricular activities in his love life. I had never heard of any during his days on the Hill, but asked among his colleagues, newspapermen and friends. I never found the slightest suspicion of any romance.

In the 1964 campaign, when I was doing everything I could to help Barry Goldwater, one of the most engaging and warmest personalities I have ever known in politics, a Texan came to me promising a strong anti-Johnson story. He said he could furnish me with proof that LBJ had chartered a plane to bring a load of call girls from Chicago to Texas in order to entertain and influence some wealthy contributors.

I told my informant I thought the story was ridiculous, because there were enough young ladies selling their beautiful bodies in the Lone Star State, so that there was no necessity for engaging in wholesale importation. However, I said I would be interested in any proof he could offer. None was ever presented. The informant gave the lame excuse LBJ had ordered all records burned. Yet, the story was to persist; I heard it many times.

I did learn that LBJ had a district tax collector in Austin removed because he would not alter income tax records as Johnson ordered. When he was preparing to reach for the 1960 Democratic nomination, LBJ went to the internal revenue official, asking him to reopen a return for 1956 or 1957, so Johnson could make an additional payment. The collector said LBJ could file an amended declaration for 1959, but declared he would not go back any further to bury any Johnson mistakes. The obdurate collector found himself replaced.

Once, in a limited conference aboard Air Force One, LBJ told a few reporters that he and his wife had a joint income of about $200,000 a year. The release of the conference was held up, but reporters could never understand why. I knew when Robert C. Young, the *Tribune*'s White House man, showed me a copy of the transcript with the reported joint earnings of $200,000.

I knew that LBJ was making annual gifts of personal papers, which he valued at $150,000, to his library. With such deductions limited to 30 per cent of income, I knew that the Johnsons' income had to be far greater than the $200,000 he mentioned.

At least LBJ made his own fortune. True he made much of it through political manipulation and influence, but it was done legally. He built a small inheritance of some $15,000 his wife received from her father into a most substantial radio-TV operation in Austin. The family fortune was valued at between $14,000,000 and $28,000,-000, depending upon whether one accepts the family count or outside estimates.

In the memoirs *Plunkitt of Tammany Hall*, written by William L. Riordon, the Tammany Hall stalwart of the turn of the twentieth century makes a distinction between honest and dishonest graft. Plunkitt sums up his discourse on how he took advantage of inside information to buy up land where he knew the city was going to build a park and making a handsome profit, by saying: "I seen my opportunities and I took 'em."

To me the dividing line between honest and dishonest graft is very thin, indeed. Both are reprehensible. Perhaps office holders would be relieved of temptation if half their salaries were to be made tax free. It might be well to pay our Presidents $500,000, of which $250,000 would be tax free. It would obviate a lot of fiscal juggling to put aside something for the declining years.

I would not say that LBJ was as American as apple pie, probably because there wasn't much pie around in his youth. But he was a great American success story in politics; he certainly saw his opportunities and took advantage of them.

Others, including Truman and Eisenhower, did quite well. Truman went into the White House broke. Friends raised a $4,000 pot to help him buy the clothes necessary for the office. At his death he left an estate of more than $747,000, not counting property he held jointly with Mrs. Truman or the value of many historical documents in his library. He did well in writings and speeches.

Ike was started on a handsome fortune by a special Internal Revenue Bureau ruling, under which he was permitted to write off the earnings of his first book, *Crusade in Europe*, as a capital gain. The theory was that he was not a professional writer and had but one book in him. No one else was ever permitted to take advantage of this ruling. He wrote several other volumes.

I broke the story of the favored treatment. It was given to me by Joseph Nunan, Truman's collector of Internal Revenue, before Ike entered politics. Nunan later went to jail; I could only believe he gave me the story because he thought I was on the trail of his misfeasance in office. I was not, I am sorry to say.

Johnson was not an ideal boss. He was not considerate of those about him. He could be cruel and even abusive. Rarely was he kindly. In the White House he was given to taking three-hour naps in the afternoon. He didn't play golf as Ike had or bowl as Truman did. For health and weight reasons he gave up drinking anything but low-calorie beverages.

He thought nothing of calling his staff members at 6 A.M. and ordering them down to work. They didn't take naps as he did and the early-morning calls frequently followed long nights at their desks.

This driving was one of the reasons why Jack Valenti left Johnson's service for the motion-picture industry. George Reedy and Bill Moyers were others who were not desolate on leaving. I was surprised when LBJ told me Moyers quit because he wanted to be Secretary of State and Johnson didn't consider him qualified.

I found the story hard to believe, but I am aware that working in the White House is a most dangerous form of intoxication. Many who write statements and speeches, as often and well as Moyers did, come to fancy themselves as great thinkers and writers, not realizing it is not their phrases but the President's power that makes their words memorable. It is no wonder then that there is a constant struggle going on behind the White House throne. Staffers are almost invariably jealous of one another and vying for favor and influence.

In the Kennedy administration, the *Tribune*'s White House man, Laurence Burd, undertook to do a series of profiles on the men around the President. He had been captured by JFK and his team, so he was suspicious when I asked him if he would ask one question for me of Arthur Schlesinger, Jr., and Theodore C. Sorenson, top White House aides. He agreed but only when I assured him he needn't run the answers if he didn't approve of them. I suggested he ask each one what the other did.

When Schlesinger was asked what Sorenson did, he told Burd that if he ever found out, Schlesinger would be glad to know. Sorenson was asked what Schlesinger did, and he replied that he often wondered himself. Jealousy doesn't stop at the White House gates. I was not popular with either of the top aides, but especially not with Sorenson, because I exposed his record of draft exemption as a conscientious objector.

LBJ could be tough with associates as well as with his staff. He made a lifelong enemy of Senator Vance Hartke of Indiana, possibly by being too truthful. LBJ called the senator to the White House and dressed him down like a schoolboy for voting against legislation the President favored.

That was bad enough, but when LBJ told Hartke that the senator was "nothing but a two-bit mayor before you rode my coattails into the Senate," Hartke never forgave the President and hamstrung Johnson whenever he could. In one instance Hartke was brighter than most of his colleagues and me, because he had long predicted Johnson would not seek re-election in 1968.

LBJ did have one recreation in the White House that I put an end to, but not actually on his account. When he first took over the White House LBJ initiated the practice of taking luncheon guests into the swimming pool for a plunge before eating. The pool was built for Roosevelt under a subscription organized by the New York *News.* LBJ didn't provide trunks for his guests, all male, but took them and himself into the pool naked.

I was intrigued by this practice, because the first series of these dunkings was for various sets of editors, all of whom boasted of their White House invitations and intimacy, but none mentioned swimming in the raw. This was something, they agreed, that the public had no right to know. The spectacle of the editors sitting on the sides of the pool, dangling their feet in the water and contemplating their navels, amused me.

So, I wrote a column reporting that LBJ had revived, for the edification of his guests, the practice of what small-town boys called "skinny dippin'" when it was done at the old swimming hole. LBJ was angered. He didn't like the column because it brought him a flood of outraged and indignant letters, charging him with desecrating the White House and conduct unbefitting a Chief Executive. However, he never exhibited any anger toward me.

Johnson also knew I was the source of another story which brought him criticism when he was running for Vice President. LBJ liked to hunt on his ranch for game birds and deer. He had a sort of forest ranger's tower built on the ranch where he could sit with sporting guests and drink and talk.

His guests on one occasion were Roy Howard, head of the Scripps-Howard newspapers, his son, Jack, the current head of the chain, Ralph Johnston, a wealthy Texas sportsman, and Lyle Wilson. The party talked and drank into the sunset. When it became dark LBJ turned on a bright outside light. In a short time a buck was drawn by the light. LBJ put down his highball, picked up his rifle, opened a window and shot the deer in its tracks. As any hunter knows this is deer jacking and not to be equated in any way with sportsmanship. Many wrote to protest his action.

While LBJ was a proud Texan and given to riding ten feet tall in the presidential saddle, he couldn't ride a horse for sour apples. When Johnson invited President Gustavo Diaz y Ordaz to his ranch on the Pedernales, LBJ asked his guest to join him on horseback. Taking a look at his host's lean, ranger build, the Latin politely demurred. But when LBJ took off in his saddle in his inimitable rocking-chair style, the Mexican chief of state whispered to Antonio Carrillo Flores, the most popular Mexican ambassador to the United States and later his country's foreign minister:

"If I had known he rode like that, I would have joined him, if only to give him a lesson."

However, LBJ, as a Texan, did much to improve Mexican-American relations. He not only had the Mexican President as an honored guest in the White House, but also had him in his home in Texas, that vast area flung away by that inept Mexican dictator, Antonio López de Santa Anna, who lies in a neglected grave above the shrine of Guadalupe in Mexico City. Johnson ceded territory claimed by a meandering river back to Mexico, which was widely appreciated south of the border.

Johnson was born at Stonewall, Texas, about thirty miles from the ranch that was his proudest possession. His father was politically ambitious but low on accomplishment. His mother was a driving woman who nursed unbounded ambition for her son. Perhaps she did not expect him to go as far as he did.

As a child he knew hunger, which is not a bad thing for an occupant of the White House to look back upon. While LBJ was given to looking on his childhood through mists of romance and nostalgia, it was often to remember that he had been poor once and didn't want to be "poor no more," as Ralph Johnston explained.

LBJ managed to get a degree at a teacher's college and went on to get a law degree in Washington, D.C. Between the two institutions he taught public speaking in a Houston high school and coached its debating team. His pupils, including Littman Danziger, capital record dealer, regarded LBJ as well intentioned but less than inspiring.

While he was attending Georgetown University's law school,

Johnson worked on Capitol Hill. He was in the office of Representative Richard M. Kleberg of Texas, one of the owners of the fabulous King ranch, but that didn't deter the congressman from demanding and accepting kickbacks from at least one member of his office staff.

On February 22, 1937, Representative James P. Buchanan of Texas died and LBJ entered a contest for the vacancy. It was shortly after this election and before Johnson took his seat in the House that I first met LBJ aboard a presidential special enroute to the Dallas exposition of that year.

Bascom Timmons introduced us. Timmons had supported and counseled the new congressman. LBJ was pledging admiration, affection and gratitude, even proposing that there should be a statue to the newsman in Texas as high as the monument at San Jacinto.

Later LBJ was to take umbrage—in large doses—over some of Timmons' criticisms. He stopped speaking to his friend, which is hardly unusual for politicians. As a group, they are generally grateful for a time but exact blind devotion as their price for continued friendship.

Shortly after we met, Johnson approached me on the special, saying he had been stopped by the train conductor who exacted a fare. LBJ pulled out and showed me a telegram from FDR inviting him to join the train.

"I paid the conductor," Johnson said, "but I want to know if I did right. After all, the President invited me aboard."

"You did," I answered. "And let this be a profitable lesson to you. The President is very generous with everybody's money but his own, and don't you forget it."

From the very beginning, LBJ established the pattern of his service in government. He was ever eager to learn; he never stopped asking questions and he was never too busy to listen to the answers. He mastered parliamentary procedure and acquainted himself with every phase of government. He did not choose to attempt to shine on the floor in spread-eagle or persuasive oratory, but to work in the cloakrooms and halls of Congress. By the time he became Senate majority leader, Johnson knew his trade far better than most of his immediate predecessors. He was a master of compromise. He was virtually infallible in counting noses on any votes. He was one of the ablest of the manipulator school of politicians, who are generally far more effective than the demagogues.

Johnson worked well behind the scenes—persuading, cajoling and threatening when he considered it necessary. He loved the taste of victory, but he also knew when to abandon a lost cause in his days in Congress. That may have been why he was moved not to seek re-election in 1968.

Johnson was fond of saying FDR was his political father, but Roosevelt barely knew the Texas congressman, although Johnson had served as Texas administrator of the National Youth Administration. Actually his political father was Speaker Rayburn, another of the great silent manipulators. LBJ often rode roughshod over those who displeased him and would have crushed many who stood in his way. But he got his share, if not more than his share, of criticism in and out of Congress.

LBJ had not been happy in the vice presidency. The best that could be said of it was Lady Bird's remark: "At least we get our pictures in the papers." As usual, there was much talk of upgrading the office when he went in, but nothing much came of it. He undertook the foreign travels that JFK didn't want to make for himself. One of these was to Pakistan.

Johnson had eaten more than his share of corn pone as a boy, so that the streak of corn in him was very close to the surface. When he met a camel driver, Bashir Ahmed, he undertook to play the role of Caliph Haroun al-Raschid of *The Arabian Nights*. He invited Bashir to Washington, his Texas ranch and had him presented with an American truck.

Unhappily the Pakistani's fate was not to be unlike that of the drunken tinker, Christopher Sly, in Shakespeare's *The Taming of the Shrew*. Sly was bamboozled into believing he was a great lord and cruelly awakened to harsh reality. Bashir went home with his truck, but soon lost everything, including his camel, the taste of prosperity proving too rich for his blood. LBJ also lost on the deal by exposing himself to considerable laughter and joshing. He never forgave some who ridiculed him.

While he was in the vice presidency, LBJ confided that he suspected JFK's brother Bobby of fanning the scandal over Robert G. Baker's influence operations. There was reason to believe that the

Senate secretary's close ties to LBJ might make it easy for JFK to dump LBJ in 1964, but whatever the motivation of the exposé, the Baker affair has become one of the imponderables of history.

Not until the scandal broke did I recognize Baker as one of a number of men who were given to recognizing me and calling me by my first name. I always felt that those who went out of their way to be nice to me at capital functions might well bear watching because they might have something to hide. But I failed to follow my own rule in the Baker case, or I might have had a part in exposing the scandal.

Johnson's accession to the presidency has been told with deep feeling and admirable restraint by both LBJ and Lady Bird. I shall not attempt to improve on their versions, although he told me the story privately as he did many others. There are few more touching stories anywhere than his honest account of fumbling for words in trying to offer sympathy to Jacqueline Kennedy, her dress still stained with her husband's blood, aboard Air Force One, which had become his plane by accident of death. His words deserve a place, in my opinion, beside the great and moving account of Robert E. Lee's surrender at Appomattox Courthouse by U. S. Grant.

Members of the Kennedy staff, although stunned by their grief, resented Johnson's assumption of the presidency, but that office does not and cannot brook a vacuum. The widow did not share this resentment, although many professed to know that she did. The evidence lies in the many lengthy handwritten notes she addressed to the new President, expressing her gratitude and appreciation for services and kindnesses. They include one in which she urged him to continue calling her "Honey," saying, "I like it." Some Kennedyites regarded the endearment as nothing short of lese majesty.

In line with his predecessors, LBJ found a name for his Administration, the Great Society, and he lived up to it. I told him that he might have been more accurate if he had termed it "the New Populism," because it went even beyond the liberalism of the Los Angeles platform. He succeeded in passing a veritable flood of legislation, giving the liberals all they wanted and more, and spending beyond the New Deal, the Fair Deal and the New Frontier. Very little of the passage was due to his wheeling and dealing, as some professed to see, but it was passed largely because it was said the martyred President wanted it. Whatever the dead chieftain wanted or was presumed to want was regarded as holy.

No doubt too much was passed too soon. There were warnings, including those of his successor as Senate leader, Mike Mansfield of Montana, that it would take years to untangle hasty and ill-considered legislation. It is still being untangled and the price is being paid, in part, in inflation of prices and deflation of currency. However, this legislation must be traced back to FDR, who promised to rule with the people, but who seized almost absolute power, certainly absolute power over currency. Johnson determined to spend on escalating the war and on his Great Society as well. This double-barreled spending is the root of many of today's problems.

Strange it is that the liberals never trusted the man who did most for them. They hated him with a passion that made me sympathetic toward him. I have seen some of my colleagues in my own home redden with rage and stammer in fury at the mere mention of his name. The only thing they would offer by way of apology was that the very mention of his name caused them to explode because they hated him so. Many times I found myself silent—an unusual role for one so gregarious—while other newsmen, almost invariably liberals, vied with one another in criticism and cruel jokes against LBJ.

I never knew quite why they hated him so, except that they could never accept his conversion to liberalism. They considered him a Texas reactionary and an economic royalist at heart. Yet, they joyously accepted Kennedy's conversion, which was not a whit less opportunistic. They could love the man of inherited wealth and hate the man who had made his own way.

The liberal distrust of LBJ's domestic policies was not fatal. The Waterloo came over Vietnam. LBJ got the full blame for this war, although what he did was to carry out and implement the policies of his predecessor. And he got no credit for the liberal domestic programs.

LBJ didn't create the situation in Vietnam, but was blamed for it even as Nixon was, although RMN inherited the great blunders of the two previous administrations. How much responsibility the military ought to bear for the intervention and escalation is another matter for the final determination. So is White House responsibility for failure to follow the military's recommendation for winning the war by cutting off land and sea supply lines from Red China and Russia.

Very likely, LBJ was blamed for Vietnam by liberals who wanted to whitewash the Kennedys of any responsibility. When he was seeking the Democratic nomination in 1960, Johnson was critical of JFK's absenteeism and his voting record as a senator. Johnson accused Kennedy of running out on the vote to condemn McCarthy and he also attacked Joe, the father, for contributing to McCarthy's campaign funds. LBJ hit Papa Joe for believing "Hitler was right" before the war. Jack may have been able to swallow all this and take LBJ as a running mate, because he needed Texas and the South, but Bobby and the other Kennedy liberals could not.

It has been written that LBJ's hatred of Nixon made his acceptance of second place with Kennedy an easy choice. This was not so, as far as I ever learned from Johnson. Lyndon regarded Nixon as a hard worker in the Senate, which Kennedy was not. LBJ invited Nixon to his ranch early in 1960 when both were seeking their party's nomination. This invitation had not been extended to Kennedy.

It has also been written that Johnson had long cherished the vice presidency as a stepping stone to the White House, having indicated his availability for that office to Stevenson in 1956. Neither he nor Stevenson ever gave me any reason to believe that this was so, but he was hardly alone in ambition. Had he allowed his name to be submitted for second place at Chicago in 1960, I am sure he would have won easily over both Kennedy and Kefauver.

When I say I liked Johnson, let me here and now unequivocally state I loved his 1964 opponent, Senator Barry Goldwater of Arizona, so far as one man can hold another in high affection or, more importantly, so far as a reporter can hold a politician in affection. It is extremely difficult to write objectively about a friend, whose company one enjoys and would enjoy even if political philosophy were not similar.

If Lyndon had a zest for life, Barry had a zest for youth. I can never see Barry growing old and crabbed, any more than I can see myself doing so, because of his capacity for enthusiasm and his affection for young people. When he was crushed in the 1964 election, he didn't retire to sulk in his Arizona tent, but came back at dawn to jest with defeat in the lists of the Senate. It is as difficult not to like Barry, as many people found it impossible to like LBJ.

I know that Barry didn't really want to run for the presidency. I am positive his fine wife, Peggy, didn't want him in the White House. Barry ran, not against Johnson, but against the memory of an all-but-sainted dead President. Barry was trapped by his own charm and party devotion into making his bid. He was a phenomenon of personality, but one who was projected into the arena as the right man, but at the wrong time and in the wrong place.

He is the only candidate for the presidency I have ever known who wrestled with doubts of his own inadequacy and purpose, while he was running for the job. He not only talked of his doubts, but wrote them down. In a startlingly frank letter, he wondered whether he would have the courage to do the things he was saying he would do if he ever got into the White House. This was a month before the election.

However, he didn't have to worry about it too much, he knew, because he was aware that victory for him would have to be one of the greatest political upsets of all time. What worried him more was that he might fail the cause of conservatism to which he was deeply and sincerely committed.

In his campaign for the nomination, Barry was to be betrayed by many he had helped when he was stumping the country for Republican candidates as chairman of the GOP Senatorial Campaign Committee. I went along with Barry—as a friend rather than a reporter—when he went to Chicago to head off a threatened break in the Illinois delegation, which had been elected to support him. There were state politicians who wanted to start a boom for Governor William W. Scranton of Pennsylvania. They were stopped cold.

On our return to Washington we stopped at Lansing, Michigan, where Barry asked Governor George Romney, who was trying to deny Barry the nomination, whether there was anything Romney wanted him to do or say. In my presence Romney said there was not. Yet he went on to attack and work against Barry, declaring that the senator had never invited his views.

However, that is all political water over the figurehead of the ship of state. Barry could not have been elected and we knew it. As a friend, I was moved to betray my own judgment by being the only correspondent to predict Goldwater's election in a news magazine poll. I knew Barry wasn't going to win, and he knew he wasn't going to win. But he called to thank me, because he knew I was the lone reporter, although I hadn't been identified in the poll. We shared a laugh over my vote.

Barry called me after I returned from a campaign survey just before the election. He said he had tried to reach me in order to ask my advice on what position he should take on an issue. Then, with a laugh, he said he knew what advice I would give, if he reached me, so he did what I would have advised. He revealed that Arthur Krock had given him the same advice.

Many blamed Goldwater's defeat on the protective team which surrounded and engulfed him, much as Al Smith's New York team did in 1928. However, if he had won, the same team would have been proclaimed the greatest, but it just wasn't in the cards for him to win.

Barry was never slow to credit those about him for their parts in helping him to write books or speeches. Most politicians I have known dismiss their ghost writers the minute the latter's words trip from their own tongues.

I know Barry was hard hit by the margin of his defeat for all his courage. His unfailing humor and his wife's obvious relief did much to sustain him. Yet, no one can fault him for rejoicing that George McGovern was defeated in 1972 by a greater margin than he had been in 1964.

I was present when Barry brought down the house at a Friendly Sons of St. Patrick dinner in the capital before his nomination. He opened by saying that if that Jewish peddler grandfather of his, who had helped to found the Democratic party in Arizona, could see where he was that night, he would be whirling in his grave. He scored an even more notable success in laughing at himself in defeat before the Gridiron Club in 1965.

At the funeral service for Julie Pegler, in Rome's St. Susanna Church in 1955, Westbrook Pegler sought to put the Episcopalian Barry at ease by suggesting the senator take his cue for rising, sitting and kneeling from this writer.

"Look, Peg," said Barry, "I've buried so many Catholics you might do better to follow my lead."

As much as I love Barry, I'm glad that he didn't win the White House, where JFK once asked him: "What in hell do you want this job for?" But even as he asked the question JFK was doing everything he could in order to win a second term.

I am sure that Barry could not have turned the country around as much as he may have wanted to. And many of those who most wanted him to turn it around would have been among the first to scream for his impeachment, so accustomed have so many become to their own particular bit of federal bounty.

Also I am glad Barry never had to contend with the struggle for power that is the White House. No man who has not suffered should ever be allowed to become President, in my opinion. And he should permit no one around him who has not demonstrated fortitude under great trial. Even then a President can expect to encounter betrayal and greed. There is nothing so stifling for a President as the protection of the White House team. Its members suffocate all ideas that are not their own and would cheerfully strangle one another to gain more power. The young men are even fiercer than the old.

Although discretion might be the kindlier course, I must reveal a bit of innocent spoofing that I persuaded Barry to engage in. Maxwell had so taunted me over what he fancied was Barry's failure to thank him adequately for *Tribune* support in 1964, which support didn't carry Illinois or any state in the *Tribune* area, that I became weary of his complaining.

I wrote to Barry enclosing a suggested letter from him to me, presumably written a few days after his defeat. The purported letter from Barry stated that although he had little to be grateful for in defeat, he appreciated my help and counsel, and the backing of the *Tribune*. Then came the dirty work. The purported letter went on to say that Barry had hoped, if elected, to offer Maxwell the post of Secretary of State, but didn't suppose that Maxwell would take it because being editor of the *Tribune* was more important than running the nation's foreign affairs.

I never heard another complaint against Barry. In fact, Maxwell hailed him as a great man. But, as so often happened with humor, at least my brand, I was soon to discover that I was only hoisting my-self on my own petard, because in 1968 Maxwell told me that if Nixon were elected he might consider an ambassadorial appointment.

Maxwell did suggest to Nixon that I get one, because he knew LBJ had offered such an appointment. I was quite sure that Johnson did so only because he knew I wouldn't take it and was flattering me. When Maxwell made his suggestion to Nixon, I was supposed to counter with the suggestion that Maxwell be named to Mexico. However, I didn't press this on Nixon before or after his election.

Few men I have known have been as obsessed with the verdict of history as LBJ. Perhaps this might be regarded as a sign of strength in most Presidents, because all are conscious that history is looking over their shoulders. But to me it was something of a weakness in Johnson. It seemed to me that he wanted to buy his way into the role of a great President by spending. The end papers of his book of White House memoirs, *The Vantage Point*, would seem to bear this out, because they contain a list of his achievements, signed by members of his Cabinet and other top officials, which glorify his spending programs.

It may have been LBJ's misfortune that he reached his White House goal—first by accident of death and then by reaction to that death—at a time when he was confronted by the choice of spending on war or spending on welfare. He chose to do both with a fearful impact on the national economy. He strove to unite all behind him and almost achieved that goal in the 1964 election. But he ended by dividing the people on the war in Vietnam. He chose to augment a policy he had inherited from his predecessor, but came to walk in its garden of Gethsemane alone, as Presidents must.

It seems to me that in his preoccupation with the verdict of history, LBJ forgot to wheel and deal, nor did he persuade and cajole as he might. He hesitated to employ the full weight of his power or even the full weight of his position as party leader, in order to silence critics in his own party.

When he came to the White House, LBJ was busy on the telephone and in appointments, begging for help from a wide variety of friends and critics. He made a melody of: "I need all the help I can get." He was still asking for help when he left.

There is an old Arab proverb that counsels: "Beware of the fulfilled wish." In 1964, LBJ wished to win and win big. When he did there was no way for him to go but down, which he did. He might have fared better with a smaller margin of victory.

There is no doubt that his six years in the White House left him so worn and perplexed that he was not loath to lay down the burden of his office. He had fulfilled his most ambitious wish, but it had not brought him the happiness and peace of mind he expected to find at the end of that rainbow of accomplishment.

No doubt he relinquished his office with regret. He might have preferred to have the nation rise up and reject his withdrawal by acclamation. Perhaps in his heart of hearts he prayed for a thunderous roar of: "No, we need you!" when he announced his retirement, but I feel sure he knew he wouldn't get it. So he went back to private life and his beloved ranch, where he was, sad enough, to die alone on a chill night in January 1973. He was by himself, through a curious set of circumstances, when he most needed someone at his side.

How many sleepless hours he spent in wondering what the verdict of history would be on him and his Administration, only he knew. It is not for me or for my time, but for all time, to make the final evaluation.

NIXON

RICHARD MILHOUS NIXON IS still running his fateful race with history so that wise men should refrain from making an assessment of his careening career. Since I have never made any claim to superior wisdom, I am impelled to undertake some analysis of the man, his policies and his future, on the basis of some twenty-seven years of acquaintance and observation.

Every man is a prisoner of his past to some extent. With Nixon that extent is great, because it will be seen he runs to patterns set long ago. He is certainly not a bad man, although some would have him insincere, utterly selfish and without principle. Even those who hate him most, and there are many, can hardly rejoice over his present state.

He had looked forward to an old age of honor, affection and respect with hosts of friends. Instead his nights must be haunted with the scorpions of what might have been and his days echo the curses of his enemies and those who deserted him in his hours, days and months of trial.

Still, I believe the pendulum will swing back, as it always does, and he will first come to be pitied and then to be loved, which is more than he ever was at the height of his power in the presidency. Americans, a blend of many dissimilar people, are more southern in character than northern, although most of us come from cooler climes where temperaments are considered to be less volatile.

Americans are quick to hate, quicker to forget and certain to feel sympathy for those suffering misfortune whether guilty or innocent. After all, Nixon has not been found guilty of any crime. Undoubtedly he would have been impeached, principally on the ground of obstructing justice, which could be taken to mean standing by associates above and beyond necessity or personal interest.

Hate is the blight of the soul, while compassion raises man closer to God than any of his actions except the creation of another life.

Nixon chose to resign rather than undergo an impeachment trial. He told his fellow countrymen he chose to do this, against his own instincts and the importunings of his family, in order to spare the nation the disruptive agony of a Senate trial, noting that the nation had already been sadly wracked by months of Watergate and attendant disclosures.

Whether or not the Senate would have voted his impeachment in the final analysis is at least open to doubt. On the eve of a congressional election, Nixon lost almost all his support in the House, and a great deal in the Senate, but an impeachment trial outside of election pressures might have ended in a personal vindication but at the cost of irreparable disunity and almost total lack of domestic legislation.

To those who knew him the resignation was not too surprising. In 1960, when he lost the presidency by an eyelash to John F. Kennedy, Nixon was urged to contest the count in Illinois and the tossing out of thousands upon thousands of favorable ballots in Texas, which many believed cost him victory. Nixon chose not to do so because such a contest would have plunged the nation into disunity and disorder. Also, it must be borne in mind, that throughout his political career Nixon frequently did what he solemnly said he would not do.

At any rate his fellow countrymen may increasingly come to believe Nixon resigned for his country and not for himself. And they may grow to feel more and more that his greatest sin was to protect himself after the fact. After all, other Presidents in our time have made their first concern their own protection, employed the full power of their office to gain their ends and worked to cut their own taxes.

Old wrongs do not make for present rights, however. Still, it has long been a universal trait of politicians to take care of friends and to punish enemies. Most of us recognize that when a politician takes a position and declares: "It isn't politics; it's the principle"—that's politics.

Nixon is not an easy man to know, nor is he an easy man to love. Some of this is due to the manner in which nature mingled the elements within him, but a great deal of it is due to what he has made of himself. He doesn't give his friendship easily and when he does he is not always wise in his choices or safe in his trust. Despite a confident public manner, he is actually insecure in many decisions. Most strangely, he is quite insensitive to others. Perhaps this insecurity and insensitivity were the hydra heads of his troubles.

In his own eyes, he is a completely honest man. And he is in the eyes of his family. He is a model husband and a good father, as is evidenced by his wife and two charming daughters. Yet, Nixon has not and does not always choose the straightforward way: He is careless with promises he has no intention of keeping; he doesn't always return loyalty that is honestly given; he frequently relies too much on his own judgment, and he is not always careful or cautious in the delegation of power.

If that reads like an indictment, it isn't so intended. His cup is full of bitter regrets. I long admired his mind, which I considered first-rate, although I disagreed with him more often than not. I had considerable respect for his mind, until he released the Watergate tapes voluntarily. Just how he or anyone around him could believe the release of the first batch of transcripts would help him or his cause, I could never understand.

I applauded his courage as much as we disagreed and I still do. I, of course, sympathize with his suffering as most Americans do, I am sure. It has certainly been well above man's allotted share, even the most ambitious of men. Yet, as a friend, I can understand, without fully approving, why he was given the soubriquet "Tricky Dick."

Benjamin M. McKelway, former editor of the Washington *Star*, recently recalled a remark I made at a luncheon Nixon gave in his quarters in the capital when he was Vice President. Nixon had assembled some two dozen newsmen, mostly of liberal persuasion, and spoke at length of Atlantic Union, welfare and the like.

"Dick," I observed when he had finished, "you make me sick to my stomach."

I was aware he was pitching his remarks to his audience.

Power is a very heady wine, indeed, and should be sipped most cautiously. It is not difficult for the drinker to convince himself he can do no wrong, and it is not difficult, when drinking, to forget all past experience, even the most trying sufferings, as mere prologue, when in office. Many politicians are convinced that their audiences believe what they say even when they don't believe it themselves.

There are lessons for future Presidents in the Nixon administration. Few Presidents have had a smoother first term or a greater nightmare in the beginning of the second. Probably the lessons will be forgotten, as they were after the regime of Warren G. Harding. More importantly, there are lessons for the American people in giving too freely of their votes and too generously of their money, but they will also be not long remembered, I fear, so let me offer a few thoughts for public instruction.

It seems clear to me that the Watergate scandal cries to heaven for the creation of a new post in the White House which, for the want of a better term, I identify as that of devil's advocate. There should be somebody of trust at every Chief Executive's elbow to argue—soundly and reasonably—against almost any course of action the President proposes or accepts, particularly those he tosses off rather casually, without due consideration and without specific instructions.

Also there should be someone in any administration, whom I call the hound of the White House, because he would be charged with baying on the trail of any delegation of power in order to see that it is exercised properly and with due restraint. Few Presidents consult their critics, as LBJ did me. I do not pretend I was an important critic or that I had a great knowledge of plans or programs in the making, but I did set a tone, along with others who gave honest opinions. It is almost impossible for a President to get an honest count, but he should try.

The American people might do well to demand a strict accounting and exact limitation of campaign funds for any and all offices. There are entirely too many loopholes in giving and still are, although one of the results of Watergate has been a vote for cutting the amount of individual giving. It is ridiculous for candidates to spend many times what they will make in order to win office. There is perpetual temptation to reward larger donors. It is less than honest that Congress should try to limit individual contributions and at the same time try to get every taxpayer to underwrite the campaign expenses.

Also Watergate and its attendant ills demonstrate that there is great danger in a man or a party having too much to spend. If there is too much money it can readily be diverted to extraneous and even dangerous objectives. I have known members of Congress who put campaign contributions into safety deposit boxes to meet personal expenses.

Finally, it might be well if the American people were to exercise wisdom, rather than enthusiasm, in voting and steer shy of making a religion of either party. But that is doubtless asking too much. The two-party system is admirable in many respects—far superior to the system of multiple parties in some countries—but it is not without faults, and the major one would seem to be that there is little or no real difference between the two parties, except one is in and the other is out of power. It might be better if the people demanded differences.

But enough of that, let us look into the acorn from which the Nixon oak grew. I have found him more of a puzzle than any of the other seven Presidents, including Gerald R. Ford, I have known in varying degrees of intimacy.

I first met Nixon when he came to Congress in 1947 with JFK. Ordinarily I would not have met a California representative so early in his career, except that he came from the home district of Bert Andrews, bureau chief of the New York *Herald Tribune*. Also I had been asked by Herbert Hoover to keep an eye on the new congressman, because he had helped to pick Nixon.

This doesn't mean that Nixon and I became fast friends immediately. I respected him but I am suspicious by nature, as all reporters should be, and often wondered whether he had an eye out for the main chance in seeking service on the House Un-American Activities Committee rather than in safeguarding internal security. I cannot say he did, but I wondered, and I find it hard to reconcile his concern about communism in 1949 with his playing ring-around-the-rosy in the White House with Moscow, Peking and Hanoi.

I regard communism as a reprehensible political system not so much for its ideologies as for the fact that it won and held on to power by terror and still does. It is not healthy or advantageous to speak out for liberty and freedom in Communist countries. While communism is still dedicated to world domination, I recognize that much of that battle cry is sounded to keep the minds of its peoples off its failures to bring the millennium at home.

I never liked Nixon's devotion to Atlantic Union, not that I don't like the British, but they are no longer a major world power. And I didn't like his libertarian leanings, but I don't approve of this in many friends.

It is not generally known, but Nixon's most admired political hero of recent times is FDR, not entirely ideologically, of course, but Nixon would have liked nothing so much as to be able to promote the wild enthusiasm that Roosevelt could by waving his right hand, flashing his smile or crooning, "My friends." Nixon tried by throwing both hands over his head, but the response was less than electric.

From the very beginning, I found Nixon more calculating than warm, more promising than performing, more self-centered than outgiving, more petty than generous, and more inclined to say what he thought a listener might want to hear than frank enough to reveal his own stand.

Just before the 1952 convention in Chicago, for example, he told Taft that he wanted to be with the Ohioan, but was under tremendous organization pressure in California. He knew that this was not so; Taft knew that it was not so, and I, who was present, knew that it was not so. Possibly he didn't want to hurt Taft's feelings, which is common in politics, but I felt then and still feel that he didn't want to disclose his own hand.

Nixon knew, even as I did, that if Taft won the nomination, he planned to name William F. Knowland, the senior senator from California, as his running mate. There was no room for advancement for Nixon under Taft, but there was under Ike.

Nixon was projected into the California senatorial race against Representative Helen Gahagan Douglas as a result of his role in the Hiss case. In that campaign he displayed his weakness for cuteness when the two contestants were invited to debate at the San Francisco Press Club. There Nixon confounded Helen by reading a letter pledging his support and wishing him success. He paused for dramatic emphasis and then confided that the letter was signed "Eleanor Roosevelt." Mrs. Douglas' jaw dropped, evidently not putting it past her heroine to betray her, because such is the nature of politics. Then Nixon explained that the letter was not from the wife of the former President, but from the daughter-in-law of Republican President Theodore Roosevelt. No one enjoyed the trick more than Nixon. He won the confrontation and the election, with the aid of accusations that Helen was soft on communism, if not a Communist.

Nixon, like Johnson, was a poor boy. He did well, but never had the same consuming desire for money that Johnson did. Nixon's father was a grocer as mine had been, which was a slender bond, and is remembered largely because he boasted to me that he could still pick a good cantaloupe, an accomplishment I envy. I can't help but wish that he could have picked a good Cabinet or friends as easily.

Nixon had only two years in the Senate before he moved into the vice presidency, so that he didn't have much time to establish a reputation in that body. As Vice President, he was not particularly happy, but then I have never known a holder of that job to be, with the possible exception of Ford, who was aware that it was a stepping stone to the presidency. He frequently complained to me that Ike never had him as a White House guest, but then Nixon belonged to Ike's official and not his intimate circle. They were never close friends.

When Nixon became involved in a 1952 campaign flap over disclosures that he had accepted contributions to a political fund from a number of California friends, including Herbert Hoover, Jr., Ike did not rush at once to his running mate's defense. Instead he asked for time to study the situation, which cut Nixon deeply. The truth was that without any knowledge of politics, Ike didn't know what to do until he consulted his advisers. It is strange that this incident didn't make Nixon shy of any contributors.

Eisenhower did embrace Nixon publicly after the latter had aroused wide public sympathy by undertaking his own defense in a TV appearance. Again his love for political cuteness prompted him to bring his daughters' cocker spaniel, Checkers, on the show with him. No doubt the response to that TV appearance prompted him to undertake his defense of himself in the Watergate affair to the public in another TV appearance, which was less than successful.

The unkindest Eisenhower cut for Nixon, he confided to me, came in 1956. Early in that campaign year, when a cabal was forming to dump the Californian from the ticket, Ike was asked at a press conference to list Nixon's political contributions to his administration.

"Give me a week and I'll try to think of one," was his devastating reply.

The fact remains that Ike did retain Nixon in 1956. Nixon was growing in the President's respect and regard, which is what Ike should have said in his answer to the press conference question. But Ike was never known for fast thinking on his political feet.

Stassen was the front man for the dump-Nixon movement, GOP Chairman Leonard Hall told me. The group included General Lucius Clay, a soldier who fancied himself as a kingmaker. Members of the cabal wanted to replace Nixon with Sherman Adams, which would have made a pretty scandal.

At the 1956 convention, Victor Johnston, Republican strategist, executed one of the most amusing and effective political gambits I have ever known. Johnston went down into San Francisco's skid row and recruited a number of its most disreputable citizens. He identified himself as Stassen and told his army he wanted to make an impression on delegates. He decked them out with Stassen ribbons and badges, and sent them into hotel lobbies with instructions to jostle anyone wearing a delegate or alternate badge. When those jostled complained to the police, the bums protested they had been hired by Stassen. One of them spotted Johnston in the lobby of the St. Francis Hotel and told the police: "There he is now." Johnston faded out of a side door.

I saw a good bit of Nixon as Vice President but more socially than politically because Vice Presidents are not tops as news sources. Now and then Nixon would call and say: "Let's go face the enemy." This would mean that he wanted to go to the National Press Club. There he would tease a drink in the bar, while trying hard to be "one of the boys," among reporters dedicated largely to his extermination. These sessions did not help him, but I suppose he must be credited with trying.

Once in the Statler-Hilton Hotel, he put his arm around my shoulder on his way to a news conference saying: "Let's go in together." I pulled away saying it would do neither of us any good, knowing that, Washington being what it is, I would be credited with briefing him on his answers.

Nixon is less of a drinker, or enjoys a drink less, than any of the Presidents I have known. Once, months after his defeat for governor of California in 1962, he announced he was going to drown his sorrow in the conviviality of Bohemian Grove, the annual encampment of San Francisco's Bohemian Club, some ninety miles north of the bay city, but he gave his intention up as a bad job after two drinks failed to bring any relaxation or pleasure.

Dick behaved admirably when Ike was stricken with his heart attack, his ileitus operation and his stroke. He moved in quietly to see that the government continued to function without disruption and did so without throwing his weight around. No doubt this prompted him to feel he deserved more of Ike than he got, but he was only a pawn in the presidential game Ike was playing.

It must ever be borne in mind that no President falls in love with his Vice President, the man he knows is only a heartbeat or a scrawled signature away from the White House. Abraham Lincoln dropped Hannibal Hamlin for a Democrat as easily as one might shed a glove. FDR shed two second men without a tear. And when he got into the White House himself, Nixon was casual in his treatment of Spiro Agnew and shed him with regret perhaps, but more over himself than over tears for Agnew.

And Nixon picked Ford, I am sure, more because he knew that he could get a man with a reputation as "Mr. Clean" accepted by Congress without difficulty, than out of personal affection. This does not mean that he didn't like Ford or was lacking in gratitude for the latter's support as House Republican leader, but I do not believe that he felt he was naming his successor.

I knew Ford. He was a redoubtable football player, who had performed well in the All-Star game, sponsored by the *Tribune* and he was a Michigan congressman. I considered him far above the average newcomer to Congress. He earned my grudging admiration. I did not consider him the best choice for Republican leader, because I thought he was slow in making up his mind and somewhat vacillating. However, he surprised me by his performance. He worked to get a team and did so.

He once asked me to write him a speech for a Gridiron dinner, but discarded mine for one fashioned by some Hollywood gagmen. Their product pleased almost no one except Ford, who relished their string of puns. He served well and conscientiously on the Warren Commission which investigated the assassination of President Kennedy. Once we shared the speaking platform before a group of citizens of Lithuanian descent or birth. He became irked, and confessed it later, when I remarked that they might have done better if they had picked me to be their principal speaker.

I thought I was leaving the way open for him to poke a bit of fun at me, but he chose to take my remarks at face value. As a tribe, politicians are not renowned for their sense of humor, although they are great storytellers because it is easier to court a laugh than to take a position and not as costly in polling booths. Also he may have been annoyed because I won the biggest hand of the evening when I observed that those attending didn't want to go back to Lithuania, but wanted desperately for their relatives there to enjoy American democracy.

Like my fellow Americans I wish Ford well, and he shall have my prayers, as he asked, because I wish my country, my fellow citizens and myself well. As the first President elected from nothing larger than a congressional district, he will need the prayers of all. It would seem to me he cannot hope for re-election in 1976, because Watergate would seem to have paved the way for a Democratic President, but two years are a long time and who can say how the ballots might bounce. Also he will continue to find it hard to explain why he pardoned an "innocent man" for attempting to cover up Watergate.

It would seem that Ford's accession dimmed the star of Senator Edward M. (Teddy) Kennedy. With almost any Democrat a probable winner, some party leaders would hardly be falling over the last of the Kennedy sons to beg him to lead them to victory, while others would fall in line automatically. Few Americans would like to see Teddy tempt fate by seeking the nomination, which might be for him an invitation for a mentally unstable figure to attempt to wipe out the last of the three political brothers. Teddy has taken himself out of contention for the Democratic presidential nomination in '76 in a strong, unmistakable language, but he has many years ahead in which to change his mind.

I was closer to Nixon in the 1960 campaign than I had been in his years in the vice presidency, but he had become big news and commanded my time. I found him a bit trying because he was forever pulling out some critical column by a liberal commentator and pointing to a favorable line or phrase, probably included merely to bolster a pretense to objectivity. I wasn't jealous but did think that he might have found a line of my immortal prose worth repeating and treasuring.

I knew Nixon had determined to name Henry Cabot Lodge as his running mate in 1960, when he was pretending to leave the choice to a committee. I was opposed to Henry, although we had worked together as reporters in the 1932 conventions. At any rate, Lodge's selection didn't prove as helpful as Johnson's by JFK. Lodge intimated Nixon might pick a Negro for his Cabinet, which made him ahead of his time and party, but this hurt the ticket in the South where Negroes didn't have the votes or the mobilization in those days.

The defeat stung for years, although I am sure it was forgotten in the 1968 victory and the 1972 triumph. I know he was glad he determined not to contest the narrow Kennedy victory. Yet, the defeat made him somewhat bitter against JFK. I know that when Nixon went to Rome as a private citizen, he called upon Robert Cartwright, then consul general, to arrange an audience with Pope John XXIII. He asked that the audience be as long as that granted Kennedy on his presidential visit because, as Nixon put it, "If the truth be told I am a better Catholic than he is." It is, at least, a debatable statement.

He made a visit to Ireland as President, partly because Kennedy had scored a triumph there. Nixon visited the grave of a Quaker missionary of his mother's family, who didn't find many converts in Ireland, but did gain a peaceful grave. Nor did he capture the Irish as his rival did, but then Kennedy was of the blood and faith. My good friend and near neighbor Patrick Lynch insists he prevailed on Nixon's favorite niece in Michael Powers' pub in Quincy to induce him to make the visit and this could be so.

In 1961, when Nixon was considering making his bid for the governorship of California, he pretended to be making up his mind, when he had already determined to run. I knew he had made up his mind because he confided to an intimate who gave the story to me. We were together at Cave Man's Camp in Bohemian Grove with GOP Chairman Leonard Hall and GOP Finance Chairman Cliff Folger. Hall and Folger were persuading Nixon to run and tried to enlist my support. I was opposed to the step and told Nixon so, although I knew he had decided to run and wrote that he would do so.

Since then Nixon has needled me over my advice, saying that if he had listened to me, he would not have been licked and would have been forgotten, so that he would never have gained the presidency. I wonder if he feels the same way now.

At the same encampment, Nixon attempted to tease me in front of our camp mates as we were seated around a blazing log fire.

"I'm going to get a great laugh in 1964, when you'll have to vote for Rocky," he taunted, knowing I was no friend or admirer of the New York governor.

"I won't have the slightest trouble, Dick. I'll do what I did in 1960," I answered. "I'll vote against Kennedy."

"You mean you didn't vote for me in '60?"

"You heard me, Dick. I voted against Kennedy."

But he won my sympathy in the California defeat, so I was solidly behind him in 1968. Although he had a lucrative New York law practice, money couldn't satisfy Nixon. He had a monkey on his back, riding him toward redemption of purpose. He never lost sight of the White House in his hours of defeat; it was ever on his mind and not the least bit gently.

No doubt the defeat for the presidency in 1960 and the loss of the governorship of California in 1962 are but pinpricks today alongside the great shame and humiliation of resignation under a heavy cloud, regardless of any concern for the country. There would seem to be no road back, except to win the sympathy and understanding of more of his fellow citizens through the passage of healing time.

What a fall we have seen! What prolonged anguish! It can never end for him or his family. Those who destroyed him have done their worst. His most dedicated enemies may have reason to regret it. So may all politicians.

I had seen and heard from him more frequently than before. He asked my advice on the appointment of staffers like William C. Strand, Jr., when he decided to stump for Goldwater in 1964. This was a commendable exercise in party loyalty and not entirely unselfish. I was annoyed when he complained that Strand didn't get him the press he thought he was entitled to, and had to emphasize that he was not a candidate so he could not expect to draw as he had in 1960.

In 1967, Nixon came to the turning point in his political life. I was not only there but played a small role in it. Nixon had embarked on world-wide travel to establish himself as an expert on foreign affairs in his second quest for a presidential nomination. Things did not look bright for him in June 1967, when he came to Bohemian Grove for relaxation.

On his first day in camp Nixon cornered Dr. George S. Johnson, founder of the Department of Psychiatry at Stanford University, and myself at the breakfast table. He talked for an hour, outlining the political situation and considering the techniques by which he might hope to oppose and beat Rocky. I thought Nixon was wound tighter than the dollar watch of my boyhood days, and said so. Breakfast is one meal at which I don't like serious conversation or politics.

A day or two later Nixon left camp, presumably not to return that summer. Herbert Hoover, Jr., came to me and asked what I thought of extending an invitation to Nixon to make the final Saturday afternoon talk at the lakeside, which had long been his late father's role. I thought it over a bit and gave it my enthusiastic endorsement. I don't take credit for his appearance, but I didn't discourage it.

Nixon spoke from a few notes. He covered every problem in every corner of the world and outlined what he thought would be the best approach to each area. When he finished, men who had been lying on the grass, leaped to their feet and cheered. It is something to get a seated man to his feet, but to pull a man off his back and onto his feet is no mean oratorical feat.

I have listened to more speeches than most and am less impressed by oratory, even my own, than many of my fellow men, but I had to go up to Nixon, shake his hand and say:

"Dick, if you make that same speech up and down the land, you will be nominated and elected."

This was one of my better predictions and was heart warming to a man who had received more criticism than encouragement from me. He insisted I sit beside him at lunch, waving me to his left. A few days later he was to twit me in a letter, saying he enjoyed lunching with me even though I "insisted on sitting at his left."

Nixon later confided that the reception of that speech gave him the impetus he needed to make his pitch. He was grateful for my part in his appearance. He unwound and did make that speech around the hustings. By way of a parenthetical note, Nixon, in that same speech, paid an impromptu tribute to Herbert Hoover, which is the best of any I have heard. Against a background of towering redwoods, he said:

"I could describe Herbert Hoover as a great statesman. I could describe him as a great businessman. I could describe him as a great humanitarian. But, above all, he will be remembered as a man of great character.

"No leader in our history was more viciously vilified. Deserted by his friends, maligned by his enemies, he triumphed over adversity. In the twilight of his life, he stood tall above his detractors. His triumph was a triumph of character. We can be thankful that he was one of those rare men who lived to hear the overwhelmingly favorable verdict of history on his career.

"Two thousand years ago, when these great trees were saplings, the poet Sophocles wrote, 'One must wait until evening to see how splendid the day has been.'

"Herbert Hoover's life was eloquent of those words."

I wonder if the words give Nixon any comfort in his dark hours. As one who liked LBJ, loved Goldwater, respected Nixon, but revered Hoover, I can only say, I wish I had uttered or written that tribute.

Before the 1968 nomination campaign began, I had lunch with Nixon in a New York club off Wall Street. He asked but did not take my advice on a man to conduct his press relations, but did accept most of my advice on other matters. I could not help but note he didn't seem to know any of his fellow club members and they didn't seem interested in him.

Shortly before the Miami convention, on my return to Washington from the opening of the Vietnam peace talks in Paris, Nixon sounded me on my impressions and invited me to his New York apartment with Maxwell, my editor. We sprawled for a couple of hours in the sunlit library of his apartment. I have a camera eye and a retentive memory for books, so I saw he was doing his homework on foreign affairs and political problems.

"Who should I pick for Vice President?" he asked looking at me, perhaps remembering my rather violent opposition to his 1960 choice.

I deferred to Maxwell, stalling for time. Besides, I knew he had put the same question to Admiral Lewis L. Strauss, former head of the Atomic Energy Commission, who worked for hours on his answer as though it were the subject of a political thesis worthy of a doctorate.

Maxwell, who hadn't given the problem any thought and didn't know the field, sidestepped, so the question came back to me. I began by saying that I was much more interested in knowing whom he had ruled out. He ticked off Senators Charles H. Percy of Illinois, Mark O. Hatfield of Oregon, Edward W. Brooke of Massachusetts, and Governor Daniel J. Evans of Washington. That was all I wanted to know because I was in complete accord.

Then I launched into a man-by-man appraisal of the field, ending by declaring myself in favor of Governor Ronald R. Reagan of California, not only because the latter had demonstrated himself to be a most effective speaker in the Goldwater campaign, but also because Nixon was running without a state base, New York being in Rocky's pocket. Nixon agreed but insisted Reagan wouldn't accept the nomination. I argued he could be drafted. If he had Reagan would be President today.

Not once in our long survey of all the possibilities did either of us mention Agnew. However, at that time the Maryland governor was on the Rockefeller team and neither of us thought he could be blasted out of the New York camp. At the time of the selection I considered Agnew an admirable choice on Nixon's part, not so much for himself as for the fact that Agnew created a diversion, which demonstrated Nixon's mastery of politics. When Nixon named Agnew, the liberals had a new target, screaming, "Spiro who?"

I had thought they would seek to destroy Nixon by replays of his 1962 speech, in which he conceded defeat for the California governorship. In that early-morning talk, an exhausted and bitter Nixon lectured the press, and not without reason, because many had done their best, not always fairly, to beat him. The liberals got so busy with their "Spiro who?" campaign they indirectly built up Nixon.

Agnew had been a liberal darling but became a target. Had the scandal of receiving payments from contractors not broken when it did, he might be President today and the country could expect to be dragged through another trying experience in the explosion of that scandal. I accompanied Agnew to the banquet of the century at Persepolis, marking the twenty-five-hundredth anniversary of the founding of the Persian empire, and came to like him and his wife.

Every conservative has his favorite liberal, and Hubert Humphrey is mine. For many years Hubert had carried the liberal flag in the ideological parades of that clan. They were to forget this at Chicago, because he had supported LBJ on the war in Vietnam.

I think the former Vice President was treated shabbily by those he had best served. In that convention, the antics of a relatively few militants—always in sight of TV cameras—divided the party. The plight of the Democrats not only made it clear that Nixon would be elected in 1968, but made it clear the party would be ready for a take-over by the inept, so that he would be re-elected in 1972. The first to see this was Marshall McNeil of the Scripps-Howard newspapers.

I had a small role in advancing Senator Edmund S. Muskie for the Democratic vice-presidential nomination, again being asked to suggest a running mate. My selection served to demonstrate my political fallibility. Muskie came to believe in his own myth, even to feeling he would have won had he been nominated in 1968, although he was hardly known. He was off and running almost from the hour of Humphrey's defeat, although he didn't declare until early 1972. Had he been less sure of himself, he might have joined Humphrey in stopping George S. McGovern at Miami and held the party not against Nixon but from capture by terrified amateurs.

Throughout the preconvention campaigning and the convention itself, I was beset by a problem more amusing than serious. My editors, whose knowledge of politics was rudimentary and intuitive, convinced themselves that LBJ had taken himself out of the race that March as a superploy to win the nomination. Nothing I could say or do could shake this conviction up to the moment of Humphrey's nomination. One of the editors always had a solution before there was any problem.

I tried hard to explain that LBJ didn't have to surrender what was his for the asking. The situation got more ludicrous when I got a scoop on Muskie's nomination and was made to subordinate it against what an editor, who should have been the candidate of the Know-

Nothing party, fancied was an LBJ move to arrive on the scene and stampede the convention. After it was all over he begged me to write a story saying the *Tribune* had an exclusive on Muskie's selection, but my heart wasn't in it.

Still more amusing, although not without its pitiful aspect, was the moment this same editor came to me, waving an AP bulletin on the Soviet employment of planes, tanks and guns to quell the uprising in Prague, and exclaiming triumphantly:

"This means Johnson will be renominated and re-elected."

I said nothing, being aware that no argument of mine could pierce such obduracy. I merely began a column declaring that the latest Soviet aggression was all that was needed to insure Nixon's victory. I expected the column to be killed—on the ground that this editor was protecting me from myself. This had happened to me before and would happen again. One thing I must say for the new breed of reporters, they have intimidated their editors, so they seldom meet with such treatment. Not all editors are difficult or impossible. I had my share of great ones in Edward Scott Beck and Stewart D. Owen. And I can say a kind word for W. D. Maxwell for all his self-dramatization.

Nixon had his uneasy moments in the campaign. Long before others, he saw the third-party candidacy of George Wallace as a greater help to Humphrey than to himself. He confided to me that for every vote Wallace would take from Humphrey he would take two from Nixon. Nixon never became overconfident, but played his cards close to his chest—coldly, calculatingly and tirelessly. He was the strongest man physically to run for the presidency in my time and he needed all that strength.

After his election I wrote that Nixon had six new crises confronting him as President. In his book on crises he had listed the Hiss case, the fund his California supporters provided, Ike's heart attack, the assault on him by a Communist mob in Caracas, the kitchen debate with Khrushchev in Moscow when he was Vice President and the 1960 presidential campaign.

My list of six new crises were: peace in Vietnam, law and order, efficiency and economy in government, the increasing confrontation with communism, the monetary problems of the West, and the re-uniting of a divided America. Of Course, I missed the greatest crises of them all—the Watergate affair, but who, in 1969, could foresee that anyone would undertake the colossal stupidity of bugging the headquarters of the Democratic National Committee? Thank God, I retired on December 31, 1971, so that I have no personal knowledge of the bugging and haven't discussed it with anyone in authority, although many of the casualties, like Maurice Stans and Richard Kleindienst, are friends.

The Watergate break-in was known in June 1972, long before the election, yet it was not built into an issue against Nixon until after he had won. Could it be that the architects of the issue didn't want McGovern to win, as much as they wanted to destroy Nixon? There would seem to be something to his charge of "outrageous, vicious and distorted" coverage of the affair from the beginning, even though his skirts are hardly spotless.

He is not the first President to have lied to the people, nor the first to favor friends and punish enemies. Spying on one's political enemies is not new. He is not the first President to attempt to bury unfavorable news.

While there is no doubt that the break-in was reprehensible as well as stupid, the effort to place the blame directly on Nixon brought about a veritable orgy of smears, unsupported accusations, wild rumors and careless assumptions. If guilt by association was bad under Joe McCarthy, it was no less so under Watergate. Not only the Nixon administration, but the American Government suffered from the waves of hysteria. The investigations paralyzed the functioning of government and destroyed prestige abroad. Investigation of scandal is commendable and necessary. However, we can wonder whether it is wise to conduct trial by press and electronic media, rather than trial by judge or jury or Senate.

Still, there was one good thing about the investigation and that is that it could only happen in America. Anywhere else it would have been suppressed by concern over national interest or by dictatorial regimes.

There have been scandals before and will be again. All the scandals have not been confined to Washington, although a host of them have been buried by concentration on Watergate. Scandals have run in a broad spectrum across the country and across party lines. Men will steal and profit in politics although they may be fools to do so.

All politicians appear to have suffered as a result of Watergate. People seem to be disposed to vote against anyone holding office. This could result in good. I have often felt the men and women most competent to hold public office would never expose themselves to the slings and arrows of outrageous partisanship. It may be that the media will suffer because of the way the press pack bayed on the heels of the President. At any length both politicians and the media have been losing public confidence. This, too, could be for the better, if it brings soul-searching reforms.

But Nixon most certainly was not without accomplishment in the White House, although these were buried under the deluge or attributed to others. Nixon ended the war in Vietnam, as he promised, an action which seemed to anger some liberals more than the war itself, because it robbed them of an issue. No man who ends bloodshed can be entirely reprehensible.

He moved firmly and promptly to end the war in the Middle East which threatened to involve the United States and Soviet Russia in a nuclear holocaust. Perhaps he gave too much credit to his acquaintance with Leonid I. Brezhnev and perhaps his ordering of a worldwide alert of U.S. forces was a bit overdramatic, but the cause of peace was served. It may be that he didn't give enough credit to dollar-diplomacy promises to rebuild North Vietnam and financial aid to Israel and Egypt.

Nixon recognized Red China and broadened the detente with Russia. Time will have to judge the value of these steps.

He did put the first American on the moon. Of course, this move was begun and furthered under Kennedy and Johnson, but the long step for mankind was taken while Nixon was in the White House.

He attacked the problems of law and order. Advances have been claimed. Our campuses have been quiet, partly because draft-dodging agitators have left the relative security of our institutions of higher learning. He halted the draft, but whether this lull can be continued without disrupting essential defense remains to be seen. Crime continues to flourish. Many feel no real solution can come until the courts and forces of protection and prosecution come to realize that nice people have rights too, rights more sacred and inherent than the rights of criminals.

Nixon moved on monetary problems and inflation, but largely by exercising FDR's dictatorial grasp of power. Twice in fifteen months Nixon devalued the dollar so that it is now worth, in purchasing power, less than a fifth of what it was when FDR reduced its value to 59 cents in 1933.

Under FDR the nation embarked on an orgy of spending abroad. Between lend-lease and foreign aid, we can account for most of our national debt of some 450 billion dollars, a debt greater than that of all the other nations in the world combined. There has been a spending of some 440 billions on welfare schemes and the poor are still with us in even greater numbers. These things have helped to speed the inflation spiral.

Nixon improved conditions in America, although hamstrung by Watergate. However, improved trade balances and a rise in the gross national product were wiped out by galloping inflation and soaring oil prices. The market is down and inflation is increasing, despite his experimentation with controls.

Nixon had tried to interest Congress in promoting efficiency and economy in government, but Watergate prevented concentration on this effort. Nixon found, as all Presidents must, he could not cut spending and clean house as he promised in his first campaign. He discovered that most spending programs are wired into the budget and all recipients of federal bounty have their hands out for more. Also he found that bureaucrats are riveted to their jobs by civil service and have a remarkable instinct for their own preservation.

In the White House Nixon found, also as all Presidents must, that it is altogether different in the Oval Office than it looks from the outside. He reached the street where he wanted to live, but soon found that it is nowhere as easy to fulfill campaign promises as it is to make them. He soon learned that the White House is not only a splendid misery but it is also a fearsome responsibility that is forever dissolving into impossible dreams. It was beset for him, as for others, by temptations and trials, marked by difficult tests and cruel necessities, and burdened by unreasonable and conflicting demands for perfection. History will decide whether he failed to meet the tests himself or was hounded into failure.

Also he was haunted by the inadequacies and ambitions of those around him. He and members of his Cabinet found it impossible to battle that faceless mechanism—bureaucracy. Executive may order but bureaucracy disposes. Its members have a fine regard for their own jugulars and possess a remarkable instinct for wringing appropriations out of Congress. Fighting this apparatus is like punching a partially deflated balloon; it gives but it returns, so that the more you attack it the more it remains the same.

Those closest to Nixon swaddled him in layers of their protection, shielding him from any ideas but their own. This is a fate common to Presidents and only the greatest have been able to break this protective custody. Friends, especially in Congress, began complaining of neglect, not understanding the captivity of the White House. In the re-election campaign he was accused of subordinating party interest to his own re-election. No doubt those about him were so concerned and spent accordingly, but they spent him into destruction.

Nixon won and he won big in 1972. However, LBJ went in with a political landslide in 1964, which had him riding high in the saddle, but he left four years later with his tail between his legs. Nixon won by the greatest margin since Washington, but his departure was the most ignominious of all time.

Congress yapped at Nixon's heels for months, partly for political reasons but partly also to regain prestige and independence. Yet Congress is but a shadow of what it was some forty years ago, when they turned over power and the purse strings to FDR. Nothing serves to demonstrate the decline of Congress so much as the fact that so many are running for the presidency and the vice presidency.

In the past, Presidents seldom sprang from the Senate, and Harding served to demonstrate the upper chamber of Congress is not the best of backgrounds, but that lesson has been lost on the people. Four of the last five Presidents have been senators and Ford was a congressman and presided over the Senate as Vice President.

The greatest of the most recent accomplishments of Congress was a most doubtful one, in my opinion. They raised their own pay by 42 per cent from $30,000 to $42,500 and are aiming to go to $50,000 or more, but not in an election year. They also doubled the pay of the President and increased that of Cabinet members, judges and their own leadership. They stepped up their pensions and increased their perquisites, including postage and telephone allowances, the size of their staffs and staff wages.

It now costs more than $600,000 a year to support a member of

Congress in a style they could not maintain for themselves. All this was done in the name of attracting better men to public service, but what we get, for the most part, are the same old faces and the same old silly performances. Yet we do get occasional good young men like Representatives Edward J. Derwinski and Philip M. Crane, both of Illinois.

When Presidents come to the White House they profess to subordinate the good of the party for what they consider the welfare of the people. Some injure the party and the people in the process, as Nixon did. It is refreshing, therefore, to find a man like Truman, who believed that in making appointments to office, Democrats should be preferred if they were experienced and fit. Of course, those Presidents who appoint members of the opposition party, frequently have their eyes out for capture of enemy votes, which is only natural.

The presidency is the world's most powerful office. Its occupant is called upon to exercise a godlike quality of justice along with divine compassion for enemies within and without. Most unfortunately a President is limited to the same twenty-four hours that measure the daily life of the humblest citizen, so that he must rely on men who are picked by him and not the electorate. Also he is subject to the same passions as the humblest of citizens—anger, hate, greed and all the rest. Most strive to control their passions or to hide them, when they erupt.

After all, the most a President can expect these days is some seventy thousand hours in the White House, if he gets re-elected and serves eight years. In these hours he must eat, sleep, relax and participate in ceremonials as well as work. He has no more than ten thousand to fifteen thousand hours for thinking and acting with the judgment of history racing down the corridors of time to meet him.

Naturally, no President can satisfy everyone. The disappointed and ambitious are forever grumbling and predicting disaster. Nixon didn't always satisfy me and he certainly didn't satisfy Congress. How he rated with the people is impossible to determine with certainty, but it would seem he did not do too well, even though most people became weary of the concentration on Watergate.

I am sure that many politicians and office seekers were unjust to Nixon in their criticism of him. Many came to feel they had elected him and complained of neglect, when the most they could honestly claim was that they hadn't hurt his chances. I found him more than generous toward my well-intentioned but hardly earth-shaking efforts.

I had letters, phone calls, dinner invitations and bids to Sunday prayer services, which forced me to get up earlier to attend my own. I must confess that had one of the prayer invitations come some forty years earlier, when I was young and unmarried, the charming wife of the presiding Presbyterian might easily have converted me.

Also I was given the VIP treatment of being invited to the President's private office for a private meeting, which was photographed. All this had happened before, but is flattering nonetheless. When I went in I was warmly greeted and Nixon opened by saying:

"Walter, I've just announced something you're not going to like."

"What is it now?" I asked.

Nixon explained he had just named John Connally, the former Democratic governor of Texas, Secretary of the Treasury. I had to acknowledge I didn't like it, because I didn't believe in any President turning over the moneybags to a convert and because if there was one thing the Republican party was supposed to have something of a monopoly on, it was financial acumen.

We had a very frank exchange on many items of policy and programs. During the course of our talk, the President said:

"You know, I am a conservative."

When I smiled, Nixon asked me why, so I replied: "As far as I am concerned, Mr. President, you have just added another color to the rainbow; conservatism has to have a very wide spectrum, if it can take in both you and me."

When Secretary of State William P. Rogers made the same statement to me, about the same time, I laughed out loud.

While he was in private life in New York, Nixon offended some people by greeting them like long-lost friends, then suggesting they have lunch or dinner soon and never setting a date. Also he had a habit of writing to acquaintances after visiting their towns, saying he was sorry he had missed them but suggesting they have lunch on his next visit. He seldom did, which annoyed the sensitive, when they should have been pleased that he was thoughtful enough to write.

In the White House he tried to bring all to whom he owed any debt and a wide range of the nation's leadership to lunch and dinner. He entertained more than any President in my time.

I was no end pleased at the outset of an awards ceremony by the President's announcement that the only reason I wasn't getting a Freedom Medal was that I wasn't old enough. I applauded lustily, because I considered it then, as now, the finest thing he ever said about me. Later he promised to bestow the award during his second term. He must now wish that he could, not for me especially, but on anyone.

Nixon hailed DeWitt and Lila Wallace on the fiftieth anniversary of the *Reader's Digest* in a White House dinner. Wally brought down the White House at the magazine commemoration, by saying that his gratitude for the ceremony was exceeded only by the national debt. Nixon joined in the laughter, which was partly at his own expense.

Nixon is to be credited with returning the Supreme Court to its traditional channels, through his appointments, although he had his troubles with two men the Senate turned down. His judicial appointments, on the whole, have been better than his executive selections.

In an original and highly unusual State of the Union message, in his first term, Nixon boldly called for a "peaceful revolution," in order to return power to the people. This program was not welcomed in Congress, where Democrats decided the best thing to do was to forget his six-point program to promote prosperity, improve environment and advance health. The Watergate affair sidetracked the plan to oblivion.

Nixon recognized that the American people are dissatisfied and angry, frustrated and frightened. He owed his re-election to fear of McGovern's indecision and uncertainty, more than to his own charisma, the antics of spy slap-happy associates and a high tide of campaign money. One of the first to recognize the significance of Watergate and its destruction of Nixon was my old friend Marshall McNeil, who retired ahead of the storm as I did.

The American way of life has changed markedly in the past forty-one years, but there is grave doubt that the people want it returned to the simple virtues of honesty, thrift, industry and self-reliance, although some may say they do.

Long, long ago Andrew Oliver, the American colonial politician, who was hanged in effigy on his appointment as stamp officer and at whose grave in 1774 patriots jeered when his coffin was lowered into the ground, said:

"Politics is the most hazardous of all professions. There is not another in which a man can hope to do so much good to his fellow creatures. Neither is there any in which, by a mere loss of nerve, he may do widespread harm, nor is there another in which he may so easily lose his own soul, nor is there another in which positive and strict veracity is so difficult. But danger is the inseparable companion of honor. With all the temptations and degradations that beset it, politics is still the noblest career that any man can choose."

I am certain that Nixon would agree that Oliver said a mouthful, if I can use that precise if unacademic expression. Most Americans would say a profound "Amen!" to this definition.

But I wonder if all Americans are fully cognizant of their own roles in making government function. George Santayana, the Spanish-American poet and philosopher, defined the role of the American people, of whom he chose to be one:

"If a noble and civilized democracy is to subsist, the common citizen must be something of a saint and something of a hero. We see, therefore, how justly flattering and profound, and at the same time, how ominous, was Montesquieu's saying that the principle of democracy is virtue."

The need for virtue cries to heaven. There has been much corruption and much indifference to corruption, but there has also been something of a sadistic orgy on Watergate in the investigations, the courts and the news media. Neither the political investigators nor the press should have acted as prosecutor, judge and jury. If this is permitted to continue, and I say this as a member of the press dedicated to tearing down politicians but by due process of law, virtue will have been outraged in the very temple of our democracy.

The people—not the politicians or the press—must decide.

INSTANT HISTORY

Some of my best friends were and are newspapermen. I am a constant reader of newspapers. There was a time when I might have said in no other trade could one meet so many interesting people—almost all of them in the newspaper business. But then I climbed aboard the water wagon and found that my newspaper associates were not so brilliant, witty, informed or engaging as I had believed when I was carousing with them. Sobriety taught me that they are guilty of all the faults they see in others.

I once thought newspapers were exciting history, something like Thomas Carlyle's *French Revolution*, with its jazz band tempo. Today I see much to support Napoleon's definition of history as the lie agreed upon, and find the instant history of the press is, all too often, the fable agreed upon.

However, newspapers are not without their public service. Perhaps the greatest of these is to teach distrust of the published word, which they have done admirably. They have been helped, of course, by politicians, who assail the press and reporters, especially those who put security of office above statesmanship, in the way so many put promotion and pay above immortality.

In the fifteen-century morality play *Everyman*, the central character of that name is summoned by death. He calls on various acquaintances to accompany him, but Kindred, Goods, Beauty and Strength refuse him, claiming more pressing business elsewhere. The Good Deeds introduces him to his sister, Knowledge, who says:

> Everyman, I wyll go with the, and be thy gyde,
> In they moost nede to go by thy syde.

Today the press is offering to be the guide of everyman in times that try men's minds. Unhappily, everyman has become suspicious of the press and is bogged down in a credibility gap. Friedrich Nietzsche, the German philosopher, defined a nation as a group of men who speak one language and read the same newspapers. In America, more and more newspapers are speaking the same language with the result there are fewer newspapers and, on the whole, fewer readers.

The world is full of tangled texts and aching eyes. Our times have been thrown out of joint around the world by false logic, doubtful doctrine and sinister intent. It would be better if the people could put their confidence in an informed and objective press. But people have lost their faith in the media—newspapers, magazines, radio and television—as polls reveal.

The fact must be faced. I don't want to become waspish about the new breed, or of sighing over the good old days, merely because they are old. Nor do I wish to hail all changes as good merely because they are new. The fault lies, where it always has, in the newsmen themselves—from the very top to the lowliest cub reporter.

The new breed are better educated and equipped than they were in my early days. But they are not writing literature as so many seem to think they are. They are writing journalese. And they are by no means as important and infallible as they seem to think they are. Certainly they are not as responsible as they should be. Many are quite unsure of themselves and, therefore, are given to running and hunting in a pack. Too many identify themselves with a political party or a social cause.

For many years, newspapermen gloried in the term "Fourth Estate." There was a solemn pride in constituting an honor guard of liberty and freedom. Politicians were regarded by newspapermen as their natural enemies, because the primary interest of most party men was to share the wealth of rich and poor alike—although they pretended to be interested in promoting the common welfare. Even when the friendliest of relations were maintained, newsmen stood ever ready to tear down politicians from their high places for wrong-doing in office by due process of law. Sadly, the tearing down was often accompanied by the building up of the opposition, subjected to the same frailties and excesses of power. In the building up, newsmen often forgot their watchdog role and enlisted in the opposition. Many deserted the Fourth Estate to become members, or at least support-ers, of the First Estate, the rulers.

This was done partly out of sincere desire to make the world a better place. Often it was done out of ambition, the same sin by which the angels fell. Some newsmen sought the way of promotion and pay and popularity, even as politicians do. They should be watched most carefully.

Neither the old breed nor the new breed approach perfection. Thus, we have conflicting views of journalism. I present the poles from two men of lofty purpose and the same faith—Pope John XXIII and Hilaire Belloc, the gifted writer.

"The popular press, as we have it today, thrusts the 'Modern Mind' lower than it would otherwise have fallen, swells its imbecility and confirms it in its incapacity for civilization and therefore for the faith," said Belloc, a happy mixture of English, French and Irish blood.

I was in the audience when Pope John gave an audience to the newsmen accompanying President Eisenhower to India in 1959. The Holy Father began by saying he had always enjoyed excellent rela-tions with the press during his days in the Vatican's diplomatic serv-ice, because he was aware of the lofty mission that responsible news-men fulfill.

The Pontiff added that, since his election to the papacy, he had come to appreciate and understand the role of the press more and more, so much so that he was often "tempted to think that if the great St. Paul were alive today, he would probably have belonged to the profession of newspapermen, because that would give him the best means of spreading the doctrine of Christ."

Pope John urged the newsmen to dedicate themselves to "truth with natural goodness and good will . . . and you will render a great service to the cause of peace in the world and to the promotion of brotherhood between men." He closed by saying that when each of the newsmen before him "come to the end of your life and are about to face your God in judgment, that you will always be able to look back and say that in fulfilling your mission you always served the cause of truth."

I suppose my own views lie somewhere between the Pope's idealism and Belloc's cynicism, but they lean toward those of the Pontiff.

In my early days in Washington, I knew each member of the House and Senate press galleries as well as members of the foreign press. Shortly before I retired, I found I knew relatively few, but even worse than that, I found there were many I did not want to know.

Most of the latter make up the new breed that is more interested in interpretation of news, for which they are not always well equipped, than in gathering facts. They pretend to know the social significance of any assignment before they leave the office. Frequently they discard facts which might upset their preconceived conclusions. What annoys me is the pretense to knowledge and background by young men with little experience.

I do not condemn the new breed entirely. There are men and women of learning and competence among them, although they are not always encouraged. Nor would I replace them with the old breed exclusively. Rather, I have sympathy for all breeds because newspapering is the toughest of trades, when it is practiced on the national and international levels. Historians must differ if we are to dig the truth out of the past, and so must newspapermen if we are to get the truth about us. There is entirely too much agreement in the news when reporters run with the pack.

There has been a dangerous tendency to interpret the past in the light of the ideologies and prejudices of today. Not even God can change the past, but there are those who try, notably the Communists. It is far easier to change the present, a temptation ever before reporters.

It is easy enough to talk of the facts of history. But who can say for certain what the guiding or crucial fact or thought of all those surrounding a leader in a single day was on any decision. It is difficult when all concerned are dead, harder perhaps, when all the principals are living. Then, all should be consulted and judged, but there isn't the time, nor the inclination.

Music critics profess to see Beethoven's growing awareness of his deafness or Mozart's worry over debts, in this or that movement of their symphonies or other works of art. Yet, if God touches any among us, it is the musicians. Many have written melodies worthy of heaven, and Mozart has written arias God would not be ashamed to sing. The great music is not the shriek of racked souls but rather the flight of lofty souls. Such genius is rarely, if ever, spiteful, hysterical or morbid. The great musicians and the great heroes are immortal for what they have done. If they are difficult to understand, because we can know only fragments of their thoughts, how much more difficult it is to know the facts of current lives and current history for which there are no "instant replays." The tragedy of our day is that few try to get the facts; they prefer to suck them out of their thumbs or to contemplate in their ivory towers.

The work of reporting and commenting upon what goes on to-day is complicated because the newsman is part of the process he is observing, supposedly with detachment. This is easy enough when reporting a scene as Pliny the Younger did of the eruption of Vesuvius, since he could attest that as an eyewitness he was part of it all. However, this is but a minor feature of the work of newsmen today. They are engaged in commenting on what has happened or what will happen, so that naturally what is written is often a compound of myth, propaganda, guesswork, pretense and mumbo jumbo.

Propaganda is the easiest to spot. Our times have come to accept the selection and manipulation of facts, not only by dictatorships, but also by parties in and out of power in democracies. More difficult to spot is the myth. Much is written and said about progress demanding this or that course of action, when what professes to be promotion of democracy is no more than concentration of power or creation of more political jobs. Politicians are the same around the world, and we should never forget it. They make a very good living, wherever they are, out of promises. Khrushchev recognized this when he said: "Politicians are the same all over. They promise to build a bridge where there is no water." Nikita also recognized that the press is a major ideological weapon, so there is no wonder the press has become a major factor of life everywhere.

In all forms of political action there is a concentrated effort to make truth the stalking horse of error, of what is good for those in power or reaching for power. In Russia the autocracy of the czars is bad, but that of the Comintern is good. Stalin condemned the vestiges of Leninism as imperialistic; Khrushchev blasted the personality cult of Stalin, and Khrushchev was blamed for failure when out of power. So the game of playing with truth goes round and round and round.

Some newsmen concern themselves with the myth of origin. They are not so interested in the mighty oak as the acorn from which it grew. Others concern themselves with the hero-villain myth, which would say it was George Washington, not the Continental Army, that suffered at Valley Forge, or that it was Adolf Hitler and not the German people who fought in World War II. Under the myth theory, a President is a hero from whom all blessings flow or a devil whose every action and word are to be distrusted.

Guesswork is to be expected and is justifiable, to an extent, because the people have, from the beginning of time, wanted to know what will happen as often as they wanted to know what has happened. Pretense to knowledge, deliberate falsification and mumbo jumbo are more difficult to spot. After all, we are simple people and like to think that others are wiser, more trustworthy and better informed than we ourselves are, so we put our reliance quite often in sieves rather than stout vessels.

Few newsmen are deliberate fakers, although I have known those who were given to planting rumors in the National Press Club and waiting until they were repeated to them. Then they could write that something or other was rumored among capital newsmen.

Other newsmen are given to believing in the most dangerous myth of all—their own. There are few things more dreadful than pompous mediocrity, and nothing gives some newsmen so much confidence as their own ignorance. This is true in the highest levels of newspapering as well as the lower.

In my time I knew, intimately, a half dozen or more of the most important news commentators of our day. When I say important, I mean those whose words were eagerly read and studied. I do not necessarily credit them with making policy decisions, even though they may not have been without influence.

Arthur Krock of the New York *Times* was the best-read and most-quoted columnist of my time and his. He was a man more chastened by his power than intoxicated by it. While I often was inclined to think him too kind to those with whom he dined, he was a man of integrity and courage; he did not hesitate to speak out, even when it meant the loss of friendship of the great, including Presidents.

Walter Lippmann was described as the philosopher in residence in Washington, although he never pretended to or aspired to that role. He was not a reporter by training, being one of the advance guard of today's new breed of commentators. At Harvard, Lippmann was to the left of John Reed, the American who glorified the Communist revolution and who is buried beside the Kremlin wall. Lippmann became disillusioned with that form of tyranny, as Reed may have, had he lived. Lippmann was prone to error, like the rest of us, although loath to confess it. This failing was frequently noted by his targets, including Acheson, Dulles and Dean Rusk, who served Kennedy and Johnson ably and well. Acheson told me that it was a good thing the memory of the American reading public didn't last longer than three days, or Lippmann would have been out of business long ago. For six months Walter belabored the Dulles policy of massive retaliation. He then astounded his readers, including me, by beginning a column one morning with the declaration that now the policy of massive retaliation has proved a success . . . thus brushing off all he had said against it.

Ray Moley also began newspapering at the top. He had been a member of the Brain Trust and a favored Roosevelt speech writer. He had been named Assistant Secretary of State, but soon became disillusioned with FDR's frivolous approach to the most serious problems, particularly world monetary policy. He knew, worked with and assisted most of the leaders of our day at one time or another. His writings demanded attention from government leaders and in the educational community where he was a luminary.

David Lawrence wrote about national and international activities for sixty-two of his eighty-five years. Without question he was one of the most kindly and charitable of all the newsmen I have ever known; his writings were widely read and effective. Frank Kent of the Baltimore *Sun* was a gentleman as well as a scholar. His comments on politics were "must" reading in my early days in Washington, when the *Sun* was more closely followed in the capital than it has been since the airplane brings the New York *Times* to many front doors. John O'Donnell, a New Dealer who left Roosevelt when he saw him heading to war, was a columnist who educated his readers as well as offered them his point of view in the New York *News*. He sprinkled his writings with literary and historical allusions, so that if he did not convert he did give instruction.

John T. Flynn was the Daniel Defoe of my day. This reporter, editor, writer, and crusading liberal was an able pamphleteer and author of many books in which he made economics and government as exciting as fiction. I suppose liberals would not count him among their number today, but he abhorred war which they professed to do until intervention became the road to power and influence.

And in a class by himself was Westbrook Pegler, God's angry man or the most sparkling and bravest of them all, as you prefer. Certainly no columnist had more vitality and vigor, wit and epithets, delight and seriousness. If he angered some readers, he was still part of their diet because he remained a master of the written word. He had a marvelous ear for the American idiom and manner of speech.

Peg once autographed a collection of his columns to me with the inscription: "To my friend, Walter Trohan, from his friend (making one for each) Westbrook Pegler (author!)." "My hates have always occupied my mind much more actively and have given greater spiritual satisfaction than my friendships," he once said. "The wish to favor a friend is not as active as the instinct to annoy some person or institution that I detest." He could be most effective when he was outrageously humorous. And for all his bile he could be the sweetest and gentlest of men to his first wife, Julie, and his widow, Maud Towart Pegler, who had been his secretary and good right hand.

George Sokolsky, of King Features, was one of the ablest and clearest thinkers in the conservative camp. He, too, started on the far left. His place has been filled, ably and well, by William Buckley, who writes and talks like Belloc. There are few men in my craft whom I envy, but I do Bill—he has a mind as sharp as Belloc's, as witty as Rabelais'. He has a joy of living as great as Mark Twain's. Even those who dislike his philosophy must admire his style and envy his gifts.

I must also say a kind word for John Chamberlain, Holmes Alexander, David Sentner and Clark R. Mollenhoff. Nor can I forget George Morgenstern and M. Staunton Evans, editorial writers, for the *Tribune* and the Indianapolis *News* respectively.

The conservatives had no corner on ability, although I knew them best and preferred their company. Others would call themselves middle of the roaders, but often listed to the left side of the street. I think of Joseph Alsop and his brother, Stewart, and William White, who did not hesitate to break step with liberals on Vietnam or other cherished issues.

Finally there are able and respected writers among those who would fight to the death to say they are objective, but seldom if ever crossed the middle of the road, like James (Scotty) Reston, the mainstay of the eastern liberal establishment; Marquis Childs, no less of a pillar in the Midwest, and David Broder, a far younger man in Washington, but scarcely less bright. The liberal roll of columnists is a long one these days. I leave it to them to take care of their own.

Among columnists and reporters, there are those who are molders of journalistic fashions and there are those who follow the styles. In the great army of the Washington press—more than fifteen hundred newsmen and newswomen—there are those who are servants and not masters in the house of the printed word. If the corps has one great fault, as a whole, it is that few dare to break away from the pack as Mowgli did by waving the red flow of flame in Rudyard Kipling's *Jungle Book*. But Mowgli was a man cub and reporters are, all too often, wolf cubs and fear to leave the pack.

To me, it has always been distressing to find young reporters so unsure of themselves that they run around the White House press room, asking: "What do you think the lead is?" whenever a presidential statement or speech is handed out. If the reporter doesn't know what the lead is, he should be put to writing obituaries, because the one central fact—the end of life—is always before him.

It is even more distressing to come upon reporters interviewing one another on what is and what is not significant. Too often these interviewees are the "informed sources" one hears so much about in so many news stories. Too often the interpreters are given to interpreting one another, so that quite often many inside stories are nothing more or less than what is going on inside journalistic minds. Some reporters think that readers are interested in the thoughts and thinking of their fellows and are given to quoting them, probably hoping to be quoted themselves.

Reporters are given to repeating one another. I must confess I have been guilty of this at times, but not often. Under the pressure of deadlines, there sometimes seems to be no other way of filling that yawning gap on the typesetter's stone in time to make the paper.

In the rush to interpret the news instead of finding it, the result has all too often been mixed-up history and mixed-up writing. The right to know has become the right to preach. Many newsmen have come to feel that no policy or program is of any importance until they lean their minds for or against it.

Newspapermen have become as bad as editors in striking attitudes about censorship and freedom of the press, when what they want is a license to do as they please. There is really only one great danger to freedom of the press, as I see it, and that is the censorship newsmen are imposing on themselves. They are not only intolerant but hostile to opposing opinion. This attitude is more dangerous than anything they may fancy that the White House, the military or the government as a whole is seeking to impose.

Newsmen have already won virtual immunity libel, as far as targets in public life are concerned, by a legislative decision of our courts. Now some newsmen seem to want legislation which would permit them to steal information, probably through agents, and protect them from responsibility on the ground that they must protect their sources. No doubt most newsmen would continue to exercise responsibility, no matter what laws are passed but the door would be flung open to the irresponsible to abuse the privileges they seek to establish. Some reporters are demanding protection of their notebooks as sacred to their trade. As one who never used a notebook in his life, I may be pardoned a smile.

When I was writing pieces critical of FDR, HST and JFK, I was accused by many of my colleagues, as well as administration spokesmen, of slanting the news. Now my colleagues are doing it; they call it interpretation. This wouldn't be so bad, except that the interpretation is generally slanted the same way for and the same way against by most of the interpreters. It has long been recognized that almost all Washington reporters are Democrats or independent against Republicans. Few would join me in saying "a plague on both your houses." This doesn't mean that there aren't many good reporters in Washington or that the new breed is without its virtues.

The party alignment of reporters is to be as expected as their liberal alignment. For a long time Democrats represented themselves as the party of the intellectuals, partly because of their now all-but-for-gotten founding father, Thomas Jefferson, as against the party of money, the Republican party. The truth is that men of money do well in both parties and men of money profit under both parties. The Democrats did attract intellectuals and reporters, on the strength of Jefferson's philosophy that the least government was the best government. The fact that Democrats were long out of power helped them to win such recruits because they became the party of protest. The intellectuals fancied themselves as working for "a new era," a political bromide, as old as any, but one that is still employed at the highest levels and not without magic effect.

Philosophers as far back as Plato and Aristotle dreamed of the perfect state, one run by their own kind, of course. There were political writers before the Greeks but none so detailed. Plato would have the state run by philosophers. He was critical of the exercise of power by all citizens and called for an ordered and structured society. It must be remembered that the glory that was Greece and the grandeur that was Rome were established on a foundation of slavery, even as Russia is today. Plato would have imposed rigid controls, established a caste system of society, imposed censorship on literature and art, but most of all he would have restricted government to an elite. All this from one whom liberals profess to venerate but seldom read.

Aristotle is recognized as the founder of political science, if anyone can call the game of power for profit a science. He made a cool analysis of the then existing political forms, which haven't really changed too much. He argued for the supremacy of the law, as the way to stability without passion. Aristotle considered numerical and proportional representation. He would have limited wealth, but he was no socialist. All in all, he viewed politics as an avenue to happy life but inclined himself toward an elite of governors. Incidentally, he placed good politicians at the top level in the afterlife, a spot we may assume is not overpopulated.

It is understandable then that some newspapermen should look upon themselves as philosophers, destined to bring political order out of chaos. The specialists in law haven't done too well. The professors, as eager for political plums as any, haven't demonstrated the genius they claimed. So some newsmen would rush into the breach, confident they can do no worse, and not without reason. Many newsmen lay claim to power without responsibility. If one must pretend to know all the answers, it is best not to be responsible to an electorate. And a good many readers are captives because there are so few papers.

Another besetting sin about newsmen is incest. If the public doesn't, reporters do read one another and talk to one another. It is difficult to cover all bases, so there is considerable trading of information, but more trading of ideas, which can be dangerous. There are caste divisions among newsmen, although they are all for leveling class distinctions and are for one man, one vote. There are some newsmen of social backgrounds, who nod to those down the scale with a great show of democracy, but prefer to spend their time among their own kind. "I don't understand why he did it," I overheard one reporter say of another to a third of the same social level. "After all, he's one of our kind, coming from the same background and going to the same school."

Many entertain well to cultivate news sources. Some join clubs for the same purpose. The game of news is a struggle and it is a neverending fight to gain sources in high places and to be able to phone the White House and other top offices.

Perhaps the operation of incest in the press is best evidenced by the way some stories are played to the point of boredom, like Watergate, the war in Vietnam, the Pentagon papers, McCarthy and various scandals in various administrations. It can't be said that any one newsman or any clique always calls the turn, but it is amply evident that some set the fashions, which are no less arresting than hot pants but generally more ephemeral.

Newshounds on the trail ought to be music to the ears of taxpayers, but they are all too often not. The baying seldom induces economy, promotes efficiency or brings down prices. In fact, it doesn't always sell papers as a startling crime once did. The new breed doesn't seem to be as interested in selling papers as in peddling a point of view.

The decline in newspaper influence has been accompanied by a decline in the number of papers. There is a tendency toward monopoly across the land. On the whole, this is not good for the readers, nor is friendship among owners. What is best for readers is to be able to purchase two papers of diametrically opposed views and study what both sides have to say before making up their minds. Today, papers are more alike than not. And they are more expensive than they were. Also, it is good for readers to have editors telling the truth about one another instead of socializing together.

Many editors are downgrading their own editorial pages by taking on columnists whose views are diametrically opposed to their own. Not all of this is undertaken in the interests of informing readers and encouraging them to make up their own minds. During the Depression many publishers found they could buy eight columns of opinion for about $40 a week, but if they hired a reporter they would have to pay him about that amount and he might not fill more than a column a day. Columns are still often cheaper than hiring digging reporters, even though editors may be fouling their own editorial nests.

Another practice, which took a great step forward, if that be the right direction, in the Depression was the general use of the by-line. In the past the by-line was reserved for long-established and proven veterans and was occasionally awarded to lesser men for a particularly fine effort, something like a decoration for valor. In the Depression years the by-line was widely distributed in lieu of money. It was not surprising that many came to look on the by-line as making them great writers and deep thinkers, something like Shakespeare or Plato.

Editors and publishers may be more to blame for the trend toward intrepreting and analysis than members of the new breed themselves. Few papers have news staffs in the capital. Most prefer to leave hard news to the wires and have their own men interpret, analyze or write sidelights on the news. Press-service men cannot be blamed if they interpret a bit in their news stories. Some editors and publishers blame loss of advertising and the slow growth or even decline of circulation on the electronic media. Perhaps this is so; I do not know. I do know that radio and TV made reporting harder for the newsmen. Reporters find their sources preferring to spill their secrets or make their observations over the airwaves.

"I'd rather have one minute on a TV show than hit the front page of any newspaper, even in my home town," one senator told me.

Newsmen are not above courting the media themselves, as the halls of the National Press Building demonstrate on presidential press conference days. By some mysterious alchemy, reporters sprout pastel-blue shirts on those days, having been told they photograph better than white on TV cameras. Many vie for recognition at such conferences, so that their editors can see them rise and intone a question, and possibly hear the President call them by name. Vanity also makes the news go round. And, after a young man has been interpreting for some years and grows weary of it, where can he go except to TV with its fabulous salaries and national recognition and identification?

News is a highly perishable commodity at best. Its gathering is complicated by the fact that what is grist to one editor is chaff to another, even on the same paper. The competition in the capital is keen. It takes considerable ingenuity and great application to race ahead of the pack. I must repeat that it was simpler in my early days than it is for the new breed. However, they face the same problem that I did— that the editor's wastebasket is a greater threat to freedom of the press than censorship. Editors talk of the right to know, but many cherish it only because they can decide what the people should know.

The press, as a whole, is quick to criticize, but even quicker to resent. I often wonder why it is that editors and reporters, who are so good at dishing it out, are so sensitive when it comes to taking it. I suppose it is only human nature.

On November 13, 1969, Vice President Agnew spoke on the liberal bias of the news media. It was a speech heard around the nation and around the world. Although his image has become tarnished, his truths have not. He said the right thing at the right time and with the right accent. As a result the media improved, although it is not yet perfect. Sometimes it seems that the right to know is confused with the right to misinform. All the distortion and confusion aren't as deliberate as some on the far right may suspect. Much of it grows out of fascination with one's own words or one's own thinking, rather than malice.

It was not unusual for me to be out of tune with both sides on most issues. Although I wrote many stories idolators would not touch, I tried to write the news straight down the middle. Often liberals came to me, after reading my stories at Chicago conventions or elsewhere where the *Tribune* was available, to say, with not a little surprise, that my story could run in their papers without change. Some even said so in Washington, at least on stories that did not hit their heroes.

I was never attracted to the liberals because they were too intolerant for my blood, going into paroxysm of rage over any point of view but their own and forever putting God on their side even when they didn't believe in Him.

Still, they never gave me as much trouble as their right-wing counterparts. I was nearly written off by the anti-Communists, because I refused to see a conspiracy under every leaf in the Red rose garden. Also I resented the profiteers on the right, those venal souls who saw largess flowing into the coffers of the professional rabble rousers and wanted their share of it. I suspect the left-wingers have the same kind of operators, but I am not familiar with them.

I have felt hopeless and helpless, but I never doubted. Nor do I despair. Most people I know recognize the sincerity of my views. I do not admire those who differ, like the Communists, but I would not silence them as some of them would silence me.

I had my own troubles with the Nazis as well as the Reds, being denounced by name in the Moscow press. The Nazis tried to adopt me as one of their own, because I was against America's entry into the war. Early in 1940, I was feted at a luncheon in Horcher's restaurant in Berlin. Guests included Hans Diekchoff, the former German ambassador to Washington, who was no Nazi, and a former professor at the University of Virginia, who was. It was quite a luncheon. My hosts assured me that all the items were on the nonration food list but, as I suspected, the average German had not seen any of them for months and months. The atmosphere became a bit cloying and I had to resort to rudeness in order to divorce myself from ideological goose stepping.

Two waiters came to our private dining room, bearing between them a roast turkey on a silver tray. Unfortunately, for them, they lost their balance and sent the creature bouncing under the table. I left the seat of honor to direct the search, to the discomfort of my hosts. Otto Horcher, the proprietor, who was never a Hitlerite was laughing in the corridor. He was to suffer because top Nazis came to his establishment and he could hardly keep them out.

When the bird was recovered, one of my hosts waved it away and commanded them to bring in the second turkey. In a few minutes the two waiters were back with the tray and a turkey, which the Nazis insisted was better than the first and I said they looked remarkably alike even to a bruise on the breast, which the first bird had sustained in its fall. This put a damper on the feast, but I was to do even worse.

I left a book at the table, deliberately, and when I returned for it, I found the rest of the party saluting one another and heiling Hitler, so I said:

"Sorry to break up the lodge meeting, gentlemen, but I've left a book."

It was a copy of Thucydide's *History of the Peloponnesian War*, about an earlier unfortunate venture into militarism.

When I got to London, I told the story of the turkey. It offered a sorely needed humorous note on the master race in an uneasy period of the phony war, so that it was given a half-page play in Lord Beaverbrook's *Daily Express*. It was through this story that I first met Winston Churchill, being introduced by Beaverbrook, in the men's room of the Savoy Hotel. I was to meet Churchill many times after that, but none so dramatic as the last time I ever saw him. I came upon him brooding alone on the platform of a private car in Washington's Union Station, which was taking him to Hobcaw Barony, Barney Baruch's Carolina estate. It was after his defeat by Clement Attlee. Not one reporter or embassy official was there. I am not sure that he recognized me as I identified myself and wished him well. I could not help but be reminded that honor is generally reserved for the powerful. Nonetheless, I was not a great admirer of Churchill, although I could respect his dedication to his country. I met King George VI and Queen Elizabeth II but only to exchange courtesies. I saw and talked with the Duke of Windsor several times and found him well versed in history and politics. I always suspected he was dropped because he was strongly against British involvement in war, as much as for his marriage.

I met many chiefs of state—kings, presidents and dictators—around the world, most of them merely while paying respects. I interviewed others, but can't claim I know them at all intimately or well. I have already mentioned Syngman Rhee, who was as close to a saint in office as I ever knew. I met Charles de Gaulle before he gained power and found him a patriot with a sharp mind. I was impressed by King Peter of Yugoslavia and King Hussein of Jordan, but probably because I found them far better informed than I had expected.

I found Konrad Adenauer remarkable and one of the few truly great men I have known. I met Jawaharlal Nehru, who was a friend of Colonel McCormick's, but never recognized his stature until I saw him in India operating among his own people. I told him I recognized he hated the white race, because of his dislike of the British. He acknowledged that this might be so. I charged him not to include Americans.

I was most impressed by Generalissimo Francisco Franco of Spain and by Antonio de Oliveira Salazar of Portugal. Franco gave me an interview which made front pages all over Spain as well as in the *Tribune*, because he confided he had picked his successor and intimated that his choice had fallen on Prince Juan Carlos. No one could have been more kindly or more courteous, nor further from the popular American conception of a dictator—a strutting, swaggering egocentric. Franco spoke slowly and distinctly, recognizing that I had some understanding of Spanish.

At one point I remarked that he surprised me because he was picking young men for his Cabinet, where other dictators seldom trusted men not of their own generation. He said quite simply that he liked young people. I said I liked young girls. His face clouded, as I knew it would, because his morals are particularly correct. Then, while he still frowned, I added, again in Spanish, "Four years old." Recognizing he had been trapped, he joined in laughter at himself. We shook hands at his desk, piled high with papers, at the door of his office, in the reception room and out in the hall, where he accompanied me for a final farewell and had the colorful mounted Spahis give me a salute. Later I was decorated with the rank of commander in the Order of Isabel the Catholic, but would not accept the decoration until a year and a half after my retirement.

My experience with Salazar, another powerful dictator, was no less pleasant. He set the interview for his office in the House of Parliament, apologizing because his residence was being repainted. I went to the building alone, explaining in my self-taught Spanish rather than in Portuguese that I had an appointment with the Premier. I was put on an elevator alone and got off at the top floor. There was no one to receive me. I entered an office and was directed to another at the end of the corridor. There I found an empty reception room. I sat down, wondering if I were in the right place. After a time a man entered, all out of breath, apologizing for being tardy and explaining he was my interpreter. I expressed myself surprised by the absence of any protection and any exercise of precaution.

"But who would want to kill the Premier?" he asked in astonishment.

A few minutes later, the door of the adjoining room was opened and there stood Salazar. I could have walked in upon him at any time I was alone. A few days later I had an interview with Johnson in the White House and could not help but mark the contrast. I went through various guards and checks and hands until we sat down in his private hideaway office, sipping Tab.

I must reveal that Johnson jolted me during our talk, which ranged over a wide variety of subjects, including my interviews with Franco and Salazar. Somehow the name of Styles Bridges, the late senator from New Hampshire came into our conversation.

"President Truman told me, in this room, to play fair with Bridges, when he was chairman of the Senate Appropriations Committee, and he would play fair with me," Johnson recalled. "Then he warned me: 'If you don't, the first thing you know he'll have you by the pecker and will be twisting it.'"

Johnson laughed and added musingly: "You know, I have always thought that it was strange language for the President of the United States to use in the White House."

"You won't mind, I'm sure," I put in, "if I am no less surprised that you, the President of the United States, should repeat it in the White House."

Bridges was an able and level-headed member of Congress, but he was thoroughly convinced the Roosevelt administration was trying to poison him. He twice told me after visits to Bethesda Naval Hospital that doctors had told him he was being systematically poisoned. I dismissed this as pardonable distortion of the importance of his opposition role.

Once I heard Senator William E. Jenner of Indiana make an attack on General Marshall on the floor of the Senate. At one point he stopped suddenly and raised his head to gaze at the ceiling. I sought him out in the cloakroom because I could see no reason for such emphasis. "I felt a twitch around my heart," Jenner, who was a bit of a hypochondriac, explained, "so I called on the good Lord not to take me, praying: 'Don't take me now, Lord, there won't be a corporal's guard of friends to carry me off the floor.'"

One of the greatest speeches I ever heard in that body was delivered by Senator Henry Fountain (What a prescient woman his mother must have been to give him such a gushing middle name!) Ashurst of Arizona on his defeat for his party's renomination in 1940 by Ernest W. McFarland. The next morning Ashurst put on striped trousers and a cutaway coat with a red carnation. He secured the floor on a point of personal privilege. The sixty-five-year-old solon began by thanking the people of Arizona for entrusting him with various political offices since 1897, including twenty-eight years in the Senate. He went on to discuss his political philosophy which made a glowing virtue of expediency. Then he closed by congratulating the people of his state on their wisdom in picking so able a man for his successor. Had the election been held the next day, Ashurst would have been renominated.

In the middle 1950s, the press gallery and then the public came to realize that colorful characters had virtually disappeared from the Senate, so they took to building up Everett McKinley Dirksen of Illinois, who had succeeded Taft as Republican leader. Dirksen had a style of oratory all his own, being a blend of the honey of the South, the folksiness of the Middle West, the erudition of the East and the camaraderie of the West, along with a generous sprinkling of spread-eagle oratory and humor. Once Dirksen turned on a colleague with the challenge: "Sir, you are interrupting the man I most like to hear."

One of the most unusual and devoted tipsters I had was Frank Murphy, former governor of Michigan and former Attorney General, who was named to the High Court in 1940. Murphy was a born feudist, possibly because FDR had taken him to the mountain top, shown him the White House below and then jerked it away from him. Anyway, Murphy regarded every case before the Supreme Court as a battleground. He was angered by any disagreement on the part of any of his colleagues, so he took to calling me and reporting on the Court's Saturday-afternoon conferences. Knowing my phones were tapped, he always made himself known by saying: "This is the underground."

Many and many a Sunday I would have an account of some dispute among the justices. These stories were among the topics of many a capital cocktail party. At one of these, I was talking to Homer Cummings, then retired as Attorney General, when Robert H. Jackson, another former head of the Justice Department joined us.

"You know Walter Trohan," Cummings began.

"Oh yes," said Jackson, with whom Murphy often differed. "And I am grateful that Walter was off of me and on to Frankfurter this morning." Jackson played a role in the war crimes trials at Nuremberg, where he picked up the free and easy morals of the military. When he died in the apartment of a female secretary in Washington, it was said he had come to the capital from his Virginia home to shop at a Sears Roebuck store, although there was one closer to his home. The explanation went on to say that when he felt himself stricken, he thought of his secretary's apartment and sped there for shelter and care.

When I first came to Washington, the justices of the Supreme Court were far above political scenes, dwelling on an Olympus of their own. The first justice I met socially, over drinks, was Owen J. Roberts, but not for some three or four years after I came to Washington. We became involved in an argument over some of his votes.

Later I came to be on a first-name basis with most of the members of the Court, although I must say I never really liked it. I think the justices should be above familiarity.

Once when Fred Vinson was Chief Justice, it fell to my lot to introduce him at the annual barbecue of Bill Dolph, radio man, and Walter Thomas, patent attorney, near Warrenton, Virginia. I began in the deepest tones I could muster in order to command the attention of guests scattered about the lawn: "Gentlemen, the Chief Justice of the United States." Nothing happened. I tried again and still nothing happened. A third try was no more successful. Finally, knowing that he had been alerted, I shouted:

"Fred, where in hell are you?"

"Right here, Walter," he replied, "and I'm coming."

Roberts became a *Tribune* target when he undertook to head the inquiry into Pearl Harbor, which was designed, in large part, to clear Washington officials of any complicity in the attack. So, in 1951, I consented to go on the "American Forum of the Air," although I generally shunned TV appearances, to debate Atlantic Union with Roberts and Senator Kefauver. Roberts backed out at the last moment—I like to think it was on my account—and was replaced by Clarence Streit, a pleasant gentleman who has long made a living out of proposing union. I was associated with Clyde Lewis, a former commander in chief of the Veterans of Foreign Wars, who had succeeded in getting a number of state legislatures to rescind resolutions they had passed favoring such union.

I lost interest in the debate when Roberts failed to appear, although I had armed myself against him. However, my heat was rekindled when Kefauver opened the debate and didn't abide by the rules, which called for a one-minute statement. He droned on for three. So when it came my turn, and Theodore Granik, the moderator, asked me what I thought of Atlantic Union, I said:

"Not much. I want to call attention to the first man to propose Atlantic Union. On October 7, 1780, eighteen months after George Washington took office, this man wrote from London: 'I am now led to devote the rest of my life to reunion of the British Empire as the best and only means to dry up the streams of human misery that have deluged the world.'"

Kefauver and Streit smiled and nodded in agreement. Then I wiped the smiles off their faces with:

"The man who wrote that was Benedict Arnold. It was the Benedict Arnold plan then and it is the Benedict Arnold plan now."

Beads of sweat gathered on Kefauver's head. He and Streit were taken aback and never regained their balance. Lewis hopped them up nicely.

After the debate, Kefauver approached me, saying: "I can't understand it; you were so nice and pleasant at lunch, and then you hit me so hard and so savagely."

"I'm sorry . . ." I began.

"Oh, not at all, you were perfectly within your rights."

"Hear me out, Estes," I admonished. "I am sorry because I contributed to your education and I regret it, because this lesson will serve you at some future date when you are taking on someone on my side, which was your old side, as you well know."

My reference was to the fact that Kefauver had been on the right in law school but joined the left when he came to realize there were more workers than bosses.

Blair Moody, a newspaper colleague as a reporter for the Detroit *News*, came to me with a related suggestion at the end of the war. He confided that he had discovered there were more people working in auto plants in his area than on the executive level, so he slanted his stories toward the workers, suggesting, out of his affection for me, he said, that I might do the same for profit.

"I am glad it isn't principle, Blair," said I.

"Oh, not at all," he confessed gaily. "But it works wonders."

It certainly worked wonders for him, because he was appointed to the Senate by Governor G. Mennen (Soapy) Williams, who traveled, I could not help but feel, the same road of expediency.

Few reporters have been closer to the FBI or its chief, J. Edgar Hoover, than I was. Two of his top aides, Louis B. Nichols and Cartha I. DeLoach, remain among my closest friends. All three helped me on occasions when I suspected I was being fed a story by a Communist or a Communist sympathizer. I never had an FBI file in my hands, but information from the files was supplied me, not to pillory anyone but to resolve my doubts.

Many mortally feared and dreaded the FBI, even though Hoover was ever vigilant against letting his organization be built into a gestapo or NKVD. There was much talk of the FBI hounding critics, but this is to be suspected and I can say it as one who wrote one of the strongest anti-Hoover pieces ever printed.

In my early days in Washington one of my managing editors, Robert M. Lee, ordered me to write a piece on Hoover, labeling him as a "drugstore cowboy," after the slang of that day, because he had never made an arrest or engaged in the roundup of any gangsters. I went around to the Secret Service, the Treasury's internal revenue unit, the narcotics division and postal inspection service. All of these units were less than impressed by Hoover. They fed me a lot of odds and ends, mostly trivia, which I fashioned into several thousand words of criticism.

Courtney Riley Cooper, a magazine writer close to the FBI, sent a telegram to the *Tribune* denouncing me as a reporter in the pay of Al Capone. The telegram didn't get anywhere because it went to Lee who best knew why the piece had been written.

The piece did help push Hoover to active duty. He did join in the capture of gangsters. Also it helped to make us friends. I knew him intimately and admired his dedication and devotion to America. Of course, I criticized him when he undertook duties and performed actions I did not like, but these didn't strain our friendship, at least for long.

Masses of information come into the FBI on millions of citizens. I know there is a considerable file on me, although I have not seen it. Some angry persons went so far as to accuse me of being a Communist. This didn't bother me because I knew such raw materials wouldn't be used against me, but would be checked. Much of the complaint against the FBI has come from those who have something to hide or have friends who have something to hide, usually Communist affiliations or associations. The FBI has never used these except as a caution when such a person might be considered for a high appointment. The FBI file serves to warn that a man who has once made a mistake may do so again in power, although often the FBI notes that the man has lived down his early mistake over the years.

I know the FBI has a file on a popular national figure who punctured his eardrum to escape the draft in World War II. I know that Kennedy dropped the man when this fact was brought to his attention. But the man came back to associate with high figures in the Nixon administration, although I know the contents of the file were made known. Also I know the FBI laid the photograph of a White House clerk on the desks of two White House secretaries. The photo was a nude. Nothing was done by the first secretary in the Kennedy administration. He could not be certain whether the girl was the playmate of the President or of a colleague. The secretary in the Johnson administration fired the clerk, who subsequently joined the staff of Senator Bobby Kennedy.

My story has been told, although much remains unsaid. It is time to close. Still it has been suggested that I offer advice to the new breed. It is difficult, not because the task is hard, but because it is so simple that I cannot expect it to be taken seriously. It is nothing more or less than a strict dedication to the old virtues of truth, honesty, integrity and justice.

There should be less striving for master's degrees and more searching for practical experience at all levels. Every reporter should have some experience at covering police and police courts, not only to learn the problems of the poor, but in order to become acquainted with the problems of law enforcement.

Every reporter should cover civil and criminal courts in order to understand the processes of law and the operations of all engaged in it—prosecutors, defense counsels, judges and juries. It might well discourage the tendency to act as prosecutor, judge and jury in their stories. Reporters should study the operation of government at town, city and state levels. They should understand the operation of the political mind at all levels. It might well teach them not to attempt to replace it in the news.

I think it is wrong for a reporter to undertake interpreting and analyzing in his twenties. This is bad for him because after ten years of such "experting," he comes to realize there is nothing in the future but more of the same, so that he is tempted to leave for more lucrative fields. Also it is bad for readers because youngsters are not qualified for such roles.

Few are born geniuses and even these must be trained. Every reporter can grow slowly and confidently into a mighty oak, not presume to become one overnight. He should learn to understand suffering, conflicts, temptations—the whole gamut of sins—but must measure them by virtues.

A reporter must learn there is good and bad in every man and good and bad in everything man makes or attempts. He should be loath to attach himself to a man or cause and thus surrender his greatest asset—objectivity. The greatest danger the country faces today is that all the news media is leaning, thinking and writing one way. Until we see both sides of any issue we cannot understand it, but also we cannot be free. Everything has been tried before in politics and found wanting. There is no reason to believe that this shall not come to pass again with this day's most promising adventures. A good reporter must ever bear in mind the opposite side. I know I have stressed my opposition to men in power throughout my career, but largely because others would not do it.

Those in the electronic media have an awesome and even frightening responsibility. Unlike most reporters, who work for a single paper or even for a service, or some columnists, who appear in hundreds of papers, some newscasters are familiar in homes across the nation five nights a week. They should strive all the harder for objectivity, but all too often they are merely readers or actors of a sort and leave the writing to others, who are not identified.

Reporters should love their fellow men. No man is an island, as John Donne said, but I would go further and say every man is as interesting as a continent if only we explore him. Over a half century,

I found men I didn't like but none to hate. Nor am I obsessed with bitter wisdom.

I might have continued writing until my seventieth birthday for the *Tribune*, and beyond July 4, 1972, if some newspaper friends had their way, but not my editors. However, almost a half century of reporting had to end and, to me, it was best to end it voluntarily. After all, I had stayed three and one-half years beyond the prescribed three score and five, but not by my own wish entirely. So I was ready and even eager to go.

I did not become a columnist, and then not without complaint, until I was fifty-six years old, or young, whichever one prefers, because I do not feel or act old. But a half century of reporting and forty years of attending conventions are more than enough for any man. My time to end it had not only come but it had passed.

There was only one way to make the break and make it stick, and that was to pull up stakes and move far away from the capital. I could not bear to spend my life fighting the old battles and to bore young people by my tales of the past.

So, I chose the land of long twilights, soft rain and softer voices. I admire the sunrises and sunsets, and am enchanted by the ever-changing face of Fin Lough and the Clare Hills outside my library window. And almost all my friends are far younger than I, so I live in the present.

Best of all there are no editors. It is true I have rebelled against authority all my life, as various bosses and politicians can testify. And now that I am my own boss, I am beginning to battle myself. I will admit I was difficult, but I like to think I was honest and had the courage of my convictions.

I fly the American flag high here in Ireland, among a people who hail me as an American, which is a far nobler and prouder title than we accord one another at home. It is also the most promising title that anyone can hold because Americans are not only the hope of a better day for themselves but for all people wherever they may dream of a brighter tomorrow.

And so, as a journalistic Fiddler Jones, I am ending up with a broken typewriter, a broken laugh and a thousand memories, and not a single regret, except of my own inadequacy in serving those I most wanted to serve, my readers.